FUNCTIONALISM AND GRAMMAR

To Sarah Groll, a teacher who cared

FUNCTIONALISM AND GRAMMAR

T. GIVÓN

JOHN BENJAMINS PUBLISHING COMPANY
AMSTERDAM/PHILADELPHIA

^{TM} The paper used in this publication meets the minimum requirements of American National Standard for Information Sciences — Permanence of Paper for Printed Library Materials, ANSI Z39.48-1984.

Library of Congress Cataloging-in-Publication Data

Givón, —, date.
    Functionalism and grammar / T. Givón.
        p.   cm.
    Includes bibliographical references (p.) and index.
    1. Functionalism (Linguistics) 2. Grammar, Comparative and general. 3. Typology (Linguistics) 4. Discourse analysis. 5. Psycholinguistics. I. Title.
P147.G58   1995
415--dc20   95-6774
ISBN 90 272 2147 2 (Eur.) / 1-55619-500-1 (US) (Hb; alk. paper)   CIP
ISBN 90 272 2148 0 (Eur.) / 1-55619-501-X (US) (Pb; alk. paper)

John Benjamins Publishing Co. • P.O.Box 75577 • 1070 AN Amsterdam • The Netherlands
John Benjamins North America • P.O.Box 27519 • Philadelphia, PA 19118 • USA

Contents

Preface

All functionalists subscribe to at least one fundamental assumption *sine qua non*, the non-autonomy postulate: that language (and grammar) can be neither described nor explained adequately as an autonomous system. To understand what grammar is, and how and why it comes to be this way, one must make reference to the natural parameters that shape language and grammar: cognition and communication, the brain and language processing, social interaction and culture, change and variation, acquisition and evolution.

The past three decades have witnessed an explosion of scholarship on grammar as an instrument for organizing, representing and communicating experience. The work of the functionalist schools that now dot the linguistic countryside spans a wide range of methodologies and databases — from discourse and conversational analysis to semiotics and iconicity; from diachrony and grammaticalization to typology and universals; from acquisition and variation to cognition and text processing. To all these schools, some versions of the non-autonomy postulate has remains neigh an article of faith.

There is something fundamentally sound about the current proliferation of functionalist approaches to grammar, in that it guarantees a diversity of perspectives, methods, and data. As in the case of biological species, internal diversity remains the best guarantor of adaptive flexibility, maximizing the species' evolutionary options. Unfortunately, the pitfalls of exploding diversity among functionalists are just as apparent — sectarianism, non-communication, and incoherence. In this too, the social dynamics of organized scholarship echoes the adaptive experience of biological populations, where excessive diversity leads to isolation, incompatibility, and speciation.

Biological species strive for the elusive dynamic balance between promiscuous diversity and stagnant uniformity. What governs the balance is, of course, natural selection, whereby a species submits its adaptive gambles to the harsh judgment of the environmental market-place. In science, a certain methodological commitment to testing and re-testing hypotheses, both deductively and inductively, is the analog of biology's adaptive environment. It is the sieve that winnows the wild from the plausible, the possible from the probable. There is nothing infallible about this enterprise. Much like biological evolution again, it can be cumbersome and ungainly, and on occasion yield spectacularly mal-adaptive results. Nevertheless, it is all we've got, this socially-negotiated commitment to method, a willingness to expose hypotheses to the harsh light of analytic rigor, to measure them up against some empirical reality. Without such a commitment, our articles of faith are little but ideological hand-waving. But the proliferous functionalist schools have yet to submit their constructs — let alone their differences — to the scrutiny of method. As the overripe Generative orthodoxy crumbles of its own weight of formal vacuity and metho-dological indifference, functionalists on their various stripes trumpet their reductive visions in a mounting cacophony of self-indulgence and parochialism.

Our propensity for reductive thinking follows the beaten track of philo-sophical (and scientific) reductionism. Here are some of my current favorites:

- Arbitrariness and motivation: Saussure's and Chomsky's arbitrariness dogma is untenable; grammar is not 100% autonomous and arbitrary. Therefore grammar must be 100% iconic and motivated.
- Rule-governedness: The generative position is untenable; grammar is not 100% rule-governed. Therefore grammar must be 100% flexible and un-governed.
- Categoriality: Grammatical categories are not 100% formal and discrete. Therefore grammatical categories must be 100% flexible and non-discrete.
- Meaning and context: Meaning is not 100% literal and non-contextual. Therefor meaning must be 100% metaphoric and contextual.
- Change and variation: Saussure's and Chomsky's dogma of idealized "competence" is untenable. Grammar is not 100% invariant. Therefore grammar must be 100% variable, pliable, emergent.
- Cognition and communication (I): Communication is transacted in a social, interpersonal space. Therefore the cognitive aspects of grammar must be reduced to its social aspects.
- Cognition and communication (II): Communication is a cognitive phenom-enon, transacted between two minds. Therefore communicative functions must be reduced to cognitive operations.
- Universality and diversity: Chomsky's dogma of near-100% universality of grammar is untenable. Therefore universals of grammar are purely heuristic, distributional.
- Structure and function (I): Grammar is overwhelmingly iconic and motivated. Therefore functional organization need not be demonstrated independently, it simply falls out of structural organization.

- Structure and function (II): Grammar is overwhelmingly iconic and motivated. Therefore structural organization need not be demonstrated independently, it simply falls out of functional organization.

Reductionism is a virulent intellectual disease of ancient vintage, an old denial reflex, an atavistic tantrum. In linguistics, reductionism embodies a refusal to come to terms with the complex, interactive nature of bio-cultural reality. In their puzzling propensity for reductionism, functionalists are slowly turning themselves into a caricature of Chomskyan linguistics.

As the reader may have divined, this book is infused with a certain measure of frustration. It is about how hard it is to do things right and how easy it is to go wrong. The social dynamics of the field seems, increasingly, to have conspired against coherence. I would be the first to cheer if I were to be proven wrong. But I see little to cheer about in the collective smugness that seems to have engulfed us.

The people I have learned from are too numerous to acknowledge here. Still, I would like to record my indebtedness to two eminent — and eminently sensible — fellow functionalists: to John Haiman for shedding much light on both the highs and lows of iconic motivation; and to Bernd Heine for reminding us of the diachronic underpinnings of grammar.

In my twelve years in the public schools and thirteen years at various universities, only one teacher had ever bothered to tell me that my ideas mattered, and that they therefore deserved critical scrutiny. It was a formative experience that turned out to last me a lifetime. She got me over the hump. Her name was Sarah Groll, she taught us humanities during my junior year at the highschool, and later became a noted Egyptologist. She was, still is, a veritable tiger. I would like to dedicate this book to her.

Eugene, Oregon
December 1994

1

Prospectus, Somewhat Jaundiced

1.1. Historical notes

1.1.1. Antecedence and antecedents

History is always written from a particular perspective by those who survived to tell the tale. Sensible scholars strive to trace their intellectual lineage as far back as their eye can see, often succeeding admirably in doing just that. But just how far does the eye see? This is where perspective rears its mischievous head. In contemplating the descent of the functionalist approach to grammar, I have elected to pursue a more modest goal, tracing mostly the lines of inquiry that have been formative to my own work. From this admittedly myopic perspective, the antecedence of functionalism in linguistics should not be sought primarily in the work of linguists, but rather in the work of anthropologists, psychologists, sociologists and biologists; and long before them in the work of philosophers.

Being honor-bound to pay homage to our immediate intellectual progenitors, however, the following quotes come to mind readily, beginning with Edward Sapir:

> "...Language is a purely human and non-instinctive method of communicating ideas, emotions and desires by means of a system of voluntarily produced symbols..." (Sapir 1921: 8)

> "...Hence we have no recourse but to accept language as a fully formed functional system within man's psychic or "spiritual" constitution. We cannot define it as an entity in psycho-physical terms alone, however much the psycho-physical basis is essential to its functioning..." (*ibid.*, 10–11)

But of course, Otto Jespersen would do just as well:

"...The essence of language is human activity — activity on the part of one individual to make himself understood by another, activity on the part of that other to understand what was in the mind of the first..." (Jespersen 1934: 17)

As would George Zipf:

"...language is primarily a representation of experience. It may represent experience as a report of direct perceptual experience, such as in an account of a football game or in a description of some scene or event. Or it may represent tendencies to act and may be viewed as representative of potential activity, such as in an oration to persuade others to modify their behavior in accord with the wishes of the speaker... a function of the linguistic representation is to preserve or restore equilibrium. This equilibrium may be of two types: (a) inter-personal and (b) intra-personal..." (Zipf 1935: 294–295)

Or Michael Halliday:

"...A functional approach to language means, first of all, investigating how language is used: trying to find out what are the purposes that language serves for us, and how we are able to achieve these purposes through speaking and listening, reading and writing. But it also means more than this. It means seeking to explain the nature of language in functional terms: seeing whether language itself has been shaped by use, and if so, in what ways — how the form of language has been determined by the function it has evolved to serve..." (Halliday 1973: 7)

Or Simon Dik:

"...a language is conceived of in the first place as an instrument of social interaction between human beings, used with the primary aim of establishing communicative relations between speakers and addressees..." (Dik 1978: 1)

Or, in tracing back our preoccupation with semiotics, Dwight Bolinger:

"...The natural condition of language is to preserve one form for one meaning and one meaning for one form..." (Bolinger 1977: x)

And earlier, C. S. Peirce:

"...In the syntax of every language there are logical icons of the kind that are aided by conventional rules..." (Peirce 1940: 106)

And ultimately Aristotle:

> "...Now spoken sounds [= words] are symbols of affections of the soul [= thoughts], and written marks are symbols of spoken sounds. And just as written marks are not the same for all men [= are language specific], neither are spoken sounds. But what these are in the first place signs of — affections of the soul — are the same for all [= are universal]; and what these affections are likenesses of — actual things — are also the same..."
> (*De Interpretatione*, tr. & ed. by J.L. Ackrill, 1963)

From my own perspective, the best point of departure for functionalism is to be found in biology, a discipline that has been profoundly functionalist for over two thousand years. Functionalism in biology harkens back to Aristotle, who more or less single-handedly dislodged the two structuralist schools that had dominated Greek biological thought up to his time. Both schools sought to understand live organisms componentially, the way they did inorganic matter. Thus Empedocles proposed to explain organisms by their component elements. While Democritus opted for understanding organisms through their component parts, or structure.

In his *De Partibus Animalium*, Aristotle first argues against Empedocles' elemental approach, pointing out the relevance of histological and anatomical structure:

> "...But if men and animals are natural phenomena, then natural philosophers must take into consideration not merely the ultimate substances of which they are made, but also flesh, bone, blood and all the other homogeneous parts; not only these but also the heterogenous parts, such as face, hand, foot..." (*De Partibus Animalium*, McKeon ed. 1941: 647)

He next notes the inadequacy of Democritan structuralism:

> "...Does, then, configuration and color constitute the essence of the various animals and their several parts?... No hand of bronze or wood or constituted in any but the appropriate way can possibly be a hand in more than a name. For like a physician in a painting, or like a flute in a sculpture, it will be unable to do the *office* [i.e. function] which that name implies..." (*ibid.*, 647; italics added)

Next, he offers his functionalist touchstone — the **teleological** interpretation of living things, using the analogy of usable artifacts:

> "...What, however, I would ask, are the forces by which the hand or the body was fashioned into its shape? The woodcarver will perhaps say, by the axe and auger; the physiologist, by air and earth. Of these two answers, the artificer's is the better, but it is nevertheless insufficient. For it is not enough for him to say that by the stroke of his tool this part was formed into a concavity, that into a flat surface; but he must state the *reasons* why he struck his blow in such a way as to affect this, and what his final *object* was..." (*ibid.*, 647–648; italics added)

Aristotle then outlines the governing principle of functionalism, the correlation — or isomorphism — between form and function:

> "...if a piece of wood is to be split with an axe, the axe must of necessity be hard; and, if hard, it must of necessity be made of bronze or iron. Now exactly in the same way the body, which like the axe is an *instrument* — for both the body as a whole and its several parts individually have definite operations for which they are made; just in the same way, I say, the body if it is to do its *work* [i.e. function], must of necessity be of such and such character..." (*ibid.*, p. 650; italics added)

Ever since Aristotle, structuralism — the idea that structure is arbitrary and thus requires no explanation or, worse, somehow explains itself — has been a dead issue in biology, a discipline where common-sense functionalism is taken for granted like mother's milk. As one contemporary introductory textbook puts it:

> "...anatomy is the science that deals with the structure of the body... physiology is defined as the science of function. Anatomy and physiology have more meaning when studied together..." (Crouch 1978: 9–10)

Likewise, from a current introduction to animal physiology:

> "...The movement of an animal during locomotion depends on the structure of muscles and skeletal elements (e.g. bones). The movement produced by a contracting muscle depends on how it is attached to these elements and how they articulate with each other. In such a relatively familiar example, the relation between structure and function is obvious. The dependence of function on structure becomes more subtle, but no less real, as we direct our attention to the lower levels of organization — tissue, cell, organelle, and so on... The principle that structure is the basis of function applies to biochemical events as well. The interaction of an enzyme with its substrates, for example, depends on the configuration and electron distributions of the interacting molecules. Changing the shape of an enzyme molecule (i.e. denaturing it) by heating it above $40°$ C is generally sufficient to render it biologically nonfunctional by altering its shape..." (Eckert and Randall 1978: 2–3)

In the early 20th Century, structuralism somehow resurfaced in the nascent social sciences. To these infant disciplines — psychology, anthropology, linguistics — positivist philosophers of science sold the deceptive analogy of physics. The intuitive post-Darwinian functionalism of the Neogrammarians, the German Romanticists, and the early pioneers of Anthropology was then dismissed as crude anthropomorphism, a convenient heuristic at best.[1] To understand the roots of extreme structuralism in positivist philosophy, consider Carnap's later reflection upon the physicalism of the Vienna Circle:

> "...The thesis of physicalism, as originally accepted in the Vienna Circle, says roughly: Every concept of the language of science can be explicitly defined in terms of observables; therefore every sentence of the language of science is translatable into a sentence concerning observable properties..." (Carnap 1963: 59)

The core notions of functionalism — teleology, purpose, function — are invisible constructs that defy translation into the physicalist "language of science", as are psychological concepts such as *meaning* and *intent*, or for that matter, *mind*.

The critical element that makes something a biological code, or in Peirce's words, "...something by knowing of which we know something more...", is always the association of some purpose or function with a physical structure of the code, or with the structured behavior governed by it. Likewise, in the definition of "biological organism", the notion of "function" is *sine qua non*; no sense can be made without it, no serious explanation can be offered. This is where the world of living organisms stands in stark contrast to the pre-biological physical universe where teleology and function have no meaning. To quote someone who should perhaps know:

> "...My view of physics is that you make discoveries but, in a certain sense, you never really understand them. You learn how to manipulate them, but you never really understand them. "Understanding" would mean relating them to something else — to something more profound..." (I.I. Rabi, in an interview in *The New Yorker*, October 20 1975: 96)

1.1.2. The legacy of structuralism

In the intellectual garden of early 20th Century Positivism, the three central dogmas of Saussure were natural growth, rising together in a symbiotic embrace. The **arbitrariness** doctrine detached the linguistic sign — the visible behavior — from its invisible mental correlates. The middle term of Aristotelian semiotics — the mind — was thus excised, leaving the two observable terms — the sign and its worldly referent — the lone participants in the equation. Bloomfield's approach to meaning, a sad caricature of positivist and behaviorist "meaning as external reference", owes its descent to similar intellectual sources:

> "...We must study people's habits of language — the way they talk — without bothering about mental processes that we may conceive to underlie or accompany habits. We must dodge the issue by a fundamental assumption, leaving it to a separate investigation, in which our results will figure as data along the results of other social sciences..." (Bloomfield 1922: 142)

And again:

> "...In order to give a scientifically accurate definition of meaning for every form of the language, one should have to have a scientifically accurate knowledge of everything in the speaker's world... In practice, we define the meaning of a linguistic form, whenever we can, in terms of some other science..." (Bloomfield 1933: 139–140)

Saussure's second dogma, the **idealization** associated with his fateful distinction between *langue* and *parole*, may be viewed as a purely methodological gambit. All facts are to some extent idealized in science, where the search for the 'ultimate' fact is an empirical bottomless pit and a philosophical mirage.[2] It is thus not an accident that the Bloomfieldians, as good empiricists, skipped over this empirical escape hatch altogether. It remained for Chomsky, within a resurgent mentalistic approach, to resurrect the distinction:

> "...Linguistic theory is concerned primarily with an idealized speaker-listener, in a completely homogeneous speech-community, who knows its language perfectly and is unaffected by such grammatically irrelevant conditions as memory limitation, distractions, shifts of attention and interest, and errors (random or characteristic) in applying his knowledge of the language to actual *performance*..." (Chomsky 1965: 3; italics added)

The fundamentally methodological nature of the idealization was indeed acknowledged by Chomsky:

> "...This seems to me to have been the position of the founders of modern general linguistics, and no cogent reason for modifying it has been offered. In the study of actual linguistic performance, we must consider the interaction of a variety of factors, of which the underlying *competence* of the speaker-hearer is only one. In this respect, the study of language is no different from empirical investigation of other complex phenomena..." (*ibid.*, 3–4; italics added)

On the surface of it, there is nothing inimical to functionalism in such methodological idealization. Except for one crucial respect — all the functional-adaptive pressures that shape the synchronic — idealized — structure of language are exerted during actual performance. This is where language is acquired, where grammar emerges and changes. This is where form adjusts itself — creatively and on the spur of the moment's opportunistic construal of context — to novel functions and extended meanings. This is also where slop, variation and indeterminacy are necessary parts of the actual mechanism that shapes and reshapes competence. To dismiss the relevance of the rich data-base of performance to the study of competence is, in point of fact, a travesty of what is done in other sciences. Performance is not *abstracted from* in other sciences, but is rather *controlled for,* and its effects are systematically studied. In the absence of commitment to do this, what may have been a methodological caution in Saussurean structuralism metamorphosed into a theoretical tenet of Generative linguistics.[3]

Saussure's third dogma, the strict **segregation** of diachronic from synchronic description, may be viewed as another aspect of idealization. The problem of change, graduality and their attendant indeterminacy has dogged analytic philosophers ever since Plato and Aristotle.[4] There is nothing inherently wrong with the structuralists' desire to ignore change under particular conditions. After all, language users are routinely obliged to make categorial choices of form under the relentless time-pressure of actual communication.[5] The problem again lies in dismissing the relevance of the data-base of change and variation to our understanding of synchronic structure. By way of analogy, this is akin to suggesting that the evolutionary mechanism that gave rise to a particular life-form is irrelevant to our understanding of that life-form.

1.1.3. Direct descent

In a narrow sense, the functionalist tradition I have been associated with traces its direct descent back to a rather paradoxical source — Chomsky's Aspects (1965). Following earlier moves by Fillmore (1963), Katz and Postal (1964) and Gruber (1965), Chomsky began in his writing from the early 1960s to license a blatantly functionalist idea — the isomorphism between deep syntactic structure and propositional meaning. What is more, lexical-semantic structure à la Chomsky (1965) seemed at first blush to be integrated into the syntactic machinery of PS ("rewrite") rules (Chomsky 1965: 79–80). But Chomsky remained ambivalent about this solution, noting its inadequacy:

"...However, G.H. Matthews...pointed out that this assumption was incorrect and that rewriting rules are not the appropriate device to effect subcategorization of lexical categories. The difficulty is that subcategorization is typically not strictly hierarchic but involves rather cross classification..." (Chomsky 1965: 79)

Soon, lexical semantics is bundled off into "complex symbols" (*ibid.*, 86–89) and thus excised from syntax:

"...The separation of the lexicon from the system of rewriting rules has quite a number of advantages. For one thing, many of the grammatical properties of formatives can now be specified directly in the lexicon, by association of syntactic features with lexical formatives, and thus need not be represented in the rewriting rules at all..." (*ibid.*, 86–87).

But of course, by packing "syntactic" features into the lexical formatives, syntax and lexicon are again intermingled. And, almost as an after-thought, Chomsky lets hierarchic syntactic structure back into the complex symbols:

"...Limitation of complex symbols to lexical categories implies that no complex symbol will dominate a branching configuration [i.e. have syntactic structure; TG], within the categorial component. Now, however, we have some evidence that within a word, branching must be permitted in a configuration dominated by a complex symbol..."[6] (Chomsky 1965: 188)

But, again almost in the same breath, a dichotomy between syntax and (interpretive) semantics is licensed, as an alternative way of dealing with semantically anomalous sentences:

"...Alternatively, if we conclude that the semantic component should carry the burden of accounting for these facts, we can allow the syntactic component to generate the sentences of (14) as well as those of (13),[7] with no distinction of grammaticalness, but with lexical items specified in such a way that rules of the semantic component will determine the incongruity of the sentences of (13) and the manner in which they can be interpreted (if at all)..." (Chomsky 1965: 78)

The Generative Semantics rebellion launched by Ross and Lakoff's paper "Is deep structure necessary?" at the 1967 La Jolla conference can be directly traced to Chomsky's fateful opening of the Pandora's Box of meaning. But the semantic functionalism of the late 1960s retained much of the generative preoccupation with logic (cf. Lakoff's *Linguistics and Natural Logic*, 1970), the algorithmic approach to rules of grammar (viz. "Generative" Semantics), and in general the fairly narrow focus on lexical and propositional meaning even when discourse-pragmatic notions were clearly at issue (viz. Chafe's *Meaning and the Structure of Language*, 1970). Methodologically too, the generative reliance on de-contextualized sentences, grammaticality judgement, the native's proverbial intuition and English as the near-exclusive data source persisted. It fell upon the next wave of functionalism in the early 1970s, a fortuitous amalgam of discourse-functional, typological, acquisitional, variational and diachronic work, to bid a decisive farewell to American structuralism.

1.2.   From faith to theory

Functionalists in linguistics recite, vigorously and often, a set of cherished premises:

- language is a social-cultural activity
- structure serves cognitive or communicative function
- structure is non-arbitrary, motivated, iconic
- change and variation are ever-present
- meaning is context-dependent and non-atomic
- categories are less-than-discrete
- structure is malleable, not rigid
- grammars are emergent
- rules of grammar allow some leakage

These principles are all valid — up to a point and within well defined contexts. In the complex, biologically-based system of knowledge representation and communication that is human language, such principles are circumscribed by competing principles that interact with them and constrain their applicability. A biological processing system is typically an interactive arena, where competing sub-systems find their dynamic balance in an often eclectic compromise. In the absence of a coherent theory that recognized this interactive complexity, the cherished premises of functionalism have often degenerated into reflexive slogans, ideological gestures, articles of faith.

The retreat from theory and methodology to ideological hand-waving is a familiar spectacle in the humanities and social sciences. In exorcising the twin dogmas of theory-as-algorithm and method-as-number-crunching, a reflexive tantrum of relativism has become the standard escape hatch from the tiresome demands of responsible scholarship. It is a trend we should do well to resist.

1.3.   Naive iconism and the reality of formal structure

Functionalists have always been committed to the proposition that grammatical structure is not arbitrary. This commitment is most commonly expressed as either one of two idealized principles:

(1)   **Idealized principle of iconic correlation**:
a. A 1:1 correlation holds between form and meaning
b. Grammatical form correlates with semantic or pragmatic
function in a non-arbitrary ('iconic') way.

But as Haiman (1985) and others have been pointing out, both (1a) and (1b)
must be taken with certain caveats. First (1a): ambiguity — but never synonymy — is rampant in grammar, as it is in the lexicon. One should thus expect a
systematic bias in the linguistic code toward one-to-many conversion from form
to meaning, and many-to-one from meaning to form. Second (1b): diachronic
change is, paradoxically, the agent of both the iconicity of grammar and its
eventual demise. In its latter capacity, diachronic change tampers systematically
with the idealized expectation (1b) (see chapter 2, section 2.6; chapter 3).

As Haiman (1992) points out, the process of grammaticalization — the rise
of morpho-syntactic structure — is inherently a process of partial rigidification,
or *ritualization*. Through this process, emergent grammatical structure to some
degree becomes *emancipated* from its formative functional motivation (Haiman
1992; see also chapters 2 and 9). Thus, while the rise and subsequent change
of grammatical structures is always functionally motivated, the resulting
product is seldom 100% iconic. In their zeal to reject structuralist reductionism
— the doctrine of arbitrariness — functionalists often fall pray to an equally
reductive logical fallacy:

(2)   **Reductionist fallacy of non-arbitrariness**:
"Because structure is not 100% arbitrary, it must be 100% iconic".

Many of us have at one time or another indulged in this brand of **naive
functionalism**, taking for granted that idealizations (1a) and (1b) must range
over 100% of form-function pairs in grammar.[8] Such an over-extended position
gives grounds to two kinds of criticism by non-functionalists, or by sympathetic
would-be functionalists:

(3)   **Common critiques of naive functionalism**:
       a. "Functionalism in grammar is untenable, because *some*
          form-function pairings are indeed arbitrary".
       b. "You people articulate a naive position; you indulge in ad-
          hoc and circular practices; first you assume iconicity or
          functional motivation — *a priori*; then you look around to
          find what you expect".

Criticism (3a) of course springs from an equally naive Platonic reductionism:

(4)   **Platonic reductionism and form-function correlations**:
       "Either all form-function relations are non-arbitrary, or else
       functionalism is empirically vacuous".

But (4) is, in essence, the very same reduction practiced by naive functionalists
who espouse (2).

Criticism (3b), on the other hand, often comes at us from sympathetic
audiences of would-be functionalists. It is directed at the seemingly *ad hoc*
fashion in which functionalists often cast about for obvious functional explanations. In their desperation to explain all, functionalists often pay no heed to the
ramifications of their explanations. Often, a quick survey of more facts, access
to related disciplines and some prudent exercise in deductive inference, would
reveal that the pursuit of transparent functional explanation at all cost serves to
satisfy our ideological aversion to **excess structure**:

(5)   **Aversion to excess structure**:
       "No structure could possibly hang around without an obvious
       function being paired to it".

But the evolution of biological design produces excess structure under many
conditions (see chapter 2, section 2.7). And while in the main all biological
design evolves under adaptive — functional — pressures, a simple isomorphism
between structures and functions is not always transparent in complex, interactive biological systems. The existence of some measure of arbitrariness in the
grammatical code is thus to be expected.

Finally, grammaticalization and ritualization mean nothing unless they mean
the rise of **formal structure**. The rise of grammar may be functionally motivated;
but once there, formal structure assumes its own reality, communicatively,
cognitively and neurologically (see chapters 8, 9). What is more, the assertion that
function correlates with structure is an empty tautology unless both function
and structure are defined independently of each other. But the only meaningful

definition of "structure" is formal (see chapters 5, 6). Another reductionist fallacy we should do well to resist is the rejection of formal structure:

(6)   **Rejection of formal structure**:
      "Because the rise of grammar is functionally motivated, and because grammatical structure is not 100% formal, therefore grammatical structure is 100% non-formal".

1.4.   The mess inbetween discreteness and graduality

Aristotle has not been alone in his worry about the no-man's-land between categoriality and flux. In the early formative decade of the functional-typological renaissance, say 1967 to 1977, there were perfectly good reasons why many of us would have wanted to view non-discreteness as an alternative to the Generative love affair with discrete categories. Following Ross (1972, 1973) and Lakoff (1973), we began to discover the less-than-categorial aspects of grammar. But as is often the case in the context of rebellion (intellectual or otherwise), excess tends to breed counter-excess, as opposing camps strive for maximal differentiation within a limited space. Thus, the extreme Platonic categoriality of the Generative dogma pushed us, in the early 1970s, into an equally dogmatic extreme. Ultimately though, trading one reductive dogma for another is a bad strategy in science. It was a lousy gambit when Chomsky (1959) insisted that we choose between his dogmatic innatism and Skinner's equally dogmatic stimulus-response. And it hasn't improved with age.

In a recent review, Petri and Mishkin (1994) point out that the human mind/brain has both rational propositional mechanisms (episodic-declarative memory) and stimulus-driven mechanisms (procedural-semantic memory). Both are necessary sub-components of a the overall complex adaptation. In the same vein, both categoriality and non-discreteness have always been necessary ingredients in the representation and communication of experience — in the appropriate context.

Most functionalists are currently working, whether explicitly or implicitly, within a distinct approach to categorization, Roschean **prototypes** (Rosch 1973a, 1973b, 1975). Unlike the unconstrained shaded fuzziness of Wittgenstein's (1953) family resemblance,[9] prototypes allow for both flux at the margins and solidity at the core of categories. And there are profound functional reasons why both are necessary. Non-discreteness and graduality are needed because:

(7) **Reasons why natural categories must retain a margin of flexibility**:

    a. Context-dependent processing cannot proceed without *some* flexibility and graduality in construing and adjusting interpretations to the relevant context.

    b. Learning and diachronic extension of categories cannot proceed without shaded graduality.

The context most appropriate to non-discreteness is thus that of new learning, diachronic change and analogical extension. These processes depend heavily on *analogy* and *similarity*, which are in principle non-discrete and logically unconstrained. But equally, some categorial rigidity is indispensible, because:

(8) **Reasons why natural categories must retain considerable rigidity**:

    a. Mental processing within realistic time constraints cannot proceed without such rigidity.

    b. Much of rapid processing is automated, and thus depends heavily on rigid on-off neurological processing modules.

In biological design in general and the neurology in particular, the balance between automated and attended processing is heavily biased in terms of frequency. Recurrent, frequent, predictable information is eventually processed by modular, automatic channels that are relatively context-free.[10] Less frequent, less predictable information is processed through more conscious, attended channels that can scan for contextual relevance.

The balance between automated (more categorial) and attended (more contextual and flexible) processing is somewhat domain-specific, but is attested in grammar, lexical-semantic activation and word-form recognition. Non-discreteness in language is thus not an alternative to discrete categories, but rather its complement in a complex hybrid system.

1.5. Clear distinctions and partial overlaps

One fringe benefit of the prototype approach to categorization is that it can accommodate distinct phenomena that are nevertheless in partial overlap. Functionalist work has been plagued by misunderstanding about how to handles partially-overlapping but vigorously distinct domains. What tends to happen is a species of reductive thinking, inferring the whole ('all not') from the part ('not all'):

(9)   **The fallacy of categorial impurity**:

"Categories that exhibit any overlap at all cannot be distinct, but rather must be contiguous sub-sections of the same category".

The fallacy (9) is indebted, once again, to Platonic categories. In biologically-based natural information processing, prototype-like categories and the distinction between automated and attended processing combine to resolve this apparent logical conundrum. The secret is of course in the frequency distribution. Typically, the bulk of the membership of a natural category distribute close enough to the population mean, so that membership is unambiguous and can be recognized and processed automatically and fast (Rosch 1973b). Only a relatively small portion of the population occupies fringe areas, where membership may be ambiguous, and where slow, attended, context-dependent processing may be required. That is, schematically:

(10)   **Distributional balance between distinctness and inde-terminacy in natural categories**

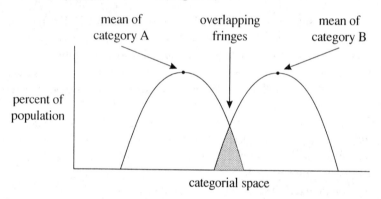

As an illustration of how serious the problem can get, let us consider one area where functionalists of various stripes have succeeded in raising a considerable amount of theoretical fog — the distinction between the three well-coded functional realms of language:

• lexical semantics (word meaning)
• clausal semantics (propositional information)
• discourse pragmatics (cross-clausal coherence)

The relation between the three areas is, in an obvious way, one of concentric inclusion or *biased dependency*.[11] It is possible, at least up to a point, to talk about the meaning of words without invoking their propositional context. But

it is impossible to specify the propositional information of an event clause
without reference to the lexical meaning of their participant entities. Likewise,
it is possible at least in principle to understand the propositional information
packed into an event clause without reference to its discourse context. But it is
impossible to understand a coherent discourse without understanding the
propositional information of its component clauses.

The distinction between the three areas persists up to a point at the code
level. Lexical concepts are coded as words by the sound code. Propositional
information and discourse coherence are coded by grammar. And it is possible
in most cases to tell which parts of the grammatical machinery code primarily
propositional information, and which code primarily discourse coherence.
Indeed, a relatively small fraction of the total machinery of morpho-syntax is
dedicated to coding propositional information (the so-called 'semantic frames',
'argument structure', "who did what to whom", etc.) This portion of the
grammar has the expected overlaps — and biased dependency — with the lexical-
semantics of verbs and subjects or object nouns, in the domain of semantic case-
roles. But there is no reason to conclude from the overlap that there exists no
useful distinction between lexical meaning and propositional information.

Once one begins to examine the distribution and use of grammatical
structure in its communicative context, the overwhelming deployment of
grammar to code discourse coherence is obvious:[12]

(11) **The most discourse-pragmatically oriented grammatical systems**:
      a. Grammatical roles of subject and direct object
      b. definiteness and reference
      c. anaphora, pronouns and agreement
      d. tense-aspect-modality and negation
      e. voice and topicalization
      f. focusing and relativization
      g. speech acts
      h. clausal conjunction and subordination

But distinctness again does not mean lack of overlap or interaction between
clause-level semantics and discourse pragmatics. Case-marking systems is one
major arena where fuzzy boundaries between propositional semantics and
discourse pragmatics can be observed. Thus, one major case-marking type —
active-stative — is oriented primarily toward semantic roles. Another —
nominative-accusative — is oriented predominantly toward the pragmatics of
topicality. While another — ergative-absolutive — straddles the fence between

those two, displaying aspects of both in the complex arena of transitivity. Likewise in the area of voice and de-transitivity, one can easily distinguish between more semantic (middle-voice, reflexive, reciprocal) and more pragmatic (passive, inverse, antipassive) processes or constructions.[13] And within the domain of pragmatic voice, both passives and antipassives retain a certain residue of propositional semantics. The list goes on and on, and in each case the pattern is the same — distinctness and categoriality in the main, overlaps at the margins.

1.6.   Taking cognition and neurology seriously

There is much cognitive and neurological evidence upholding the distinctness of the three functional realms coded by language. But the evidence suggests both modularity and vigorous interaction between modules. Much cognitive and neurological work has been done on the lexicon under the rubric of **semantic memory** (Just and Carpenter 1987; Squire 1987; Squire and Zola-Morgan 1991; Petri and Mishkin 1994). Likewise, a vast literature describes the visual and auditory word-recognition modules and their connectivity to semantic memory (Posner and Raichle 1994; see also chapter 9). The mental and anatomical reality of **episodic memory** as the repository of both single-events experience and coherent multi-propositional discourse is equally well established, in both cognitive psychology (van Dijk and Kintsch 1983; Just and Carpenter 1987) and neurology (Squire 1987; Squire and Zola-Morgan 1991; Petri and Mishkin 1994; see again chapter 9). There is, likewise, a considerable body of evidence about Broca's area in the left-frontal lobe and its role in grammatical processing, in both speech production and speech comprehension (Lieberman 1984; Schnitzer 1989; Menn and Obler 1990; Greenfield 1991). And a growing if tentative body of evidence suggests that grammar, like word-recognition, involves automated processing (Lieberman 1984; Blumstein & Milberg 1983; Schnitzer 1989; Givón 1979; Greenfield 1991). In formulating our hypotheses about the functional correlates of grammar, we must begin to pay attention to relevant work on the cognition and neurology of language, memory and attention. Findings in allied disciplines are, if nothing else, an important constraint on our theoretical search-space. All other things being equal, a hypothesis that converges with evidence from neighboring disciplines ought to be preferred to of one that shows no such convergence.

Lastly, when we invoke cognition, it behooves us to familiarize ourself with the vast cognitive literature that is relevant to our work, lest "cognitive" becomes an ideological slogan. Simply assuming that the categories we derive from studying language by our traditional methods are — by definition — "cognitive" renders the term empty. If language and cognition are indeed closely associated, the only meaningful way of showing the association is to define each one independent of the other, and then study the correlations. Otherwise we are in danger of sliding into tautology.[14]

1.7. Typological diversity and language universals

While recognizing cross-language typological diversity, most functionalists remain committed to the existence of language universals, presumably both of meaning/function and grammatical structure. But the universals we propose, at whatever level, must be based on a study of representative diversity of types. Here too, an empirically-responsible universalist position must navigate a middle course between two extremes — Whorf's and Bloomfield's naive anti-universalism and Chomsky's equally naive universalism.

In two subsequent chapters (3, 4) I try to address some of the problems we face. They seem to involve a peculiar failure of functionalist resolve, in distinguishing between the *domain* of grammatical typology and the actual diversity of *types* within a domain. There is no question that grammatical types within each domain are types of *structure*. If Japanese has zero coding of the coreferent argument inside a relative clause, Hebrew codes them as anaphoric pronouns, German as relative pronouns and Bambara as full nouns, these are all variant structures. But in order for the domain "relative clause" to be defined in a non-arbitrary, non-circular way, it could *not* be defined in terms of structure. Rather, it must be given an independent functional definition. The procedure to be adopted in the study of grammatical universals and grammatical typology is roughly this:

(12) **A functionalist approach to grammatical typology**:
   a. Define by independent criteria all grammar-coded functional domains.
   b. Determine then what structure in each language codes each functional domain.
   c. Group those structures into major types and sub-types.
   d. Discover universal principles that constrain the range of structural variation within each functional domain.
   e. Attempt to explain those universal constraints.

There is of course a silent partner lurking around this procedure — the question of universality of propositional-semantic and discourse-pragmatic functions. It is fairly clear that these functions are much more universals than the variant grammatical structures that code them. But a non-reductive approach to universals must remain informed of the fact that universality of function remains a matter of *degree*. First, different languages may combine the very same universal features in different ways.[15] This is well known, for example, in the study of tense-aspect-modality and voice.[16] Second, cross-language diversity, whether culturally motivated, diachronically explained or merely accidental, may cut even deeper. Some semantic features, pragmatic functions or their combinations may be attested only in a few languages, or even only in one language.

Finally, we know that the lexicon represents the bulk of culture-specific cross-language diversity. The diversity represented in the lexicon is that of world-view, i.e. a group's perspective on its relatively-stable conceptual universe. We also have good reasons to believe that the two grammar-coded functions — propositional semantics and discourse pragmatics — exhibit *greater* universality than lexical-semantics. But again there is no need to suppose that grammar-coded functions are 100% universal. An empirical approach to the study of universals commits us only to finding ways of evaluating both structural and functional diversity without pre-judging the ultimate results.

1.8.   Methodology

1.8.1.   Intuition and its limits

Reductionist philosophers of science have been militating for either one of two extremes in methodology, **inductivism** (cf. Carnap 1950; *inter alia*) and **deductivism** (cf. Popper 1934/1959; Bach, 1965, *inter alia*). Linguistics has been the hapless victim of such reductionism, oscillating between the two extremes. For several decades, Bloomfieldian inductivism reigned:

> "...The only useful generalizations about language are inductive generalizations..." (Bloomfield 1933: 20)

The Chomskyans followed with an equally rabid deductivism. What unites both positions is of course their unfailing reductionism; or, as Bach (1965) put it:

"...Whereas the Baconian stresses caution and 'sticking to the facts' with a distrust of theory and hypothesis...the Keplerian emphasizes the creative nature of scientific discovery, the *leap to general hypotheses* — often mathematical in form, whose value is judged in terms of fruitfulness, simplicity and elegance...The prevailing assumptions of American linguistics prior to 1957 were essentially Baconian in character...[Chomsky's approach, on the other hand, is a] deductively formulated method..." (Bach 1965: 113–114]

More mature and realistic philosophers of science (e.g. Hanson 1958) observe that neither extreme is by itself viable, and that empirical science involves a mix of many strategies, of which the three most prominent ones are:
- deductive reasoning
- inductive reasoning
- abductive-analogical reasoning

These three strategies are used at different contexts in the course of a scientific investigation. Deductive reasoning is used primarily in hypothesis testing, in deriving testable implications of the hypothesis, in designing falsificatory tests, and in deciding whether test results are or are not compatible with the hypothesis. Inductive reasoning is also used in testing hypotheses, but from a different perspective. Whole populations can seldom be tested. In selecting a small sample to be tested, inductive inference allows generalizing the results to the population — provided the sample indeed represents stable trends rather than random fluctuation. Abductive-analogical reasoning is used in a wide range of contexts during an empirical investigation:
- hypothesis formation
- pre-empirical decisions on the relevance of some facts and the irrelevance of others
- pre-empirical decisions on the theoretical relevance of some domains and the irrelevance of others
- post-empirical decisions about when to quit testing a hypothesis
- theoretical explanations

Abductive-analogical reasoning also goes by the name of common sense or intuition. Both extreme deductivists and extreme inductivists have short-changed abduction and intuition, by not recognizing that it is fact-driven, albeit in a very different way than induction (see chapter 7).

Functionalists have traditionally relied — heavily, overwhelmingly — on intuition, analogy and abduction. This is to some extent understandable, given our extreme preoccupation with explanation. But it may be costly, since intuition is both the fastest discovery tool in the arsenal science and, potentially, the most distortive. As Raimo Anttila (1977) has noted, abduction is like high-stake gambling against long odds: When you are right, you save yourself a load of drudgery. When you are wrong, you earned yourself a lot of grief. And without deduction and induction, you may rest aggrieved for a long eternity.[17]

1.8.2.   Induction and quantification

Quantification and eventually inferential statistics are fundamental to induction and hypothesis testing. But in spite of 30-odd years of tireless preaching by Labov and others,[18] functionalists have remained disgustingly Chomskyan in their disdain for population variation, sampling and induction. A putative form-function correlation is only valid — i.e. predictive — if it can be tested on a sample of the general population over which it makes predictions. But communicative behavior like other biological phenomena is often less-than-uniform. And this is especially true given the heuristic nature of our definition of communicative functions. One cannot thus take it for granted that the sample will faithfully represent the population; this needs to be shown. And the only way it can be shown is by quantification and inferential statistics.

Unfortunately, the most common functionalist approach to method is roughly this:

(13)   **The Pull-em-out-of-the-text functionalist methodology**:
   a. Make a hypothesis that grammatical *Form A* has the commu-
      nicative *Function X*.
   b. Look for some real text ('communication').
   c. Identify (one, some, or many) instances in the text where
      Form A is paired with *Function X*.
   d. Declare your hypothesis proven.

This sad caricature of method glosses over a number of relevant questions. First, how many instances of *Form A* in the text were not paired with *Function X*, but rather with *Functions Y,Z,Q*? Second, how many instances of *Function X* in the text were not paired with *Form A*, but rather with *Forms B,C,D*? Third, given the percent of *Form A* that indeed correlates with *Function X*, is it statistically significant, in view of (i) the size of the total population; (ii) the size of the sample; and (iii) the amount of variation within the sample? Without answering these questions, we perpetuate the bad habit of testing hypotheses by attempting to *verify* them. Whereas what we should be doing is attempting — and hopefully failing — to *falsify* them.[19]

1.8.3. Deductive reasoning

Having rejected the dogmatic deductivism of Popper and Chomsky, functionalists often neglect to take advantage of the legitimate and salutary uses of deductive reasoning in the empirical cycle. This failure is often deliberate and self-congratulatory. It is also another version of Platonic reductionism:

(14) **The fallacy of the perfect method**:
 "If a method is not by itself 100% reliable, it must be therefore 100% useless".

There is, of course, a well-known precedent for this reductionist reasoning in Philosophy of Science, Feyerabend's (1975) tantrum *Against Method*. But it seems to me that another version of reductionism also lurks here:

(15) **The fallacy of switched domains**:
 "Since Chomsky's model of grammar as a deductive algorithm
 is empirically useless, deductive logic is a useless tool in our
 methodology".

But how does one derive testable implications of one's hypotheses? Or expose their self-contradictory features? Or decide whether empirical results are compatible or incompatible with hypotheses? Or discover whether two hypotheses are incompatible with each other? In our zeal to reject Chomsky's deductivism, we have developed a great tolerance for self-indulgence and sloppy reasoning.

Our neglect of deductive logic is nowhere as glaring — and costly — as in our approach to conditional associations. Correlations between forms and functions, or between particular form-function pairs, are the life-blood of our text-based methodology. But such correlations come in a variety of logical types:
• one-to-many
• many-to-one
• one-to-one

The first two are biases (one-way) conditional associations; the third is a two-way (bi-conditional) association. There is much to be gained from learning to appreciate the difference, an exercise that requires relatively little formal training. And many glaring fallacies in our work can be directly traced to our disdain for the logic of conditional association (see chapter 7).

1.8.4. Community

I left the issue of communal coherence for last because I am somewhat wary of raising it. My discomfort is due to the fact that the sociology of our loose network of would-be-science is still vulnerable. But in all good science, the issue of communal consistency and how disagreements are handled and hopefully resolved is an integral part of the methodology.[20]

We have, I think for good reasons, rejected the authoritarian strictures of many current schools of linguistics. We have refrained from anointing — or even electing — leaders. We have refused the label of "theory", "grammar", "school". *Network* or *framework* are as close as we have ever come to that, so that often we go by labels conferred upon us by others.[21] We have also resolved to treat each other with civility, to listen without legislating over differences, and to accommodate a healthy range of diversity in both theory and method. This has been, fundamentally, a healthy strategy and a source of strength for our network. But like all strategies, an extreme application beyond the relevant context may yield distortive results.

The flip side of our great patience with each other and our respect for internal diversity is our reluctance to argue over differences that may be profound, to expose logical contradictions, to resolve conflicting empirical claims. This reluctance has indeed preserved our community, and good science is profoundly communal. But a good community of science manages, somehow, to balance *two* opposing strategies. It fosters cooperation, mutual respect and an appreciation for diversity and unfettered investigation. But it also strives to make some decisions, however tentative and temporary, about conflicting claims. In availing itself of the second strategy, the community moves, however lurchingly, toward settling contradictions the only way they can be settled in science — empirically if possible, deductively when appropriate. It would be a bloomin' shame if, having survived and perhaps transcended the rigidity and vituperation of the 1960s, we would have only succeeded in creating for ourselves a cozy nest of fuzzy ideological like-mindedness. Such an obsession with comfort is, well, uncomfortable.

Notes

1) See e.g. discussion in Hempel and Oppenheim (1948) and Hempel (1959) concerning the functionalism of Radcliffe-Brown and Malinowski.

2) The inherent partial contamination of fact by theory as well as by the observer's perspective is a way of life in science (Hanson 1958).

3) This may be an unintended corollary to Hanson's (1958) notion of theory-laden facts: a methodologically contaminated theory.

4) Aristotle labored heroically over this problem of gradual growth and maturation in biology, which he saw as a threat to his theory of universal discrete *forms*. The best account he managed to come up with was rather *ad hoc* (see Tweedale 1986).

5) Roughly speaking, one word per 250 milliseconds, or one clause per 2-3 seconds.

6) In his footnote 44, Chomsky cites neither J. Gruber's nor P. Chapin's dissertation research in this connection. The internal "syntactic" structure of lexical items was a big chunk's of Gruber's (1965) dissertation. It was also the main point of Chapin's (1967) dissertation on derivational morphology.

7) Sentences (13) were semantically totally anomalous:

     (i)   the boy may frighten sincerity
     (ii)   sincerity may admire the boy
     (iv)   John amazed the injustice of that decision
     etc.

They contrasted with the metaphorically interpretable (14):

     (i)   sincerity may frighten the boy
     (ii)   the boy may admire sincerity
     (iii)   the injustice of that decision amazed John
     etc.

8) One of the most articulate expressions of this extreme position can be found in Erica García's (1979) "discourse without syntax". This is of course not surprising in the context of the Diverian form-function school.

9) And Rosch and Mervis's (1975) use of the Wittgensteinean metaphor notwithstanding. For an extensive review see Givón (1989: chapter 2).

10) See chapters 8 and 9, as well as Givón (1989: chapter 7) for review.

11) For a more detailed discussion see chapter 9.

12) See overview in chapter 8, as well as chapters 3 (voice) and 4 (modality). One of the most astute functionalists I know titled her book on the functional correlates of grammar *The Semantics of Grammar* (Wierzbicka 1988).

13) See extensive review in chapter 3.

14) Tautological thinking bedevils functionalist linguistics elsewhere; see discussion in chapters 3, 7 and 9.

15) This is what Peter Harder has been calling recently "the structure of meaning"; see e.g. Harder (1992).

16) See, respectively, Givón (1984: chapter 8) and chapter 3 below.

17) Though of course you may not know it.

18) See in particular Labov (1975).

19) See Popper (1934/1959) as well as extensive discussion in chapter 7.

20) One does not need to buy into Kuhn's (1962) thesis in its entirety to appreciate the role that the social network of a field can play in its methodology. This may be even more pertinent in a would-be-science such as linguistics.

21) This is comforting, if one recalls that the *Bantu* people's name for themselves is 'people', as is the *Dine*'s (Athabaskan) or *Nuuci*'s (Ute). In a recent e-mail discussion I suggested, I think in the same spirit of unmarkedness, that we call ourselves *linguistics*.

2

Markedness as Meta-Iconicity: Distributional and Cognitive Correlates of Syntactic Structure

2.1. Introduction*

2.1.1. Markedness and explanation

The notion of markedness has been implicit, under one guise or another, in linguistic analysis since antiquity. The tradition of describing declaratives before imperatives and interrogatives, actives before passives, main clauses before subordinate clauses and affirmatives before negatives is testimony to the seductive appeal of markedness. Thus, in opening his discussion of negation, Aristotle proceeds:

> "...The first statement-making sentence is the affirmation, next is the negation..." (*De Interpretatione*, in J. Barnes, ed. 1984, p. 26).

And it would have indeed been bizarre for him to proceed: "...The first statement-making sentence is the negation, next is the affirmation...". What I hope to show here is that the intuitive appeal of markedness is not only a methodological convenience for the linguist, but also a cognitive imperative for the information-processing organism.

As a theoretical construct, markedness presupposes the notion of **formal complexity**, whereby the marked is structurally more complex and the unmarked more simple. But issues other than formal complexity are just as central to our understanding of markedness. First, there is the matter of biased **frequency distribution**, where typically the marked category is less frequent, while the unmarked is more frequent. A succinct demonstration of this skewing over a wide range of phonological, semantic and grammatical categories is found in Greenberg (1976). Second, there are the **substantive grounds** for markedness — communicative, cognitive, socio-cultural or neuro-biological.

Some such grounds must be invoked if one is to explain why the marked and unmarked have their observed formal and distributional properties.

Seeking substantive grounds for markedness of course makes sense only if one subscribes to the fundamental assumption that — in principle — all biologically-supported structures are adaptively motivated. In biology proper, this assumption has been taken for granted ever since Aristotle, who likened body organs to instruments:

> "...If a piece of wood is to be split with an axe, the axe must of necessity be hard; and if hard, it must of necessity be made of bronze or iron. Now exactly in the same way the body, which like the axe is an instrument — for both the body as a whole and its several parts individually have definite operations for which they are made; just in the same way, I say, the body if it is to do its work, must of necessity be of such and such character..." (*De Partibus Animalium*, in McKenon, ed., 1941, p. 650)

In the same vein, a contemporary biologist has this to say in his introduction to human anatomy:

> "...anatomy is the science that deals with the structure of the body...physiology is defined as the science of function. Anatomy and physiology have more meaning when studied together..." (Crouch, 1978, pp. 9–10)

Describing structures independently of the multiple adaptive contexts that constrain both their use and their evolution is a luxury not available to functionalists. Functionalists are burdened with having to explain the facts of structure by reference to some surrounding adaptive context.

A meaningful discussion of markedness in grammar — and its near kin, iconicity — must contend with questions such as: Why is the structural code called syntax (or 'grammar') the way it is? What is natural about it? How is it constrained by its communicative task environment, or by the socio-cultural, cognitive or biological contexts within which it has evolved? This is a tall order, and the recurrent theme of the book.

2.1.2. Brief historical note

The notion of markedness entered structural linguistics via the Prague School, initially as a refinement of Saussure's concept of the *valeur linguistique* in binary distinctions. The Pragueans noted that binary distinctions in phonology and grammar were systematically skewed, or asymmetrical.[1] One member of the contrasting pair acted as the "presence" of a property, the other as its "absence". What is more, the systematic skewing of linguistic contrasts was a necessary reflection of the hierarchic nature of linguistic structures (Shapiro

1983). The discussion below, while compatible with this general scheme, is not bound by the limits set by early structuralist schools.

2.1.3. The context-dependence of markedness

Markedness is a context-dependent phenomenon par excellence. The very same structure may be marked in one context and unmarked in another. This can be illustrated with two simple examples. Subject NPs are characteristically definite, referential and highly topical. Instrumental NPs are characteristically indefinite, non-referential and non-topical. Now, which determiner category is the marked one — definite or indefinite? In the context "subject NP", indefinite is marked.[2] In the context "instrumental NP", definite is marked. In the same vein, active clauses predominate — in terms of frequency — in oral communication about everyday human affairs. Passives and other impersonal clauses predominate in academic discourse about abstract topics. Which clause-type is the marked one then, and which the unmarked? In the context of "everyday oral communication", the passive is marked. In the context "written scientific discourse", the active is marked.

Eventually, one is forced into categorizing the markedness of not only linguistic categories, but also of the various types of contexts within which they are embedded. For example, it is probably reasonable to assume that formal academic discourse is a more marked discourse-type, and everyday oral communication a less-marked one. Similarly, one may wish to conclude that the instrumental case-role is more marked than the subject case-role. Once a context is categorized as marked, a category that is marked within that context is in fact the *unmarked* case in human language. The active clause is thus the unmarked case globally, as is 'definite'.[3]

The assignment of markedness status to linguistic contexts must be justified by the very same criteria used to support the markedness of morphemes or constructions — most particularly frequency distribution.[4] For example, in the totality of human linguistic activity, everyday oral language is the overwhelmingly frequent norm, and academic discourse an infrequent counter-norm. And similarly, the subject NP is overwhelmingly the most frequent clausal participant in text, while the instrumental is a relatively infrequent participant.

One important logical consequence of the context dependence of markedness is that substantive explanations of markedness must be domain-specific. So that the communicative, socio-cultural, cognitive or biological correlates of markedness vary from one domain to the next. For example, placing the agent

in the subject (thus topic) role in transitive-clauses, and thus making the active
clause the unmarked case, probably reflects a cultural norm, that of talking
egocentrically more about purposeful human actants than about dumb non-
human objects. The fact that definite referents are more frequent in discourse
than indefinites, on the other hand, reflects a communicative norm, that of
talking about the same topic over long equi-topic chains of clauses. And the
fact that voiced vowels are the unmarked norm in phonology no doubt reflects
some perceptual universal of the human ear.

While the functional correlates of markedness vary from context to
context, its structural and distributional correlates remain the same for all
domains; so much so that structural approaches often ignore its domain-specific
substantive aspects, and construct context-free theories of markedness.[5]

2.1.4.   Criteria for markedness

Three main criteria can be used to distinguish the marked from the unmarked category in a binary grammatical contrast:

(a)   **Structural complexity**: The marked structure tends to be more com-
       plex (or larger) than the corresponding unmarked one.
(b)   **Frequency distribution**: The marked category (figure) tends to be
       less frequent, thus cognitively more salient, than the corresponding
       unmarked category (ground).
(c)   **Cognitive complexity**: The marked category tends to be cognitively
       more complex — in terms of mental effort, attention demands or
       processing time — than the unmarked one.

The general tendency in language is for these three criteria to coincide. This
coincidence — the common association of structural markedness, substantive
markedness and low frequency — is the most general reflection of **iconicity** in
grammar. And it is this correlation that one must explain by invoking both
general principles and detailed developmental mechanisms.[6]

The criterion of frequency distribution (b), while seemingly a formal
property, is intimately associated with the cognitive phenomenon of **figure–
ground**. Most perceptual and cognitive contrasts tend to pair up so that the
more salient, important figure is less frequent. It thus stands out vis-à-vis the
more frequent ground. This skewed distribution must itself be explained,
presumably by reference to substantive domains such as communication, socio-
culture, cognition or biology.

Firm data on the cognitive complexity (c) of morphemes and syntactic construction in context are not always available, so that other substantive considerations must often be taken into account. As elsewhere in language and cognition, a category is not identified by the presence or absence of a single criterial feature. Rather, categories are defined by clustering of a number of central features, those that tend to characterize the **prototype**. This is important particularly in cases when structural markedness does not match distributional or substantive markedness.[7]

2.2.   Markedness of discourse types

In dealing with the markedness of grammatical categories or constructions, one faces again and again the question of markedness of discourse types. This is so because, as noted above, the same grammatical category may have different markedness value when placed in the context of different discourse types. This is probably not the place to undertake a comprehensive treatment of the subject, so that the following may be considered an exploratory survey at best.

2.2.1.   Oral-informal vs. written-formal discourse

2.2.1.1. Structural complexity

There is a continuum, in terms of degree of grammaticalization and syntactic complexity, between extreme oral-informal and extreme written-formal discourse.[8] The features that characterize the two extremes closely parallel those that characterize pre-grammatical (pidgin) vs. grammaticalized communication, respectively.[9] However, in the case of oral vs. written discourse these features manifest themselves in terms of skewed distributional tendencies (relative frequency) rather than in absolute presence or absence. These tendencies may be summarized as follows:

(1)   **Properties of oral vs. written discourse**

parameter	oral-informal (unmarked)	written-formal (marked)
syntactic complexity:	conjoined	embedded
grammatical morphology:	sparse	abundant
word order:	flexible, pragmatic	rigid, grammatical
processing speed:	slower, halting	faster, fluent
context dependence:	higher	lower

2.2.1.2. Frequency distribution

Since language has evolved almost exclusively as an oral face-to-face instrument of communication; since the vast majority of speech communities to date remain profoundly pre-literate; and since even in so-called literate societies the vast majority of speakers spend the bulk of their communicative interaction within the oral-informal medium, a good argument exists for assuming that face-to-face communication is the unmarked norm.

2.2.1.3. Cognitive complexity

In the natural acquisition of both first and second language, the pre-syntactic, pre-grammatical **pidgin** mode of communication is invariably acquired before the grammaticalized mode.[10] One may assume, at least in this case, that the order of acquisition reflects the order of cognitive complexity, and that the prevalence and universality of pre-grammatical pidgin communication reflects its greater cognitive simplicity. In addition, with respect to each one of the parameters listed in (1), it can be shown that the marked member is cognitively more difficult to process than the unmarked.[11]

2.2.2.   Human-affairs vs. abstract-academic discourse

Subject matter does not by itself entail formal complexity. However, a strong frequency-association exists between everyday human affairs topics and informal face-to-face communication, on the one hand, and abstract or academic topics and written formal discourse, on the other. Such an association makes the structural arguments advanced above applicable here as well. That is, abstract academic discourse tends to be syntactically more complex.

The same strong association also entails that discourse about everyday human affairs is the more frequent, unmarked human norm; while abstract academic discourse is the less frequent, marked counter-norm. The same strong association also entails that discourse about everyday human affairs is cognitively easier to process, while discourse about abstract academic subject matter is cognitively more complex. The acquisition data from both L1 and L2 are compatible with this assumption.

2.2.3.   Conversation vs. narrative/procedural discourse

One may define the difference between conversation and narrative (and procedural discourse) along several parameters, with three of those being perhaps the most salient. While each of the three can be construed separately, they exhibit strong dependencies. And further, they each represent a continuum.[12]

(2)   **Conversation vs. narrative: Defining parameters**

parameter	conversation	narrative/procedural
control of perspective:	shifts between participants	retained by one participant
dependence on hearer feedback:	higher	lower
text coherence:	disruptive	continuative

There is a strong association between conversation and oral-informal communication. This association, however, is a one-way conditional:

conversation ⊃ oral/informal
(but not necessarily: oral/informal ⊃ conversation)

On the basis of this conditional association, one can argue that conversation is the less complex, more frequent, evolutionary-prior unmarked norm; while narrative or procedural discourse is the less frequent marked counter-norm. However, if one considers **continuative coherence** to be the norm of human discourse (see further below), than the shifting perspective of conversation may be viewed as a more marked, cognitively more complex discourse type. For the moment it is clear that more empirical research into the nature of coherence of conversation is needed before the cognitive issue can be resolved.

There are no data on the frequency distribution of conversation vs. narrative/procedural discourse. Further, one would expect that the choice of cultural context would pre-determine the results. For example, the theater presents mostly dialogue — i.e. conversational discourse; while novels tend to be skewed more toward narrative. What is more, narrative and conversation are often intermingled: A narrative may include embedded conversations of any length, and any single conversational turn may be long enough to qualify as narrative.

From both the developmental and evolutionary perspective, face-to-face communication is prior. Short turns — thus shifting perspective — is indeed the early childhood norm.[13] But in this respect early child discourse may not represent the adult norm. And further, Ervin-Tripp (1970) has shown that the coherence of early childhood dialogue extends over adjacent short turns, again suggesting that continuative coherence is the unmarked norm even in conversation. Finally, the study of verbal modalities (see below) suggests that perhaps a more revealing grouping of discourse genres would be conversation/narrative vs. procedural.

2.3.   Markedness of clause types

2.3.1.   Preamble

The main, declarative, affirmative, active clause has been tacitly assumed, in grammatical description ever since the Greeks, to be the privileged, unmarked clause type. In this section we will discuss the four binary contrasts underlying this tradition, adding one more — continuative coherence; that is, the contrast between chain-medial (maximally coherent) vs. chain-initial (minimally coherent) clauses in connected discourse. The markedness status of these five categories can be given as:

(3)   **Markedness status of clause-types**
       unmarked   **marked**

       main/conjoined   subordinate
       declarative   manipulative
       affirmative   negative
       active   passive
       continuative   disruptive

2.3.2.   Main vs. subordinate clauses

2.3.2.1. Complexity and finiteness

2.3.2.1.1. Finiteness in subordinate clauses

Finiteness has been traditionally discussed as a property of verbs, but it clearly applies to other parts of the clause. Consider, for example:

(4)   a. **Finite**:   They categorically reject   the offer
       b. **Non-finite**: Their categorical   rejection of the offer

The structural changes from the finite (4a) to the nominalized, non-finite (4b) involve the following adjustments:

(5)   **Adjustments in finiteness in nominalized clauses**:

	locus	finite		non-finite
(a)	**Verb**:	Verb	⇒	noun
(b)	**Verbal inflections**:	Full	⇒	absent
(b)	**Case**:	Nominative	⇒	genitive, accusative
(c)	**Modifiers**:	Adverb	⇒	adjective
(d)	**Articles**:	Subject	⇒	determiner

Out of the formal adjustment from finite to non-finite clause seen in (4), (5), two central grammatical foci are of particular interest. Both are indispensable to the independent main clause, and both tend to be either reduced or altogether zeroed out in non-finite clauses:

- Marking of the subject NP
- Marking of tense-aspect-modality

The reduced marking of the two grammatical foci is already apparent in tightly-bound verb complement clauses:

(6)   a. **Finite:**   He left
      b. **Non-finite:** He wanted **to leave**
                        She told him **to leave**

A similar reduction can be seen in equi-subject participial ADV-clauses:

(7)   a. **Finite:**   He left in a hurry
                        She came back home
      b. **Non-finite:** **Leaving in a hurry**, he then proceeded...
                        Instead of **coming back home**, she...

The conventional wisdom in linguistics has always been that non-finite clauses such as (4b), (6b) and (7b) are the marked case, and the corresponding finite clauses are the unmarked. But there are grounds for suspecting that the conventional wisdom is somewhat off the mark.

In support of the conventional wisdom — i.e. a more marked status of non-finite clauses — one may cite the fact that in spoken informal discourse some types of dependent non-finite clauses — especially nominalized clauses such as (4b) — are rare (see further below). But non-finite complement clauses such as (6b) abound in all discourse types, and are thus, by the frequency criterion, less-marked.

2.3.2.1.2. Finiteness in conjoined main clauses

More serious problems for the conventional approach identifying non-finite clauses as marked arise when one examines more closely the syntactic marking of the most frequent clause-type in connected, coherent discourse — conjoined chain-medial clauses. Such clauses reveal, upon careful cross-linguistic study, systematically impoverished (reduced) grammatical marking. This lower markedness is reflected at exactly the same two grammatical sub-systems where one finds it in non-finite dependent clauses:

- Unexpressed subject
- Reduced tense–aspect–modality

The grammatical structure of conjoined chain-medial clauses is clearly reduced and simplified. The cross-linguistic evidence for this is overwhelming,[14] but the evidence is just as clear in English, where one finds two types of **clause-chaining**. In the first, only the chain-final clause is finite, the others are reduced, participial, non-finite:[15]

(8)   Coming out,
        stopping to check the mailbox,
        taking a look at the driveway
        and pausing to adjust his hat,
        he turned and walked to his car.

In the second clause-chaining strategy, predominant in English, conjoined main clauses have been traditionally considered finite. The chain-initial clause here is indeed finite, but all non-initial clauses bear reduced grammatical marking in one way or another. Thus, (8) above may be translated into this second type as:

(9)   **He came out,**
        stopped to check the mailbox,
        took a look at the driveway,
        paused to adjust his hat,
        turned
        and walked to his car.

Chain-medial clauses in either clause-chaining type tend to be the most thematically continuous ('coherent'). This can be measured in terms of three major components of thematic coherence:

- Referential continuity
- Action continuity
- Tense–aspect–modal continuity

The study of clause-chaining systems cross-linguistically reveals the following correlation between these elements of coherence and the finiteness of the clause:[16]

(10) **Correlation between finiteness and thematic coherence**:
    a. "Clauses with higher referential continuity tend to receive less-finite marking".
    b. "Clauses with higher sequential action continuity tend to receive less finite marking".
    c. "Clauses with higher tense-aspect-modal continuity tend to receive less finite marking".

In both clause-chaining types in English, correlations (10) are borne out by the low finiteness of equi-subject or equi-object V-complements (6b), and by the lower finiteness of equi-subject participial ADV-clauses (7b). In the classical New Guinea type clause-chaining languages, these predictions are borne out by the lower finiteness of SS-medial clauses vis-à-vis DS-medial clauses; by the lower finiteness of DS-medial clauses vis-à-vis chain-final clauses; and by the lower finiteness of sequential-medial clauses vis-à-vis non-sequential medial clauses.[17]

The zero subject marking of conjoined chain-medial clauses, as in (9), is indeed a well known phenomenon, under the label of VP-conjunction. Of even more interest is the systematic reduction in the second main sub-system of the finiteness of clauses — tense–aspect–modality. Consider first:

(11) a. Mary **has been** com-**ing** here every summer,
    b. gathe**ring** plants,
    c. watch**ing** birds,
    d. collect**ing** rocks
    e. and just rest**ing** and hav**ing** a quiet time.

The scope of both the perfect and durative aspects in (11) applies to the entire chain, as does the equi-subject (SS) condition. But the continuative medial and final clauses (11b,c,d,e) are largely unmarked for these aspect, with the relevant auxiliaries appearing only once in (11a). And since subject agreement is marked on the auxiliary in English, these SS-medial clauses also dispense with subject agreement. The only fully-finite clause in (11) is the chain-initial (11a), appearing at the point of maximal disruption of coherence. In sum, the chain-medial clauses in (11) code maximal coherence — equi-subject, equi–tense–aspect–modality, continuing sequential action. In such clauses, the very same reduced tense-aspect-modal and reduced subject marking is found, under the very same conditions of maximal thematic continuity, as in the classical New Guinea clause-chaining systems.

Consider now the consequences of breaking tense-aspect-modal continuity in English:

(12) **Increased finiteness due to aspectual break:**
   a. She was writing to her parents,
   b. telling them about her new flat,
   c. describing the furniture
   d. and poking fun at the neighbors. ⇐ **break in aspectual**
   e. She also **told** them... **continuity**
   f. * , also **told** them... ⇐ **unacceptable**
   alternative to e.

The shift in aspectual coherence between (12d) and (12e) demands terminating the chain with a period in (12d), explicitly marking the new aspect in the new chain-initial clause (12e), and explicitly re-coding the subject in (12e).

Consider next the consequences of breaking the continuity of sequential action:

(13) **Increased finiteness due to sequential action break:**
   a. He **came** into the room,
   b. **stopped,**
   c. **saw** the woman on the couch,
   d. **looked** at her briefly
   e. and **wondered** why she was there. ⇐ **break in sequential**
   f. He **had** been told about her... **action continuity**
   g. * , (**had**) been told about her... ⇐ **unacceptable**
   alternative to f.

The break in sequential action between (13e) and (13f) requires an explicitly-marked perfect aspect (including the auxiliary 'have'), the termination of the chain with a period in (13e), and re-coding the subject more explicitly in (13f).

The same rules seem to govern modal continuity:

(14) **Increased finiteness due to modal discontinuity:**
   a. She **should** go there,
   b. stop by,
   c. pick up a pound of salami
   d. and take it home. ⇐ **break in modal**
   e. She **can** rest then... **continuity**
   f. * , **can** rest then... ⇐ **unacceptable**
   alternative to e.

The break in modal continuity between (14d) and (14e) again requires explicit marking of the unpredictable modality, period intonation, and explicit re-coding of the subject.

Consider, finally, the consequences of a break in referential coherence:

(15) **Increased finiteness due to referential discontinuity**:
  a. He **came** into the room,
  b. **stopped**,
  c. **saw** the woman on the couch,
  d. **looked** at her briefly
  e. and **wondered** why she was there.　⇐ **break in referential**
  f. After a minute she **looked** at him...　**continuity**
  g. * , (she) **looked** at him and...　⇐ **unacceptable**
  　　　　　　　　　　　　　　　　　　　alternative to f.

The lower finiteness of chain-medial clauses seems to be a consequence of their maximal thematic coherence (continuity, predictability) in tense–aspect–modality, sequential action and reference.[18] A break in any of these sub-components of coherence precipitates more finite marking of the clause.

If subordinate clauses were to be considered structurally more complex, and if such presumed complexity had any cognitive basis, then the relevant notion of complexity must be **norm-dependent**. That is, one must first demonstrate independently that main clauses constitute the cognitive norm ('ground'). One must then demonstrate that the speaker/hearer harbors a cognitive expectancy of that norm, and thus finds them easier to process than counter-norm dependent clauses.

2.3.2.2. Frequency distribution

The frequency distribution of main vs. subordinate clauses in discourse is partly genre-dependent. As suggested earlier above (1), oral–informal face-to-face communication tends to have a higher proportion of conjoined clauses, while written–formal academic discourse tends to have a higher proportion of subordinate clauses. Thus, consider the following text-frequency counts from English.

(16) **Frequency distribution of main vs. subordinate
clauses in English narrative**[19]

written-academic						oral-informal					
conjoined		subordinate		total		conjoined		subordinate		total	
N	%	N	%	N	%	N	%	N	%	N	%
43	36%	77	**64%**	120	100%	120	**86%**	20	14%	140	100%

2.3.2.3. Cognitive complexity

We noted earlier above that the oral-informal discourse genre, in which conjoined clauses predominate over subordinated clauses, is acquired earlier and is cognitively easier to process than the written-formal genre. Slobin (ed. 1985) notes in this connection:

> "...Conceptual development determines the order of acquisition..." (1985, vol. I, p. 9).

This general principle seems to underlie the parallelism between the cognitive markedness and order of acquisition. But in addition, a considerable body of experimental psycholinguistic studies seems to suggest that embedded clauses are more difficult to process than conjoined main clauses.[20]

2.3.2.4. Other substantive considerations

As noted in (16) above, conjoined chain-medial clauses predominated in coherent discourse. Such maximally-coherent, less-marked clauses tend to contain, on the average, one chunk of new information and at least one chunk of topical (grounding) information per clause.[21] Subordinate clauses (REL-clauses, ADV-clauses, sentential subjects/objects and verb complements) tend to have a much higher proportion of topical (grounding) information. Given the preponderance of the conjoined clauses in oral discourse, it makes sense that the clause-type that carries the bulk of new information in discourse is also the less-marked norm, both structurally and cognitively.

2.3.3.   The markedness of speech-act types

The argument for the unmarked status of the declarative speech-act is complex. Nonetheless, as any descriptive linguist knows, using the declarative clause as the reference point for grammatical description is as intuitively obvious as any methodological decision that a field linguist must make.

2.3.3.1. Structural complexity

Of the two main non-declarative speech-acts, questions are clearly more complex. Some of their grammatical complexity vis-à-vis declarative clauses is absolute, as in the case of the extra question-morpheme of yes-no questions, or the residual REL-clause structure of some WH-question patterns.[22] Some of the complexity is norm-dependent, as in the variant word-order or intonation pattern of questions.[23] Imperative clauses, the most prototypical manipulative clause type, tend to have a reduced, less-finite structure in the two main grammatical foci: Unexpressed subject NP and reduced verbal inflections.[24] If imperatives are to be considered more complex, their complexity must be norm-dependent, i.e. primarily cognitive.

2.3.3.2. Frequency distribution

There are specialized discourse genres, such as exams, questionnaires, penal codes or the Ten Commandments, where non-declarative clauses predominate. These discourse types are clearly marked, i.e. not the human-universal norm. In both oral and written narrative about everyday human affairs, declarative clauses predominate. In informal–oral conversation, or in the embedded dialogue within written narrative, the percent of non-declarative clauses is higher than in narrative, but still not predominant. These distributional tendencies are illustrated in the following two tables.

(17)   **Frequency of non-declarative clauses in English oral narrative and conversation**[25]

narrative						conversation					
non-decl.		declar.		total		non-decl.		declar.		total	
N	%	N	%	N	%	N	%	N	%	N	%
/	/	109	**100%**	109	100%	46	**46%**	53	53%	99	100%

(18) **Frequency of non-declarative clauses in English written narrative and embedded dialogue[26]**

narrative						dialogue					
non-decl.		declar.		total		non-decl.		declar.		total	
N	%	N	%	N	%	N	%	N	%	N	%
/	/	81	**100%**	81	100%	22	**16%**	115	84%	137	100%

The 46% non-declarative clauses in the conversational text in (17) is probably an over-representation, due to the specific nature of the conversation — an interview between a fluent native speaker and a disfluent pidgin speaker. The 16% manipulative clauses in the embedded conversation in (18) is probably nearer the distributional norm. This suggests that even in conversation, declarative clauses predominate.

2.3.3.3. Cognitive complexity

It is not clear that an argument can be made for a norm-independent lower cognitive complexity of declarative clauses.

2.3.3.4. Other substantive considerations

Early childhood speech-acts are predominantly manipulative (Carter 1974; Dore 1976; Bates *et al.* 1975; Lamendella *ms*). Similarly, primate communication is overwhelmingly manipulative. But both of these facts reflect a prior evolutionary stage of both socio-culture and language, one that is characterized by the following salient features:[27]

(19) **Characteristics of early human socio-culture and communication ('the society of intimates'):**

(a) **Social group**: Intimate, stable, uniform, kin-based
(b) **Cultural universe**: Stable, simple, familiar
(c) **Physical environment**: Stable, familiar
(d) **Subject matter**: Predominantly concerning entities, events, times and places within the immediate speech-situation
(e) **Shared background information**: Derived primarily from situational and generic sources

Under such conditions, most background information necessary to establish the propriety of a manipulative speech-act is either generically shared by all members of the **society of intimates**, or is inferred from the shared speech situation. One way or another, the background requires no overt coding, and communication may proceed directly to its real purpose — manipulating the behavior of the interlocutor.

The major evolutionary change toward the current stage of human communication involved an increase in the social, physical and informational complexity of human culture (i.e. in factors (19a,b,c)). As a result, the informational background necessary to justify — i.e. establish the context for — manipulation could not be assumed anymore to be shared by all members of the speech-community, now a **society of strangers**. Rather, it must be explicitly coded — through declarative propositions. The predominance of declarative speech-acts in human communication as we know it now is an adaptive response to the rise of a complex society, one in which one frequent communicates with non-intimates. The considerable residue of manipulative clauses remains in informal face-to-face communication, and its higher frequency, represents a vestigial survival of an antecedent society of intimates.

2.3.4. Markedness of affirmative and negative clauses

2.3.4.1. Structural complexity

Negative clauses tend to have at least one extra morpheme as compared to the affirmative, and often two, as in e.g. French or Ute. As an example from the latter, consider:[28]

(20) **Negation in Ute**
    a. **Affirmative**:
        mamach   sivaatuch-i paxa-y
        woman/SUBJ goat-OBJ   kill-IMM
        'The woman is killing the goat'
    b. **Negative**:
        mamach   **kacu**-'u sivaatuch-i paxa-**wa**
        woman/SUBJ **NEG**-3s goat-OBJ   kill-**NEG**
        'The woman is not killing the goat'

Further, in many languages negative clauses are historically embedded ('dependent'), with the accompanying syntactic complexity. Thus, in Kru (Niger-Congo), embedded clauses have the OV order, while main clauses are VO:[29]

(21) **Negation in Kru**
  a. **Affirmative main clause** (VO):
     nyeyu-na bla nyino-na
     man-the hit woman-the
     'The man hit the woman'
  b. **Negative** (OV):
     nyeyu-na **si** nyino-na bla
     man-the NEG woman-the hit
     'The man didn't hit the woman'
  c. **Complement clause** (OV):
     nyeyu-na **mū** nyino-na bla
     man-the **go** woman-the hit
     'The man will hit the woman'

2.3.4.2. Frequency distribution

Negative clauses are much less frequent in text than affirmative clauses. This is illustrated in (22) below.

(22) **Frequency distribution of affirmative and negative clauses in English narrative**[30]

	clause type					
	affirmative		negative		total	
text	N	%	N	%	N	%
academic	96	95%	5	**5%**	101	100%
fiction	142	88%	20	**12%**	162	100%

2.3.4.3. Cognitive complexity

The higher cognitive complexity of negative clauses has been documented extensively, in terms of later acquisition by children and higher processing difficulties (H. Clark 1969, 1971a, 1971b, 1974; E. Clark 1971; Hoosain 1973; Hoosain and Osgood 1975). The higher presuppositional complexity of negative clauses, as compared to their corresponding affirmatives, has been discussed elsewhere.[31]

2.3.5. Markedness of active and passive voice

2.3.5.1. Structural complexity

The argument for a norm-independent higher structural complexity of passive clauses is not overwhelming. In passive clauses marked by verbal morphology or an auxiliary, one could argue that more structure is there relative to the active clause. On the other hand, the most common passive clause-type is missing the agent, and is thus shorter and less complex. As an illustration of both features in the same language, consider the following example from Ute (Givón 1980a):

(23) a. **Active**
mamach   sivaatuch-i paxa-qa
woman/SUBJ goat-OBJ   kill-ANT
'The woman killed the goat'
    b. **Impersonal passive**:
sivaatuch-i paxa-**ta**-xa
goat-OBJ   see-**PASS**-ANT
'The goat was killed'

The case for higher structural complexity of the passive is thus stronger in passive types — perhaps better called *inverse* — that retain the agent in an oblique case, as in English:

(24)   The goat **was** kill-**ed by** the woman

2.3.5.2. Text frequency

Clauses in informal, human-oriented everyday discourse are overwhelmingly active. The percentage of passives or other de-transitives is much higher in academic discourse, but still seemingly much lower than actives. Typical active/passive frequency distributions in written English text are given in (25) below.

(25) **Frequency distribution of active and passive clauses in written English**[32]

	clause type					
	active		passive		total	
text type	N	%	N	%	N	%
academic	49	82%	11	**18%**	60	100%
fiction	177	91%	18	**9%**	195	100%
news	45	92%	4	**8%**	49	100%
sports	64	96%	3	**4%**	67	100%

The lower text-frequency of passives (and other de-transitive voice clauses) is further discussed in chapter 3, below.

2.3.5.3. Cognitive complexity

A number of psycholinguistic studies have shown that passive clauses are processed with more difficulty, and acquired later by children, than active clauses.[33] Whether this difficulty is independent of the frequency norm is for the moment unclear.

2.3.5.4. Other substantive considerations

The unmarked status of active clause has its roots in a number of cognitive and cultural domains. The prototypical semantically-transitive event has a salient agent/cause, a salient patient/effect and a bounded, realis, perfective, fast-changing verb (Hopper and Thompson 1980). Prototypical semantically-transitive events are thus perceptually more salient. The prototypical pragmatically-transitive active voice in connected discourse, with the agent occupying the subject/topic grammatical role, reflects the anthropocentric orientation of human culture and human discourse.

2.4. Markedness of nominal modalities

2.4.1. Preamble

The nominal modalities — or grammatical categories that cluster around the noun or noun phrase — to be discussed here are:

(a) case-role
(b) referentiality and individuation
(c) definiteness
(d) anaphoric status
(e) topicality

These categories are not fully independent of each other, and their interactions are asymmetrical, with two categories predominating. First, case-role interacts with all the other categories, so that the markedness of each is computed relative to case-role. Second, topicality also interacts with all the other categories.

2.4.2.   Case-role and markedness

2.4.2.1. The topic hierarchies

The familiar hierarchy of the major semantic roles, as in (26a), reflects the likelihood of a case-role occupying the more topical position(s) in the clause, as well as in discourse.

(26)   **The topicality hierarchies of case-roles**:

    a. **Semantic role**: AGT > DAT/BEN > PAT > LOC > INSTR > OTHERS
    b. **Grammatical role**: SUBJ > DO > IO

The hierarchy of grammatical roles (26b) reflects the grammaticalization of the semantic hierarchy (26a).[34]

2.4.2.2. Structural complexity

The subject and object grammatical roles are the more likely to be morphologically unmarked. This generalization applies primarily to nominative languages. In ergative languages, the transitive subject is most likely to be morphologically marked. Morphologically unmarked indirect objects are relatively rare.[35]

2.4.2.3. Frequency distribution

The more topical semantic roles — agent, dative-benefactive and patient — are the ones most likely to occupy the subject or direct-object grammatical roles. Predictably, subjects and direct-objects are the most frequent grammatical case-roles in text.[36]

2.4.2.4. Cognitive complexity

The unmarked cognitive status of the subject/agent and object/patient case-roles is upheld by their earlier acquisition by children (Slobin, ed. 1985). Since they are the more topical (i.e. recurrent and cognitively activated) participants in the clause, their higher cognitive accessibility may be taken for granted.[37] The subject and direct-object grammatical roles thus code the cognitively more salient participants in states and events.

2.4.3. Referentiality and individuation

Grammatically-marked referentiality of nominal participants turns out to closely coincide — in actual discourse — with topicality (Wright and Givón 1987). The topic-hierarchy literature of the 1970s (cf. in particular Timberlake 1978) also correlates individuation and topicality. And Hopper and Thompson (1980, 1984), in their discussion of prototype events and prototype nominal participants, note that referential and individuated nouns are the prototypical event participants, thus presumable the unmarked case. This generalization is not absolute, but is rather relative to the case-role of the referent. It is true primarily of the three more topical case-roles — subject/agent, object/patient, and dative-benefactive.[38] The predictable relation case-role, referential status and anaphoricity is summarized in (27) below.

(27) **Most likely reference (REF) and definiteness (DEF) status of main clausal participant-types:**[39]

    a. **Verb/predicate**: Nearly 100% NON-REF
    b. **Agent/subject**: Nearly 100% REF & DEF
    c. **Patient/object**: 50%-80% REF & DEF
    d. **Dative/benefactive**: Nearly 100% REF & DEF
    e. **Manner, instrument**: Nearly 100% NON-REF
    f. **Locative**: Nearly 80% REF & DEF
    g. **Time**: Nearly 100% REF & DEF

Since reference and individuation correlate so strongly with topicality, we will defer their discussion till the appropriate section below.

2.4.4. Definiteness

2.4.4.1. Structural complexity

There are no overwhelming grounds for considering definite full NPs structurally more complex than indefinites, at least in languages that mark both

with articles. It has been said that in many languages indefinite are morphologically unmarked. Thus, for example, Li and Thompson (1975) suggested that
this is the case in Mandarin Chinese. A closer examination of the facts reveals
that it is only non-referring — non-topical — indefinites that are unmarked.
Referring, topical indefinite nouns in Mandarin are marked with the numeral
one (plus a classifier).[40] At issue here is thus the markedness status of topical
(important) vs. non-topical (unimportant) NPs.

2.4.4.2. Frequency distribution

The distributional facts, taken at face value, do not support the cognitive
markedness of definites. As can be seen in (27) above, the three most common
case-roles   — subject, direct object and dative-benefactive — tend to be
definite, referring and topical, a tendency that is overwhelming for subjects and
dative-benefactives. However, the bulk of the definite subjects, direct objects
and dative-benefactives accounting for this are either anaphoric pronouns or
zero anaphors. These two grammatical devices code cognitively activated —
thus highly accessible — referents. Whatever its ultimate resolution, the
markedness status of definite vs. indefinite NPs is not independent of case-
roles, anaphoric status and topicality (see below).

2.4.4.3. Cognitive complexity

The argument for considering definite NPs cognitively more complex than
indefinite NPs hinged on the number and complexity of the cognitive operations required for the processing of definite and indefinite referents in coherent
discourse. A summary of suggested cognitive operations triggered by the
grammar of referential coherence is given in (28) below (see also chapter 8).

(28)   **Major grammar-coded cognitive operations
in the grammar of referential coherence:**[41]

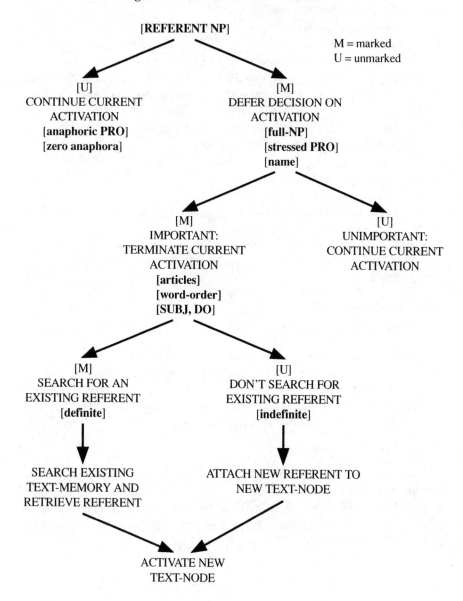

To summarize, definite (and topical) full-NPs are indeed cognitively accessible ('identifiable') to the hearer, with their accessability coming from either one of three distinct sources:

- the immediate speech situation
- some generic-lexical source
- a pre-existing "file" in episodic memory.

While being accessible, definite full-NPs are not currently activated. Processing such referents must involve at least the following grammar-cued cognitive operations:

(a) Determine that the referent is topical/important.
(b) Determine the source of definiteness
    (situational vs. generic vs. episodic)
(c) Search and retrieve their co-referent from the
    episodic memory-file (if that is the source)
(d) De-activate the currently-active topical referent
(e) Activate the new topical referent.

The processing of important indefinite full-NPs, on the other hand, does not require the decision in (b), nor the memory search in (c), but only operations (a), (d) and (e).

2.4.5.   Anaphoric status

2.4.5.1. Structural complexity

The contrast we deal with here is between zero anaphors or unstressed pronouns (also verb agreement), on the one hand, and full NPs (or stressed independent pronouns), on the other. In terms of morphemic size, zero anaphors and unstressed pronouns are the smallest referent-coding devices. They are thus structurally less marked in the most obvious sense.

2.4.5.2. Frequency distribution

In connected coherent discourse, zero anaphors and unstressed pronouns are the most common referent-coding device. This is illustrated in table (29) below with text-distribution data from oral English, Ute and two English-based pidgins, comparing the relative frequency of zero anaphors and pronouns with that of definite full-NPs.

(29) **Text frequency of anaphoric subject pronouns (and
zeroes) and DEF-noun in spoken Ute, spoken English
and two spoken Pidgins** (Givón 1983a, 1983b, 1984a)

	pronoun/zero		def-NP		total	
	N	%	N	%	N	%
Ute	288	**93.5**	20	6.5	308	100.0
English	540	**74.4**	185	25.6	725	100.0
Spanglish	109	**68.9**	54	31.1	163	100.0
Filipinglish	132	**73.3**	48	26.7	180	100.0

2.4.5.3. Cognitive complexity

There are strong grounds for considering zero anaphors and unstressed
pronouns to be cognitively the least-marked — the default processing choice —
referent-coding device in discourse. The argument can be briefly outlined as
follows:[42] Zero anaphors and unstressed pronouns code maximally-continuous
referents, those that are currently activated. They precipitate neither termination,
nor activation, nor search for a co-referent. They thus signal no change in
current cognitive operation — thus default continuation — of the current
activation status.

2.4.6. Topicality and referential continuity

2.4.6.1. Continuous vs. discontinuous topics

The markedness status of topical (i.e. important) vs. non-topical (unimportant) referents is not absolute, but is rather relative to the coherence structure
of the discourse. It depends primarily on whether one is dealing with a continuous or discontinuous referent. As noted above, continuous topical referents —
most commonly coded as zero or anaphoric pronouns — must be considered
the unmarked referent-coding device. In the discourse context of maximal
referential continuity, an important ('topical') referent is thus the unmarked
case, since it merely continues the current activation status.

The markedness situation is reversed for full NPs, which are used to code
discontinuous referents. A full NP coding a discontinuous referent may be
either definite, cuing a search for an existing ('accessible') file, or indefinite
full-NP, cuing the opening of a new file. In the context of referential disconti-

nuity, unimportant (non-topical) referents are the unmarked case and important (topical) are the marked case. This is so because an unimportant referent does not precipitate a change in the current activation status. No cognitive re-orientation takes place; the currently-active important topic continues as such; and the equi-topic thematic chain continues. In contrast, when a full NP — definite or indefinite — is coded as an important (topical) referent, a change-of-topic is precipitated, involving a number of cognitive operations (see (28) above).

2.4.6.2. Structural complexity

Important (or referring) full-NPs are morphologically more marked vis-à-vis unimportant (or non-referring) NPs. Thus, in the most typical case, the numeral 'one' codes important indefinite referents, while unimportant referents are zero-coded. This is the case in Mandarin, Turkish, Hebrew, Creoles and many other languages. As an illustration, consider the following example from Krio.[43]

(30) a. **Referring/important participant**:
          wan-man don   wok as meseynja na   **wan**-fam
          REF-man finish work as messenger LOC REF-firm
          'A man (once) finished his career as a messenger
          in a commercial firm'

     b. **Non-referring/unimportant participant**:
          di moni wey denh go-gi-am   foh grachuiti
          the money REL they FUT-give-him for gratuity
          'the money that they were going to give him
          as gratuity'

Both 'man' and 'firm' in (30a) are important, referring, recurring topics in the narrative. In contrast, 'gratuity' appears only once in the entire story, and is used in a non-referring sense.

2.4.6.3. Frequency distribution

Important full-NPs are less frequent in text than unimportant ones. The bulk of full NPs in text are unimportant or non-referring topical. This contrasts sharply with of the frequency situation in zero anaphors and pronouns, which are both important and frequent in text. This reversal is not surprising. For important entities to be salient, they must stand out as the less frequent figure vis-à-vis the more frequent unimportant referents (ground). Few important topics are introduced into the discourse as full NPs; but they recur a lot — as zero-anaphors or pronouns. As illustration of this, consider the frequency distribution of important (recurrent) and unimportant (non-recurrent) indefinite NPs in spoken Mandarin and spoken English:[44]

(31) **Frequency distribution of important and unimportant indefinite NPs in spoken Mandarin Chinese text**
(Wright and Givón, 1987)

important (ave. persistence 3.1 clauses)		unimportant (ave. persistence 0.23 clause)		total	
N	%	N	%	N	%
40	38%	65	**62%**	105	100%

(32) **Frequency distribution of important and unimportant indefinite NPs in spoken English text**
(Wright and Givón, 1987)

important (ave. persistence 0–2 clauses)		unimportant (ave. persistence 3–10 clauses)		total	
N	%	N	%	N	%
37	22.7%	113	**77.3%**	150	100%

2.4.6.4. Cognitive complexity

One can make an argument, again based on the number of mental processing operations involved (see (28) above), to support the higher cognitive complexity of important full-NPs. Being either definite or indefinite, their processing will require:[45]

(a)   terminating the currently-active topic;
(b)   activating a new topic; and either
(c)   searching for an existing memory file (DEF), or
(d)   opening a new file (INDEF).

In contrast, unimportant references are themselves filed as new information under the currently-active topic file, thus continuing current activation.

2.5.   Markedness of verbal modalities

2.5.1.   Suggested markedness values

The binary contrasts discussed here are given in (33) below, together with their suggested markedness status.

(33)   **Markedness of verbal modalities**:

category	unmarked	marked
(a) **Modality**	realis	irrealis
(b) **Perfectivity**	perfective	imperfective
(i) Termination	terminated	incompletive
(ii) Compactness	compact	durative
(c) **Perfectness**	preterit	perfect
(i) Sequentiality	in-sequence	off-sequence
(ii) Relevance	event-anchored	speech-anchored

2.5.2.   Structural complexity

The unmarked morphological status of the realis, terminated, compact, in-sequence, event-anchored categories has been discussed extensively elsewhere.[46] Thus, for example, in Creoles languages, where all grammatical markers arise at roughly the same diachronic stage, the zero-marked verb form codes the realis, perfective, preterit aspect. This zero verb-form contrasts, for each category, with a marked morpheme. As illustration, consider the verb-forms of Krio:

(34) **Krio verb morphology**

    a. **Preterit** (unmarked):
       i   rayt
       he write
       'he wrote'
    b. **Irrealis**:
       i   **go**-rayt
       he FUT-write
       'he **will** write'
    c. **Durative**:
       i   **de**-rayt
       he DUR-write
       'he is writing'
    d. **Perfect (i)**:
       i   **bin**-rayt
       he PERF-write
       'He has/had written'
    e. **Perfect** (ii):
       i   **bin-rayt-don**
       he PERF-write-PERF
       'He has/had already finished writing'

2.5.3. Frequency distribution

The distributional evidence supporting the markedness assignment suggested in (33) has been discussed in Hopper and Thompson (1980) and elsewhere. Recapitulating briefly, the realis, perfective, preterit verb-form tends to be the most common in discourse. But this distributional norm is genre-dependent, and is typical primarily of everyday action-oriented narrative discourse. This norm is part of the transitive clause prototype (Hopper and Thompson 1980). Other discourse genres may show different distributional profiles. For example, both academic and procedural discourse display a predominance of the habitual tense-aspect, which is a sub-category of both irrealis and imperfective. As an illustration of this genre-dependence of the text-frequency of tense–aspect–modality, consider their distribution in action-oriented fiction vs. academic text in English.

(35)   **The distribution of aspect and modality in action-oriented fiction and academic English text**[47]

category	academic		fiction	
	N	%	N	%
preterit	2	2%	74	**56%**
irrealis	18	**20%**	8	6%
habitual	62	**70%**	/	/
durative[48]	/	/	43	**32%**
perfect	7	8%	8	6%
total:	89	100%	133	100%

In the following sections we will discuss each verbal modality briefly, concentrating on the substantive aspects of its markedness.

2.5.4. Substantive considerations

2.5.4.1. Modality

The unmarked cognitive status of the realis modality (vs. irrealis) is probably due to both cognitive and socio-cultural factors. For realis to be cognitively the unmarked modality, one must then assume that events that did occur in real time and space, or are occurring at the time of speech, are more salient in the mind than events that did not occur, or might occur at some hazy future date. The basis for this assumption must be found in properties of human perception and memory: Directly-witnessed events are more memorable than unwitnessed ones.[49] And memory traces of the past, arising from either direct experience or the testimony of a reliable witness, are more salient, stored better and retrieved faster, than potential, hypothetical or future events that are yet to occur. The higher text-frequency of realis in everyday human discourse may also reflect its higher socio-cultural relevance: Events that did happen or are happening are more likely to affect one's life than hypothetical future events.

2.5.4.2. Perfectivity

Perfectivity involves two related aspects of boundedness: (a) The presence (unmarked) vs. absence (marked) of a terminal boundary; and (b) the degree of temporal diffusion of the event at both boundaries — i.e. whether it is compact (unmarked) or diffuse (marked). A sharply-bounded event is perceptually and cognitively more salient. And the terminal boundary feature of the perfective also relates it, in most languages, to the unmarked realis-past modality.

2.5.4.3. The perfect

The marked category perfect involves in many languages two distinct aspects — counter-sequentiality and current relevance — each with its own grounds for markedness.[50]

2.5.4.3.1. Counter-sequentiality

As noted earlier above, connected discourse is highly continuous in all sub-elements of coherence, including temporal coherence. High temporal coherence, i.e. events related in-sequence in the thematic paragraph, is coded grammatically by the less-marked preterit aspect. The unmarked status of the preterit vis-à-vis the marked counter-sequential perfect thus reflects the asymmetry of the discourse-coherence norm.

Sequentiality involves not only temporal coherence, but also action coherence. Human action sequences are complex, and come in natural, culture-based routines. Compare for example:

(36)   a. He opened the door, came in, sat down and started to eat.
       b. ?He came in, opened the door, started to eat and sat down.
       c. ?He started to eat, sat down, came in and opened the door.
       d. ?He opened the door, started to eat, sat down and came in.

There is nothing illogical or physically implausible in the counter-normative (36b,c,d). But they do not represent the conventional norm.

2.5.4.3.2. Relevance

The unmarked sequential preterit tends to signal that the event was relevant at the time when it occurred. The marked perfect, on the other hand, codes events that are relevant at some later time — either speech-time ('present perfect') or some past time following the event ('pluperfect'). It is not clear what the basis for the marked status of the perfect is, especially given the privileged position of speech-time as the deictic anchor of human verbal communication. However, events whose relevance is dissociated from their own time-axis tend to be rendered off-sequence. They are presented in discourse at the time when they are relevant rather than in the natural order they occurred.

Consider for example the contrast between the preterit in (37c) and the pluperfect in (38c):

(37) **In-sequence**:
   a. So she left,
   b. went back home,
   c. **ate** dinner
   d. and went to sleep.

(38) **Off-sequence**:
   a. So she left
   b. and went back home.
   c. She **had already eaten** dinner,
   d. so she went to sleep.

The perfect may be thus marked for another reason — not because of its delayed relevance feature, but because in breaks the unmarked norm of narrating events in the same order in which they occurred (see section 2.5.4.3.1. above).

2.6.   Markedness as meta-iconicity

2.6.1.   Meta-iconicity and naive iconism

The discussion of markedness above raises, implicitly, an issue that has been central for our understanding of the natural relation between the linguistic code and its *designatum*. That is, the traditional if often tacit assumption:

(39) **The meta-iconic markedness principle**:

> "Categories that are structurally more marked
> are also substantively more marked".

Assumption (39) is a ubiquitous article of faith for functionalists, reflecting their belief in some idealized one-to-one correlation between form and meaning. To cite Bolinger (1977):

> "...The natural condition of language is to preserve one form
> for one meaning, and one meaning for one form..." (1977, p. x)

As Haiman (1985) points out, Bolinger's "natural condition" is a useful idealized benchmark, but like all useful idealization it is somewhat over-extended, for two independent reasons. First, both polysemy and homophony are common fare in human language, but synonymy is rare, a mirage. Form-to-function correlations thus tend to be often one-to-many, but never many-to-one, respectively. Second, the ideal iconicity ('fidelity') between the linguistic code and its designatum is subject to corrosive diachronic pressures from both ends of the diachronic cycle of grammaticalization. First, the code is constantly eroded by phonological attrition. And second, the message is constantly modified by creative elaboration. Thus, the general tendency toward iconicity is undeniable, but it is not an absolute tendency; it is strongly mitigated by diachronic change.

Bolinger's idealization often becomes an ideological trap for functionalists, a trap that may be called **naive iconism**. The naive iconist, or ideological functionalist, assume that substantive markedness — distributional, cognitive — *always* goes along with structural markedness. But the facts turn out to always be more complex. Finally, as noted above, the various aspects of markedness — structural complexity, frequency distribution and substantive markedness — must be examined independent of each other, in order for their "correlation" to be real rather than circular. Their correlations must then be noted as a matter of empirical fact rather than ideological faith.

2.6.2.   Diachronic change and markedness reversal

2.6.2.1. Ritualized structure

There is a very common type of **re-grammaticalization** that is found when the functional range of a grammatical construction is extended — much like in lexical sense-extension — to new contexts. One mechanism driving such extension of the functional range of constructions is analogy or similarity. But due to the inherent conservatism of structure, grammatical structures that had been previously quite isomorphic with their functions lose their isomorphism. For quite a while, such structures may continue to be isomorphic to their older functions. One consequence of this is an increase in what Haiman (1992) calls **ritualization** — the correlation between form and function has become, at least for the moment, somewhat arbitrary.

Consider, for example, the formal behavior of serial verbs that have become, functionally, prepositions or post-positions. In their extended capacity they now mark nominal case-roles. But for quite a while after their functional re-grammaticalization they may still carry formal — morpho-syntactic — verb properties. Thus in Akan (Niger-Congo), serial verbs must carry the same tense-aspect marker as the main verb in their clause, regardless of whether their meaning is verbal or not (Osam, 1993):

(40) a. **Verb meaning**:
Araba ma-**a**   Ebo nam
Araba give-PAST Ebo fish
'Araba gave Ebo (a) fish'
  b. **Verbal meaning in chained clause**:
Araba tǫ-ǫ   nam ma-**a**   Ebo
Araba buy-PAST fish give-PAST Ebo
'Araba bought (a) fish and gave (it) to Ebo'
  c. **Case-role meaning**:
Araba yę-ę   edwuma ma-**a**   Ebo
Araba do-PAST work   give-PAST Ebo
'Araba worked *for* Ebo'

There is nothing natural about nominal case-markers carrying tense-aspects, which are prototypically verbal inflections. Suffixed to a nominal case-marker, a tense-aspect morpheme is indeed highly marked.

2.6.2.2. Cyclic fluctuations of markedness

In one sense, a new function coded by an old structure is **under-marked**. It shares the extended structure with some other function(s). Only gradually does the new function begin to acquire its own distinct structural characteristics. When that has occurred, the new function is not under-marked any more, but rather well-marked. Isomorphism between structure and function has been restored.

But a newly-grammaticalized function is often structurally **over-marked**. This is common in the rise of grammatical morphology, when new morphemes tend to be larger and more distinct, while decaying old morphemes are eroded or zeroed out. In the rise of new tense-aspect-modal morphology, for example, the last shreds of decaying old inflections are replaced by new, large, de-verbal auxiliaries, without portmanteau or morpho-phonemics. In the same vein, in the rise of new case-marking morphology, large, distinct relational nouns or serial verbs displace decaying older case morphology. At the tail end of the grammaticalization cycle, the converse situation is often found. An old form-function pairing may be structurally under-marked, due to eroded morphology.

As an example of the entire cycle, consider the evolution of the indefinite article in English. In Old English, the numeral 'one' was pressed into use as marker of referential (important) indefinite nouns. This gave rise to a contrast between the marked 'one' and the unmarked zero (as in Creole or Mandarin). Schematically:

(41) a. **Non-referring object**:
     She wanted to buy house
     (but couldn't find any. 'house' = not a specific one)
   b. **Referring object**:
     She wanted to buy **one** house
     (because she liked it. 'one house' = a particular one)

At this early stage, structural markedness fully matched substantive markedness. But over time 'one' bleached out both semantically and phonologically, to become the unrestricted indefinite marker *a(n)*. Now the referring and non-referring noun are equally marked:

(42) a. **Non-referring object**:
     She wanted to buy **a** house
     (but couldn't find any. 'a house' = not a specific one)
   b. **Referring object**:
     She wanted to buy **a** house
     (because she liked it. 'a house' = a particular one)

Finally, in current spoken American English a new marker for referring (important) nominals has arisen, the unstressed 'this'. The old *a(n)* is by now morphologically almost a *zero,* so that the contrast between *a* and *this* in the spoken language re-establishes the referring noun as marked, and the non-referring noun as unmarked:

(43) a. **Non-referring object**:
     She wanted to buy **a**-house
     (but couldn't find any. 'a house' = not a specific one)
   b. **Referring object**:
     She wanted to buy **this** house
     (because she liked it. 'this house' = a particular one)

Given the discrepancy between structural and substantive markedness that characterizes both the beginning and the end of grammaticalization cycles, it may well be that only at some mid-point in the life of a grammatical construction — after its structural differentiation but before its structural erosion — do we find maximal correspondence — iconicity — between the structural and substantive aspects of markedness.

2.7.   Naive functionalism and excess structure

Whenever naive functionalists confront a structure whose semantic or pragmatic functions are less than obvious, they feel compelled to come up with a functional correlate, come what may. This compulsion carries with it the germs of logical *non sequitur*:

(44)   **Naive functionalist faith**:
"Because most structures reveal a considerable measure of iso-morphism with paired functions, no structure could possibly hang around without some obvious function paired to it."

As a heuristic exercise, (44) is sometime beneficial, in that it compels the linguist to look around for less-than-obvious communicative functions. It thus serves as useful antidote to extreme structuralism. But given what we know about markedness reversal through diachronic change, naive functionalism must be surely tempered by caution.

One notion that must temper naive functionalism is known in biology as **excess structure**. Some component of biological structure cannot be paired isomorphically in an obvious way to any specific function. In many cases, such excess structures perform more abstract global functions that are harder to pin down. In other cases, excess structures are the bio-design consequence of the way more concrete — obvious — functions are represented isomorphically. An example of this can be seen in the design of DNA as a code for protein produc-tion.[51] The most concrete elements in this code are sequences of nucleotide triplets. Each triplet on the DNA chain codes for a particular amino acid on the protein chain. This correspondence is 100% isomorphic. However, interspersed between such concrete segments of the DNA code are occasional nucleotide sequences that do not correspond to any amino acid in the protein chain. Some of these seemingly redundant nucleotides function as higher-level governors, they block or release entire sequences of the more concrete — isomorphic — code. Their function is thus more global and abstract. But other segments in the linear DNA chain are apparently fillers, they seem to be there in order to ensure a particular spacing of the more concrete elements in the code. And others yet may be there as mere by-products of the way other elements of the complex structure, elements with more obvious functions, are organized.

Complex hierarchic functions most often map onto complex hierarchic structures. The greater the complexity of function, with higher and higher hierarchy levels, the more hierarchic and abstract is the structure; and the less obvious is the correlation between structure and function.

2.8.   Markedness, cognition and communication

2.8.1.   Saliency and frequency

Markedness is fundamentally an adaptive cognitive strategy for economy of processing. It tackles the potentially-random continuum of "external reality" with a strong innate bias, converting it into strongly asymmetrical cognitive dimensions. The bias yields two seemingly contradictory tendencies:

(a)   **Saliency:**
       Salient experience types are filtered in, non-salient
       experience types are filtered out.

(b)   **Frequency:**
       Frequent experience types are accorded more efficient,
       automated processing. Infrequent experience types are
       processed less efficiently.

The unmarked end of cognitive dimensions is the **default** choice in processing. One of the best illustrations for this is paired antonymic adjectives. It is well known that the positive member of such pairs, the one that denotes the presence of a quality, is the unmarked member, covering the entire scale. The negative member, on the other hand, is marked and covers only its own extreme. This may be seen in the biased acceptability of answers to questions:

(45) a.   **Affirmative adjective question:**
            How long is it?
            =Very long.
            =Very short.

      b.   **Negative adjective question:**
            How short is it?
            =*Very long
            =very short

The positive member of paired adjectives denoting perceptual or physical dimensions denotes, without exception, the perceptually more salient pole:

(46) **Paired adjectives and perceptual saliency:**

positive	negative	perceptual property
big	small	ease of visual perception
long	short	,, ,, ,, ,,
tall	short	,, ,, ,, ,,
wide	narrow	,, ,, ,, ,,
fat/thick	thin	,, ,, ,, ,,
high	low	,, ,, ,, ,,
light	dark	,, ,, ,, ,,
near	far	,, ,, ,, ,,
fast	slow	ease of visual perception
loud	quiet	ease of auditory perception
high note	low note	,, ,, ,, ,,
sharp	dull	ease of tactile perception
heavy	light	ease of weight perception
rough	smooth	ease of tactile perception
spicy	bland	ease of taste perception

On the face of it, the relation between salience and frequency is contradictory. Salient experience is clearly the less frequent **figure**, standing out on the more frequent **ground**. How is it then that the more salient positive adjectives — and positive events and states in general — are the unmarked case in language?

The paradox turns out to be only apparent. Once the vast continuum of possible experience has been filtered out, only the small portion of salient experience remains to be dealt with cognitively. That portion now constitute the presence of experience, the totality — 100% — of experience that is cognized and communicated. Salient events and states have thus become the more frequent, unmarked norm. Communication about non-events or non-states is now the more rare, marked counter-norm. Cognition is thus not the simple Aristotelian mirror of external ('real') experience. Rather, it is a constructive filter that shapes experience in adaptively-advantageous ways.

2.8.2. Cognitive vs. cultural saliency

The markedness values that emerge past the filters of cognition and language are not biased only by the saliency of physical perception, but also by cultural perspective. A clear demonstration of this is found in Cooper and Ross's (1975) account of order preferences in frozen noun-conjunctions.

(47)

preferred order (unmarked > marked)	less-preferred order (marked > unmarked)
a. **Near > far**:	
now and then,	*then and now
here and there,	*there and here
this and that,	*that and this
b. **Adult > young**:	
father and son,	*son and father
mother and daughter,	*daughter and mother
c. **Male > female**:	
man and wife,	*wife and man
d. **Male > female > young**:	
men, women and children,	*children, women and men
e. **Singular > plural**:	
one and all,	*all and one
ham and eggs,	*eggs and ham
cheese and crackers,	*crackers and cheese
f. **Large > small**:	
large and small,	*small and large
g. **Singular/large > plural/small**:	
hammer and nails,	*nails and hammer
h. **Animate > inanimate**:	
life and death,	*death and life
i. **Human > non-human**:	
a man and a dog,	*a dog and a man
j. **Agent/large > patient/small**:	
cat and mouse,	*mouse and cat
k. **Whole/one > part/many**:	
hand and finger(s)	*finger(s) and hand
whole and parts	*parts and whole
l. **Salient > non-salient**:	
day and night	*night and day
m. **Whole/visible > part/invisible:**	
body and soul	*soul and body
n. **Possessor > possessed**:	
John and his brother,	*his brother and John
o. **Positive > negative**:	
more or less,	*less or more
plus or minus,	*minus or plus
good and bad,	*bad and good

The ordering hierarchies in (47) correspond closely to well-known marked-ness assignments, with the unmarked member always preceding the marked one. Some, like near > far (47a), singular > plural (47e)/(47g), large > small (47f)/(47g), salient > non-salient (47l), visible > invisible (47m) and positive > negative (47o), are firmly grounded in the perceptual saliency noted in (46). But others are grounded — at least partly — in **cultural perspective**. Thus, while adults are larger than children (47b) and males larger than females (47c), it is the cultural reality of power and social control that makes 'adult' and 'male' the unmarked case vis-à-vis the marked 'young' and 'female'. Similarly, while animates move and inanimates are stationary (47h), it is our egocentric cultural perspective as an animate species that makes 'animate' the unmarked and 'inanimate' the marked case. Likewise, it is our egocentric cultural perspective again that makes 'human' the unmarked and 'non-human' the marked category (47i). And it is no doubt the cultural perspective of power and control that makes the 'possessor' unmarked and the 'possessed' marked (47n).

The role of culture in the assignment of markedness does not contravene what we know about perceptual saliency. Rather, it suggests that cognitive saliency — and with it linguistic markedness — is not a purely physiological phenomenon, but rather the product of interaction between the more perceptual and the more cultural aspect of cognition. That reality is constructed at the intersection of the two is not exactly a surprise.

Notes

*) I am indebted to John Haiman, Winfred Lehmann and the late Dwight Bolinger for many helpful comments and suggestions.

1) In their work on markedness; see in particular Troubetzkoy (1958/1969, 1975), Jakobson (1932/1971, 1939/1962, 1974), Jakobson and Waugh (1979), Jakobson and Pomorska (1980). For extensive discussion, of both history and substance, see Greenberg (1966a, 1976), H. Andersen (1966, 1973, 1974, 1979), and in particular Shapiro (1983).

2) So that indefinite-subject ('presentative') clauses have well known exceptional ('marked') syntactic characteristics, in terms of word-order, pronominal agreement, and nominal morphology. They are thus syntactically more complex (see Givón, 1990b, ch. 17).

3) In connected discourse, definite referents outnumber indefinite ones by a wide margin. See discussion further below as well as in chapter 8.

4) Using criteria of cognitive complexity to argue for the markedness of contexts is a more tricky enterprise. In both perception and cognition, quite often frequency of exposure is a major factor in determining processing speed. In the same vein, frequency is the major factor in motivating automated (fast) vs. attended (slow) processing.

5) This is one clear distortion in my earliest treatment of syntactic markedness (Givón, 1979a, ch. 2), where a single substantive dimension (new vs. old information) was used to explain markedness in a multiplicity of grammatical domains. The same also applies to schools that endeavor to explain markedness by reference only to the internal properties of the semiotic system (e.g. Shapiro 1983, ch. 2). From the perspective adopted here, semiotic explanations that do not refer to entities outside the code system are functionalist in a weak sense (Givón 1979a, ch. 1; 1989, ch. 8).

6) An exceptionless isomorphism between the substantive and formal correlates of markedness — perfect iconicity — is seldom found in human language, where both the exceptions to iconicity and the common iconic tendencies arise via diachronic pathways of grammaticalization and structural erosion. See discussion further below.

7) See note 6 above. The most common source of this pervasive conservatism of structure, as compared to function, is diachronic functional change, which normally outpaces structural adjustment; see Givón (1979a, ch. 6).

8) See Keenan and Bennett (eds. 1977), Ochs (1979) or Givón (1979a, ch. 5), *inter alia*.

9) See discussion of the pre-grammatical vs. grammatical mode of communication in Givón (1979a, ch. 5; 1989, ch. 7), as well as in chapter 8 below.

10) For first language acquisition see Bloom (1973), Bates (1976), Scollon (1976), Limber (1973), Slobin (1977, ed. 1985), Givón (1979a, ch. 5), *inter alia*. For natural second language acquisition see Bickerton (1981), Schumann (1976, 1978) R. Andersen (1979), Givón (1979a, 1984b, 1989), *inter alia*.

11) For evidence on the greater processing difficulty of complex and embedded clauses, which are much more frequent in the grammaticalized written-formal mode, see Bever (1968), Bever and Townsend (1979), Brown and Hanlon (1970), Fodor and Garrett (1967), Gough (1965), Kornfeld (1974), McMahon (1963), Mehler (1963), Savin and Perchonok (1965), Slobin (1966, ed. 1985) *inter alia*. While the discussion in many of the earlier studies is couched in terms of "transformational complexity", and while some of the data — particularly those measuring immediate recall — may be subject to different interpretations (see Gernsbacher 1985), the results correlate fairly consistently syntactic complexity, order of acquisition by children, and processing difficulty. One feature in (1) — processing speed — seems to belie these cognitive claims, since grammaticalized communication indeed proceeds much faster than pidgin communication. However, this seeming exception is due to the fact that grammar is a more automated, streamlined mode of communication, and automaticity is associated with speeded processing (cf. Schneider and Shiffrin 1977; Schneider 1985, *inter alia*).

12) For extensive discussion see Goodwin (1981).

13) See Ervin-Tripp (1970), Bloom (1973), Limber (1973), Keenan-Ochs (1974a, 1974b, 1975a, 1975b), Scollon (1976) or Slobin (ed. 1985), *inter alia*.

14) See Givón (1990b, ch. 19).

15) Generative accounts have considered these to be conjoined verb phrases, thus "governed" clauses under a single PS tree. See e.g. Stockwell *et al.* (1973) or McCawley (1988).

16) See Givón (1990b, chapter 19).

17) *Ibid.*

18) Thematic coherence is a multi-strand composite, with these three strands being the most concrete and easiest to quantify; see chapter 8.

19) The oral text was pp. 1–3 of the transcript of a life-story narrative, told by a retired New Mexico rancher (see Givón, 1983a). The written text was pp. 4–7 of Chomsky (1971).

20) See references in note 11, above.

21) See chapter 8.

22) See Givón (1990b, ch. 18).

23) *Ibid.*

24) *Ibid.* In many languages the imperative is the simplest, shortest verb-form.

25) The oral narrative was the first 3 pp. of transcript of a Korean-English Pidgin life-story, originally recorded by D. Bickerton in his Hawaii English Project (Bickerton and Odo, 1976) and described in Givón (1984b). The oral conversation is the first 3 pp. of transcript of a conversation between an English speaker and a Spanish-English Pidgin speaker, originally recorded by J. Schumann and discussed in Givón (1984b).

26) The written text, narrative interlaced with dialogue, was pp. 68-71 of McMurtry (1963).

27) For discussion see Givón (1979a, chs. 5, 7).

28) From Givón (1980a).

29) From Givón (1975a).

30) The academic text is pp. 119–120 of Haiman (1985). The fiction text is pp. 76–77 of McMurtry (1963).

31) See Givón (1979a, ch. 3).

32) From Givón (1979a, ch. 2), where the original sources of the various texts are cited. The category "passive" does not include various active-impersonal clause types. Academic discourse is thus probably much richer in de-transitive clauses than these figures imply.

33) See references cited in note 11, above.

34) See Keenan and Comrie (1972), Hawkinson and Hyman (1974).

35) In few languages, such as the Arawak languages of Peru, all object nouns are morphologically unmarked. Their semantic role is coded on the verb. The lone exception is the patient, whose semantic role remains uncoded. However, the patient is the prototypical direct object, a syntactic role that is pronominally marked on the verb (David Payne, in personal communication; see also Givón, 1990b, ch. 17) as well as chapter 5 below.

36) Regardless of anaphoric status.

37) See discussion further below as well as in chapter 8.

38) While the 'locative' and 'time' semantic roles are highly referring and anaphoric, they are not thematically important, a fact corroborated by their low cataphoric persistence in the discourse.

39) The data are summarized from Greenberg (1974) and Givón (1979a, ch. 2).

40) See discussion in Givón (1984b, ch. 11) as well as Wright and Givón (1987).

41) For full details see chapter 8 below, as well as Givón (1990b, ch. 20) and Chafe (1987).

42) See note 41 above.

43) See extensive details in Givón (1984b, ch. 11) as well as Wright and Givón (1987).

44) Comparable figures are not yet available for definite NPs. Further, there are grounds for suspecting that the majority of definite NPs in text code *important* referents.

45) See Givón (1982a).

46) See Givón (1977, 1982a).

47) The academic text was pp. 21–23 of Haiman (1985). The fiction text was pp. 83–85 of L'Amour (1962).

48) The paucity of the durative verb-form in the academic text is to some extent misleading. Of the 62 verb tokens in the habitual category, 47 — 76% — were 'be' (or 'exist') with adjectival, participial or nominal predicates. The remaining 15 tokens of non-be verbs were: 'think', 'believe', 'have', 'seem' (2), 'assert', 'share', 'denote', 'include', 'express', 'define', 'allow', 'survive', 'cite', 'come' — overwhelmingly stative verbs.

49) The strongest evidential category is used when the event was eye-witnessed. In the grammar of evidentiality, that category tends to be morphologically the unmarked. For further details, see Chafe and Nichols (eds. 1986).

50) In some languages the two are not united. Thus, for example, in Ute the perfect has only the counter-sequence function, while the current relevance function is merged with the 'immediate'/-'present' aspect (see Givón 1982a; 1984b, ch. 8).

51) See Leder (1982), Tonegawa (1985), Alt *et al.* (1987), Rajewsky *et al.* (1987).

3

The Functional Basis of
Grammatical Typology

3.1.   Introduction*

The underlying theme of this chapter has been lurking in the cellars of functional linguistics in an unresolved form, an embarrassing family skeleton that somehow refuses to die. Traditionally and intuitively, the functional approach to grammar has tended to coincide with strong interest in a systematic approach to cross-language diversity; that is, to **grammatical typology**. True, the relative emphasis on these two associated traits — functionalism and typology — has tended to shift from one linguist to the next. So that some functionalists (say Comrie) may emphasize typology more than function; others (say Halliday or Lakoff) may pull in the opposite direction. But a strong current of association, as best exemplified in the work of Joseph Greenberg, has persisted. Still, typologists often behave as if the practice of grammatical typology takes place in a functional vacuum.

In this chapter I use the (functional and typological) analysis of de-transitive voice, and in particular of inverse constructions, as a cautionary tale. The tale suggests why the practice of function-blind typology is unworkable and indeed logically bizarre — not only for functionalists but also for all linguists. A second theme is a bit more familiar, the profound interaction between diachronic change — grammaticalization — and grammatical typology.

Voice is probably the most complex grammar-coded functional domain in language. On the functional side, it spans a range of clause-semantic and discourse-pragmatic dimensions, ones that interact in complex ways across the oft-permeable boundary between semantics and pragmatics. On the structural side, voice is coded in any natural language by a large family of distinct grammatical constructions. Given the relative permeability of the boundary between semantics and pragmatics, it is not always easy to tell apart constructions that code more semantic aspects of voice from those that code its more pragmatic aspects. In spite of this potential overlap, clear prototypes of "more semantic" and "more pragmatic" voice constructions do exist. For the purpose of this chapter, I will zero in on constructions that involve primarily the pragmatics of de-transitive voice.

3.2.   The functional basis of grammatical typology

A cross-linguistic grammatical typology is nonsensical unless it is based on an independent functional definition of the domain to be "typed".[1] This ought to be such an obvious truism that one is surprised how often it is ignored, not only by structuralists but also by many *bona fide* functionalists.

The following fundamental logical assumption is indeed made by all cross-linguistic typologists, regardless of theoretical orientation:

(1)   **The logical assumption of taxonomy**:
       "In different languages we find different **types** of structures
       that somehow must be grouped together as members of the
       same **meta-type**".

But "same meta-type" of what?

The naive traditional assumption, whether explicit or not, has always been that types of structures are grouped by typologists into the same meta-type of structures. It should take only a brief examination of the facts to convince ourselves that this simple-minded taxonomic approach to typology — grouping structural sub-types into their structural meta-types — could not possibly be right. This is so because in following such a procedure we have no secure way of deciding by purely structural criteria why structure A (in language *a*) and structure B (in language *b*) should be grouped together as sub-types of structural meta-type X; while structure C (in language *c*) and structure D (in language *d*) should be grouped together as sub-types of structural meta-type Y.

One could of course argue that a purely structural criterion for such sub-grouping does exist, namely **structural similarity**. One can then observe the pattern of structural similarities between A,B,C,D and then group them accordingly. This sounds feasible in principle, but one concrete example will demonstrate the total bankruptcy of such an approach in real typological space.

Consider cross-linguistic diversity of passive construction. A quick typological survey would reveal the following major structural sub-types:

(A) **Adjectival-stative:**
In some languages, such as English, a passive clause arose diachronically from, and still structurally resembles, a predicate-adjective or stative-resultative clause, as in:

(2)   a. **Passive:**   It was broken (by someone)
       b. **Adjectival-stative:**   It is broken
       c. **Perfect-resultative:** It has been broken
       d. **Predicate-adjective:** It is big

(B) **Nominalization:**
In some languages, such as Ute, a passive clause arose diachronically from, and still structurally resembles, a nominalized clause:[2]

(3)   a. **Passive:**
          múusa-ci p<u>a</u>xá-**ta**-p<u>u</u>ga
          cat-OBJ   kill-PASS-REM
          'The cat was killed'
       b. **Nominalization:**
          múusa-paxá-**ta** ka-'áy-wa-t<u>u</u>   'ura-'ay
          cat-kill-**NOM**   NEG-good-NEG-NOM be-IMM
          'Cat-killing is bad'

(C) **Reflexive:**
In some languages, such as Spanish, a passive clause arose diachronically from, and still structurally resembles, a reflexive-reciprocal middle-voice clause:[3]

(4)   a. **Impersonal passive:**
          se-curó   a   los brujos
          REF-cure/**3s** OBJ the sorcerer
          'Someone cured the sorcerers'
       b. **Reflexive:**
          se armó de   todas sus armas
          REF arm/3s with all   his weapons
          'he armed himself with all his weapons'
       c. **Reciprocal:**
          se   combatían
          RECIP fight/IMPF/3p
          'they fought each other'

    d. **Middle-voice**:

       se   curaron   los brujos

       REF cure/PAST/3p the sorcerers

       'The sorcerers got well'

       'The sorcerers cured themselves'

(D) **L-dislocation**:

In some languages, such as Kimbundu, a passive construction arose diachronically from, and still structurally resembles, a left-dislocation construction:[4]

    (5)   a. **Passive**:

          Nzua **a-mu**-mono   kwa meme

          John **they-him**-saw by   me

          'John was seen by me'

          (lit.: 'John, they saw him by me')

       b. **L-dislocation**:

          Nzua, aana   **a-mu**-mono

          John   children **they-him**-saw

          'John, the children saw him'

       c. **Impersonal-subject with L-dislocation**:

          Nzua, **a-mu**-mono

          John   **they-him**-saw

          'John, they saw him' (anaphoric)

          'John, he was seen' (impersonal)

(E) **Inverse clause**:

Finally, in some languages, such as Bella Coola, the passive clause arose diachronically, and still structurally resembles, an inverse clause. In Bella Coola, one surviving vestige of the clause's erstwhile inverse function is the obligatory semantic inversion when the subject/agent is *3rd person* and the object/patient is *2nd person,* as in (Forrest 1994):[5]

    (6)   a. **Intransitive**:

          ɬ'ap-**s**   ti-'imlk-tx

          go-**3s/int** ART-man-ART

          'The man goes'

   b. **Active-transitive:**
   k'x-**is**   ti-'imlk-tx   ci-xnas-cx
   see-3sOBJ/3sSUBJ/ACT ART-man-ART ART-woman-ART
   'The man sees the woman'
   c. **Passive-detransitive:**
   k'x-**im**   ci-xnas-cx   **x**-ti-'mlk-tx
   see-3sSUB/PASS ART-woman-ART OBL-ART-man-ART
   'The woman is seen by the man'
   d. **Active-transitive with 3>2:**
   *k'x-**nu-s**   ti-'imlk-tx
   see-2sOBJ-3sSUBJ/ACT ART-man-ART
   *'The man sees you'
   e. **Obligatory passive-detransitive with 3>2:**
   k'x-**ct**   **x**-ti-'imlk-tx
   see-2sSUBJ/PASS OBL-ART-man-ART
   'The man sees you'

The reason why such typological diversity of passive constructions exists is because each passive type A through E above arose diachronically from a different source construction. That source construction shares some functional features of the passive in the various sub-domains of de-transitivity. This partial functional similarity — partial overlap — is what made possible the diachronic extension from the various source domains towards the same target passive function.[6] But while the synchronic function of these re-analyzed constructions may now be that of passive voice, their structure still reflects many features of their earlier point of origin. Structure, as we noted in chapter 2, always lags behind functional re-analysis in grammaticalization; it takes structure a while to readjust and regain a measure of isomorphism vis-à-vis its new function.

If we were to construct taxonomy of the passive sub-types A-E above by structural similarity alone, we would group the English passive (A) with other predicate-adjective-like copular constructions; the Ute passive (B) with agent-suppressing VP-nominalization; the Spanish *se*-passive (C) with reflexive, reciprocal and middle voice; the Kimbundu passive (D) with topicalizations such as L-dislocation and Y-movement; and the Bella Coola passive (E) with other classical inverses. And we would have not landed then very far from the classical position of generative structuralists, who have doggedly refused to consider any construction a passive unless it matched the structural characteristics of the English passive.[7]

The alternative to the structuralist approach to grammatical typology is to recognize explicitly what has been implicit in the practice of grammatical typology all along; namely that in human language there is always more than one structural means of performing the same communicative function. And that grammatical typology is the study of the diversity of structures that can perform the same type of function.[8] In other words:

(7)   "In grammatical typology, we enumerate the main **struc-tural means** by which different languages code — or per-form — the **same function.**"

3.3.   The semantics of transitivity

Three semantic dimensions are central to our understanding of transitivity and de-transitivization. They are the three features that define semantically-transitive clause, thus also the semantic underpinnings of the active-transitive voice. Each of those corresponds to one core aspect of the **prototypical transitive event** (Hopper and Thompson 1980):

(8)   **Semantic definition of transitive event**
    a. **Agent**: The prototypical transitive clause involves a volition-al, controlling, actively-initiating agent who is responsible for the event, thus its **salient cause**.
    b. **Patient**: The prototypical transitive event involves a non-volitional, inactive non-controlling patient who registers the event's changes-of-state, thus its **salient effect**.
    c. **Verbal modality**: The verb of the prototypical transitive clause codes an event that is perfective (non-durative), sequential (non-perfect) and realis (non-hypothetical). The prototype transitive event is thus fast-paced, completed, real, and perceptually-cognitively salient.

In studying the pragmatics of voice, it is often useful to confine oneself to clauses that code semantically-transitive events, i.e. those that abide by the transitive semantic prototype (8). In such a restricted domain, one can study the variant clause-types that code changes in the pragmatic perspective, subtracting such changes from other possible effects of semantic de-transitivization. That is, one studies the pragmatics of voice while holding the transitive semantic frame more or less constant.[9] For this reason, I will exclude from the discussion here a group of de-transitive voice constructions that, in one way or another, tamper with the semantic core of the transitive event — in terms of features (8a,b,c). These semantic de-transitive constructions are most commonly:

(a)   reflexive clauses
(b)   reciprocal clauses
(c)   middle-voice constructions
(d)   perfect-adjectival-resultative clauses

3.4.   The pragmatics of de-transitive voice

Pragmatic perspective on transitive events is a complex phenomenon. I will assume, however, that the major component of this phenomenon is the **relative topicality** of the agent and patient in the semantically-transitive event. The pragmatic definition of the four main voices we will focus on here has been given initially by Cooreman (1982, 1985, 1987):[10]

(9)   **Relative topicality of the agent and patient**
       in the four main pragmatic voice constructions:

voice	relative topicality
active/direct	AGT > PAT
inverse	AGT < PAT
passive	AGT << PAT
antipassive	AGT >> PAT

The transitive **active-direct** voice is thus defined pragmatically as the voice construction in which the agent is more topical than the patient, but the patient retains considerable topicality. Relative to this benchmark — the unmarked case — the three main pragmatic de-transitive voices are then defined as:[11]

(10)   **Definition of main de-transitive voices:**
        a. **Inverse:** The patient is more topical than the agent, but the agent retains considerable topicality.
        b. **Passive:** The patient is more topical than the agent, and the agent is extremely non-topical ('suppressed, 'demoted').
        c. **Antipassive:** The agent is more topical than the patient, and the patient is extremely non-topical ('suppressed', 'demoted').

In defining the main pragmatic voices as in (9), (10), one must keep in mind that these are but the most commonly attested prototypes. As Thompson (1989) has noted in his work on Navajo, many more-subtle voice contrasts can be grammaticalized in a particular language. One functional dimension often associated with inverse constructions is that of obligatory **semantic inversion**. Since this turns out to be one of the main typological dimensions of inverse clauses, I will defer discussing it until further below.

3.5.   Definition and measurement of topicality

3.5.1.   Anaphoric and cataphoric dimensions

Defining the pragmatics of voice in terms of topicality of the agent and patient of the event, and their promotion to or demotion from topicality, raises an urgent methodological issue — the structure-independent definition, and measurement, of topicality. Two important aspects of the topicality of nominal referents are both cognitively significant and methodologically measurable:[12]

(a) **Anaphoric accessibility**: Whether the current referent has prior text antecedence, and if so how far back, and thus presumably how cognitively **accessible** that antecedence is.

(b) **Cataphoric persistence**: Whether the current referent recurs in the following text, and if so how frequently, and thus presumably how thematically **important** or attentionally **activated** it is.

Two quantitative text-based measures for assessing the topicality of referents have been used in previous studies, adapted from Givón (ed. 1983b; 1991), Wright and Givón (1987), and Givón (ed. 1994). These methods are based on the assumption that more topical — thematically important — referents tend to be both more anaphorically accessible ('continuous') and more cataphorically persistent ('recurrent'). Neither measure assesses topicality directly; both are plainly heuristic. They measure the referential continuity properties of referents, in two — opposite — textual directions. It is assumed then that the two measures correlate with the two respective cognitive dimensions of topicality.

3.5.2.   Quantitative identification of voice constructions

3.5.2.1. Topicality measures

a.   **Referential distance**

The first method measures the referential distance (RD) of the referent, or its anaphoric gap; that is, the number of clauses separating its present occurrence from its last occurrence in the preceding text. When the coreferent antecedent is found in the directly preceding clause, the value 1 is assigned. When the antecedent is found in the second or third clause from the present occurrence, the value 2/3 is assigned. When no antecedent is found in the preceding 3 clauses, the value >3 is assigned. The results are then expressed as the frequency distribution of these three RD values in the total population of agents or patients. Mean or median values for the whole population can also be computed. In general, highly topical referents, such as pronouns or zero anaphors, tend to have the RD value of 1. Emphatic and topicalized NPs, or independent contrastive pronouns, tend to have the RD value of 2-3 clauses. Anaphorically less-accessible referents tend to have the RD value of >3. The diagnostic cut-off point between topical and non-topical referents is thus either between the values 1 and 2/3, or 2/3 and >3.

b.   **Topic persistence**

The second measure, of cataphoric continuity, is that of topic persistence (TP). One counts the number of times the referent recurs within the next (cataphoric) 10 clauses following its present occurrence. Most commonly, TP values between 0 through 10 are recorded. The results are again expressed as frequency distribution of the various persistence values in the total population of agents or patients. Mean or median values for the whole population may also be computed. The Topic Persistence measure has proven particularly useful in assessing the topicality of referents regardless of anaphoric antecedence (Wright and Givón 1987). In general, more topical referents tend to have TP values above 2. Less topical referents tend to have TP values of 0–2.

A typical distribution of the population of agents and patients in semanti-cally-transitive events according to their RD and TP measures is given in (11), taken from Cooreman's (1982) study of Chamorro. In this early study, the measurement methods were a bit different and the results were expressed as averages rather than percent distributions.

(11)   **Relative topicality of agents and patients of semantically transitive clauses in the various pragmatic voices in Chamorro** (Cooreman 1982):

voice	mean RD (scale 1–20)		mean TP (scale 0–3)	
	agent	patient	agent	patient
direct-active	1.42	4.25	2.45	0.81
passive	6.33	3.33	0.44	1.44
inverse	4.03	1.38	1.33	2.00
antipassive	1.86	20.00	1.29	0.00

3.5.2.2. Frequency distribution in text

In her study of the four main pragmatic-voice constructions in Chamorro, Cooreman (1982, 1985, 1987) established a bench-mark for the likely frequency distribution of the four main voices in narrative text. Her frequency counts are reproduced in (12).

(12)   **The frequency distribution of voice constructions in semantically-transitive clauses in Chamorro narrative text** (Cooreman, 1987)

voice construction	N	%
active-direct	601	72.0
inverse (in-)	134	16.1
passive (ma-)	35	4.2
antipassive	64	7.7
total:	834	100.0

While frequencies vary with text-type, genre, author and more subtle sub-functions, the distributional profile established by Cooreman is remarkably stable cross-linguistically, and has been repeatedly validated in other studies (T. Payne 1982; Cooreman *et al.* 1984; Shibatani 1985, 1988; Rude 1987; Thompson 1989; Givón ed. 1994). This distributional profile can be used as a partial — corroborative — diagnostic for telling voice constructions apart. It has also been used successfully to decide whether a construction is a passive or active-ergative, in languages undergoing a diachronic shift to ergativity (Cooreman

1988; Cooreman *et al.* 1984; T. Payne 1982; Shibatani 1985, 1988; Tsunoda 1986; Brainard 1994). It can equally well be used as a partial diagnostic for telling apart a passive from an inverse construction. All other things being equal, inverse constructions tend to be much more frequent in text than passive constructions.

3.5.2.3. Frequency of non-anaphoric agent or patient deletion

The third quantitative diagnostic test for telling apart pragmatic voice constructions involves the text-frequency of clauses with a non-referring, non-anaphoric absent ('deleted') agent or patient. This diagnostic is particularly useful in differentiating the active-direct from the antipassive via the frequency of non-anaphoric patient deletion; and the inverse from the passive via the frequency of non-anaphoric agent deletion. Here again, Cooreman's (1982, 1987) reported frequencies for Chamorro will serve as an illustration.

(13)   **Frequency of non-anaphoric *zero* agents and patients in the four voice constructions in Chamorro** (Cooreman 1987)

voice construction	% of *zero* argument
	patient:
active-direct	0.0%
antipassive	61.4%
	agent:
inverse	3.6%
passive	90.5%

While not by themselves conclusive, such differential frequencies are very useful as a diagnostic, and have been validated repeatedly by later studies (Cooreman *et al.* 1984; Rude 1985; Cooreman 1988; Thompson 1989; Givón ed. 1994). Not only are these frequencies a useful heuristic, but they are also somewhat predictable on general theoretical grounds. The *zero* expression of referents occurs in language under two distinct circumstances:

(a)   high anaphoric predictability
(b)   low topicality or non-referentiality

The antipassive and the passive are both topicality-suppressing ('demoting') constructions *par excellence*, but they suppress the opposite arguments — the patient in the antipassive, the agent in the passive. In terms of iconicity, the "deletion" of non-topical, non-referring arguments is the most natural expression of suppression or demotion.[13]

3.6.   Syntactic-typological correlates of de-transitive voice

3.6.1.   Subjecthood and voice

In the unmarked active-direct clause, the topical agent has the highest probability — of all voice construction — of being the grammatical subject of the clause. This is most conspicuous in nominative-accusative languages, where (a) the nominative-subject is a morphologically unified entity; and (b) a large cluster of grammatical properties are loaded on the nominative NP (see chapter 6). Among those grammatical properties, three "overt" ones have been singled out by Keenan (1975):

   (a)   nominal subject case-marking
   (b)   control of verb-subject agreement
   (c)   characteristic word-order position

But other — "behavioral" — syntactic properties must also be recognized, such as various constraints on:

   (d)   deletion under coreference (equi-NP deletion, anaphoric deletion, relativization)
   (e)   control of role-changing syntactic processes (dative-shift, relativization, passive, raising)

While some subject properties, particularly nominal case-marking, are not quite as clearly clustered around a single NP in ergative-absolutive languages (Dixon 1972; Woodbury 1975; Anderson 1976; Brainard 1994), the exceptional nature of the ergative subject in so-called "deep ergative" languages has probably been exaggerated (Cooreman et al. 1984; Tsunoda 1986; Cooreman 1988).

3.6.2. Grammatical relations in the de-transitive clause

3.6.2.1. Syntactic demotion

All other things being equal, one would expect arguments that are pragmatically suppressed — the agent in the passive, the patient in the antipassive — to also be syntactically demoted. That is, one would expect the agent of the passive to be demoted from subjecthood, and the patient of the antipassive to be demoted from direct objecthood. This indeed tends to be the case in the vast majority of passives and antipassives cross-language. But the converse — syntactic promotion of the more topical non-agent — is much less universal.

3.6.2.2. Syntactic promotion

In the case of the promotion of non-patients to the role of **direct object**, some languages (KinyaRwanda, Nez Perce) make such pragmatically-promoted objects the grammatical direct-object, but others (Hebrew, Sherpa, Spanish) do not. And this is indeed a major typological dimension in the cross-linguistic typology of direct objecthood and dative-shifting.[14]

More germane to our discussion here are the grammatical correlates of pragmatic promotion of non-agents in de-transitive voice clauses — passive and inverse. In passivization first, the pragmatically-promoted patient is promoted to grammatical subjecthood in some languages (English, Nez Perce, Plains Cree, Koyukon, Chamorro) but not in others (Ute, Spanish *se-*). In other languages one finds semi-promotion of the topical patient to subjecthood, along the hierarchic lines suggested by Keenan (1975) (as in Chepang, Thompson 1989, 1994; Bella Coola, Forrest 1994). Syntactic promotion of the topical non-agent to grammatical subjecthood is thus not a criterion for defining a passive construction, but rather one of the major typological dimensions in the cross-linguistic typology of passive clauses.[15]

Returning now to the inverse, it has been argued (Dahlstrom 1986; Thompson 1994) that promotion of the non-agent to subjecthood might be a reliable criterion for distinguishing between passive and inverse constructions; that is, that unlike passive, inverse clauses tend to be non-promotional. This seems to be true in Algonquian (Dahlstrom 1986) and Athabaskan (Thompson 1989).[16] But it is clearly false for Chamorro (Cooreman 1987), where the patient in both the passive (*ma-*) and inverse (*in-*) clauses is equally the grammatical subject. Nor is it true in the languages surveyed by Keenan (1975), where non-agents in the de-transitive clause — be it inverse or passive — are only semi-promoted to subjecthood.

Equally vexing for the typologist is the impact of diachronic change on clean structure-guided identification. Thus, for example, an inverse clause can become a passive-voice clause over time (Forrest 1994; see above). And an erstwhile passive may assume the function of a pragmatic inverse (Hidalgo 1994; Zavala 1994). What is more, the very same clause-type can code *both* the inverse and passive voice functions, as in Squamish (Jacobs 1994), Cebuano (T. Payne 1994), Karao (Brainard 1994) or Spanish (Hidalgo 1994). There is thus no reason to assume that a clear syntactic distinction in terms of grammatical promotion of the topical non-agent must exist between de-transitive clauses that pragmatically demote the agent — passive voice — and those that do not — inverse voice. Indeed, both the passive and the inverse can be either promotional or non-promotional, so that for both, promotion to subjecthood is a typological variable.

3.6.3.   Toward a cross-linguistic typology of inverse constructions

3.6.3.1. Syntactic-typological dimensions

An exhaustive cross-linguistic typology of inverse-voice clauses is some-what premature, given the relatively little attention that has been paid until now to inversion in most language families. The typology offered here is but an opening, designed to initiate rather than close the discussion. At the very least, this first move must establish the two necessary prerequisites for an eventual typology:

(a) **Language-independent functional definition**

By defining the inverse voice functionally, in a language-independent and structure-independent fashion, one lays down the foundation for identifying — in any language — the clause-type that performs inverse-voice function. The discussion of inverse constructions has traditionally suffered from a great amount of language-specific parochialism and structure-bound circularity.[17]

(b) **Syntactic dimensions and typological variability**

Having defined the inverse voice functionally, one can now open the door for the search, in any language, of clause-types that perform this function. This search is at its very infancy in spite recent efforts.[18] For this reason, the cross-linguistic inventory of structural variants of inverse voice is still incomplete. The discussion here should be thus regarded as exploratory.

I will begin by identifying what seem to be the four main syntactic dimensions along which the already-known inverse constructions seem to vary. They are:

(14) **Syntactic-typological dimensions of inversion**:
     a. Pronominal inverse vs. word-order inverse
     b. Case-marking of full-NP arguments in the inverse
     c. Semantic vs. pragmatic inversion
     d. Promotional vs. non-promotional inverse

3.6.3.2. Pronominal (morphological) vs. word-order inverse

3.6.3.2.1. Pronominal inverses

In the classical Algonquian voice alternation described by Dahlstrom (1986), of the two 3rd-person arguments of the semantically-transitive clause, agent and patient, the more topical one is case-marked as **proximate**, and the less topical one as **obviate**. In the active-direct clause, the agent is the proximate and the patient the obviate. In the inverse clause, the patient is the proximate and the agent the obviate. On full-NP arguments, the proximate is unmarked and obviate is morphologically marked. In addition, a complex pronominal verb-agreement pattern marks the contrast between the active-direct and the inverse clause. Thus compare (Dahlstrom 1986):

(15) a. **Direct**
     aya.hciniw-**ah** nisto e.h-nipaha.t   awa na.pe.sis
     Blackfoot-**OBV** three kill/**DIR-3/OBV** this boy/**PROX**
     'The boy [PROX] killed three Blackfoot (men) [OBV]'
    b. **Inverse**
     osa.m e.-sa.khikot   ohta.wiy-**ah**   wa o.skini.kiw
     much love/**INV/OBV-3** his/father-**OBV** this young.man/**PROX**
     '(For) his father [OBV] loved this young man [PROX] too much'

When the agent and/or patient are zero anaphors, the same contrast is signalled by the verbal pronominal-agreement pattern alone:

(16) a. **Direct**
     ite.w.
     say.to/**DIR/3-OBV**
     'He [PROX] said to him [OBV]'

b. **Inverse**
itik.
say.to/**INV/OBV-3**
'He [OBV] said to him [PROX]'

According to Dahlstrom (1986), the agent is the grammatical subject in both the active-direct and the inverse clause, and the latter remains active-transitive. In contrast in the passive clause, which is agentless, the topical proximate patient is the grammatical subject. It controls proximate pronominal agreement on the verb, and the verb itself is marked as a derived intransitive:

(17) **Passive:**
awana.pe.sis e.kwa aw o.skini.kiw   mawi.hka.ta.wak
this boy/**PROX** and   this young.man/**PROX** mourn/**PASS-3p/PROX**
'This boy [PROX] and this young man [PROX] are being mourned'

A more purely pronominal direct-inverse system is seen in Athabaskan, where the contrast occurs only when the patient-object is pronominal. In the active-direct clause, the proximate agent pronoun is *zero*-marked, and the obviate patient pronoun is *ye-*. In the inverse clause, the proximate patient pronoun is *be-* and a pronominal agent is then the obviate *ye-*. With 3rd-person arguments in Koyukon, the contrast is (Thompson 1989):

(18) a. **Direct**
ye-ni-ɫ-'an
3/**OBV**-THM-TR-see
'He [PROX] is looking at her [OBV]'
b. **Inverse**
be-ye-ni-ɫ-'an
3/**PROC**-3/**OBV**-THM-TR-see
'He [OBV] is looking at her [PROX]'

In both the active-direct and the inverse, the same transitive prefix marks the verb. In the passive clause in Koyukon, no overt 3rd-person agreement on the verb is shown for either argument. One may argue, however, that this is the same nominative agreement pattern of 3rd-person subjects of both intransitive clause and the active-direct clause (see (18a) above). The passive verb is coded by the intransitive prefix:

(19) **Passive**
ni-**Ł**-'an
THM-**INTR**-see
'She [NOM] was seen'

3.6.3.2.2. Word-order inverses

One clause type that hitherto has never been considered an inverse is distinguished from the active-direct purely by word-order. In such a clause, the more-topical non-agent argument is made topical — i.e. "proximate" — by placing it in a more fronted position, before the less-topical agent. In some languages, such fronting has an added syntactic effect — post-posing the less-topical agent and thus marking it "obviate" by word-order. The word-order contrast between the active-direct and inverse is therefore rendered as (schematically):

active-direct: AGENT (...) PATIENT
inverse: PATIENT (...) AGENT

Word-order inverse clauses have been described traditionally as **Y-movement** or **L-dislocation** clauses.[19] It can be shown, however, that the pragmatic characteristics of these object-topicalizing clauses are the same as those of all other types of inverse clauses: They all topicalize non-agent arguments without strongly de-topicalizing the agent. And they involve the same broad range of **topic-shifting** and **switch-reference** in discourse. There is thus no reason for not attaching to these construction their rightful functional label.[20]

Word-order inverses have been identified in several languages — Modern Greek, Korean, Chepang, Maasai, Cebuano (Givón ed. 1994). So far, the agent and patient in all of these seem to retain the same grammatical case-roles — subject and object, respectively — in the inverse as in the active-transitive clause. In other words, these word-order inverses are non-promotional. In this respect they thus conform to the pattern described in Algonquian (Dahlstrom 1986) and Athabaskan (Thompson 1989, 1994). However, unlike the Algonquian and Athabaskan inverse, the word-order inverses described thus far involve no pronominal-morphological marking. In this typological dimension they are rather different from the Algonquian-Athabaskan type.

We have already noted that inverse clauses may be either promotional or non-promotional. Since the five described word-order inverses are all non-promotional and non-pronominal, one is tempted to posit a one-way conditional association between word-order inversion, on the one hand, and promotionality and pronominality on the other:

(20) **Correlation between typological features of inverse clauses**:
"If word-order inverse, then also non-promotional and non-pronominal inverse".

However, as we shall see further below, neither association is necessary.[21]

As an example of a typical word-order inverse construction, consider the object-fronting clause in Early Biblical Hebrew. Like all other object-topicalizing clauses in this language, the subject in this clause is post-posed, precipitating the characteristic OVS order of the inverse. The OVS word-order is not attested in the unmarked preterit (so-called 'imperfect') clause. Word-order in preterit-marked clauses is invariably VS(O):

(21) **Active-direct (preterit, VSO)**
va-ye-**varex**   'elohim 'et-noaḥ   ve-et-ban-av
and-3s-bless/**PRET** God   ACC-Noah and-ACC-sons-his
'...and God blessed Noah and his sons...' (Genesis, 9.1)

The word-order inverse clause in EBH requires the perfect aspect. This may be seen in the passage in (22) below, where in the preterit-marked (22a) the subject-agent is topical ('proximate'), while in the perfect-marked (22b) and (22c) a non-agent/subject is topicalized ('made proximate'):

(22) a. va-yi-**vra'**   'elohim 'et-ha-'adam be-tsalm-o,
       and-3sm-**create/PRET** God   ACC-the-man in-image-his
       '...and God created the man in his image,
    b. be-tselem   'elohim **bara'**   'ot-o,
       in-image/GEN God   **create/PERF/3sm** ACC-him
       in God's image he created him,
    c. zaxar ve-neqeva **bara'**   'ot-am.
       male and-female **create/PERF/3sm** ACC-them
       male and female he created them'. (Gen. 1.27)

In the perfect-marked active-direct clause with a topical ('proximate') agent/subject, the unmarked word-order is SVO. The OVS-ordered inverse contrasts with that unmarked order:

(23) a. **Direct (perfect, SVO):**
　　　ve-ha-'adam yada"　　　　'et-Ḥava
　　　and-the-man knew/PERF/**3sm** ACC-Eve
　　　'And Adam knew Eve' (Gen. 4.1)
　　b. **Inverse; fronted direct-object (perfect, OVS):**
　　　ḥamesh "esrey　'ama gavr-u　**ha-mayim**
　　　five　　ten/GEN arm　rose-they **the-water/PL**
　　　'...the water rose fifteen arms [measure]...' (Gen. 7.20)
　　c. **Inverse; fronted indirect-object (perfect, OVS):**
　　　'et-ha-'elohim hithalex　**Noaḥ**
　　　with-the-God walked-he **Noah**
　　　'...Noah walked together with God...' (Gen. 6.9)
　　d. **Inverse; fronted adverb (perfect, OVS)**
　　　be-re'shit　　bara'　　**'elohim** 'et-ha-shamayim
　　　in-beginning created-he **God**　ACC-the-heaven
　　　'...in the beginning God created the heaven...' (Gen. 1.1)

Characteristically, the SVO-ordered active-direct clause (23a) is paragraph initial, while all the topic-switching OV(S) inverse clauses are paragraph medial. The double word-order adjustment — fronted non-agent, post-posed agent — is characteristic of VO languages with flexible subject position, such as Spanish, Classical Arabic, Modern Greek, and many Bantu languages.[22]

3.6.3.3. Full-NP case marking in the inverse clause

As noted earlier, the purely pronominal inverse clause in Athabaskan involves no case-marking of the proximate or obviate full-NPs. In Algonquian an obviate full-NP — in both the direct and inverse clause — is morphologically marked. The proximate NP, on the other hand, is unmarked in both clauses. Thus recall (Dahlstrom 1986):

(24) a. **Direct**
　　　aya.hciniw-**ah** nisto e.h-nipaha.t　awa na.pe.sis
　　　Blackfoot-**OBV** three kill/**DIR-3/OBV** this boy/**PROX**
　　　'The boy [prox] killed three Blackfoot (men) [obv]'
　　b. **Inverse**
　　　osa.m e.-sa.khikot　　ohta.wiy-**ah**　wa o.skini.kiw
　　　much love/**INV/OBV-3** his/father-**OBV** this young.man/**PROX**
　　　'(For) his father [obv] loved this young man [prox] too much'

Other typological situations of full-NP case-marking are apparently more frequent. In many languages the full-NP obviate agent in the inverse clause is case-marked as oblique. Sahaptin, for example, has two oblique obviate-agent suffixes, one used in the obligatory semantic inverse, the other in the pragmatic inverse; as in (Rude 1989, 1991, 1994):

(25) a. **Active-direct**:
ɨwínsh i-q'ínu-shan-a   yáamash(-na)
man   3/NOM-see-IMPFV-PAST mule.deer(-OBJ)
'The man [PROX] saw a/the mule-deer [OBV]'

b. **Semantic inverse**:
i-q'inu-sha-ash   ɨwínsh-nɨm
3/NOM-see-IMPFV-1s man-OBV
'The man [OBV] sees me [PROX]'

c. **Pragmatic inverse**:
ɨwínsh-in pá-q'inu-shan-a   yáamash-na
man-OBV INV-see-IMPFV-PAST mule.deer-OBJ
'The man [OBV] saw the mule-deer [PROX]'

The obviate suffix -*in* of the pragmatic inverse (25c) is the associative suffix 'with', as in (Rude 1991):

(26)   **pa**-wiyánawi-ya   tílaaki miyánash-**in**
3p/NOM-come-ASP woman child-ASSOC
'The woman came with (her) child'

The obviate suffix -*nm* of the semantic inverse, on the other hand, apparently comes from the so-called 'hither' ('cis-locative', motion toward the speaker) verb suffix, as in (27b) below (Rude 1991):

(27) a. wina-tk
go-IMP/PL
'Y'all go (away from here)'
b. wina-**m**-tk
go-CIS-IMP/PL
'Y'all come (this way)'

One may as well note that an oblique case-marking of the non-topical (obviate) agent in the de-transitive clause, with the original meaning 'from', 'with', 'by', 'through', 'because of' or even the genitive 'of', is a common marking pattern in both passive and inverse clauses. Thus, in two related Salish languages, Squamish (Jacobs 1994) and Bella Coola (Forrest 1994), an oblique obviate prefix marks the determiner preceding the non-topical (obviate) agent in the de-transitive clause. But the Squamish de-transitive clause is functionally an inverse, while its etymological equivalent in Bella Coola is functionally a passive. In the same vein, in the non-promotional de-transitive clause in Nepali, the non-topical obviate agent is marked with the oblique postposition 'because':[23]

(28) a. **active-direct**:
      Omi-**le**   Maya-**lay** mar-**in**
      Omi-**ERG** Maya-**OBJ** kill-PAST/**3sf**
      'Omi killed Maya'
    b. **De-transitive**:
      Omi-**dwara** Maya-**lay** mar-**i-yo**
      Omi-**because** Maya-**OBJ** kill-**PASS/INV**-PAST/**3sm**
      'Maya was killed by Omi'

In the direct-active (28a) the proximate agent controls verb agreement. In the de-transitive (28b) verb agreement neutralizes into the 3d-person-masculine.

3.6.3.4. Obligatory semantic inversion

In the classical Algonquian inverse described by Dahlstrom (1986), the direct vs. inverse variation described thus far was that of the so-called 'optional' **pragmatic inverse**, with 3rd-person agents and patients. The choice of the inverse vs. direct clause here is controlled by the relative topicality of the two participants in the discourse. When the agent is more topical, it claims the proximate case-role, the patient claims the obviate case-role, and the clause is marked as active-direct. When the patient is more topical, the case-roles reverse and the clause is the inverse.

In Algonquian and many other languages, the very same inverse clause also has another, seemingly obligatory use, one that on the surface of it seems to be controlled by semantic factors, better know as the **generic topic hierarchies**. The hierarchies are indeed familiar, and in general can be given as:[24]

(29) **The generic topic hierarchies**:
    a. **Discourse participation**: speaker > hearer > 3rd-person
    b. **Animacy**: human > animate > inanimate
    c. **Agentivity**: agent > dative > patient
    d. **Gender**: male > female
    e. **Age**: adult > child
    f. **Size**: large > small
    g. **Possession**: possessor > possessed
    h. **Definiteness**: definite > indefinite
    i. **Anaphoricity**: pronoun > full-NP

These hierarchies set up a preference, so that the higher an event participant is on the hierarchy, the more it is likely to be the topic — and grammatical subject — in the unmarked active-direct clause. This is true statistically for all human languages.[25] What is unique to languages that have an obligatory **semantic inverse** is that some sub-set of the generic topic hierarchies (29) also controls obligatory inversion. When the agent out-ranks the patient on the relevant hierarchy, the active-direct clause is used. When the patient out-ranks the agent, the inverse clause must be used.

One can, of course, detect a fundamental unity in the use of the semantic and pragmatic inverse in a language that codes both functions with the very same construction. What is at issue is **norm reversal** vis-à-vis the expected relative topicality of event participants. The pragmatic inverse involves norm reversal in the feature of agentivity (29c). While the obligatory semantic inverse involves norm reversal in one or more of the other features. This unity may be given as follows:

(30) **Use of inverse clause in contexts of norm reversal**:
    a. **Pragmatic inverse**:
        "If the agent is more topical than the patient (cf. norm (29c)), the direct-active clause is used. If norm (29c) is reversed and the patient is more topical, the inverse clause is used".

    b. **Semantic inverse**:
        "If the agent outranks the patient on the relevant generic topic hierarchy (cf. norms (29a,b,d-i)), the direct-active clause is used. If the relevant norm is reversed and the patient outranks the agent on the relevant hierarchy, the inverse clause is used".

The exact details of which hierarchy or hierarchies in (29) exercises control over semantic inversion, and how conflicts between different hierarchies are resolved, are all highly language specific. In general, the pragmatic inversion rule (30a) applies only when both participants are *third persons*.

A cursory survey of even the few inverse constructions already known to us makes it fairly clear that the existence of obligatory semantic inversion could not be a criterion for determining whether a clause-type is or is not an inverse. Rather, semantic inversion is one typological dimension along which inverse clauses vary. Thus for example, the Algonquian (Dahlstrom 1986) and Chamorro (Cooreman 1985, 1987) inverses unite both the pragmatic (29a) and semantic (29b) inversion. In Maasai (D. Payne *et al.* 1994) and Sahaptin (Rude 1994), on the other hand, the two functions are carried out by two separate constructions. Thus, compare the two constructions in Sahaptin (Rude 1989, 1991, 1994):

(31) a. **Semantic ('obligatory') inverse:**
          i-q'ínu-sha-ash   ɨwínsh-**nɨm**
          3/NOM-see-IMPFV-me man-OBV
          'the man [OBV] sees me [PROX]'
      b. **Pragmatic ('contextual') inverse:**
          ku **pá-'ɨn**-a   pch'íimya-**n** piyáp-**in**
          and INV-tell-PAST wild.cat-OBJ elder.brother-OBV
          'And the elder brother [OBV] told the wild cat [PROX]'

In Bella Coola, as noted above (see Forrest 1994), what must have been an earlier inverse construction, to judge by surviving vestiges of semantic inversion, is synchronically — in terms of its pragmatic function — a passive voice construction. While in Squamish (Jacobs 1994) the cognate construction, with similar vestiges of semantic inversion, functions currently as the inverse voice, perhaps ambiguously as also the passive voice. In the same vein, Gildea (1994) has noted that an erstwhile inverse clause may preserve the feature of semantic inverse in spite of having become functionally neither an inverse nor a passive, but perhaps an active-direct clause.[26] Finally, none of the pragmatic word-order inverses surveyed in Givón (ed. 1994) — Modern Greek, Korean, Chepang, Maasai, Cebuano — show any trace of obligatory semantic inversion. The presence vs. absence of obligatory semantic inversion must be thus considered one — important but not by itself criterial — typological dimension along which inverse clauses vary. That the association between pragmatic and semantic inversion is not accidental goes without saying, given the topicality-related nature of the hierarchies in (29).

3.6.3.5. Promotional vs. non-promotional inverse

Just like the passive, an inverse clause can be either promotional or non-promotional. That is, it may or may not involve profound changes in grammatical relations, such as:

- Promotion of the topical proximate-patient to subjecthood
- Demotion of the non-topical obviate-agent from subjecthood

As noted earlier, the topical proximate patient of inverse clauses in both Algonquian (Dahlstrom 1986) and Athabaskan (Thompson 1989, 1994) is not promoted to grammatical subjecthood.[27] On the other hand, the topical proximate patient in the Chamorro inverse (*in*-clause) is as much a grammatical subject as is the topical patient of the *ma*-passive (Cooreman 1985, 1987).

Of even more interest is the phenomenon of partial promotion or demotion in both passives (Keenan 1975) and inverses. Thus, Rude (1994) shows partial demotion in the Sahaptin inverse clause: The patient-NP retains its object case-marking, but the obviate agent-NP is demoted to oblique marking, and verb agreement is neutralized in the pragmatic inverse clause (cf. (31b)).[28] Clearly then, grammatical relations, and in particular the feature of promotion vs. non-promotion of the proximate patient, are not a reliable criterial feature for identifying inverse clauses. Rather, they are one typological dimension along which inverse clauses may vary.

3.7.   Diachronic change and the typology of inverse

3.7.1.   The diachronic underpinnings of synchronic typology

Diachronic considerations occupy a central position in our understanding of grammatical typology. This is so because universals of form=function pairing exert their shaping and re-shaping effect on synchronic grammar primarily via the two developmental processes of **grammaticalization**:

- language learning
- diachronic change.

In this section I will show that the typology of syntactic constructions that code the inverse voice-function makes sense only if one considers such a typology — the inventory of known types of inverse clauses — in the context of the grammaticalization pathways via which the various types arose.

The idea that synchronic typology is inexorably linked with diachronic developmental pathways is neither new nor particularly surprising.[29] Much like the variation of synchronic types in biology, the typology of the grammatical structures that perform the same communicative function is nothing but an enumeration of the possible pathways of grammaticalization — primary or secondary — via which those types have come into being.

The grammaticalization of source domains into target domains is guided by **functional similarity** of potential sources and targets. Functional similarity — or partial overlap — between grammar-coded domains is thus central for our understanding of what is natural and universal about grammaticalization, and thus about grammatical typology. Functional similarity is one of the prime natural constraints on the possible range of synchronic structural types that can code the same domain. The reason why the study of voice constructions is so revealing of natural constraints on syntactic typology is now transparent:

- When a functional domain is complex, it has a wide network of functional similarities with other domains.
- Having a wide network of functional similarities means having an equally wide range of potential diachronic sources that can grammaticalize the domain.
- Having a wide range of potential grammaticalization sources means having a wide range of different structure types that can code the domain.

3.7.2.   From word-order inverse to pronominal inverse

A major typological contrast noted above was between word-order inverses (Biblical Hebrew, Chepang, Modern Greek, Korean, Maasai, Cebuano) and pronominal ('morphological') inverses (Algonquian, Athabaskan, Squamish/Bella Coola, Kutenai, Sahaptin).[30] This distinction is not absolute, since the two features are often associated. For example, the pronominal inverse of Squamish (Jacobs 1994) and the passive of Bella Colla (Forrest 1994) both involve post-posing the obviate, oblique-marked agent — thus a VOS word-order contrasting with the VSO order of the direct-active clause. Further, given the pragmatically determined word-order of Algonquian,[31] one suspects that proximate full-NP patients in the inverse clause of Plains Cree (Dahlstrom 1986) more often then not precede obviate full-NP agents.[32] One is thus tempted to suggest that the coding of relative topicality of the agent and patient by word-order is typo-

logically the more wide-spread — unmarked — feature of inversion, while pronominal-morphological marking is the more restricted — marked — feature.[33]

What I would like to demonstrate now is that there is a natural diachronic
pathway that links the two inverse types, so that — at least under some conditions — what begins as an object-topicalizing word-order inverse can give rise
to a pronominal morphological inverse. To illustrate this potential, I will cite the
object-topicalizing constructions of two Bantu languages. But I think there is
enough evidence to suggest that this is a major diachronic pathway. Consider
first the development of the de-transitive — either passive or inverse — clause
in Kimbundu from a blend of object L-dislocation and an impersonal-subject
clause:[34]

(32) a. **Active — plural subject:**
         aana   **a-**mono Nzua
         children **they-**saw John
         'The children saw John'
      b. **Anaphoric or impersonal plural subject:**
         a-mono   Nzua
         they-saw John
         (i)   'They saw John' (anaphoric)
         (ii) 'John was seen' (impersonal)
      c. **L-dislocation:**
         Nzua, aana   **a-mu-**mono
         John   children **they-him-**saw
         'John, the children saw him'
      d. **L-dislocation with anaphoric or impersonal subject:**
         Nzua, **a-mu-**mono
         John   **they-him-**saw
         (i)   'John, they saw him' (anaphoric)
         (ii) 'John, he was seen' (impersonal-subject)
      e. **De-transitive:**
         Nzua **a-mu-**mono   kwa meme
         John **they-him-**saw by   me
         'John was seen by me'
      f. **De-transitive:**
         meme **a-ngi-**mono   kwa Nzua
         I   **they-me-**saw by   John
         'I was seen by John'

Structurally, the Kimbundu de-transitive clause resembles the Sahaptin pragmatic inverse (Rude 1994) in two ways:
- A frozen relic of the impersonal 'they' occupies the characteristic subject pronoun prefixal slot on the verb.
- The less-topical (obviate) agent takes an oblique case.

However, due to the L-dislocation origin of the construction, it differs from the Sahaptin inverse in two other features:
- the more topical (proximate) occupies the clause-initial subject position (Kimbundu is a rigid-SVO language); and
- the more topical (proximate) patient controls a new set of pronominal subject agreement — what used to be the object agreement set in the active-direct clause.

What we see in Kimbundu is the rise of a distinct pronominal set in the object-topicalizing de-transitive clause. In other words, a word-order inverse has given rise to a pronominal-morphological inverse.

Consider next the contrastive-topic ('Y-movement') construction in Dzamba, another rigid-SVO Bantu language. This object-topicalizing construction displays two word-order adjustments relative to the direct-active SVO clause:
- The more topical (proximate) patient/object is fronted.
- The less topical (obviate) agent/subject is post-posed.[35]

In addition, the construction also displays two morphological adjustments relative to the direct-active clause:
- Subject agreement is eliminated.
- The verb must agree with the proximate object.

Thus (following Bokamba 1971, 1976):

(33)   a. **Active-direct**:
      o-Poso   **a**-tom-aki   mukanda
      DEF-Poso **he**-send-PAST letter
      'Poso sent a letter'

    b. **Active-direct, anaphoric object pronoun**:
      o-Poso   **a-mu**-tom-aki
      DEF-Poso **he-it**-send-PAST
      'Poso sent it' (it = the letter)

    c. **Object topicalization ('inverse', OVS)**:
       i-mukanda **mu**-tom-aki o-Poso
       DEF-letter **it**-send-PAST DEF-Poso
       (i)   'The letter Poso sent (away)'
       (ii) 'The letter was sent by Poso'
    d. *i-mukanda **a-mu**-tom-aki   o-Poso
       DEF-letter   **he-it**-send-PAST DEF-Poso
    e. *i-mukanda o-Poso   **mu**-tom-aki
       DEF-letter   DEF-Poso **it**-send-PAST
    f. **L-dislocation (OSV)**:
       i-mukanda o-Poso   **a-mu**-tom-aki
       DEF-letter DEF-Poso **he-it**-send-PAST
       'The letter, Poso sent it'

An object-topicalizing clause — a word-order inverse — has once again yielded a construction in which the proximate patient/object controls a pronominal agreement pattern that is distinct from the agent-controlled subject agreement of the active-direct clause.

The implications of the change described above are indeed profound: Word-order inverses are, to judge by all the evidence available to us thus far, purely pragmatic inverses. On the other hand, all semantic inverses known to us are pronominal-morphological. If it turns out that the major diachronic venue for the rise of pronominal-morphological inverses is from erstwhile word-order inverses, then a strong inference is virtually certain here: Semantic inversion arises from pragmatic inversion.

3.7.3.   From pragmatic to semantic inversion

The distribution of inverses known to us thus far reveals the following association or dissociation between pragmatic and semantic inversion:

(34)   **The typology of inverse clauses:**

(A) **Purely pragmatic inverse clause**
  (i)   **Purely word-order inverse**
         (Chepang, Modern Greek, Korean, Biblical Hebrew,
         Cebuano, Maasai-I)
  (ii)   **Mixed word-order and pronominal inverse**
         (Kimbundu, Dzamba; probably Sahaptin-I)[36]
  (iii) **Purely pronominal-morphological inverse**
         (Koyukon)

(B) **Shared pragmatic-semantic inverse clause**
  (iv)   **Purely word-order inverse**
         (none)
  (v)   **Mixed word-order and pronominal inverse**
         (Chamorro *in-*, Squamish, Bella Coola,[37] probably Plains Cree)[38]
  (vi)   **Purely pronominal-morphological inverse**
         (Kutenai)

(C) **Purely semantic inverse clause**
  (vii) **Purely word-order inverse**
         (none)
  (viii) **Mixed word-order and pronominal inverse**
         (Sahaptin type-II)
  (ix)   **Purely pronominal-morphological inverse**
         (Maasai-II, Tupi-Guaraní)

In the preceding section it was suggested that word-order inversion precedes — and gives rise to — pronominal morphological inversion. Since all word-order inverses known to us are purely pragmatic, we may conclude tentatively that pragmatic inversion is the diachronically-early, general, un-marked case, and that semantic inversion is the more special marked sub-case within it. This conclusion is supported by the absence of the logically-possible inverse types (B-iv) and (C-vii). However, if this hypothesis is to prevail, the existence of the purely-semantic, purely pronominal inverses of type (C-ix) in Maasai-II (D. Payne *et al.* 1994) and various Tupi-Guaraní languages (D. Payne 1990) must be interpreted as a vestigial survival of an erstwhile functionally mixed semantic-pragmatic inverse.

Given the synchronic inventory of inverse types in (34), the diachronic pathways connecting the various types are now given as hypothesis (35):

(35) **Diachronic pathways connecting the main inverse types:**

Pragmatic word-order inverse (A-i)

**Pragmatic word-order and
pronominal inverse** (A-ii)

**Pragmatic pronominal
inverse** (A-iii)   **Mixed pragmatic-semantic
word-order and pronominal
inverse** (B-v)

**Mixed pragmatic-semantic
pronominal inverse** (B-vi)   **Purely-semantic word-order &
pronominal inverse** (C-viii)

**Purely-semantic pronominal
inverse** (C-ix)

Three diachronic changes in hypothesis (35) requires more explicit justification:

(a) The loss of word-order flexibility, yielding the purely-pronominal inverse types (A-iii) and (C-ix).

(b) The change from a purely-pragmatic to a mixed pragmatic-semantic inverse, yielding types (B-v) and (B-iv);

(c) The change from a mixed pragmatic-semantic inverse of types (B-v) and (B-vi) to the purely-semantic inverses of types (C-viii) and (C-ix), respectively.

I will take those in order.

(a) **Loss of word-order flexibility**

There is nothing here that is unique to inversion. Languages with pragmatically-controlled, fully or partially flexible word-order have been shown to rigidify, or re-rigidify, their word-order.[39] A language with an inverse type (A-ii) may undergo word-order rigidification, losing the word-order difference between the direct-active and inverse but retaining the morphological difference, thus winding up with a purely-pronominal inverse type (A-iii).

(b) **The rise of obligatory semantic inversion**

A very well-known principle of grammaticalization is at play here, one that has been described variably as:[40]

(36) **The relationship between text-frequency and grammaticalization:**

   (a) "A high-frequency pragmatically controlled behavior can easily be grammaticalized as an obligatory 'semantic' rule". (Givón 1979, ch. 5)

   (b) "Languages grammaticalize most explicitly what speakers do most frequently". (DuBois 1985)

   (c) "Semantics is grammaticalized or frozen pragmatics". (Langacker 1987)

The topic hierarchies in (29), where both semantic and pragmatic ranking is involved, are behaviorally real in the following sense — these hierarchies represent the **frequency** or likelihood of topicalization in discourse. When a language has a purely pragmatic inverse, coded either by word-order (Modern Greek) or by pronominal morphology (Koyukon), the frequency of the ranking member in each hierarchy (29a-i) being the topical participant in the direct-active clause is very high. Speaker and hearer participants consistently out-rank third person participants. Definites outrank indefinites, anaphoric pronouns outrank full NPs, possessors outrank possessed NPs, etc. As noted in chapter 2, high text-frequency is associated with the unmarked norm. Relative to this, inversion is the counter-norm.

Semantic inversion is nothing but a diachronic extension — via rigidification or semantification — of the more general rule of **norm-reversal** that is already extant in pragmatic inversion. Presumably, reinterpreting the high frequency-association between the pragmatic feature of topicality and the various 'ranking' (unmarked) semantic features in (29) as obligatory semantic inversion is a slow process. But however slow, it eventually gives rise to an obligatory rule. Inverse clauses that display semantic inversion are thus diachronically older than purely-pragmatic inverse clauses. And those that display only semantic inversion are diachronically older yet; whereby one would expect an eventual re-grammaticalization of pragmatic inversion.

(c) The loss and re-emergence of pragmatic inversion

Once a mixed pragmatic-semantic inverse clause is in place, there are good reasons why its communicative efficacy as a pragmatic inverse would be diminished. The rules of obligatory semantic inversion apply automatically — even in cases that go against the pragmatics of topicality. In such circumstances, the rise of a new purely pragmatic inverse construction is just a matter of time. This is clearly evident in Maasai (Payne *et al*. 1994) and perhaps Sahaptin (Rude 1994). In both languages, a purely-semantic pronominal inverse exists. What must have been added to it is a purely-pragmatic inverse construction. In Maasai, the new pragmatic inverse is indeed a word-order inverse, thus repre-senting an early stage in the rise of a new inverse (type A-i). In Sahaptin, the purely-pragmatic construction is already a word-order *cum* pronominal inverse, representing the later diachronic stage of type (C-viii).

Within the framework of hypothesis (35), Tupi-Guaraní — with a single type (C-ix) purely-pronominal, purely-semantic inverse — represents a language just prior to the re-emergence of a new pragmatic inverse. More likely, Tupi-Guaraní is simply another language group where linguists have not yet come around to identifying the word-order pragmatic inverse that is already there, and calling it by its rightful name.

3.7.4.   From inverse to ergative

A complex grammatical domain is not only a target zone for multi-source grammaticalization, but also itself a potential source. And the inverse clause is not an exception. It has been taken for granted in many past studies (Chung 1977; Anderson 1977; *inter alia*) that one way ergative clauses arise is from the reanalysis of erstwhile passive clauses. Given the fact that passive clauses are overwhelmingly agent suppressing and agent deleting, this source for ergativity seems puzzling. Rather, it seems more likely that the de-transitive construction that gives rise to an active-ergative clause is the inverse, which is typically agent preserving. And not any old inverse, but probably an inverse clause with an oblique-marked obviate agent.

Sahaptin and Sahaptian is a case in point. As Rude (1988, 1989, 1991) has suggested, the Nez Perce ergative clause comes from an earlier inverse. The Nez Perce ergative-NP suffix *-nim* is cognate with the obviate-agent suffix *-nim* of the semantic inverse clause in Sahaptin. Thus, compare the Nez Perce ergative clause with the Sahaptin semantic inverse (Rude 1988, 1991):

(37) a. **Ergative clause (Nez-perce):**
wewúkiye-**ne pée-**'wiye   háama-**nm**
elk-**OBJ**   **3.3.**/TR-shot man-**ERG**
'The man shot the elk'

b. **Semantic inverse clause (Sahaptin):**
i-tuxná-na-ash   ɨwínsh-**nɨm**
3/NOM-shoot-ASP-1s man-**OBV**
'The man [OBV] shot me [PROX]'

In the same vein, the ergative-transitive verb prefix *pée-* in Nez Perce (cf. (37a) is cognate with the *pá-* prefix of the pragmatic — and some semantic — inverse in Sahaptin (Rude 1988, 1991):

(38) a. **Pragmatic inverse:**
ku **pá-**'ɨn-a   pch'íimya-**n** piyáp-**in**
and **INV**-tell-**PAST** wild.cat-**OBJ** elder.brother-**OBV**
'And the elder brother [OBV] told the wild cat [PROX]'

b. **Semantic inverse:**
pá-q'inu-sha-nam
INV-see-**IMPFV**-2s
'You see me'

Probably the clinching argument for the universality of the grammaticalization pathway inverse-to-ergative is the existence of the very same obligatory semantic restrictions on ergative clauses in many **split-ergative** languages as those found in semantic inverse clauses. This has been described most succinctly by Silverstein (1976) and Dixon (1977):

(39) **Hierarch of features in ergative languages:**
a. **Participants:** 1st person > 2nd person > 3rd person
b. **Anaphoricity:** pronoun > full NP
c. **Definiteness:** definite > indefinite
d. **Individuation:** singular > plural

The constraint on the choice of an ergative vs. nominative morphology for the semantically-transitive clause in Australian languages may be given roughly as follows:

(40) **Split-ergativity constraint**:
"If the agent is high on the hierarchies in (39), use *nominative* morphology. If the agent is low on the hierarchies — and thus is outranked by the patient — use *ergative* morphology".

As noted elsewhere,[41] constraint (40) makes little synchronic sense for an active-direct ergative clause in which the agent is the more topical (proximate) argument. They make perfect sense, however, for a de-transitive inverse clause in which the patient outranks the agent. If the ergative clause in Australian languages arose from diachronic re-analysis of an inverse, we have here nothing but the frozen vestige of obligatory semantic inversion.

A similar state of affairs can be seen in Indonesian, where an inverse-to-ergative shift is still ongoing. Thus, Chung (1976) reports that the Indonesian *di*-marked "passive" — an agent-preserving construction that performs both the ergative-active and inverse voice functions[42] — cannot be used if the agent is a 1st/2nd person. In other words, an agent must be low-ranking relative to the patient on the semantic hierarchy (29a)/(39a) in order for the *di*-marked clause to be used. This is again a strange synchronic restriction for a direct-active (ergative) clause, but a perfectly good — if frozen — reflection of obligatory semantic inversion in an erstwhile inverse clause.

Finally, the so-called 'goal-focus' clause in Philippine languages, an active-ergative and inverse-voice functional mix (see Brainard 1994; T. Payne 1994, *inter alia*), shows at least one vestige of obligatory semantic inversion, when the patient outranks the agent on the hierarchy of definiteness (39c): Semantically transitive clauses with indefinite patients retain the so-called 'actor-focus' form, currently more likely the functional antipassive (cf. Cooreman *et al.* 1984; Brainard 1994; T. Payne 1994). Those with definite patients must obligatorily take the 'goal-focus' construction. In addition to being the new active-direct ergative clause, the 'goal-focus' construction still performs the function of pragmatic inverse (T. Payne 1994; Brainard 1994).

3.7.5. Diachronic connections between inverse and passive

3.7.5.1. From promotional passive to promotional inverse

As suggested above, inverse clauses arise diachronically from other, functionally-related constructions. One such source construction may be a passive. When that occurs, the grammatical features of the passive simply carry over onto an inverse clause. And if the passive was promotional, the resulting inverse is also promotional. An example of this may be the *ser*-marked passive of Spanish. Hidalgo (1994) notes that when this BE-passive clause has an oblique-marked agent (the minority of cases in text), its function resembles more that of an inverse than passive voice. A similar observation was made by Zavala (1994) in his work on Acateco (Mayan). If an agent-preserving passive clause with an oblique-marked agent also assumes the function of inverse voice, the oblique case-marking of the agent-of-passive now becomes the obviate-agent marking in the inverse. The history of the English BE-passive is somewhat similar, beginning as an agentless semantic de-transitive — an adjectival-resultative middle-voice, and slowly becoming a pragmatic passive with an oblique-marked agent. One may perhaps suggest that agent-preserving passive clauses in English are functionally inverse clauses. The history of the Sahaptian inverse is perhaps similar. Rude (1994) has suggested that the *pa-* prefix of the Sahaptin inverse verb traces back to the plural pronoun *pa-*, which in the absence of any other person marking functions as the third person plural 'they', as in (Rude 1994):

(41) a. **Intransitive**:
    kuk **pa**-wínan-a
    then **3p/NOM**-go-PAST
    'Then they went'

   b. **Semantic inverse**:
    cáw-nash **pa**-tq'ix-sha   q'ínu-t-yaw
    NEG-1s   **3p/NOM**-want-IMPFV see-NOM-ALL
    'They [NOM/OBV] don't want me [PROX] to see'

The fact that the proximate patient of the Sahaptin inverse does not control subject agreement, and that it also retains the direct-object (topical object) case-marking, can be interpreted as a diachronic relic of the grammatical properties of an agent-deleting impersonal passive clause. When used as passive voice, such a clause tends to be non-promotional. With diachronic re-shaping, an erstwhile agentless passive can become an agent-preserving inverse clause. All that is required is the addition of an oblique-marked obviate agent. In Sahaptin, this oblique case-marking in the pragmatic inverse clause derives from the associative case, as in (Rude 1992):

(42) ku **pá-ɨna**   pch'íimya-**n** piyáp-**ɨn**
    and **INV**-tell-PAST wild.cat-**OBJ** elder.brother-**ASSOC**
    'And the elder brother [OBV] told the wild cat [PROX]'

3.7.5.2. From agent-of-inverse to agent-of-passive

Given the functional overlap between inverse and passive, a diachronic shift from inverse to passive is also possible. An example of this is perhaps the Salish de-transitive clause. Jacobs (1994) has noted that in Squamish this construction performs both inverse and passive pragmatic functions. But a residual semantic inversion suggests that the inverse function is older. In Bella Coola, on the other hand, the same construction is functionally more like a passive (Forrest 1994). The oblique-marked obviate agent in the Squamish inverse thus becomes the oblique-marked agent-of-passive in Bella Coola.

3.8.   Conclusion

One of the more ingenious arguments functionally-oriented typologists use to justify persisting in a non-functional approach to typology runs as follows:[43]

(43)   **The naive iconism argument for structure-guided typology**:
    (a)   Grammatical structures tend to be iconic, i.e. iso-morphically matched to their functions.
    (b)   This means that structures that are formally similar are also functionally similar.
    (c)   Therefore, if one bases a syntactic typology on the criteri-on of structural-similarity alone, the resulting typology is also going to be function-guided.

In an ideal world of 100% iconicity, this argument — structural similarity as a heuristics for functional similarity — would indeed be valid. But in such a world there would be no typology, and thus no meaningful cross-language variation in grammar. All languages in such a world would use exactly the same structures to code the same communicative functions. But of course, we don't live in such a world.[44] Rather, the world we live in is one in which functional domains have fuzzy boundaries, and semantic and pragmatic functions are defined as prototypes with multiple similarities and overlaps. It is thus a world where grammatical constructions — especially those that code complex domains — display functional similarity to many constructions that are structurally distinct. It is, finally, a world in which structure is much more discrete than function. In such a world, speakers observe patterns of partial overlap and multiple similarities during sporadic acts of metaphoric extension — that is, grammaticalization. And they make context-dependent judgements of communi-cative need, task urgency, utility and costs — all relatively unconsciously — as part and parcel of grammaticalization.

Grammatical innovations take place in a startlingly complex cognitive, communicative and social environment. When speakers innovate by functional extension under such conditions, they can and often do grammaticalize into the same diachronic target from a number of functionally similar but structurally distinct sources. The birth of grammatical typology can be traced to this complex, context-guided interaction between less-than-discrete functional categories and much more discrete structures.

Functional linguists are burdened with having to pay attention to both the relative subtlety of fuzzy-edged functions and the relative rigidity of discrete structures. The difference between the two sides of the semiotic equation goes to the very heart of natural biological information-processing codes: A code must be reductive and discretizing. And such reduction and discretization are essential for the main task at hand — processing the incredible richness and unboundedness of experience within the finite bounds of real time.

Notes

* I am indebted to Ann Cooreman, Spike Gildea, Doris Payne and Noel Rude for many helpful comments and suggestions.

1) For antecedent discussions of this, see Givón (1981, 1983a, 1984b); Wierzbicka (1992).

2) For more details see Givón (1990b, ch. 14).

3) See *Ibid.* as well as Kemmer (1993).

4) See *Ibid.*

5) In Squamish, a related Salish language, the very same detransitive construction functions as an inverse rather than passive (Jacobs 1994).

6) See discussion of this functional overlap in Givón (1981).

7) See e.g. Marantz (1983).

8) In the same way in biology, comparative anatomy gives rise to the typology of different anatomic solutions to the same adaptive — physiological or behavioral — tasks.

9) That is, one studies verbs that code events involving a prototypical agent, a prototypical patient, and a prototypical transitive verb. This deliberate methodological gambit does not prejudge the use, in many languages, of the very same pragmatic voice constructions — passive or inverse — with intransitive verbs. Such events tend to not involve a patient-object, but do involve an agent/subject, whose pragmatic status (i.e. topicality) is re-framed vis-à-vis the active construction. Non-promotional passives tend to apply to a wide range of clause-types, both transitive and intransitive (Givón 1981). Likewise, the inverse in many languages seems to apply to intransitive clauses.

10) In her study of Chamorro voice constructions, Cooreman identified the inverse construction as "the *in*-passive". The re-interpretation of that construction as a functional inverse is due originally to Shibatani (1985, 1988).

11) The basis for designating the active-direct clause as the unmarked has been discussed in chapter 2, above.

12) The discussion here follows the line of research developed cumulatively in Givón (ed. 1983), Wright and Givón (1987), and Givón (1988, 1991f, 1992).

13) See Givón (1985a, 1991d) as well as chapter 9 below.

14) See Givón (1984a). One may wish to argue that promotion to or demotion from direct objecthood is another, albeit minor, voice alternation.

15) For the distinction between promotional and non-promotional passives, see Givón (1981; 1990b, ch. 14).

16) Rhodes (1992) has recently challenged Dahlstrom's analysis, contending that the patient of the inverse in Algonquian is promoted to subjecthood.

17) For a useful discussion of some language-specific parochialism and its consequences, see Dahlstrom (1986) and Thompson (1989).

18) Givón (ed. 1994).

19) See Givón (1990b, ch. 16).

20) To my knowledge, no word-order inverse involves obligatory semantic inversion. But semantic inversion is not a criterial feature for identifying inverse voice clauses. Rather, it is one of the main typological dimensions along which inverse constructions may vary (see further below).

21) See discussion of the Dzamba and Kimbundu de-transitive clauses.

22) See discussion in Givón (1988). We will return to one such language (Dzamba) further below, but see also Roland (1994).

23) See Givón (1990b, ch. 14). It is yet to be decided whether the Nepali de-transitive clause is an inverse or a passive. Gildea (in personal communication) notes that the frequency of this construction with an overt agent NP in the spoken language approaches *zero*, and that it seems to appear only in writing. This suggests that the construction may be a non-promotional passive rather than an inverse.

24) See Hawkinson and Hyman (1974), Givón (1976a), Timberlake (1978), *inter alia*. The feature 'agentivity' (29c) is of course the independent variable in this case, and thus not at issue in the semantic inverse, though it is central to the pragmatic inverse.

25) See discussion in Givón (1984b, chapters 4, 5).

26) See discussion of the inverse-to-ergative connection further below.

27) Rich Rhodes (1992) disagreeing with Dahlstrom's (1986) analysis of Plains Cree, argues that the proximate topic of the inverse in Algonquian is indeed the grammatical subject. So even in the same language, the status of grammatical relations in the inverse clause can be controversial.

28) In Sahaptin, the inverse verbal prefix *pa-* is transparently the (nominative) plural pronoun. In the absence of first or second person marking, this pronoun is interpreted as the third-person 'they' (Rude in personal communication). This suggests that an impersonal-subject, non-promotional, agent-suppressing passive construction may have been the diachronic source of the Sahaptin inverse.

29) See explicit discussion beginning with Givón (1971, 1978, 1979a, ch. 6), Greenberg (1978, 1979), *inter alia.*

30) 'Primarily' is used here deliberately, since many 'pronominal'-inverse clauses probably also exhibit a strong tendency toward placing the more topical proximate-patient before the less topical obviate-agent.

31) See e.g. Rhodes and Tomlin (1992).

32) Dahlstrom (1986) presents no text-based frequency counts of word-order in the direct vs. inverse.

33) This markedness interpretation is also implicit in Keenan's (1975) hierarchy of grammatical subject properties in passive clauses (case-marking > agreement > word-order); see also Givón (1988).

34) See Givón (1976a; 1990b, ch. 14). In my earlier discussion of the Kimbundu de-transitive clause I did not consider the possibility of an inverse construction. A text-based, quantified functional determination is yet to be undertaken.

35) In this way, the Dzamba object-topicalizing clause resembles Biblical Hebrew (see earlier above) as well as Modern Greek (Roland 1994).

36) Sahaptin (and Sahaptian in general) has 'free' — pragmatically controlled — word order (Rude 1985, 1994), where the more topical proximate patient of the inverse is more likely to be fronted.

37) Forrest (1994) describes the function of the Bella Coola de-transitive clause as, synchronically, that of passive voice. The designation here refers to a presumed earlier diachronic stage, the one still extant in Squamish.

38) Like Sahaptin, Plains Cree (and Algonquian in general; see Rhodes and Tomlin 1992) has pragmatically controlled word-order. The more topical proximate patient of the inverse clause is thus more likely to be fronted.

39) See Givón (1977; 1979a, ch. 7; 1983c; 1988).

40) See Givón (1979a, ch. 5); DuBois (1985); Langacker (1987).

41) Givón (1984b, ch. 5, pp. 159-161).

42) See also Rafferty (1984), Verhaar (1983a, 1983b, 1985), Kaswanti Purwo (1988).

43) This argument was raised by Anne Cooreman during the discussion of her paper on the typology of antipassives (see Fox and Hopper eds. 1994).

44) Although it has been suggested that Creole grammars represents an approximation to this idealized state of affairs (Bickerton 1981).

4

Modal Prototypes of Truth and Action

4.1. Introduction*

One flesh; to lose thee *were* to lose myself.
John Milton
Paradise Lost

4.1.1. Perspective

Many of the themes running through this chapter recapitulate the discussion in chapter 3. Like voice, modality is a complex functional domain. Like voice, it comprises of some more semantic and some more pragmatic sub-domains. As in the case of voice, a strictly structure-guided typological account of modality turns out sour. And as in the case of voice, a synchronic typology of modality is opaque without access to the relevant diachrony. But the similarities go only a certain distance, beyond which modality challenges functionalist theory in ways that are peculiarly its own.

The semantic and pragmatic sub-components of modality are not as easy to tease apart as in the case of voice. They seldom cluster quite as clearly around constructions that serve either primarily-semantic or primarily-pragmatic functions. And this persistently holistic aspect of modality emerges in spite of the lingering echoes of a well-known analytic tradition, one that divides the modal pie into two distinct regions: the seemingly more semantic region of **epistemics**, and the seemingly more pragmatic region of **deontics**. This old tradition that has come down to us from philosophy has proven itself quite useful — up to a point. But it has also inculcated in us a sense of false security about the existence of purely epistemic grammatical categories, relatively untainted by the pragmatic mess of deontics. A more careful examination of modality reveals a paradoxical situation. On the one hand, the study of grammaticalization patterns re-validates the conceptual independence of the epistemic and the deontic — as **prototypes**. On the other hand, the study of communicative use reinforces our intuitive conclusion that epistemics in human language is not really about truth or certainty, but rather, still and probably forever, about willful human interaction.

4.1.2. Goals

This chapter aims to outline some coherent principles by which one can predict the range of grammatical environments in which a **subjunctive mood** is most likely to grammaticalize. These grammatical environments turn out, on even the most cursory inspection, to represent a coherent sub-set of **irrealis**. But to understand both irrealis and the subjunctive, one must first understand the place of irrealis within the wider range of propositional modalities. In the course of trying to make sense of the subjunctive, we thus wind up having to make sense of irrealis both as a cognitive-communicative (functional) and a grammatical-typological (formal) category.

4.2. Propositional modalities

4.2.1. Traditional view of modality

The propositional modality associated with a clause may be likened to a shell that encases it but does not tamper with the kernel inside. The kernel is the **propositional frame** of clause:

- participant roles
- predication type
- grammatical roles
- transitivity ('event type')

as well as the actual lexical items that fill the various slots in the frame. All these remain relatively unaffected by the propositional modality encasing the clause. What the modality seems to signal is the **speaker's attitude** toward the proposition. By 'attitude' we mean primarily two main types of judgement, perspective or attitudes concerning the information packed in the clause:

(a) **Epistemic attitudes:**
    truth, belief, probability, certainty, evidence
(b) **Valuative attitudes:**
    desirability, preference, intent, ability, obligation, manipulation

These two main modal dimensions, epistemic and valuative ('deontic'), are not always mutually exclusive, but can intersect in some specific ways (see section 4.3.6. below). As a simple-minded illustration of how changes in modality leave the propositional kernel relatively unaffected, consider:

(1)   a. Darla shot the tiger
       b. It's too bad that Darla shot the tiger
       c. If Darla shoots the tiger,...
       d. Darla didn't shoot the tiger
       e. He told Darla that she should shoot the tiger
       f. Shoot the tiger, Darla!
       g. Did Darla shoot the tiger?

Each one of the utterances in (1) is encased in a different modal envelope. But the propositional kernel, identifying 'Darla' as the agent/subject, 'the tiger' as the patient/object, and 'shooting' as the transitive event type, is left relatively constant throughout.

Both the epistemic and valuative mega-modalities can display, at least in principle, many shades and gradations (see Palmer 1979, 1986; Coates 1983; *inter alia*).[1] But the range of grammar-coded modalities found in any particular language is usually limited to a sub-set of what is universally possible.[2]

4.2.2. The communicative definition of modality

Four main propositional modalities display the strongest functional and grammatical consequences in human language. While many of us are inclined nowadays to formulate their functional definition in either cognitive or communicative terms, it behooves us to acknowledge the long tradition that passed these modal categories on to us, a tradition going all the way back to Aristotle. This tradition, with its near-exclusive preoccupation with the epistemic aspects of modality, has indeed run its natural course. But it did manage to come up with modal notions that bear close resemblance to our present-day communicatively-defined modalities. The four traditional epistemic modalities are (Aristotle/Ackrill 1963; Carnap 1947):

(2)   **Epistemic modalities:**

logical tradition	communicative equivalent
a. necessary truth	presupposition
b. factual truth	realis assertion
c. possible truth	irrealis assertion
d. non-truth	NEG-assertion

The logical tradition treated modality as a property of propositions detached from their natural communicative context. The communicative-pragmatic interpretation of the four modalities, on the other hand, recasts them in terms of the epistemic states and communicative goals of the two partici-pants in the **communicative transaction** — speaker and hearer. This approach in linguistics owes a certain historical debt to post-Wittgensteinean philosophy, e.g. Austin (1962), Searle (1969) or Grice (1968/1975). The present re-formula-tion follows Givón (1982b, 1984, 1989):[3]

(3)   **The communicative re-definition of epistemic modality:**
        a. **Presupposition:**
           The proposition is **assumed** to be true, either by definition, by prior agreement, by generic culturally-shared convention, by being obvious to all present at the speech situation, or by having been uttered by the speaker and left unchallenged by the hearer.
        b. **Realis assertion:**
           The proposition is **strongly asserted** to be true; but challenge from the hearer is deemed appropriate, although the speaker has evidence or other grounds to defend their strong belief.
        c. **Irrealis assertion:**
           The proposition is **weakly asserted** to be either possible, likely or uncertain (epistemic sub-modes), or necessary, desired or undesired (valuative-deontic sub-modes). But the speaker is not ready to back up the assertion with evidence or other strong grounds; and challenge from the hearer is readily entertained, expected or even solicited.
        d. **NEG-assertion:**
           The proposition is **strongly asserted** to be **false**, most com-monly in contradiction to the hearer's explicit or assumed beliefs; challenge from the hearer is anticipated, and the speak-er has evidence or other grounds to back up their strong belief.

Our understanding of the functional and grammatical distribution of the subjunctive mood depends on our understanding the functional and grammatical distribution of irrealis — both its epistemic and valuative/deontic sub-modes.

One unfortunate legacy of the logic-bound approach to modality is the definition of the contrast between realis and irrealis as a contrast between, respectively, "real" and "unreal" events. This throwback to our logical antecedence is just as evident in the writing of those who would like to deny the cross-linguistic validity of irrealis (e.g. Bybee *et al.* 1992), as it is in the writing of those who find irrealis useful and valid (e.g. Chafe 1992; Mithun 1992; Roberts 1990, 1992). When realis and irrealis are defined in cognitive and communicative terms, the focus of their difference shifts in two important ways:

- **Cognitively**: From matters of logical truth to matters of **subjective certainty**.
- **Communicatively**: From speaker-oriented (semantic) meaning to **socially-negotiated** interactive (pragmatic) meaning involving both speaker and hearer.[4]

While the more pragmatic, interactive, aspects of irrealis are traditionally better recognized in the valuative/deontic sub-modes, they turn out to be just as ubiquitous in the epistemic sub-modes.

4.3.   The distribution of irrealis over grammatical contexts

There are few if any languages where the grammatical marking of all irrealis sub-modes (or 'environments') is totally uniform. Nonetheless, the distribution of the modal category irrealis across grammatical contexts is far from chaotic, and is largely predictable on universal grounds. In this section I will re-capitulate briefly some of the major predictabilities. A fuller account has been given elsewhere (Givón 1984, chapter 8). The main grammatical contexts to be discussed are:

(a) tense-aspect
(b) modal adverbs
(c) verb complements
(d) non-declarative speech acts
(e) adverbial clauses
(f) modal auxiliaries

4.3.1. Tense-aspect and irrealis

The following correlations between tense-aspect and epistemic modality are highly predictable:

(4)   **Correlations between tense-aspect and modality**
   a.   **Past/perfective** $\Longrightarrow$ realis (or presupposition)
   b.   **Perfect** $\Longrightarrow$ realis (or presupposition)
   c.   **Present-progressive** $\Longrightarrow$ realis
   d.   **Future** $\Longrightarrow$ irrealis
   e.   **Habitual** $\Longrightarrow$ irrealis *or* realis

The status of the habitual, a swing modal category par excellence, is murky for good reasons. From a communicative perspective, habitual-marked clauses tend to be strongly asserted, i.e. pragmatically like realis. Semantically, however, they resemble irrealis in some fundamental ways. To begin with, unlike realis, which typically signals that an event has occurred (or state persisted) at some specific time, a habitual-marked assertion does not refer to any particular event that occurred at any specific time. Further, the reference properties of NPs under the scope of habitual resemble those of NPs under the scope of irrealis. Briefly, the rule for predicting reference from modal scope is as follows:[5]

(5)   **Reference under modal scope:**
   (a)   Under the scope of 'fact' modalities — realis and presup-
          position — NPs must be interpreted as referring.
   (b)   Under the scope of non-fact modalities — irrealis and
          negation — NPs may be interpreted as non-referring.

To illustrate the consequences of rule (5), consider the interpretation in English of indefinite objects marked with the article 'a':

(6)   a. **R-assertion:**   He bought a new car
       b. **Presupposition:**   She knew that he bought a new car
       c. **IRR-assertion:**   He may buy a new car
       d. **NEG-assertion:**   He didn't buy a new car
       e. **Habitual:**   He buys a new car every year

In the two *fact* modalities (6a) and (6b), 'a new car' must be interpreted as referring. In the two *non-fact* modalities (6c) and (6d), 'a new car' can be interpreted as non-referring. In the habitual (6e), 'a car' is most likely interpreted as non-referring.

Given the habitual's mixed functional properties, it is not surprising that it has been grouped in some languages with realis and in others with irrealis.[6] When a functional category is complex and involves both semantic and pragmatic features, it is common for some languages to group it by its semantic features and others by its pragmatic features.[7]

4.3.2.   Irrealis-inducing adverbs

Many epistemic adverbs, such as 'maybe', 'probably', 'possibly, 'likely', 'supposedly', 'presumably', 'surely' or 'undoubtedly', create an irrealis scope over the proposition in which they are lodged, in this way overriding realis tense-aspects such as past, present-progressive or perfect:

(7)   a. **Maybe** she left.
       b. He is **probably** reading in the library.
       c. She has **undoubtedly** finished by now.

Some valuative adverbs, such as 'hopefully', are also irrealis-inducing:

(8)   a. **Hopefully**, she'll leave on time.
       b. **Hopefully**, she has left on time.
       c. **Hopefully**, he is leaving right now.
       d. **Hopefully**, she left on time.

Other valuative adverbs, such as 'preferably' or 'ideally', are so future-projecting that they are incompatible with realis tense-aspects altogether:

(9)   a. She should do it **preferably** tomorrow.
       b. **Ideally** they should finish Tuesday.
       c. *She did it **preferably** yesterday.
       d. *She is **preferably** doing it right now.
       e. *She has **preferably** done it already.
       f. ***Ideally** they did it Tuesday.
       g. ***Ideally** they are doing it right now.
       h. ***Ideally** they have done it already.

These adverbs of strong preference also seem incompatible with the future-modal 'will' and 'be going to'. They thus seem to require a stronger valuative/deontic modal, such as 'should' in (9a,b). Thus compare:

(10)   a. ?She will do it **preferably** tomorrow.
     b. ?She's going to do it **preferably** tomorrow.
     c. ?**Ideally** they'll finish Tuesday.
     d. ?**Ideally** they're going to finish Tuesday.

Finally, some valuative adverbs, such as 'fortunately' and 'regrettably', are factive, and thus preserve the realis modality:[8]

(11)   a. **Fortunately**, she left on time.
     b. **Regrettably**, she is still talking.
     c. **Fortunately**, she has already left.

4.3.3.   Irrealis in verb complements

Many complement-taking verbs induce an irrealis mode over their complement clauses, even when the main verb itself is marked by a realis tense-aspect. All three main type of complement-taking verbs can exhibit this phenomenon.

(a)   Complements of modality verbs

Non-implicative modality verbs, i.e. those that do not imply that the event in their complement has taken place, induce a valuative/deontic irrealis mode over their complements:

(12)   a. She wanted **to find another job**
     b. He planned **to build a new house**
     c. She decided **to quit her job**
     d. He intends **to write a new proposal**
     e. She tried **to leave**

(b)   Complements of manipulation verbs

Non-implicative manipulation verbs induce a valuative/deontic irrealis mode over their complements:

(13)   a. She wanted him **to buy a new car**
     b. He asked her **to write his boss**
     c. She told him **to find a house**
     d. He forbade her **to see another man**

(c) Complements of perception/cognition/utterance verbs

Non-factive perception-cognition-utterance verbs (or adjectives), i.e. those that do not presuppose their complements, induce an irrealis mode over their complements. The sub-mode induces by some non-factive predicates is epistemic, as in:

(14) a. He thought **that she loved another man**
      b. She imagined **that he loved her sister**
      c. He believed **that an evil spirit had invaded him**
      d. She was sure **that he was with a friend**
      e. He said **that the letter had arrived late**

For other non-factive predicates, the sub-modality is tinted with valuative features, such as preference or aversion:

(15) a. He wished **that she could find a new house**
      b. She hoped **she could find a job**
      c. They preferred **that another woman do it**
      d. She decided **that he should write a book**
      e. He was afraid **she might never have enough room**

4.3.4. Non-declarative speech-acts and irrealis

Two non-declarative clause types — manipulative clauses and yes-no questions — are inherently under irrealis scope. Manipulative speech-acts — command, request, exhortation — fall under the scope of irrealis for two related reasons. First, they are future projecting, depicting events that have not yet occurred. Second, they involve valuative/deontic sub-modes of irrealis:

(16) a. **Command**:
         Get me a drink!
      b. **Request**:
         Could you please get me a drink?
      c. **Exhortation**:
         Let's go get you a drink.
      d. **Jussive**:
         May he rot in hell!

The strong association of yes-no questions with irrealis, on the other hand, is due primarily to the epistemic sub-mode of **uncertainty**. The degree of uncertainty may be further modulated by the various grammatical forms of the yes-no question (Bolinger 1978):

(17) a. You didn't buy a new car, did you?
     b. Did you buy a new car?
     c. Didn't you buy a new car?
     d. You bought a new car, didn't you?

4.3.5.   Irrealis in adverbial clauses

Several types of ADV-clauses fall under irrealis scope. The most prominent among those are irrealis temporal ('when') clauses, irrealis conditional
('if') clauses and counter-fact clauses:

(18) a. **Irrealis temporal clause**:
        When you get a loan, I'll sell you my car.
     b. **Simple conditional**:
        If you get a loan, I'll sell you my car.
     c. **Subjunctive conditional**:
        If you got a loan, I would then sell you my car.
     d. **Counter-fact conditional**:
        If you had got a loan, I would have sold you my car.

The counter-fact modality need not be lodged in an ADV-clause:

(19) a. **I would have sold you my car**, but it's too late now.
     b. **She could have passed**, she missed by one point.

The association of counter-fact clauses with irrealis requires some discussion. Since the counter-fact clause is under negation scope, one may count it as
an instance of the mega-modality *non-fact* rather than of the narrower modality
irrealis. But the association may in fact be with irrealis itself, although in an
indirect, diachronically-mediated fashion (see section 4.6.3.2. below).

4.3.6.   Modal auxiliaries and the markedness status of
the irrealis sub-modes

Modal auxiliaries, in languages that have them as a grammatical category
distinct from modality verbs, are irrealis-inducing operators par excellence.
Diachronically, they are almost always derived from non-implicative modality
verbs (see 4.3.4. above). The modality associated with such verbs tends to start
as valuative — ability, intent, purpose, preference, obligation, necessity or
permission. But epistemic senses of low certainty eventually develop, regardless
of whether the modality verb attains the distinct grammatical status of modal

auxiliary (Coates 1983; Sweetser 1984; Fleischman 1989; Traugott 1989; Abraham 1992; Bavin 1992; Bybee 1992; Heine 1992; Guo 1992; Zavala 1992; *inter alia*).

One seeming exception to the modality-verb source of modal auxiliaries is the motion verb 'go', which routinely gives rise to future-tense auxiliaries. However, the source of this sense is not simply the spatial motion sense of 'go', but rather the non-motion sense found in purpose-clause complements. In this capacity, 'go' tends to display the complementation pattern of modality verbs; and it is this purposive deontic sense that is responsible for the eventual emergence of a future meaning. Thus compare:

(20) a. **Motion verb**:
          She is going **to Chicago**
      b. **Purpose clause**:
          She is going there **to buy a house**
      c. **Future modal auxiliary**:
          She is going **to leave him**

The emergence of an epistemic sense of 'go' from an earlier deontic sense thus parallels the historical development of English modals — from deontic to epistemic.

One way of interpreting the widespread and largely uni-directional development of epistemic modal senses from earlier deontic senses is by invoking semantic markedness and **semantic bleaching**. If there is a semantic common denominator to all sub-modes of irrealis, it must be the feature of epistemic uncertainty. This is so because valuative-deontic sub-modes carry, in addition to their deontic value, also an inherent sense of futurity, thus of epistemic uncertainty. Deontic modality is thus the marked case. Epistemic modality, on the other hand, need not have any deontic sense, and is thus the unmarked case. That is:

(21) a. **Deontic**: She **should** go home
              > She **hasn't yet** gone home
      b. **Epistemic**: She **will** go home
                  > She **hasn't yet** gone home
                  *> She **should** go home
      c. **Deontic**: He **wants** to leave
              > He **hasn't yet** left
      d. **Epistemic**: He **will** leave
                  > He **hasn't yet** left
                  *> He **wants** leave

The one-way-conditional association between the marked deontic and the unmarked epistemic sub-modes of irrealis may be given as:[9]

(22)   If deontic, then epistemic uncertainty
        (but not necessarily vice versa)

As noted earlier (chapter 2), a marked-unmarked relation between two categories is often revealed via a one-way conditional association between them. Thus, for example, negative clauses pragmatically presuppose their corresponding affirmatives, but not vice versa (Givón 1979a, ch. 3). Likewise, both WH-questions and yes/no questions pragmatically presuppose their corresponding declarative, but not vice versa (Bolinger 1978; Givón 1990b, ch. 18).

The general directionality of diachronic extension of modal senses — deontic-to-epistemic — has one conspicuous exception. It is found in so-called indirect speech-acts of manipulation. In some of these, an erstwhile epistemic irrealis clause assumes the speech-act value of weak manipulation:

(23)   a. **What if** you came Friday instead?
        b. **Suppose** you did it anyway?
        c. **How about** coming tomorrow?
        d. Are you **going to** do it?

In Korean, the most common strategy for forming obligative modal expressions involves the use of an 'if'-clause, which of itself typically carries a low-certainty epistemic mode. Thus (Kim 1986):

(24)   a. i   ch'aek-un an ilk-**o-myon**, an   twe-n-ta
           this book-TOP NEG read-**MOD-if** NEG be.good-PRES-PRT
           'You must read this book'
           (*lit.*: 'If you don't read this book, it won't be OK')
        b. i   ch'aek-un an ilk-**o-to**,   twe-n-ta
           this book-TOP NEG read-**MOD-even/if** be.good-PRES-PRT
           'You may not-read this book'
           'You don't have to read this book'
           (*lit.*: 'Even if you don't read this book, it'll be OK')
        c. i   ch'aek-un an ilk-**o-ya**,   twe-n-ta
           this book-TOP NEG read-**MOD-only/if** be.good-PRES-PRT
           'You must/should/may not read this book'
           (*lit.*: 'If you only not read this book, it'll be OK')

However, the valuative 'be good' in the second clause is no doubt the real source of deontic modal value here. A similar combination of valuative clause and 'if'-clause can be seen in English:

(25)   a. It would be **nice if** you **came** early and...
      b. I would **appreciate if** you **come** and...
      c. It would be **better if** they didn't show up...

Eventually, the valuative 'nice', 'appreciate', 'better' is dispensed with, as in the following example of invitation, from a recent television episode:[10]

(26)   "...Well, **if** you come with me now..."

The potential for full grammaticalization of such 'if'-clauses is evident in frozen expressions such as:

(27)   a. **If** you only knew how much this means to me!
        (> I **wish** you knew)
      b. **If** it's all the same to you...
        (> I **would like** to...)
      c. **If** it pleases His Majesty...
        (> we **may** now proceed to...)

If irrealis indeed has a semantic common denominator — epistemic uncertainty — then the widespread sharing of grammatical marking between the two sub-modes of irrealis (cf. Palmer 1979, 1986; Coates 1983; Traugott 1989) becomes non-accidental. It is simply part of the evidence supporting such a common denominator. The sharing of overt marking between the two sub-modes is thus the consequence of a predictable, uni-directional process of semantic bleaching during grammaticalization.[11]

4.4.   The distribution of the subjunctive across irrealis subordinate clauses

4.4.1.   Preamble

Having surveyed modality in general and irrealis in particulary, we turn now to focus more narrowly on the irrealis environments in which a grammaticalized subjunctive is most commonly found. I will begin by surveying the distribution of the subjunctive in subordinate clauses. Section 4.5 below then treats its distribution in main clauses. The distribution of the subjunctive across these various contexts turns out to be coherent rather than capricious. Some day, when more cross-language evidence becomes available, one should be able to rank all irrealis environments according to the likelihood of finding a grammaticalized subjunctive in them. The survey here is only a first stab at such a task.

An air-tight, categorial definition of "subjunctive" remains an unrealistic goal. One can, however, identify the most likely **subjunctive foci** along the two scalar sub-dimensions of irrealis — epistemic and valuative/deontic. The two are:

- **Epistemic**: lower certainty
- **Deontic**:   weaker manipulation.

The predictive power of this identification has the familiar ring of a one-way conditional association:

(28) **Prediction**:
"If a language has a grammaticalized subjunctive, then it is most likely to appear at those two foci along the two irrealis sub-dimensions".

Being a one-way conditional, the logical relation between subjunctive and irrealis is that of inclusion, whereby the subjunctive is a sub-set of irrealis. One should thus not expect the reverse prediction:

(29)   *"Since all languages have those loci along the two irrealis sub-dimensions, all languages should display a grammaticalized subjunctive".

Indeed, functional predictions of grammaticalization patterns most often have this one-way-conditional form — one can predict that if a change will occur, it would start at particular loci and proceed in a particular direction. But one cannot predict whether the change will or will not occur. Put another way, one can predict *how* languages would grammaticalize, but seldom *whether* they would.

4.4.2. The subjunctive in verb complements

4.4.2.1. The complementation scale

A grammaticalized subjunctive appears most commonly in two verbal complement types — of manipulation verbs and of perception-cognition-utterance verbs. The verbs in the two groups can be rank-ordered along a continuum scale of two iconically-matched parallel dimensions — the semantic dimension of **event integration** and the syntactic dimension of **clause integration**. The scale is illustrated in (30) below with English verbs.[12]

(30)	Semantic scale of verbs	syntax of COMP-clause
a.	She **let go** of the knife	CO-LEXICALIZED VERB
b.	She **made** him **shave**	
c.	She **let** him **go** home	BARE VERB-STEM COMP
d.	She **had** him **arrested**	
e.	She **caused** him **to switch** jobs	
f.	She **told** him **to leave**	
g.	She **asked** him to leave	INFINITIVE COMP
h.	She **allowed** him **to leave**	
i.	She **wanted** him **to leave**	
j.	She **expected** him **to leave**	
k.	She'**d like** him **to leave**	
l.	She'd **like for** him **to leave**	FOR-TO COMP
m.	She **suggested** that he **leave**	MODAL-SUBJUNCTIVE COMP
n.	She **wished** that he **would leave**	
o.	She **agreed** that he **could leave**	(deontic)
p.	She **preferred** that he **leave**	
q.	She **hoped** that he **might leave**	
r.	She **was afraid** that he **might leave**	
s.	She **thought** that he **might leave** later	(epistemic)
t.	She **knew** that he **left**	INDICATIVE COMP
u.	She **said**: "He **left**"	DIRECT QUOTE. COMP

The semantic dimension underlying scale (30) is that of **event integration** — the extent to which the two events in the main and complement clause are integrated into a single complex event. The syntactic dimension is that of **clause integration** — the extent to which the two clauses are integrated into a single complex clause. On both scales, example (30a) shows maximal integration and (30u) minimal. The main modal-semantic steps along the semantic continuum of the complementation scale may be given as:

(31) **Main semantic steps on the complementation scale**:
    a. successful causation ("implicative"; realis)
    b. intended manipulation ("non-implicative") ‖ MOST LIKELY
    c. preference/aversion   ‖ RANGE OF
    d. epistemic anxiety   ‖ SUBJUNCTIVE
    e. epistemic uncertainty ("non-factive") ‖ COMPLEMENTS
    f. epistemic certainty ("factive"; realis)
    g. direct quote (dissociation from the speaker's perspective)

4.4.2.2. The subjunctive of weak manipulation

Subjunctives forms of complement verbs tend to crop up in the mid-section of the complementation scale (30)/(31), covering a contiguous transition region of the valuative-deontic sub-mode **weaker manipulation** and the epistemic sub-mode **lower certainty** ((30m-s), (31b-e)). Typical verbs along this mid-section are:

(32)   **deontic (manipulative) side**

    a. weak intended manipulation ('tell', 'ask', 'suggest')
    b. preference ('want'/'wish', 'prefer', 'expect')
    c. epistemic anxiety ('hope', 'fear')
    d. low epistemic certainty ('not-sure', 'doubt', 'suspect',
                          'ask if', 'not-know if')

      epistemic side

The subjunctive range along the complementation scale thus seems to bridge over the two main sub-modes of irrealis. In both cases, the subjunctive covers the lower section of the sub-modality scale — weaker deontic force and lower epistemic certainty. On the deontic side, the subjunctive always appears in complements of non-implicative, weak manipulation verbs. But the exact cut-off point on the scale, i.e. the specific verb where the subjunctive begins to appear, is a matter of considerable cross-language variation. To illustrate this, let us compare the verbs along this sub-region in English and Spanish.

In Spanish, the verbs 'order' and 'advise' allow both an infinitive and a subjunctive complement, with the infinitive predictably coding a stronger

manipulation, the subjunctive a weaker one. I will consider modal-marked verbs
as the subjunctive form in English in such contexts, and will justify this choice
further below. Thus consider:[13]

(33) a. **Infinitive complement:**
    le   mandaron   **callar**
    him order/PAST/3p shut-up/INF
    'They ordered him **to keep quiet**'

    b. **Subjunctive complement:**
    le   mandaron   que se   **callara**
    3s/OBJ order/PAST/3p SUB REFL quiet/PAST/SUBJUN3s
    ?'They ordered him **to keep quiet**'[14]
    *'The ordered him that he **should keep quiet**'
    'They told him that he **should keep** quiet'

(34) a. **Infinitive complement:**
    le   mandaron   **seguir**les
    him order/PAST/3p follow/INF/them
    'They ordered him **to follow** them'

    b. **Subjunctive complement:**
    le   mandaron que les   **siguiera**
    him ordered   SUB them follow/3s/PAST/SUBJUN/3s
    ?'They ordered him **to follow** them'[15]
    *'They ordered him that **he should follow** them'
    'They told him that **he should follow** them'

The English 'order' is too strong a manipulative verb to accept a modal-
subjunctive complement, so that (31b) and (32b) above cannot be rendered with
'order', but only with 'tell'. The verb 'advise', on the other hand, allows both
complement types in both languages:[16]

(35) a. **Infinitive complement:**
    le   aconsejaron   no   **decir**   nada
    him advise/PAST/3p NEG say/INF nothing
    'They advised him not **to say** anything'

    b. **Subjunctive complement:**
    le   aconsejaron   que no **dijera**   nada
    him advise/PAST/3p SUB NEG say/PAST/SUBJUN/3s nothing
    'They advised him that **he should** not **say** anything'

The verbs 'tell' and 'ask' in Spanish cannot take an infinitive complement, but require the subjunctive. Their English equivalents, on the other hand, can take both infinitive and subjunctive complements (Butt and Benjamin 1988):

(36) a. le dijeron que les   **siguiera**
             her told   SUB them follow/3s/**PAST/SUBJUN**
             ?'They told her **to follow** them'[17]
             'They told her that she **should follow** them'
     b. *le dijeron **seguir**-les
             her told   follow/**INF**-them
     c. le pidieron que les   **siguiera**
             her asked   SUB them follow/3s/**PAST/SUBJUN**
             ?'They asked her **to follow** them'[18]
             'They asked her **if** she **could follow** them'
             'They ask that she **follow** them'
     d. *le pidieron **seguir**-les
             her told   follow/**INF**-them

In English, the switch to an obligatory modal-subjunctive complement appears only at a lower portion of the scale, with verbs of weaker-yet manipulation such as 'suggest', 'wish', 'insist', 'prefer', 'expect':

(37) a. I prefer that she **not leave**   (subjunctive)
     b. *I prefer that she **doesn't leave**   (*indicative)
     c. I suggest that she **leave** right away   (subjunctive)
     d. ?I suggest that she **leaves** right away (?indicative)
     e. He wished that she **would leave**   (modal-subjun.)
     f. *He wished that she **left**   (*indicative)
     g. We expect that she **would accept**   (modal-subjun.)
     h. *We expect that she **accepts**   (*indicative)
     i. She insists that it **be** done right away (subjunctive)
     j. ?She insists that it **is** done right away   (?indicative)

The difference between English and Spanish is thus in the exact switching-point from indicative (or infinitive) to subjunctive complementation. This is also evident with the verb 'want'. In Spanish, the single verb *querer* must take a subjunctive complement, thus approximating the grammatical behavior of the English 'wish'. In English, 'want' takes an infinitive complement, and is a verb of more direct manipulation, not simply a verb of private volition. 'Wish', on the other hand, is primarily a verb of volition and only marginally (if at all) of manipulation. Thus compare (Butt and Benjamin 1988):

(38) a. Quiero que   **estudies**   más
          want-I COMP study/2s/SUBJUN more
          ?'I want you **to study** more'[19]
          'I wish that you **would study** more'

In sum, then, whenever a contrast is possible between an infinitive and a subjunctive complementation of the same lexical verb, the infinitive invariably signals stronger manipulation, and the subjunctive weaker. This prediction has the force of a typical implicational universal. Typical examples of such a contrast in Spanish are (Butt and Benjamin 1988):

(39) a. Te   prohibo   **cantar**
          You prohibit/I sing/**INF**
          'I forbid you **to sing**'

      b. Te   prohibo   que **cantes**
          you prohibit/I SUB sing/2s/**SUBJUN**
          ?'I prohibit it that you **sing**'

(40) a. Le   obligan a **llegar**   pronto
          him make/3p to come/**INF** early
          'They make him **come** early'

      b. Le   obligan a que **llegue**   pronto
          him make/3p to SUB come/3s/**SUBJUN** early
          'They make it so that he **can come** early'

(41) a. Le   mandan a **recoger** el correo
          him send/3p to fetch/**INF** the mail
          'They send him **to fetch** the mail'

      b. Le   mandan a que **recoja**   el correo
          him send/3p to SUB fetch/3s/**SUBJUN** the mail
          'They send him so that he **(would) fetch** the mail'

In Bemba, a Bantu language, the very same contrast between infinitive and subjunctive complementation is found, semantically aligned in exactly the same direction. However, the cutoff point in Bemba is higher on the complementation scale — between the implicative manipulation sense of 'force' (infinitive complement) and the non-implicative sense of 'order' (subjunctive complement). Both senses are signalled in Bemba by the same lexical verb. However, an intermediate subjunctive form is possible in Bemba, with the manipulee **raised** to object.[20] This form, (42b) below, signals an intermediate degree of manipulative force, although it defies exact translation. Thus compare (Givón 1971b):

(42) a. **Infinitive complement**:
         n-à-mu-koonkomeshya **uku**-ya
         I-REM-force   INF-go
         'I forced him **to leave**'
         (> He left)
      b. **Subjunctive complement with raising**:
         n-à-**mu**-koonkomeshya (ukuti) a-y-**e**
         I-REM-**him**-order   (SUB) he-go-SUBJUN
         'I ordered him **to leave**'
         (> He may or may not have left)
      c. **Subjunctive without raising**:
         n-à-konkomeshya ukuti a-y-**e**
         I-REM-decreed   SUB he-go-SUBJUN
         'I ordered that he **should leave**'
         (> He may or may not have left)

With a lexical verb that carries a lower manipulative force, such as 'tell'/'say', the Bemba contrast between infinitive and subjunctive yields a similar gradation of manipulative force (Givón 1971b):

(43) a. **Infinitive complement**:
         n-à-mu-ebele **uku**-ya
         I-REM-him-tell INF-go
         'I told him **to leave**'
      b. **Subjunctive complement with raising**:
         n-à-mu-ebele (ukuti) a-y-**e**
         I-REM-him-tell (SUB) he-go-SUBJUN
         'I told him that he **should leave**'

      c. **Subjunctive complement without raising**:
         n-à-ebele ukuti a-y-**e**
         I-REM-say SUB he-go-SUBJUN
         'I said that he **should leave**'

4.4.2.3. The subjunctive of low certainty

4.4.2.3.1. From deontic to epistemic modality

One of the more compelling arguments for the graduality of the complementation scale — and thus indirectly also for the semantic integrity of irrealis — is the gradual semantic transition at the mid-section of the scale, from weak deontic to weak epistemic modal values. The subjunctive grammatical form, whenever it occurs, spans a contiguous mid-scale region here, regardless of whether the subjunctive is an old verbal inflection (Spanish) or a modal auxiliary (English). The crucial transition link seems to be verbs of **epistemic anxiety** such as 'hope' and 'fear' ((32c) in (32) above, reproduced below). Verbs of this type code, seemingly in equal measures, uncertainty about a future event (or state), and preference or aversion toward it.

(32)   **deontic (manipulative) side**

    a. weak intended manipulation ('tell', 'ask', 'suggest')
    b. preference ('want'/'wish', 'prefer', 'expect')
    c. epistemic anxiety ('hope', 'fear')
    d. low epistemic certainty ('not-sure', 'doubt', 'suspect',
                                      'ask if', 'not-know if')

       epistemic side

One must acknowledge that distribution of subjunctive forms across the modal transition zone is subject to considerable typological variation. The main typological contrast is between languages in which a single subjunctive form covers the entire modal range, and those in which the modal range is covered by two subjunctive forms — a valuative-deontic subjunctive (upper range) and an epistemic subjunctive (lower range).

4.4.2.3.2. Unified subjunctive

In Spanish (and other Romance languages), the very same subjunctive form spans the entire mid-range of the complementation scale (as well as in other subjunctive regions or irrealis). This parallels the use in English of the modal auxiliaries in many of the same environments. Thus compare (Butt and Benjamin 1988):

(44) a. **Weak manipulation**:
le   digo que **venga**
him say/I SUB come/3s/**SUBJUN**
'I tell him that he **should come**'
b. **Preference**:
quiero que **venga**
want/I SUB come/3s/**SUBJUN**
'I wish that he **would come**'
c. **Epistemic anxiety**:
espero que   **venga**   pronto
hope/I COMP come/3s/**SUBJUN** soon
'I hope that he **would come** soon'
d. **Low epistemic certainty**:
dudo   si **esté**   aquí
doubt/I if be/3s/**SUBJUN** here
'I doubt that (she) is here'
e. **Low epistemic certainty**:
no sé   si **tenga**   dinero
NEG know/I if have/3s/**SUBJUN** money
'I don't know if she has any money.'

The transition further down, to verbs of higher epistemic certainty, takes us out of the subjunctive range and into a fully finite indicative complement verb:

(45) **High epistemic certainty**:
sé   que **tiene**   dinero
know/I SUB have/3s/**INDIC** money
'I know s/he has money'

The syntactic transition along the relevant portion of the complementation scale, in terms of the verb-form in the complement clause, may be characterized in terms of **degree of finiteness**:

(46)

semantic scale	syntactic scale	
strong manipulation	infinitive	(least finite)
weak manipulation	subjunctive	(intermediate)
preference	subjunctive	(,,)
low certainty	subjunctive	(,,)
high certainty	indicative	(most finite)

Within this scalar framework, subjunctive-marked verbs are more finite than infinitives but less than the indicative, which allows a fuller range of tense-aspect distribution.[21]

4.4.2.3.3. Split subjunctive

In Bemba (and probably other Bantu languages), the subjunctive modal range is split right down the middle between two forms. The first is the deontic subjunctive of manipulation, as in (Givón 1971b):[22]

(47) a. **Subjunctive of manipulation (unmarked):**
a-à-ebele   Peta ukuti a-y-**e**
s/he-REM-tell Peter SUB he-go-SUBJUN
'S/he told Peter that he **should go**'
b. **Corresponding indicative:**
Peta a-y-**a**
Peter he-go-INDIC
'Peter **goes**.'

(48) a. **Subjunctive of manipulation (future):**
a-kà-eba   Peta ukuti a-kà-y-**e**
s/he-FUT-tell Peter SUB he-FUT-go-SUBJUN
'S/he will tell Peter that he **(should) go**.'
b. **Corresponding indicative:**
Peta a-kà-y-**a**
Peter he-FUT-go-INDIC
'Peter **will go**.'

The second form is the epistemic subjunctive of uncertainty, which has an invariant form across all main-clause tenses (Givón 1971b):[23]

(49) a. **Subjunctive of uncertainty (past main clause):**
n-à-twiishika nga Peta a-**inga**-isa
I-REM-doubt SUB Peter he-SUBJUN-come
'I doubted that Peter **would** come'
b. **Subjunctive of uncertainty (progressive main clause):**
n-déé-twiishika nga Peta a-**inga**-isa
I-PROG-doubt SUB Peter he-SUBJUN-come
'I doubt that Peter **would come**.'

c. **Corresponding indicative**:

Peta a-kà-isa

Peter he-FUT-come

'Peter will come'

The subjunctive-of-manipulation verb suffix -*e* ((47a) and (48a)) is an old Proto Core-Bantu suffix, one that may have overlapped with the negative verb suffix. The subjunctive-of-uncertainty verb prefix -*inga*- (49a,b) is more restricted to Bemba, at least in this context. It is, most likely, a relatively recent extension of the conditional subordinator *nga* 'if'.[24] In Swahili, reflexes of this suffix appears in lower certainty (subjunctive) 'if'-clauses, in the forms -*nga-li*-, -*nge*- and -*nge-li*- (Salone 1983). The formative -*li*- is a reflex of the verb 'be' which in Swahili has become the past tense. The -*nge*- form probably involve -*nga*- plus the subjunctive verbal suffix -*e*, which tags -*nga*- itself as an erstwhile verb.[25]

4.4.3. The subjunctive in adverbial clauses

4.4.3.1. Preamble

Many adverbial clauses carry an inherently irrealis modality, invariably its epistemic sub-mode. Whenever a grammaticalized subjunctive appears in ADV-clauses, it is thus invariably the subjunctive of low certainty. The epistemic modal space of ADV-clauses is commonly divided into a finer, often three-point, scale:

(50) **Most common modal scale of irrealis ADV-clauses**:

epistemic certainty	grammatical form
(a) Higher certainty	future/modal marking
(b) Lower certainty	subjunctive/modal marking
(c) Lowest certainty	counter-fact marking

In individual languages, the difference between points (50a) and (50b) may be coded by two distinct subjunctive forms, by two different modal forms, or by a contrast between subjunctive and non-subjunctive form. Sometimes the contrast is not coded in the ADV-clause, but rather by different irrealis forms in the associated main clause. The difference between point (50b) and (50c) may be marked by subjunctive vs. non-subjunctive form, by different modal forms, or by different irrealis marking in the main clause. Some of these typological variations are surveyed below.

4.4.3.2. English

> "...Honey, I have an uh... unusual request... uh...
> Y'see, I've been on this uh... island... for a long
> time without uh... the companionship of a uh...
> female... So I been wonderin'... uh... if I **gave**
> you two coconuts..."
>
> > Ed Sanders as "Robinson Crusoe"
> > The Fugs, *It Crawled into my Hand, Honest*
> > Reprise Records RS-6305 (ca. 1967)

With 'when'-irrealis clauses included, the continuum of epistemic certainty for irrealis ADV-clauses in English can be given as a four-point scale:

(51)　**Epistemic certainty scale for irrealis
　　　ADV-clauses in English**:
　　　　higher certainty

---

　　　a. **Irrealis 'when'**:
　　　　When she **comes**, we **will** consider it.
　　　b. **Irrealis 'if'**:
　　　　If she **comes**, we **will/may** consider it.
　　　c. **Subjunctive 'if'**:
　　　　If she ever **came**, we **would/might** consider it.
　　　d. **Counterfact 'if'**:
　　　　If she **had come**, we **would/might have** considered it.

---

　　　lowest certainty

The gradation of grammatical forms in the irrealis conditional clauses in (51) is:

(52)　**Scale of verb forms coding degree of certainty
　　　in English conditional clauses**:

　　　HABITUAL/UNMARKED > **PAST** > PAST-PERFECT

The gradation of grammatical marking on the scale is even more detailed in the associated main clauses in (51):

(53)　**Scale of verb forms coding degree of certainty
　　　in English associated main clauses**:

　　　FUTURE > FUTURE/MODAL > **PAST-MODAL** >
　　　PERFECT-PAST-MODAL

While the subjunctive of uncertainty in English is not a unified grammatical category, the relative position of English subjunctive verb forms in both ADV-clauses and their associated main clauses — past or past-modal — is in the predictable low-certainty range of the epistemic scale, just above counter-fact.

The use of the past-form of the verb as a subjunctive of uncertainty in 'if'-clauses is apparently well-entrenched in American English, both oral and written. A natural example from newspaper writing may be seen in:[26]

(54) "...The people responsible [for destroying our lives] have never even apologized," Wade said. "And even if they **did** apologize, they **could** never apologize enough..."

There is in fact an even more subtle contrast in English 'if'-clauses, between *two* subjunctive forms:

(55) a. **Future-modal**:
       What will you do if I **tell** you that...
      b. **Past-Subjunctive**:
       What would you do if I **told** you that...
      c. **Past-be subjunctive**:
       What would you do if I **were** to tell you that...
      d. **Past-perfect (counterfact)**:
       What would you have done if I **had told** you that...

4.4.3.3. Bemba

The subjunctive of uncertainty form *-inga-* that appears in complement clauses in Bemba (see earlier above) is synchronically distinct from the 'if'-clause marker *-nga-* but historically derived from it.[27] Thus compare (Givón 1971b):

(56) a. **'If'-clause**:
       nga Peta a-kà-isa,...
       if   Peter he-FUT-come
       'If Peter comes,...'
      b. **Verb complement**:
       n-déé-twiishika nga Peta a-**inga**-isa
       I-PRES-doubt   SUB Peter he-SUBJUN-come
       'I doubt that/if Peter **would** come'
      c. *****nga** Peta a-**inga**-isa,...
       if   Peter he-SUBJUN-come

4.4.3.4. Swahili

As noted earlier, the morphemes *nga*, *nge* (or occasionally *ngo*)[28] are widely attested across the core-Bantu area as low-certainty irrealis subordinators in various contexts. The spreading of 'if'-clause subordinators to complements of verbs of low certainty, such as 'not know', 'not be sure' or 'doubt' is wide-spread cross-linguistically. Most likely, the initial beach-head for such an extension is found in embedded conditional complements, as in:

(57) a. I doubt **if** he could make it
b. She's not sure **if** that's possible
c. They don't know **if** she's there

In Swahili, a number of reflexes of *nga* appear in 'if'-clauses. When contrasted with other 'if'-clause markers, these reflexes of *nga* consistently signal lower epistemic certainty. At the top of the certainty scale in irrealis ADV-clauses one finds the modal prefix *-ki-* ('when', 'if'),[29] as in (Salone 1983):

(58) a. **Higher certainty** (*ki* = 'when'):
ni-na   uhakika   kwamba ni-ta-mw-ona kesho,
I-have certainty SUB   I-FUT-her-see tomorrow
'I **am sure** I'll see her tomorrow,

   na   ni-**ki**-mw-ona, ni-**ta**-m-pa   ujumbe
   and I-MOD-her-see I-FUT-her-give message
   and **when** I see her, I **will** give her the message'
b. **Lower certainty** (*ki* = 'if'):
n-a-dhani   ni-ta-mu-ona kesho,
I-PRES-think I-FUT-her-see tomorrow
'I **think** I'll see her tomorrow,

   na   ni-**ki**-mw-ona, ni-**ta**-m-pa   ujumbe.
   and I-MOD-her-see I-FUT-her-give message
   and **if** I see her, I **will** give her the message'

With the subordinators *i-wa-po* ('it-be-that') and *i-ki-wa* ('it-if-be') one gets a lower epistemic certainty without resorting to modal or subjunctive operators, but simply with the future tense (Salone 1983):

(59) a. si-tegemeni ku-enda, lakini **iwapo** ni-**ta**-kwenda
          neg/I-expect INF-go   but   **if**   I-FUT-go
          '**I don't expect** to go, but **if** I go,

              ni-**ta**-ku-nunu-lia   mchele
              I-FUT-you-buy-BEN rice
              I **will** buy you rice'
      b. ni-na   mashaka kuwa John a-ta-kuja,
          I-have doubts   SUB John he-FUT-come
          '**I doubt** that John will come,

              lakini **ikiwa** a-**ta**-kuja,   ni-**ta**-mw-amb-ia
              but   **if**   he-FUT-come I-FUT-him-tell-BEN
              but **if** he **comes**, I **will** tell him'

With lower epistemic certainty, one enters the subjunctive range, first with the so-called *present* subjunctive (Salone 1983):

(60) **kama** ni-**nge**-kuwa tajiri, ni-**nge**-jenga   nyumba.
      if   I-SUBJUN-be rich I-SUBJUN-build house
      'If I **were** rich, I **would** build a house'

Finally, with the *past* subjunctive, one crosses over into the range of counter-fact (Salone 1983):

(61) **kama** ni-**nga-li**-kuwa   tajiri, ni-**nga-li**-jenga   nyumba.
      if   I-SUBJUN-PAST-be rich i-SUBJUN-PAST-build house
      'If I **had been** rich, I **would have** built a house'

In her discussion of the relationship between the present and past subjunctives in Swahili, Salone (1983) observes:

> "...while *nge*-sentences rarely refer to any unreal [events], *ngali*-sentences are understood either to be contrary-to-fact, or to suggest a low likelihood of fulfillment..." (1983, p. 322)

Often, only the real-world pragmatic context tips the scale between unlikely-but-possible and counter-fact. Thus (Salone 1983):

(62)   a. **Unlikely but possible:**
      ni-**ngeli**-enda   soko-ni, ni-**ngeli**-nunua   viazi
      I-SUBJUN/PAST-go store-LOC I-SUBJUN/PAST-but potatoes
      'If I **were** to go to the store, I **would** buy potatoes'
    b. **Counter-fact:**
      ni-**ngeli**-kuwa   malkia, ni-**ngeli**-badilisha   siasa.
      I-SUBJUN/PAST-be Queen I-SUBJUN/PAST-change politics
      'If I **had been** the Queen, I **would have** changed politics'

This overlapping, indeed bridging, use of the same grammatical marking — often past-subjunctive or perfect — at the lower extreme of the epistemic certainty scale is very common cross-linguistically (see further below).

4.4.3.5. Spanish

The same subjunctive forms that appear in complements of uncertainty verbs in Spanish also appear in a large variety of irrealis ADV-clauses.[30] With one conspicuous exception (see below), all these ADV-clauses fall under irrealis modal scope. The contrast between a simple indicative and the subjunctive can be found in irrealis 'when'-clauses. Predictably, the indicative signals higher epistemic certainty and the subjunctive lower certainty (Butt and Benjamin 1988, p. 235):[31]

(63)   a. **Present indicative (higher certainty):**
      Me saludará   cuando **llega**
      me greet/FUT/3s when   arrive/3s/**PRES**
      'She'll greet me when she **arrives**'
    b. **Present subjunctive (lower certainty):**
      Me saludará cuando **llegue**
      me greet/3s when   arrive/3s/**SUBJUN**
      'She will greet me when(**ever**) she **may** arrive'

Similarly with a habitual main clause (Butt and Benjamin 1988):

(64)   a. **Present indicative (higher certainty):**
      Me saluda   cuando **llega**
      me greet/3s when   arrive/3s/**INDIC**
      'She greets me when she **arrives**'
    b. **Present subjunctive (lower certainty):**
      Me saluda   cuando **llegue**
      me greet/3s when   arrive/3s/**SUBJUN**
      'She greets me when(**ever**) she **arrives**'

(65) a. **Indicative-past (realis):**
Tan pronto como se   **acabó**   la huelga,
as soon as   REFL end/3s/**PRET** the strike
'As soon as the strike **ended**,

      todo se   **arregló**.
      all REFL arrange/3s/**PRET**
      everything **became** alright'

  b. **Subjunctive-present (irrealis):**
Tan pronto come se   **acabe**   la huelga,
as soon as   REFL end/3s/**SUBJUN** the strike
'As soon as the strike **is** over,

      las cosas **marcharán** mejor
      the things go/3p/**FUT**   better
      things **will go** better'

(66) a. **Indicative-past (realis):**
A medida que **iban**   entrando,
at measure SUB go/3p/**PAST/IMPF** entering
'As they came in,

      se   lo **decía**
      them it told/**IMPF/I**
      I **told** it to them'

  b. **Subjunctive-present (irrealis):**
A medida que **vayan**   entrando, se   lo diré
at measure SUB go/3p/**SUBJUN** entering   them it say/**FUT/I**
'As they **come** in, I **will tell** it to them'

(67) a. **Indicative-past (realis):**
Hasta que no **llegó**   a ser ministro
till SUB neg come/3s/**PRET** to be minister
'Until he **became** minister,

      no se   **quedó**   contento.
      NEG REFL stay/3s/**PRET** satisfied
      he **wasn't** satisfied'

  b. **Subjunctive-present (irrealis):**
Hasta que no **llegue**   a ser ministro
until SUB neg come/3s/**SUBJUN** to be minister
'Until he **becomes** a minister,

      no se   **quedará**   contento
      neg REFL stay/3s/**FUT** satisfied
      he **won't** be satisfied'

A similar distinction between two grades of irrealis, one marked with the indicative-habitual, the other with the past-form subjunctive, is as viable in English 'until'-clauses as it is in English 'if'-clauses. The epistemic gradation is the very same as in English 'if-'clauses — higher vs. lower certainty, respectively:

(68)   a. **Indicative (higher certainty)**:
          Until he **comes**, we **will do** nothing.
       b. **Past-form subjunctive (lower certainty)**:
          Until he **came**, we **would do** nothing.

In Spanish, obligatory past-tense agreement makes this morphological distinction impossible within irrealis. The simple preterit, as in (59a), (60a), (61a), is a realis-indicative form. And the past-subjunctive form, while indeed irrealis, is governed by obligatory tense agreement. Thus compare (Butt and Benjamin 1988):[32]

(69)   a. **Past indicative (realis)**:
          cenamos   cuando **llegaron**   los demás
          dine/PAST/1p when   arrive/3p/PAST the rest
          'We **ate** when the others **arrived**'
       b. **Past-subjunctive (irrealis)**:
          Ibamos   a cenar cuando **llegaran**   los demás
          go/2p/IMPF to dine   when   arrive/3p/PAST/SUBJUN the rest
          'We **were going** to eat when**ever** the others **arrived**'

In Spanish conditional clauses, the contrast between present and past subjunctive is likewise governed by tense agreement without any certainty gradation (Butt and Benjamin 1988, p. 237):

(70)   a. **Present subjunctive**:
          Venderán la finca,
          sell/3p/FUT the estate
          'They **will** sell the estate,

          a pesar de que el abuelo   se   **oponga**.
          at weigh of que SUB the grandfather REFL oppose/3s/SUBJUN
          even if the grandfather **may/will/should** oppose it'

b. **Past subjunctive:**
Dijeron   que **iban**   a vender la finca,
say/3p/**PRET** SUB go/3p/**PAST/IMPF** to sell   the estate
'They said they **were going** to sell the estate,

a pesar de que el abuelo   se   **opusiera.**
at weigh of SUB the grandfather REFL oppose/3s/**PAST/SUBJUN**
even if the grandfather **would** oppose it'

However, with the concessive conditional subordinator *aun que* ('even if/though'),
a true three-way epistemic contrast is possible, with the present indicative
signalling highest certainty, the present subjunctive intermediate, and the past
subjunctive lowest:[33]

(71) Venderán   la   finca...
sell/**FUT**/**3p** the estate
'They'll sell the estate...

a. **Higher certainty (present indicative):**
...aunque el abuelo   se   opone
even-if the grandfather REFL oppose/**PRES**/**3s**
...even though the grandfather **opposes** it'
b. **Lower certainty (present subjunctive):**
...aunque el abuelo   se   opon**ga**
even-if the grandfather REFL oppose/**SUBJUN**/**3s**
...even if the grandfather **opposed** it'
c. **Lowest certainty (past subjunctive):**
aunque el abuelo   se   op**usiera**
even-if the grandfather REFL oppose/**PAST/SUBJUN**/**3s**
even if the grandfather **were to oppose** it'

In conditional clauses marked with the subordinator *si* 'if', Spanish displays
a three-point epistemic scale of certainty (as compared with the four-way
contrast in English, cf. (49)). The present-subjunctive form cannot be used here,
but the past-subjunctive now assumes an *irrealis* modal value (Butt and Benjamin, p. 292):[34]

(72) a. **Higher certainty (present indicative):**
Si **viene**,   me **quedaré**
if come/3s/**PRES** 1s stay/1s/**FUT**
'If he **comes**, I **will** stay'

b. **Lower certainty (past-subjunctive):**
   Si **viniera**,   me   **quedaría**
   if come/3s/PAST/SUBJUN REFL stay/1s/COND
   'If he **came**, I **would/might** stay'
c. **Counter-fact (perfect-subjunctive):**
   Si **hubiera**   venido, me **habría**   quedado.
   if have/3s/PAST/SUBJUN come   REFL have/COND stayed
   'If he **had come**, I **would have** stayed'

At least under some conditions, the past-subjunctive by itself — without
the auxiliary 'have' — can be used to mark counter-fact conditional clauses, as
in (Butt and Benjamin 1988, p. 297):[35]

(73) a. Si yo **fuera**   tú, me **habría**   quedado.
         if I be/PAST/SUBJUN you REFL have/I/COND stayed
         'If I **were** you, I **would have** stayed'
      b. Si **tuviera**   dinero, lo **habría**   comprado.
         if have/1s/PAST/SUBJUN money it have/I/COND bought
         'If I **had** money, I **would have** bought it'

4.5. The subjunctive in main clauses

4.5.1. Preamble

The two main-clause contexts where subjunctives most commonly appear
divide predictably into the two sub-modes of irrealis — the deontic subjunctive
of weak manipulation and the epistemic subjunctive of low certainty. One may
conceive of them, at least diachronically, as instances of **syntactic liberation**,
whereby a form that evolved in embedded clauses "surfaces" into main clauses.
The diachronic mechanism for such liberation, via which subjunctive grammatical markers are transmitted from subordinate to main clauses, most likely
involves so-called **indirect speech-acts**. It may be given schematically as:

(74) a. **From indirect to direct weak manipulative:**
         It would be nice **if** you **could** do for me ⟹
                          If you **could** (only) do this for me!
      b. **From indirect to direct low certainty:**
         I guess he **might** be late ⟹
                          He **might** be late

4.5.2. The subjunctive of weak manipulation

4.5.2.1. English

When a subjunctive form is used in a manipulative main clause, it contrasts with the imperative the same way it did with the indicative or infinitive in verb complements: It codes weaker manipulation. The deontic use of the English modals in toned-down manipulation is an example of this, in some cases involving a three-way contrast of manipulative strength:

(75) a. **Strongest manipulation (imperative):**
Leave!

b. **Weaker manipulation (future/modal):**
$\begin{Bmatrix} \textbf{Will} \\ \textbf{Can} \end{Bmatrix}$ you leave now?

c. **Weakest manipulation ('past'-modal/subjunctive):**
$\begin{Bmatrix} \textbf{Would} \\ \textbf{Could} \end{Bmatrix}$ you please leave now?

(76) a. **Imperative:**
Come!

b. **Weaker manipulation:**
You $\begin{Bmatrix} \textbf{can} \\ \textbf{may} \end{Bmatrix}$ come now.

c. **Weakest manipulation:**
You $\begin{Bmatrix} \textbf{could} \\ \textbf{might} \end{Bmatrix}$ come.

The modals 'should' and 'must' inherently code stronger manipulative force than 'could' and 'might'.

4.5.2.2. Spanish

In Spanish, a similar contrast is observed between the strong-manipulative ('familiar') imperative and the weak-manipulative ('formal', 'polite') subjunctive:

(77) a. **Imperative ('familiar'):**
Ven!
come/2s/IMPER
'Come!'

b. **Subjunctive-imperative ('formal'):**
   Venga.
   come/2s/SUBJUN
   'Come'

But the use of the subjunctive shades further into weaker valuative modes such as hortative, hope and weak preference:

(78) a. **Hortative:**
   Que **venga!**
   SUB come/3s/SUBJUN
   'Let him come!'
   b. **Subjunctive of hope:**
   Ojalá que **venga!**
   hope SUB come/SUBJUN
   'Let's hope he comes!'
   c. **Subjunctive of preference:**
   Mejor que **venga**   pronto.
   Better SUB come/3s/SUBJUN soon
   'He better come soon'

4.5.2.3. Bemba

In Bemba, the same contrast is seen between the stronger manipulation with the imperative and the weaker manipulation with the subjunctive, which again shades into the weak-preference hortative (Givón 1971b):

(79) a. **Imperative:**
   isa!
   come/IMPER
   'Come!
   b. **Subjunctive-imperative:**
   mu-is-e
   you-come-SUBJUN
   'You should/must come'
   c. **Hortative:**
   a-is-e!
   he-come-SUBJUN
   'Let him come!'
   'He must/should come'

4.5.3. The subjunctive of low certainty

4.5.3.1. English

In English main clauses, the two modal forms — 'present' and 'past' — partake in the same three-way contrast seen earlier in 'if'-clauses:[36]

(80) a. **Future (higher certainty):**
          He **is** coming.
          He **will** come.
      b. **'Present' modal (lower certainty):**
          He **may/can/shall** come.
      c. **'Past' modal-subjunctive (lowest certainty):**
          She **would/might/could/should** come.

4.5.3.2. Spanish

In Spanish, the subjunctive form is used in main clauses of lower epistemic certainty, usually together with epistemic adverbs such as *quizá* ('maybe'), *tal vez* ('perhaps') *puede ser* ('may be') etc. In such contexts, the subjunctive contrasts with both the present-indicative and the future:[37]

(81) a. **Present indicative (higher certainty):**
          Quizá **viene**
          maybe come/PRES/3s
          'Maybe he's coming'
      b. **Future (lower certainty):**
          Quizá **vendrá.**
          Maybe come/3s/FUT
          'Maybe he'll come'
      c. **Subjunctive (lowest certainty):**
          Quizá **venga**.
          maybe come/3s/SUBJUN
          'Perhaps he **might** come'

A similar contrast may obtain in past-tense clauses, this time between the past and the past-subjunctive (following Butt and Benjamin 1988, p. 243):[38]

(82) a. **Past-imperfect (higher certainty):**
Tal vez esa noche **estaba**   cuidando al   niño...
perhaps that night was/3s/IMPF caring   DAT/the child
'Perhaps that night she **was** caring for the child...'
   b. **Past-subjunctive (lower certainty):**
Tal vez esa noche **estuviera**   cuidando al   niño...
perhaps that night was/3s/SUBJUN caring   DAT/the child
'Perhaps that night she **may have been** caring for the child...'

4.5.3.3. Bemba

The use of the subjunctive of uncertainty in main clauses is also found in Bemba, where it contrasts with the higher-certainty future (Givón 1971b):

(83) a. **Future (higher certainty):**
a-**kà**-isa
s/he-**FUT**-come/INDIC
'S/he **will** come'
   b. **Subjunctive (lower certainty):**
a-**inga**-isa
s/he-**SUBJUN**-come
'S/he **may/might/could** come'

4.6.   Three subjunctive puzzles

We turn now to three puzzling facts about the distribution of the subjunctive in some languages. At first glance, these facts seem to challenge our description of the subjunctive as a sub-mode of irrealis. I hope to show that such challenges are only apparent.

4.6.1.   Subjunctives in Spanish relative clauses

It seems odd to find the subjunctive in restrictive REL-clauses, given that such clauses are typically presuppositional, and that presupposition is a *fact* modality. More careful inspection reveals that this use of the subjunctive remains firmly within the bounds of irrealis. Subjunctive-marked REL-clauses are used to modify **non-referring** indefinite head nouns. Since the head is non-referring, the REL-clause is automatically under the scope of irrealis. Thus consider (Butt and Benjamin 1988, pp. 237–240):

(84) a. **Indicative (referring head):**
   Coge   la maceta   que mas te   gustaba
   take/IMP the flower-pot SUB most you please/3s/**IMPF**
   'Take the flower pot you **liked** best'
   b. **Subjunctive (non-referring head):**
   Escoge   la maceta   que mas te   **guste.**
   choose/IMP the flower-pot SUB most you please/3s/**SUBJUN**
   'Pick whichever flower-pot you **like** best'

Headless REL-clauses whose implicit head is non-referring exhibit a
similar use of the subjunctive:

(85) a. Las camelias, cualquiera que **sea**   su   color,
   the camellias whatever   SUB be/3s/**SUBJUN** their color
   'Camellias, whatever **may be** their color,

        son bonitas.
        are pretty
        are pretty'
   b. Cualquiera que te   **vea**
   whoever   SUB you see/3s/**SUBJUN**
   'Whoever **may see** you

        pensará   que vas   a una fiesta.
        think/3s/FUT SUB go/3s/PRES to one party
        will think that you're going to a party'
   c. Por mucho que se   lo **digas,**   no lo hará.
   for much SUB him it say/2s/**SUBJUN** neg it do/3s/FUT
   'However much you **may tell** him, he won't do it'

The contrast between the indicative and the subjunctive in the REL-clause
in fact serves to disambiguate the referential status of indefinite head nouns.
This may be illustrated with indefinites under the scope of an irrealis-creating
verb, first in the present tense:

(86) a. **Indicative = referring head:**
   Busca a   una mujer que **conoce**   a   su madre.
   seek/3s OBJ one woman SUB know/3s/**INDIC** OBJ his mother
   'He's looking for a woman who **knows** his mother'
        (> a particular woman)

b. **Subjunctive = non-referring head:**
   Busca a   una mujer   que **conozca**   a   su madre.
   seek/3s OBJ one woman SUB know/3s/SUBJUN OBJ his mother
   'He's looking for a woman who **might know** his mother'
   (> any such woman)

Similarly in the past tense:

(87) a. **Indicative = referring head:**
      Buscaba a   una mujer   que **conocía**   a   su madre.
      seek/IMPF OBJ one woman SUB knew/IMPF OBJ his mother
      'He was looking for a woman **who knew** his mother'
      (> a particular woman)
   b. **Subjunctive = non-referring head:**
      Buscaba a   una mujer   que **conociera**   a   su madre.
      seek/IMPF OBJ one woman SUB knew/SUBJUN OBJ his mother
      'He was looking for a woman **who might know** his mother'
      (> any such woman)

4.6.2. Subjunctive in Spanish factive complements

The verbal complements of factive predicates are presupposed by definition, and are thus if anything *super* realis. For this reason, it is puzzling to find that many factive predicates in Spanish can take subjunctive complements. The predicates that take such complements are not merely factive, but are also **valuative**. They all signal either strong preference, aversion or surprise vis-a-vis a state or event. For example (Butt and Benjamin 1988, pp. 224-225):[39]

(88) a. Les   sorprendió   que no   lo **supiera**
         them surprised/3s SUB neg it know/3s/PAST/SUBJUN
         'They were surprised that she **didn't know** it'
      b. Me molesta   que te   **quejes**   tanto
         me bother/3s SUB REFL complain/2s/SUBJUN so
         'It bothers me that you **should complain** so much'
      c. Me   alegra   que te   **guste**
         REFL cheer/3s SUB you please/3s/SUBJUN
         'I'm happy that you **like** (it)'

d. Es   natural que le **conozca**
be/3s natural SUB him know/3s/**SUBJUN**
'It's only natural that she **should know** him'

e. Fué   una lástima que no me lo **dijeras**
was/3s one pity   SUB neg me it say/2s/PAST/**SUBJUN**
'It was a pity that you **didn't tell** me!'

f. Qué rabia   que no nos **suban**   el sueldo
what nuisance SUB neg us   raise/3p/**SUBJUN** the salary
'What a nuisance that they **aren't raising** our salary!'

g. Lo siento   que **esté**   enfermo
it   regret/I SUB be/3s/**SUBJUN** sick
'I'm sorry that she **is** sick'

The distribution of mood in the complements of emotive factive predicates is not governed by a simple rule. When the emotive attitude concerns a future/irrealis event, a contrast between an indicative and a subjunctive complement is possible, signalling the by-now predictable difference of degree of certainty (Butt and Benjamins 1988, p. 225):[40]

(89) a. **Indicative (stronger conviction):**
Mejor lo **dejamos**   para más tarde
better it leave/1p/**INDIC** for   more late
'We better **leave** it for later'

b. **Subjunctive (weaker conviction):**
Es Mejor que lo **dejemos**   para más tarde
be better SUB it leave/1p/**SUBJUN** for   more late
'It **would** be better if we **left** it for later'

A contrast between the subjunctive and indicative is apparently also possible in the complements of at least some factive predicates followed by the subordinator *de que*. The exact semantic value of the contrast is not easy to determine, but it may signal the degree of emotional reaction (Butt and Benjamin 1988, p. 225):[41]

(90) a. **Indicative (less emotion/surprise):**
Se horrorizaba   de que la **trataban**   así
3s be/shocked/IMPERF of SUB her treat/IMPERF/**INDIC** so
'S/he was shocked that they **treated** her this way'

b. **Subjunctive (more emotion/surprise):**
   Se horrorizaba   de que la **trataran**   así
   3s be/shocked/IMPF of SUB her treat/PAST/SUBJUN so
   'S/he was shocked that they **should treat** her this way'
c. **Indicative (less surprise):**
   Lo increíble era que Pedro no lo **sabía**
   it incredible was SUB Pedro neg it know/IMPF/INDIC
   'The incredible thing was that Pedro **didn't know** it'
d. **Subjunctive (more surprise):**
   Lo increíble era que Pedro no lo **supiera**
   it incredible was SUB Pedro neg it know/PAST/SUBJUN
   'The incredible thing was that Pedro **should not know** it'

Finding subjunctives in factive clauses seems a clear violation of our earlier prediction about the subjunctive appearing only in distinct sub-regions of irrealis. There are at least two ways of showing this to be a less-than-destructive counter example.

(a) **A synchronic explanation**

In dismissing irrealis as a valid grammatical category, Bybee *et al.* (1992) suggest that irrealis is a simple, uni-dimensional semantic feature, essentially dependent on the logician's binary distinction of 'real' (realis) vs. 'unreal' (irrealis). The failure of irrealis to abide by this simple logical definition is taken as grounds for rejecting its unified category status. But suppose irrealis and with it modality are, as I have suggested all along, a complex, multi-dimensional semantic-pragmatic domain. On the epistemic side, it involves the scalar dimension of certainty. On the deontic side, it involves the equally scalar dimensions of preference (or aversion), power, obligation, need, intent or ability.

As noted above, there is a strong association between the epistemic and valuative sub-modes of irrealis, both of which are typically future-projecting. This association is not absolute, however. Valuative attitudes of happiness or regret may also be directed toward the present and past — i.e. toward realized states or events. Such a valuative attitude toward a past event is not future-projecting, since it is directed toward a real event. This appears to be a case where the valuative and the epistemic part company. In terms of grammatical marking, some languages (English) resolve this conflict in favor of a unified marking of epistemic modality, marking factive complements with an indicative form. Other languages (Spanish) resolve the conflict in favor of unified marking of valuative modality, extending the — typically irrealis — subjunctive form to factive complements of valuative verbs.

One may as well note that even in Spanish, where a single grammaticalized subjunctive codes both sub-modes of irrealis, the valuative sub-mode does not win outright in all complements of emotive factive predicate. As seen in (90) above, subtle contrasts between the indicative and the subjunctive are found in some contexts, whereby the subjunctive always signals a higher degree of emotional involvement and the indicative a lower one. In English, modal-subjunctive forms are used in the same emotive factive contexts as in Spanish to make the very same distinction. Often in such cases, the valuative-emotive category turns out to have a strong epistemic component of **unexpectedness**:

(91) a. I'm a bit surprised that you **came** to me with such junk.
         (> it was somewhat unexpected)
      b. I'm shocked that you **should come** to me with such junk!
         (> it was totally unexpected)
      c. It's incredible that he **got** away with it.
         (> it was indeed unexpected)
      d. It's absolutely incredible that he **should get** away with it!
         (> It was extremely unexpected)
      e. He was disappointed that she **rejected** him.
         (> rejection was not wholly unexpected)
      f. He was shocked that she **should reject** him.
         (> rejection was very unexpected)
      g. She was pleased that he **agreed** to come.
         (> his agreement was not unexpected)
      h. She was so happy that he **should agree** to come.
         (> his agreement was rather unexpected)

What one sees in such examples is a consistent pairing of the two sub-modes of irrealis, a pairing that suggests the following one-way-conditional pragmatic implication:[42]

(92) "If an event is epistemically less expected, chances are that one's emotional valuative reaction to it — surprise, preference, aversion — is stronger."

In sum, the use of the subjunctive in factive-emotive complement is consistent with what we have seen so far about both the subjunctive and irrealis; provided one accepts irrealis, and modality in general, as a complex, multi-dimensional semantic-pragmatic domain, rather than as a simple, binary, logical category.

(b) A diachronic explanation

Natural synchronic form-function pairing is the product of natural dia-chronic changes. Natural grammaticalization pathways are the mechanisms through which natural synchronic states come into being. A diachronic explana-tion is thus not necessarily an alternative explanation. Rather, it may comple-ment a synchronic explanation, or illuminate what is natural about it.

A diachronic explanation of the use of the past subjunctive in emotive-factive clauses in Spanish is implicit in a recent paper by Lunn (1992). Lunn notes that the contrast between past-subjunctive and past-indicative in peninsu-lar Spanish is often used to code the distinction between, respectively, presup-posed ('factive') and asserted clauses in connected discourse. As an example, Lunn cites the contrast between the use of the indicative in a newspaper headline (first mention = asserted new information) vs. the use of the subjunctive in the subsequent full report (subsequent mention = presupposed old information; Lunn 1992):

(93) **Headline, preterit (new information):**
La bandera que **besó**   es la   que, en su día,
the flag   SUB kiss/3s/**PRET** is that SUB in his day
'The flag that he **kissed** is the one that one day

tambien **besó**   el Rey don Juan Carlos,
also   kiss/3s/**PRET** the King don Juan Carlos
King Juan Carlos also **kissed,**

y   **bordó**   su tatarabuela
and embroider/3s/**PRET** his great-grandmother
and (that) his grandmother the queen D.M.C.

la Reina doña María Cristina.
the Queen doña María Cristina
and that his great-grandmother Queen Maria Christina
embroidered'

(94)   **Main text, past-subjunctive (old information):**
Y, al final, besó   la   bandera roja y   gualda
and at end   kiss/3s/PRET the flag   red and gilded
'...And, at the end, he kissed the red-and-gold flag

que hace treinta años **besara**   su padre el Rey
SUB do   thirty   years kiss/PAST/SUBJUN his father the King
that his father the King **had kissed** thirty years ago,

y   que un   día **bordaba**   su tatarabuela...
and SUB one day **embroider/3s/PAST/SUBJUN** his g.-g.m.
and that his great-grandmother **had embroidered**...'

There are several reasons why Lunn's identification of the past subjunctive as a marker of old information, i.e. the super-realis modality of presupposition, is not a damaging counter-example to the idea that the subjunctive codes a subdomain of irrealis. First, Lunn notes (1992, p. 4) that the past-subjunctive form with the suffix -*ra* was until the late 19th Century the *pluperfect indicative* form (see also Lunn and Cravens 1990; Kline-Andreu 1990; Wright 1932). The shift of this form to past subjunctive use, where it wound up in competition with the -*se* form, is relatively recent. Second, the vast majority of Lunn's text examples translate rather naturally into the English pluperfect (rather than simple past). So that it is just as plausible to interpret the cited examples of putative old information use of the -*ra* form as conservative ('relic') uses of the old pluperfect. Finally, pluperfects (and perfects) in general tend to distribute with high frequency in grammatical environments that tend to be presuppositional: REL-clause, ADV-clauses and V-complement. As an illustration of this tendency, consider the distribution of Early Biblical Hebrew tense-aspects in the various clause-types in (95) and (96) below.

(95) **The distribution of tense-aspects in main and subordinate clauses in Early Biblical Hebrew** (Givón 1991f)[43]

	CLAUSE TYPE					
	MAIN		SUBORDINATE		TOTAL	
tense/aspect	N	%	N	%	N	%
PERFECT	42	49.5	43	**50.5**	85	100.0
PRETERIT	279	**100.0**	/	/	279	100.0
IRREALIS	41	**80.4**	10	19.6	51	100.0
PARTICIPIAL	7	26.9	19	**73.1**	26	100.0
NOMINAL	/	/	16	**100.0**	16	100.0

(96) **The distribution of tense-aspects in the three dependent clauses in Early Biblical Hebrew** (Givón 1991f)

	DEPENDENT CLAUSE TYPE					
	REL		V-COMP		ADV-CLAUSE	
tense/aspect	N	%	N	%	N	%
PERFECT	22	**48.8**	9	**81.9**	12	37.5
PRETERIT	/	/	/	/	/	/
IRREALIS	4	9.0	2	18.1	4	12.5
PARTICIPIAL	19	**42.2**	/	/	/	/
NOMINAL	/	/	/	/	16	50.0
total:	45	100.0	11	110.0	32	100.0

Both the total absence of the preterit (the main narrative tense) and the preponderance of the perfect in subordinate clauses — 81% of V-complements, nearly 50% of REL-clauses and nearly 40% of ADV-clauses — are striking. Our diachronic explanation has now led us to consider the naturalness of a diachronic pathway through which super-realis perfect or past forms may penetrate the seemingly incompatible irrealis domain of the subjunctive.

4.6.3.   The use of past or perfect as subjunctive forms

4.6.3.1. Realis-marked subjunctives

Our third puzzle concerns the common participation of past or perfect morphology in the marking of subjunctive clauses. This is puzzling because the subjunctive has such a strong association with irrealis. Past and perfect, on the other hand, are quintessential realis tense-aspects. In English, this association is apparent in two related developments already noted above. The first is the use of the past-form of main verbs or auxiliaries to mark the subjunctive of uncertainty in 'if'-clauses:

(97)   a. If you **told** them the real story, they **would** understand.
       b. If you **were** to tell them the real story, they **would** understand.

The second development is the historical shift of the past forms of the modals to non-past use (Bybee 1992). This shift has made it possible to have an epistemic contrast between the two modal forms, with the old past form now signalling subjunctive-like lower epistemic certainty:

(98) | **present modal**
 (higher certainty) | **'past' modal**
 (lower certainty) |
       |---|---|
       | She **may** be there | She **might** be there |
       | She **can** be there | She **could** be there |
       | She **will** be there | She **would** be there |
       | I **shall** return soon | I **should** return soon |

The same directionality in gradation can also be shown in at least some of the deontic uses of the modals, as in:

(99)   a. **Present form (more assertive):**
          You **can** leave right away.
       b. **Past form (less assertive):**
          You **could** leave soon, right?
       c. **Present form (more assertive):**
          You **may** do it right away.
       d. **Past form (less assertive):**
          You **might** consider doing it.

In the same vein, the Spanish historical shift discussed by Lunn (1992) is first and foremost an extension of an old past-perfect form to code subjunctive functions. And a similar invasion of the past tense was shown in the marking of low-certainty conditional clauses in Swahili (Salone 1983).

A similar shift seems to have occurred in Early Biblical Hebrew. In this language, the main aspectual contrast in narrative is between the in-sequence preterit verb form and the off-sequence perfect. The preterit is actually a diachronic merger of two formerly-distinct forms — the irrealis ('jussive') and the preterit. This form is used as the future tense, in routine high-certainty predictions, and in a wide range of modal senses:

(100) a. ki   navi'   hu'   ve-**yi-tpalel**   ba''ad-xa
          SUB prophet he(is) and-3m/IRR-pray for-you
          '...because he is a holy man and so he **will/may** pray for you...'
                                                    (Genesis, 20.7)

      b. ki   mot   **ta-mut**   'ata ve-xol 'asher le-xa
          SUB death 2/IRR-die you and-all REL   to-you
          '...so that you **will** die with all your people...'   (Genesis, 20.8)

      c. ma''asim 'asher lo'   **ye-''as-u**   ''asita   ''imad-i
          deeds   REL   neg 3m/IRR-do-PL do/PERF-2sm with-me
          '...you have done to me deeds that **should** not be done...'
                                                    (Genesis, 20.9)

      d. ze   h.asd-ex   'asher **ta-''as-i**   ''imad-i:
          this favor-your REL   2/IRR-do-3fs with-me
          '...You **should** do this favor for me:

      e. 'el kol   ha-maqom 'asher **na-vo'**   shama
          to every the-place REL   2p/IRR-come there
          whatever place that we **may** come to...'   (Genesis, 20.13)

When a contemplated future event is either highly **unexpected** or too dreadful to contemplate, the perfect verb-form is used — as a subjunctive:

(101) a. ki   'amar-ti   'eyn yir'at 'elohim ba-maqom   ha-ze
          SUB say/PERF-1s no   fear/of God   in/the-place   the-this
          '...because I said (to myself) there was no fear of God in this place,

          va-**harag-u**-ni   ''al dvar   'isht-i
          CONJ-kill/PERF-3p-me on thing/of wife-my
          so that they **would** kill me because of my wife...'
                                                    (Genesis, 20.11)

   b. ki   yodea" 'elohim ki   be-yom   'axal-xem mi-meno
     SUB knows God   SUB LOC-day/of eating-your from-it
     '...Because God knows that on the day you ate from it

     ve-**nifqḥ-u**   "eyney-xem ve-**hayi-tem**   ke-'elohim
     and-open/**PERF**-2p eyes-you   and-be/**PERF**-2pm like-God
     your eyes **would open** and you **would become** like God...'

                                   (Genesis, 3.5)

   c. va-'ani hineni mevi'   'et ha-mabul....
     and-I   lo-I   bring/**PART** ACC the-flood
     '...And behold, I am bringing the flood...

     kol 'asher b-a-'arets yi-**gva**".
     all REL   LOC-earth 3sm-perish/**IRR**
     everything on earth **will perish**.

     va-**haqimoti**   'et brit-i   'it-xa
     but-keep/1s/**PERF** ACC pact-my with-you
     But I **would keep** my pact with you,

     u-**va'ta**   'el ha-teva...
     and-come/2sm/**PERF** to the-ark
     and you **would come** into the ark...'   (Genesis, 6.17-18)

The perfect-marked subjunctive form is also used as a strong obligative modality, in contexts of **uncertain compliance**. This usage appears routinely in strong injunctions delivered by God to the Israelites, whose propensity for straying was legendary:

  (102) a. ve-**shamar-tem**   'et kol h.uqot-ay
        and-guard/**PERF**-2pm ACC all laws-my
        '...And you **should adhere to** all my laws...'   (Leviticus 19.37)

b. ve-zo't tihyeh   torat ha-metsora":
and-this 3sf/be/IRR law/of the-leper
'...And this is how lepers will be treated:

be-yom   ṭaharat-o,   ve-**huva'**
LOC-day/of purifying-his and-PASS/bring/PERF-3sm
on the day of his purification he **should be brought**

'el ha-kohen;
to the-priest
to the priest;

ve-**yatsa'**   ha-kohen   'el mi-ḥuts l-a-maḥaneh,
and-exit/**PERF**/3sm the-priest to from-out of-the-camp
and the priest **should go out of** the camp,

ve-**ra'a**   ha-kohen   ve-hineh **nirpa** ...'
and-saw/**PERF**/3sm the-priest and-lo PASS/cure/**PERF**/3sm
and the priest **should make sure** that indeed (the man)
had been cured...'   (Leviticus, 14.2-3)

The contrast between the preterit-marked and perfect-marked irrealis is also found in ADV-clauses. When the event in the ADV-clause is more likely, the preterit-like irrealis is used, as in:

(103) a. ve-xi   yi-**mkor**   'ish 'et bit-o   le-'amah,
and-SUB 3sm/**IRR**-sell man ACC daughter-his for-maid
'When a man **sells** his daughter to be a maid,

lo' te-**tse'**   ke-tse't "avadim
neg 3sf-exit/**IRR** like-exit/of slaves
she **shall not go out** like a slave...   (Exodus, 21.7)

b. ki-**yi-sh'al-un**   bney-xem maḥar   le-'mor
when-3m/**IRR**-ask-p sons-your tomorrow to-say
'...so when your children **ask** you tomorrow...'   (Joshua, 4.7)

When an event is either of low-certainty or extremely undesirable, the preterit-like irrealis is used once in the ADV-clause, then the perfect-marked subjunctive is used in all subsequent clauses:

(104) a. ve-"ata   pen   **yi-shlaḥ**   yad-o
and-now lest 3sm/**IRR**-send hand-his
'...and now lest he **sent** his hand

ve-**laqaḥ**   gam me-"ets   ha-ḥayim
and-take/**PERF**/3sm also from-tree/of the-life
and **took** (fruit) from the tree of life

ve-**'axal**   ve-**ḥay**   le-"olam
and-eat/**PERF**/3sm and-live/**PERF**/3sm for-world
and **ate** and **lived** forever...'   (Genesis, 3.22)

b. 'im **'e-mtsa'**   bi-sdom   ḥamishim tsadikim...,
if 1s/**IRR**-find in-Sodom fifty   just-men
'...If I **should find** fifty just men in Sodom...,

ve-**nasa'ti**   le-xol ha-maqom ba-"avur-am...
and-spare/1s/**PERF** to-all the-place in-sake-their
I **would forgive** the whole place for their sake...'

Genesis, 18.26)

Finally, in Ute (Uto-Aztecan), an extensive use of either the perfect-anterior suffix *-ka/qa-* or the remote past suffix-*pụga*, in combination with the irrealis suffix *-vaa-*, is made in low-certainty modal subjunctive clauses, as in (Givón 1980b, ch. 5):

(105) **Low-certainty subjunctive:**

a. náaĝa picǔ-**kaa**-va-ci
maybe come-**ANT-IRR-NOM**
'Maybe s/he did come'

b. náaĝa picǔ-**pụgaa**-va-ci
maybe come-**REM-IRR-NOM**
'Maybe s/he did come (long ago)'

c. ta'wá-ci 'uway tụkúa-v**i**   'úr**u**   tụká-vaa-**qa-pụ**
man-GEN DET/GEN meat-NOM DET/NOM eat-IRR-ANT-NOM
'The man may/could/should/might/should have eaten the meat'
(but I'm not sure whether he did or didn't)

The irrealis-perfect combination used in (105c) is also used in counter-fact clauses (see further below). Before solving the puzzle, I'd like to add another piece to it, one that is even more common cross-linguistically: the use of past or perfect to mark counter-fact clauses.

4.6.3.2. Past or perfect marked counter-fact clauses

The past and/or perfect are used almost universally to mark another non-fact clause-type that often overlaps with the subjunctive of uncertainty — **counter-fact** clauses. This use is attested in Creole languages (Bickerton 1975 1981), where the combination perfect plus modal can code either counter-fact or future-in-past, as in Hawaii English Creole:[44]

(106) a. **Counter-fact**:
  ... I **bin   go** give-am downpayment...
  I **PERF IRR** give-him down-payment
  '...I **would have given** him a down-payment
  [had the guy asked]...'
  b. **Future-in-past**:
  he say he **bin   go** order, see...
  he said he **PERF IRR** order, see
  '...he said he **was going** to order, see...'

English presents a similar situation:

(107) a. If she **had come** on time, I **would have** waited.
  b. **Had** she **come** on time, I **would have** waited.

A similar development has taken place in Israeli Hebrew, with the past form of the auxiliary 'be':

(108) im hi **hayta** roa   et   ze, az   hi **hayta** ozevet.
  if she **was/3sf** seeing ACC it then she **was/3sf** leaving
  'If she **had seen** it, she **would have left**'

One must note, further, that in Early Biblical Hebrew the perfect was probably the only available verb-form for marking counter-fact clauses. This use can be seen in the story of Abraham's near-sacrifice of his son Isaac. God, after intervening at the very last minute, commends Abraham:[45]

(109) ki   "ata yada"-ti   ki yre'   elohim 'ata
  SUB now know/PERF-1s fear/NOM/sm/POSS God   you
  '...because now I have learned that you fear God,

  ve-lo'   ḥasax-ta   'et-bin-xa   yeḥid-xa mime-ni
  CONJ-neg spare/PERF-2sm ACC-son-your lone-your from-me
  that you { **would not have spared** } your only son from me...'
           { **had not spared**   }
  (Genesis, 22.12)

We noted earlier that in Spanish the past-subjunctive with -*ra* arose from the erstwhile pluperfect (Lunn 1992). This re-analyzed form is now used — most commonly augmented with the perfect auxiliary 'have' — to mark counter-fact conditional clauses:[46]

(110) **Counterfact (perfect-subjunctive):**
Si **hubiera**   venido, me **habría**   quedado.
if have/3s/PAST/SUBJUN come   REFL have/COND stayed
'If he **had come**, I **would have** stayed'

In Uto-Aztecan languages, the use of past/perfect markers in counter-fact conditionals is widespread (Steele 1975). Thus, in Ute one finds the perfect-anterior suffix -*ka/qa*- in both main and subordinate counter-fact clauses (Givón 1980b, ch. 5, 13):

(111) a. náaĝa-sụ-ni ta'wá-ci 'uwa-y   pic̣ụ́-**kay-kụ**
maybe-MOD man-GEN that-GEN arrive-ANT-SUB
'If the man **had** arrived (but he didn't),

mamá-c̣i   'u   maĝá-**qa**-tụ-'u
woman-SUNJ DET/SUNJ feed-ANT-NOM-him
the woman **would/could have** fed him'

Often, the perfect combines with an irrealis suffix -*vaa* in counter-fact clauses:

(112) a. 'uwás-'uru   wụ́ụka-vaa-**qa**-tụ   'urá-'ay
s/he/SUNJ-TOP work-IRR-ANT-NOM be-IMM
'S/he **should/would/could have** come'
(but s/he didn't)

    b. 'uwás-'uru   wụ́ụka-vaa-**qa**-tụ
s/he/SUNJ-TOP work-IRR-ANT-NOM
'S/he **should/would/could have** worked'
(but s/he didn't)

The *remote-past* form can also be used in such contexts in Ute:

(113) 'uwás-'uru   wụ́ụka-vaa-**pụga**-tụ
s/he/SUNJ-TOP work-IRR-REM-NOM
'S/he **should/would/could have** worked (long ago)'
(but s/he didn't)

Finally, James (1982) in her cross-linguistic survey of the use past or perfect forms to mark counter-fact ('hypothetical') clauses, shows it to be widespread in many unrelated languages and language families.[47]

4.6.3.3. Explanations

(a) **The distance metaphor explanation**

Fleischman (1989), citing many of the facts surveyed above, suggested that the use of past or perfect in subjunctive may be viewed as an instance of a **metaphoric change**, centering on the feature of temporal distance ("remoteness from time-of-speech reference point") associated with the past. This feature of temporal distance is said to metaphorically transform into either the domain of inter-personal distance (in valuative-deontic sub-modes) or the domain of evidentiary distance (in the epistemic sub-mode).

In spite of its undeniable elegance, the metaphoric distance explanation, which had been anticipated to some degree by both Steele (1975) and Langacker (1978),[48] is problematic. First, Fleischman herself notes (1989, p. 18) that the *future* — an irrealis sub-mode — is also temporally remote from the time-of-speech, and thus is also amenable to metaphoric shifts toward remoteness in non-temporal domains. One thus needs to explain why the future is consistently associated with higher-certainty (or stronger manipulation) irrealis, while the past or perfect are consistently associated with lower-certainty (or weaker manipulation) irrealis, i.e. with subjunctives.

Second, unlike the past, the perfect is not a remote aspect, but rather typically an aspect of **current relevance**. That is, it marks a past event that is still relevant at the designated temporal reference point, most commonly the unmarked time-of-speech. But the perfect is just as common as the past in marking the lower-certainty or weaker-manipulation subjunctives, and it is even more common in marking counter-fact conditionals.

Third, the metaphor hypothesis as it currently stands is not specific enough. It does not supply an actual mechanism for grammaticalization. In particular, it designates no point of penetration for the metaphoric extension. It thus implies that speakers can recognize the aptness of the distance metaphor across the entire range of irrealis constructions — conditional ADV-clauses, iffy main clauses, future tense, weak-command or request clauses, yes/no-questions, counter-fact clauses, etc. From the little that is known about grammaticalization and metaphoric extension, such an unconstrained mechanism is not likely to exist. The more typical pattern in grammaticalization is for a metaphoric extension to invade a scalar domain at a small point of penetration, where the metaphoric relation is most obvious. At that **diachronic beach-head**, the metaphoric meaning exhibits greatest similarity with the literal meaning.

From that beach-head, the metaphoric change spreads gradually to other members of the domain or paradigm.

(b) **The counter-fact clause as diachronic beach-head**

The diachronic data, whenever available, support a much more specific hypothesis about the pathway of grammaticalization. One example of such specificity is the complex diachronic shift noted by Lunn (1992) in the marking of the pluperfect, past-subjunctive and counter-fact clauses in Spanish. The shift represents two independent changes:

(114) a. pluperfect $\Longrightarrow$ past-subjunctive
     b. pluperfect of 'have' $\Longrightarrow$ counter-fact

The sum total of both shifts is a synchronic overlap between the counter-fact and past-subjunctive grammatical forms. There are reason to believe, further, that shift (114a) was a more complex, mediated process:

(115) a. pluperfect $\Longrightarrow$ counter-fact
     b. counter-fact $\Longrightarrow$ past-subjunctive

As noted earlier, the epistemic sub-mode of irrealis is a scalar dimension (degree of certainty) with at least three grammaticalized levels observed in most languages surveyed:

(116) a. higher certainty irrealis (modal/future)
     b. lower certainty (subjunctive)
     c. lowest certainty (counter-fact)

If the past or perfect penetrated this paradigm initially at point (116c), then its spreading on to point (116b) may be viewed as gradual subsequent extension of the initial beach-head. What needs explanation are thus three steps of gradual analogic extension:

(117) **HYPOTHESIS: Extension of past/perfect forms**
     into the subjunctive modal domain:
     a. past/perfect $\Longrightarrow$ counter-fact
     b. counter-fact $\Longrightarrow$ past subjunctive
     c. past subjunctive $\Longrightarrow$ subjunctive

The Swahili data surveyed by Salone (1983) are just as compatible with explanation (117). The modal operator -*nga*-, with or without the old subjunctive suffix -*e* (thus -*nge*-), codes low-certainty conditional clauses ('present subjunctive'). Only with the past-marker -*li*- (thus -*ngali*- or -*ngeli*-) can it code both counter-fact and the possible-but-unlikely subjunctive of low certainty ('past subjunctive'). In the same vein Bybee (1992), in her study of the history of the past-form English modals, has traced a case of 'colonization' of the irrealis range by a realis-past form: from past to counter-fact, and from counter-fact to possible-but-less-likely modal-form subjunctives. The best support for this interpretation should of course come from implicational-hierarchic distribution of realis forms in contexts (116b,c):

(118) **Predicted implicational-hierarchic distribution**:
"Whenever one finds a realis form marking a subjunctive of low certainty (116b), one always finds that form also marking counter-fact clauses (116c); but not necessarily vice versa."

While all the facts surveyed above are compatible with this prediction, they remain for the moment sketchy and less than complete.[49]

There are good reasons why a diachronic extension such as (117b) — counter-fact forms extended to low-certainty subjunctives, especially in conditional ADV-clauses — is natural. Counter-fact conditionals are already an intermediate case, a **modal blend** of realis and irrealis. They involve a past event (realis), one that didn't occur (neg-real), but still placed under the scope of hypothesis (irrealis). They most commonly already share the 'if' marker with irrealis conditional clauses. To find that the morphology of such modal blends reflects these mixed modal properties — some realis markers (past, perfect), some irrealis markers (modals, future, 'if') — is not exactly shocking, and does not require the grand machinery of a metaphoric explanation (Bybee 1992, p. 14). Thus, in rejecting the distance metaphor explanation on essentially the same grounds, Bybee (1992) notes:

"...It is not the past tense alone that is contributing the hypothetical meaning, but rather the past in combination with a modal verb, a subjunctive mood, a hypothetical marker (such as 'if')..." (1992, p. 26)

In sum, counter-fact clauses, the modal hybrids for whose association with the past or perfect we have an independent natural explanation, remain the most likely beach-head through which realis grammatical forms first penetrated into the irrealis modal range. Once such a beach-head has been established, the spreading of past or perfect forms to the nearest point up the certainty scale — the subjunctive of low-certainty in conditional clauses — is but a small local step that does not require heavy metaphoric machinery.

4.7.   Functional universals and typological variation

4.7.1.   The reality of irrealis

We come back now to the question of irrealis and its validity in two related domains: first as a coherent functional— semantic or pragmatic — entity; and second as a grammatical-typological phenomenon. The validity of irrealis in both senses has been challenged recently by Bybee *et al.* (1992). Their arguments may be summed up as follows:

(i)   **Functional argument**:
   (a) Irrealis groups a large array of miscellaneous functions that have no coherent core meaning.
   (b) Irrealis is defined logico-semantically in terms of the reality ('truth') of states/events, rather than — as it should be — in communicative-pragmatic terms [i.e. strength of assertion or strength of manipulation; TG]

(ii)   **Grammatical-typological arguments**:
   (c) No two languages mark the same range of functions as irrealis.
   (d) The realis/irrealis distinction is seldom realized in any language as a simple binary morphological distinction.
   (e) There is no language in which *all* irrealis functions are marked by the same grammatical morpheme.
   (f) Some realis functions are occasionally marked as irrealis, such as the habitual-past in PNG languages (Roberts 1992).

(iii)   **Diachronic argument**:
   (g) Since grammaticalized modality and mood arise via many distinct channels each with its own specific dynamics, irrealis by itself does not explain these diachronic changes.

These arguments will be evaluated in order.

4.7.2.   The functional coherence of irrealis

The first argument is based on a straw-man definition of the epistemic sub-mode of 'irrealis'. As noted earlier above (section 2.), this logical-semantic definition has been supplanted at least ten years ago by a communicative-functional definition, not only of irrealis but of propositional modalities in general (Givón 1982b; 1984b, chapters 7, 8; 1989, ch. 4). The crux of the communicative definition of modality is that epistemics is not purely a matter of truth, speaker's belief or subjective certainty. Rather, epistemics typically involves **hearer-directed** considerations, such as possible challenge, supporting evidence, relative status and power, control and authority — in other words, inter-personal relations. Guo (1992) shows this clearly with his Mandarin child-language data. But the same thing has been shown by Coates (1987) in her study of the use of epistemic modal expressions in adult English conversation. And similar observations were made earlier by Syder and Pawley (1974). To quote Coates' conclusions:

> "...In conversation, it seems, the establishment and maintenance of good social relations are of paramount importance. As a result, speakers rarely state simple facts or make unqualified assertions...   ...The epistemic modals...are used to convey the speaker's attitude toward the proposition being expressed [i.e. the traditional definition; TG], to express the speaker's sensitivity to the addressee, to avoid making grandiose claims about oneself, to negotiate sensitive topics, and in general to facilitate open discussion..." (1987, p. 129)

The arguments of Bybee and her associates, both functional and grammatical, seem to presuppose that modality — and the realis/irrealis distinction — is a simple, binary, discrete mental category, much like the progressive, perfective or habitual. But modality is a much more complex mega-category. And irrealis in particular is a complex scalar dimension. As such, it intersects with a host of other grammar-coded semantic and pragmatic categories. This sort of complexity can of course be counted as more evidence of functional incoherence and the absence of core meaning of irrealis. But such conclusions are not necessary, and do not spring from careful study of either the semantics or pragmatics of modality. A careful study will reveal that the great bulk of the 'disparate' clause-types traditionally grouped under irrealis have a considerable measure of coherence and commonality:

- They tend to be future-projecting ('not-yet-real').
- They allow non-referring interpretation of NPs under their scope (Givón 1973b; 1989, chapters 4, 5)
- They tend to group into two broad sub-modal clusters, epistemic and valuative-deontic.
- Whether epistemic or deontic, they all tend to involve interaction under low certainty and thus anxiety.
- Unlike realis, they tend to involve greater flexibility of modal perspective in the interaction with the interlocutor.

The past-habitual is cited by Bybee *et al.* (1992) as a prime example of the unprincipled nature of irrealis grammatical grouping. But as we have already noted earlier, the habitual is a hybrid modality, sharing some features of realis (higher assertive certainty) and some of irrealis (lack of specific temporal reference; lack of specific evidence; non-referring NPs under its scope). The fact that some languages group the habitual with irrealis is not exactly surprising. The inconsistent grammatical marking of such a category merely underscores its semantic-pragmatic complexity.

4.7.3. The grammatical marking of irrealis and the functional basis of grammatical typology

Taken together, the four grammatical-typological arguments against the universality of irrealis boil down to a simple proposition:

(119) **Structure-guided approach to functional universals**:
      "Only cognitive-communicative categories that are marked uniformly by a single language, or are grouped in the same way by most languages, have mental reality".

As noted in chapter 3, (119) is a rather extreme approach to both functional universals and grammatical typology. Complex functional categories that involve clusters of both semantic and pragmatic features seldom if ever abide by such simple expectations. Indeed, the whole field of grammatical typology springs into existence because complex grammatical categories are not grammaticalized exactly the same way in all languages. The functional approach to cross-linguistic typological variation is founded explicitly on what has always been implicit in the practice of grammatical typology — that in human language there is always more than one structural means for gaining the same communicative ends. And that:

(120) "In grammatical typology, one enumerates the main **structural means** by which different languages code — or perform — the **same function**."[50]

4.7.4. Typological diversity as diachronic source diversity

As noted above, inconsistent grammatical marking of a functional domain, especially a complex one, is not much of an argument against its universal validity. But the grammatical marking of irrealis is not quite as chaotic cross-linguistically as Bybee *et al.* (1992) have suggested. There exist, after all, whole language families where the binary split between realis and irrealis is the major verb-inflectional distinction. This includes Austronesian (see Dixon's magnificent grammar of Boumaa Fijian 1987), as well as many languages in Papua-New Guinea (Roberts 1992) and North America (Chafe 1992; Mithun 1992; Bradley and Hollenbach, eds. 1988-1992). Bybee *et al.* argue that such languages do not count because none of them group *all* irrealis categories together, and some group irrealis with borderline categories such as the habitual. The intellectual force of such an argument is that linguistic categories — and their grammatical expression — is a matter of either-or. A Roschian clustering — **prototype** — approach to complex linguistic categories is probably more appropriate. Within such an approach, a category is not invalidated by possessing fuzzy margins, nor does membership demand the presence of *all* features of the cluster. And marginal membership of less prototypical exemplars — e.g. habitual, yes/no-questions and negation, in the case of irrealis — is also possible.

Ultimately, typological diversity is produced by the diversity of diachronic paths through which a language — any language — can grammaticalize the same functional domain. This is as true in the diachronic evolution of grammatical structures as it is in the biological evolution of body organs. In both, it is common for the very same target function to be structuralized from multiple sources. But the converse is also true — the same diachronic source can grammaticalize diverse functional targets (see Heine *et al.* 1991; Heine and Traugott eds. 1991; *inter alia*). What is often involved in multi-source grammaticalization is the choice among multiple grammatical options for coding the same functional domain. These choices involve several important considerations, some more local, others more global:

- **Economy**: Which target functional features are already predictable from available ('redundant') information inherent in the complex category?
- **Communicative potential**: Which among the cluster of features in a complex category would be communicatively the most important and useful to grammaticalize?
- **Saliency and iconicity**: Which of the possible source constructions would supply the most salient and iconic coding?
- **Availability**: Which of the possible source constructions has a low functional load and thus can be appropriated with minimal communicative loss or ambiguity?
- **Costs**: Which of the alternative channels would incur the lowest costs to the coding of other important functional domains?

Within a single language, the choice among alternative grammaticalization pathways is not made in a grammatical vacuum. The grammatical coding and grammatical behavior of related functional domains exert considerable influence on such choices. A grammar in this respect behaves much like a biological organism: Choices in one functional domain have wide ramifications in other domains.

4.8. Conclusion

The distribution of the subjunctive, either as a language-specific or a universal typological category, is best understood within the context of a rich, communicatively-based theory of propositional modality, and within it of irrealis. Likewise, irrealis and the subjunctive are best understood within the context of a rich, functionally-informed theory of grammaticalization.

The fact that our antecedents in philosophy, be they Aristotle or Carnap, chose to define modality in purely logical term, does not bind us to all details of their analysis. Given their orientation and intellectual goals, it is all the more remarkable how close to target they had come in slicing up the modality pie. The semantic and pragmatic sub-dimensions of modality may be much more closely associated than we have thought. So that starting from either semantics or pragmatics, one arrives at — roughly but recognizably — the same cluster of modal categories. Whether we should derive comfort from this observation depends, I suppose, on our view of the nature of human progress.

A strong frequency-association of features, especially a one-way conditional association, should not be taken to mean their conceptual identity. Much like the strong association between 'agent' and 'subject' in active-transitive clauses, or the strong frequency association between agent-demotion and patient-promotion in de-transitivization, the association between the epistemic and the deontic sub-modes of irrealis does not obviate their cognitive distinctness. Rather, it merely illuminates the adaptive — cognitive, cultural, inter-personal or communicative — imperatives that drive both language use and language change.

Notes

* I am indebted to Joan Bybee, Jennifer Coates, Bernard Comrie, Erica García, Bernd Heine, Flora Klein-Andreu, Marianne Mithun, Edith Moravcsik, Mickey Noonan, Eve Sweetser and Elizabeth Traugott for many valuable comments on various precursors of this chapter.

1) The valuative/deontic mega-modality has also been called "agent-oriented"; see Bybee *et al.* (1992), Heine (1992).

2) Linguists are ultimately more interested in modal — and indeed functional — categories that have the widest grammatical consequences across the largest number of languages. Such grammatical consequences do not involve only morphology, but also more abstract constraints on the distribution and interaction of grammatical sub-systems, such as constraints on coreference, deletion, movement, semantic interpretation or lexical selection.

3) But see also Chafe and Nichols (eds 1984). In terms of a number of logical-semantic properties — most conspicuously reference (Jackendoff 1971; Givón 1973b) — the four main modalities may be grouped into two mega-modalities: *fact*, taking both presupposition and realis-assertion; and *non-fact*, taking both irrealis-assertion and NEG-assertion. For more extensive discussion see Givón (1984b, ch. 8; 1989, chapters 4, 5).

4) Holmes (1984) uses the terms 'speaker-oriented' and 'hearer-oriented' in roughly the same sense.

5) For a fuller account see Jackendoff (1971) or Givón (1973b; 1984b, ch. 8; 1989, chapters 4, 5).

6) It is perhaps more surprising to find the status of the habitual figuring so prominently in Bybee *et al.*'s (1992) attack on the functional coherence and universality of irrealis: "...For instance, Roberts (1990: 399) confronts the problem of Bargam (a Papuan language) which treats the past-habitual as irrealis. Roberts suggests that the interpretation of the notion 'real world' differs across languages. We suggest that if this binary distinction differs so much across languages that a past tense, which is usually considered one of the prototypical cases of realis (Foley 1986: 158f), can be irrealis in some languages, this binary distinction is not cross-linguistically valid..." (1992, p. 63).

7) The same is also true of negation, which is grouped in some languages with irrealis, with which it shares the semantic property of "unrealized" (Chafe 1992), but is at the same time a strongly-asserted modality, and thus pragmatically more like realis. And it also is pragmatically presuppositional, and thus may be also grouped with the mode of presupposition (See Givón 1984b, ch. 9).

8) These adverbs thus resemble typical factive predicates such as 'regret', 'be happy', 'be sad', 'it is good', 'it is bad' etc.

9) As we shall see further below, this logical one-way-conditional association is not the whole story, since epistemic modal expressions are seldom used in a complete valuative/deontic vacuum in natural communication.

10) Addressed by Captain Jean-Luc Picard to two young guests, in a recent episode of "Star Trek: The Next Generation".

11) While semantic enrichment ('particularization') is not unheard of in diachronic semantic change, semantic bleaching and generalization is by far the most common direction in the rise of grammatical morphology. In the process, semantically richer and more specific lexical words lose much of their specificity but retain some of their more generic, classificatory features. The rise of most tense-aspect-modality markers from verbs, of semantic case-markers from verbs or nouns, of articles from quantifiers or demonstratives, of directionals from motion verbs, of temporal expressions from spatial ones, and of complementizers from verbs or adpositions, all attest to these tendencies (see Traugott 1982, 1986, 1987, 1988; Heine *et al.* 1991; Givón 1989, ch. 2).

12) For the original discussion and much detail see Givón (1980a; 1990b, ch. 13).

13) These examples were originally taken from Butt and Benjamins (1988, p. 223), where most cited examples are from written texts. A few examples were slightly modified in consultation with Flora Klein-Andreu (in personal communication).

14) There is nothing ungrammatical about this English sentence *per se*, but its infinitive complement may code a manipulation that is stronger than its seeming Spanish equivalent.

15) See note 14, above.

16) See note 13.

17) See note 14, above.

18) See note 14, above.

19) See note 14, above.

20) Coding the manipulee and agent of the complement verb as object of the main clause (rather than subject of the complement) is one of the general mechanisms for coding higher manipulative force, a higher level of event integration, and thus perforce also a higher level of syntactic integration of the two clauses (Givón 1980b; 1990b, ch. 13).

21) For an extensive discussion of finiteness as a scalar, clausal property see Givón (1990b, chapters 12, 13, 19). For a discussion of finiteness and markedness of verbal forms, see Givón (1991c) as well as chapter 2 above.

22) Other verbs that take this pattern are 'want', 'ask', 'order'; a negative-subjunctive form may follow 'forbid'.

23) Other predicates that take this pattern are 'not sure', 'not know', 'hope' and 'fear'. For the distribution in Bemba of tense-aspects in subjunctive-marked clauses and their associate main clauses see Givón (1972, ch. 4).

24) The infusion of grammatical forms from 'if'-clauses to complements of uncertainty verbs is a well-known channel, as in 'I don't know *if* he's here'. See discussion further below.

25) The likely reconstruction here is -*ni-ga- or -*ni-ka-, with the first element most likely the oldest Bantu copula -ni 'be', and -ga/ka perhaps a reflex of PB *kala (Swahili -kaa) 'sit', itself a common source of 'be'.

26) A report on Family Service practices in San Diego County; the Register Guard, Eugene, Oregon, 3-8-92, p. 4A.

27) For the distribution of tense-aspect forms in 'if'-clauses, see Givón (1972, ch. 4). The first element in the form -i-nga- is most likely the pronominal subject prefix/agreement of the neutral noun class 9/10 singular, widely used as 'it' for abstract and adverbial roles. The reconstruction is probably then *i-ni-ga or *i-ni-ka 'it be that'. Similar expressions are attested elsewhere in Bantu, such as the Swahili subordinator i-a-ku-wa 'it-GEN-INF-be', i-wa-po 'if'(*lit.* 'it-be-there-that') or i-ki-wa 'if' (*lit*: 'it-MOD-be'). The English 'being that' is a similar subordinator.

28) See e.g. Givón and Kimenyi (1974). The form *ngo* can be probably reconstructed to *ni-ga-o, with the suffix -o being most likely the old Proto Bantu relative suffix. The reconstructed form should then be glossed 'be (it) that' or 'being that'.

29) The etymology of -ki- 'if', which occupies the tense-aspect prefixal slot to the exclusion of all other aspectual distinctions, is not clear. Most core-Bantu TAM prefixes are derived from verbs. In Bemba, the reflex of the Swahili -ki-(-ci-) is a progressive marker. And in Swahili itself -ki- also marks progressive participial clauses, as in (Salone 1983):

ni-**ki**-mw-ona, ni-**li**-shangaa.

I-**PROG**-her-see I-**PAST**-surprised

'Seeing her, I was surprised'

30) See Butt and Benjamin (1988, pp. 231-237). Their examples include various purpose-clause subordinators, many conditional subordinators, many time-ADV subordinators, and a host of concessives, substitutives, manner-ADV clauses, and others.

31) With minor adjustments due to Flora Klein-Andreu (in personal communication).

32) See note 31.

33) Flora Klein-Andreu (in personal communication).

34) While the present-subjunctive form cannot participate in this gradation, it can be used in 'if'-clauses that are embedded in the complement of uncertainty verbs.

35) One suspects that in spoken Spanish the 'have'-less use of the past-subjunctive to code counter-fact is much more widely attested. The bulk of the examples with which Butt and Benjamin illustrate their reference grammar are taken from written texts.

36) Jennifer Coates (in personal communication) suggests that the three-way contrast is not as clear-cut in British English. In particular, she suggests that some of the present-tense modals can be used for lower certainty, interchangeably with the past modals, with the appropriate intonation.

37) Flora Klein-Andreu (in personal communication).

38) The tense-agreement requirement for the Spanish past subjunctive (Butt and Benjamin 1988, pp. 244-246) makes for interesting complications in the system.

39) These emotive-factive predicates are the most consistently factive of the entire group (Kiparsky and Kiparsky 1968).

40) With some modification suggested by Flora Klein-Andreu (in personal communication).

41) Butt and Benjamin (1988) cite many examples of either a contrast or the use of the indicative in emotive-factive complements, but they are silent on the semantic nature of the contrast.

42) Pragmatic implications do not have the full force of logical conditionals, but are rather observations about behavioral propensities, likelihoods or norms. Taking the association to be a one-way conditional is a matter of temporary caution. It may very well be that the strength of association in the other direction is just as strong. That is:

"If one's valuative reaction to an event is stronger, chances are the event is epistemically less certain."

43) See also Givón (1977).

44) The data is originally from Bickerton's Hawaii Creole transcripts; see Givón (1982a).

45) The interpretation of (108) is ambiguous, depending on whatever perspective one adopts. If one focuses on the process, i.e. Abraham's behavior, then Abraham made all the intended moves of "not sparing his son", and the clause should be interpreted as past-perfect. If on the other hand one focuses on the end result, then since Isaac was indeed spared, the clause must be interpreted as counter-fact.

46) In many spoken varieties of Spanish, the past-subjunctive form with *-ra* — erstwhile the pluperfect — can be still used without the perfect auxiliary 'have' in counter-fact conditional clauses, as in:

> si lo **supiera**,   te **habría**   llamado
> if it know/1s/**PAST/SUBJUN** you have/1s/**COND** call/PARTICIP
> 'If **I had known** it, I would have called you'

This use may be viewed as another vestige of the old meaning of the *-ra* form as pluperfect.

47) James lists French, Latin, Classical Greek, Russian and Old Irish (Indo European); Tongan (Austronesian); Cree, Chipewyan, Nitinaht and Uto-Aztecan (Amerindian); Haya (Bantu); Garo (Tibeto-Burman).

48) At the conclusion of her survey, James (1982) reviews the "remoteness of past" explanation in counter-fact clauses, but ultimately hedges her bets.

49) The test case is, probably, that it should be possible to find a language where the past or perfect mark only counter-fact clauses but not subjunctives; but one should not find a language where those realis forms mark only the subjunctive but not counter-fact.

50) Edith Moravcsik (in personal communication) notes, from a methodological perspective, that it is also possible to "go from structure to function". While the structure-to-function discovery procedure has indeed been common in the early days of typology, when our understanding of the communicative correlates of syntax was rather limited, the theoretical foundations of this procedure are dubious; see chapter 3, above.

5

Taking Structure Seriously, I:
Constituency and the VP Node

5.1.   The grammar denial syndrome*

One of the most curious aspects of current functionalist thinking is the extent to which many *bona fide* members of the fraternity are willing to go in denying both the mental reality and the surface manifestations of syntactic structure. This denial is all the more baffling coming from people who profess belief in two of the most central tenets of contemporary functionalism — iconicity and grammaticalization. If iconicity stands for the functionally-motivated isomorphism between grammatical structures and their paired semantic or pragmatic functions, then what are these functions isomorphic to if grammatical structure is deemed unreal?[1] Likewise, if by grammaticalization one means the emergence over time of new morpho-syntactic structures, from paratactic, syntactic or lexical precursors, then what is it that emerges over time, and how real is it once it has successfully emerged, if grammatical structure is deemed ureal?[2] The grammar-denial syndrome among contemporary functionalists appears to embrace the logic of self contradiction:

(1)   **The logic of grammar-denial**:
   a. G maps onto F; but G doesn't exist
   b. G emerges; but G doesn't exist

One could perhaps understand this curious lapse of logic in a historical perspective, by viewing it as an over-reaction to the three core structuralist dogmas perpetrated upon linguistics ever since Saussure:

(2)   **Three core dogmas of structuralism:**
  a. The dogma of the arbitrariness of sign
  b. The dogma of separation between synchrony and diachrony
  c. The dogma of detached "knowledge" (competence) and "use" (performance)

The three dogmas in (2) are inferentially linked, a fact that many present-day functionalists accept as an unexamined premise. But unexamined premises have a way of fostering self-defeating behavior in science. In this case, functionalists are bound to discover the obvious link between the irrelevance of function (2a) and the irrelevance of diachrony (2b): Communicative function is the driving force behind the emergence, via grammaticalization, of *motivated* form:meaning pairings. Just as compelling is the link between the irrelevance of diachrony (2b) and the irrelevance of use (2c): Grammaticalization occurs in real use-space, and is finely attuned to variation and frequency of live communicative behavior.

One can understand excess without necessarily condoning it. Overreaction to one reductionist dogma has seldom got anyone much beyond another — converse but equally reductionist — dogma.[3] It is thus perhaps time to once again state the obvious:

(a) Human communication does not proceed directly from mind to mind. Rather, it proceeds via multiple steps of **coding** and **re-coding**.
(b) Without the coding instrument called grammar, a very distinct form of human communication has been observed, one called **pidgin**.
(c) The coding instrument called grammar has well-documented, unimpeachable **cognitive reality** in discourse processing, a reality that can be manipulated and measured experimentally.[4]
(d) The coding instrument called grammar likewise has unimpeachable and well documented **neurological reality**.[5]
(e) Finally and perhaps most compelling for linguists who are shy of crossing disciplinary boundaries, the coding instrument called grammar also has many behavioral consequences that can be observed, recorded and analyzed in natural communication. And the methods used in such observation and analysis have been the stock-in-trade of linguistics for as long as the discipline has existed.

It is the observations generated by the traditional study of surface grammatical structure, in both clausal and textual contexts, that are the focus of this chapter.

5.2.   Constituency and hierarchic structure

Few functionalists deny the reality of morphology, given its concrete links to the sound-coded lexicon. Functionalist denial of syntactic structure is most commonly expressed as denial of the most down-to-earth notions of traditional parsing — **constituency** and **hierarchy**. This is indeed curious, given that one of the most striking ways in which grammaticalized language differs from pidgin communication is in the presence of nested hierarchic constituent structure. To deny the heuristic notions of **syntactic slot** and **substitution class**, both of which virtually license our discovery of constituency, is indeed to deny the obvious.

The observable reality of grammar, in so far as it is accessible to the speech receiver, boils down to four signal components that can be extracted — by whatever means — from the stream of speech:

(3)   **Observable components of grammatical structure**:
 a. Linear order
 b. Nested hierarchic structure
 c. Grammatical morphology
 d. Rhythmics: intonation and pauses

Within this cluster of properties, however, **nested hierarchic structure** (3b) retains a distinct ontological status. Its existence is confounded with and inferred from the existence of both **serial order** (3a) and **rhythmics** (3d). That is, hierarchy and constituency are more abstract and cannot be observed directly. It is because of the behavior of serially-ordered adjacent constituents under re-ordering and substitution tests that one can infer that two or more items are governed by a more abstract constituent-node. That is:

(4)   **Attested variants of string X**:
 a. A
 b. *B
 c. A, B
 d. *B, A
 Inferred constituency of X:
 e. X → A (B)

Similarly, it is because of the incompatibility of two or more items placed serially in the "same slot", combined with the fact that each item by itself does fit the "slot", that one can infer that they are members of the same syntactic class ('substitution-slot'). That is:

(5) **Attested orders of string X:**
   a. A, B
   b. C, B
   c. *A, C, B
   d. *C, A, B
   e. *A
   f. *C

   Inferred constituency of X:

   g. $X \rightarrow \begin{Bmatrix} A \\ C \end{Bmatrix} B$

And likewise, it is because of the rhythmic properties of natural speech delivery that one can infer, this time by abduction only,[6] that two slots are independent of — or coordinate to — each other, rather than being a single two-item slot. That is (... = large pause; , = small intonation break):

(6) **Attested rhythmics of strings X, Y, Z:**
   a. (X)...A, B...(Z)
   b. *X, A, B...(Z)
   c. *(X)...A, B, Z
   d. *(X)...A...B...(Z)

   Inferred constituency of Y:

   e. $Y \rightarrow A, B$

Of the four overt properties of syntactic structure, two — nested hierarchic structure (3b) and morphology (3c) — are virtually absent in pidgin communication. Further, spoken natural communication often utilizes both embedding and morphology at a much lower frequency than tightly edited written text.[7] But however infrequent, the facts of substitution in the English noun phrases in (7) below, and of exclusivity of the determiners in (8), are eloquent testimony to the reality of both constituency and hierarchy:

(7) a. **She** left
   b. **The woman** left
   c. **The tall woman** left
   d. **The tall woman who came in late** left

(8)   a. **The** house
      b. **This** house
      c. **My** house
      d. *The my house
      e. *My the house
      f. *The this house
      g. *This the house
      h. *This my house
      i. *My this house

Of course, our knowledge — both as speakers and linguists — of constituency and other facets of syntactic structure does not derive only from structural evidence, but also from our knowledge of functional organization. For example, there is a strong tendency in language for functionally-related operators to be placed next to their relevant operands, so that:

(9)   **The adjacency principle:**[8]
      "Spatio-temporal distance in the stream of speech
      tends to reflect conceptual distance".

Like all iconicity principles in grammar, principle (9) is not an inviolable law of nature, but rather an explanatory principle that predicts frequency distributions. It would predict, for example, that in (10) below, orders such as (10a) and (10b) should be much more frequent in natural language(s) than orders such as (10c) and (10d). Operands are marked in (10) by capital letters, operators by lower case letters, and operand–operator relevance by having the same letter value.

(10) a. ...A,a,B,b,C,c...
      b. ...B,b,C,c,A,a...
      c. *...A,c,B,a,C,b...
      d. *...B,a,C,b,A,c...

The adjacency principle (9) thus makes the following prediction about both proximity and cliticization in English:

(11) a. the-HORSE is-STAND-ing on-the-BARN
      b. *is-HORSE the-on-STAND-the BARN-ing

We know already that predictions (11) are not absolute, since English auxiliaries tend to cliticize on the preceding word, which is more likely to be the subject than the verb:

(12) a. I've seen it
      b. She'll leave soon
      c. They're not here

But in spite of counter-examples such as (12), principle (9) remains highly predictive, as is evident from the relative rarity of structures such as (11). Functional knowledge is thus an important, accessible if often intuitive ingredient of our knowledge of grammatical structure. In chapter 6, below, we will survey another grammatical domain where strong interaction between structural and functional categories is evident.

5.3.   The VP node

5.3.1.   Preliminaries

The VP node in a language like English presumably groups together ("dominates") at least the following major constituents, one *sine qua non*, the others negotiable:

(13) **Likely VP constituents**:
      a. verb (obligatory)[9]
      b. auxiliary
      c. direct object
      d. indirect objects
      e. optional obliques or adverbs
      f. embedded verbal complements

Being abstract and problematic, the VP node affords us an opportunity to examine the reasons — stated or implicit — for having invisible elements of structure as part of our theoretical baggage, and for considering them real. Meaning and function are by definition invisible. But our intuition insists that the code elements of grammar should be more concrete, perhaps like the sound-code of the lexicon. It is thus not surprising that no functionalist has ever risen to challenge the validity of the more concrete, lexical **terminal nodes**: They are overtly attested. Nor has anyone ever seriously objected to the most abstract **highest node**, the clause (S). Its reality is manifest both rhythmically and semantically. It is the status of **intermediate nodes**, those that group two or more lexical items into mid-level abstract constituents, that has given grammarians most headache. That is:

(14)

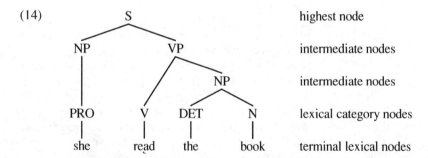

S	highest node
NP VP	intermediate nodes
NP	intermediate nodes
PRO V DET N	lexical category nodes
she read the book	terminal lexical nodes

Some of the reasons for having an intermediate VP node are traditional and methodologically transparent. Others turn out to be more opaque and implicit, often rooted in the theorist's pre-empirical assumptions. Whether one would ultimately accept them or not, pre-empirical assumptions must be first made explicit. But as in grammatical typology (chapters 3,4), functionalists must strive for independent theoretical and methodological access to structure, lest they succumb to the logical tautology of circular definitions (chapter 3), or the logical contradiction of denied presuppositions (see (1)).

5.3.2. Criteria

The VP node emerged onto the turbulent scene of late-1950s linguistics as early Transformational Grammar was struggling to unseat the then-current dogma of strictly manifest surface syntactic structure, the much reviled **immediate constituents analysis**. Whatever that dogma "couldn't handle" — discontinuity, recursion, and the systematic paraphrase relations noted by Harris (1956) — was said to exceed the formal capacities of its implicit underpinning, **phrase-structure grammar** (PSG), and then "handled" by transformations.[10] Long before the advent of "government" and "control", and long before a more explicitly account of grammatical relations became an issue, the VP node — direct if unacknowledged descendent of Aristotle's **predicate**[11] — was touted through a mix of surface-structural, semantic and formal arguments. Interlaced with the latter two was a subtle appeal to grammatical relations. Thus Postal (1964), in his condescending appended reference to Halliday's "Categories of the Theory of Grammar" (1961), writes:

"... But if we attempt to use this characterization for *derived* P-markers, there is no way to account for the presence of the subject relation in cases like *John is eager to please, the killing of the tigers* (ambiguous), *John was seen by Mary*, etc. But in a TG it can be shown that in the simplest grammar, construction like this are derived from underlying P-markers in which the appropriate elements *are* represented by configurations of the form NP VP. Thus the great effectiveness of the above configurational approach to grammatical relations is necessarily lost in *exclusively* PSG grammars, since these can provide only P-markers equivalent to the final derived P-markers of TG descriptions ..." (Postal 1964:111)

The semantic arguments for the VP node have not changed much since Aristotle. They still revolve, in Aristotle's terms, around what falls under the **logical scope** of assertion or denial and what is excluded; or what the predicate (VP) is "all about" (its subject). At issue is also what, in the more updated terms of Bybee (1985), is more relevant to what; or which constituents are semantically more closely connected. In this vein, one may argue that the auxiliary is semantically part and parcel of the VP because temporally-related notions of tense and aspect, or epistemic or deontic notions of modality, are semantically more relevant to the predicate, or to the state- or event-verb which is its core. A similar argument can be made for manner adverbs, whose semantic scope most often pertains to the verb. But the argument is considerably weaker when applied to the direct and indirect object. True enough, in Aristotle's semantic terms they fall under the scope of the predicate that is either affirmed or denied ("of the subject"). But their stronger semantic relevance to the verb — stronger than the subject's — is not all that obvious, given that even transitive verbs are sub-categorized semantically for all their obligatory semantic arguments.

Surface-structural criteria for the VP node will be central to our discussion here, though some of them will be treated at more depth than others. They are (excluding rhythmics):

(15) **Surface-structural criteria for the VP**:
   a. adjacency
   b. joint extraction/movement
   c. joint anaphoric reference
   d. NP incorporation
   e. unifying VP morphology

Formal and deep-structural criteria, those that depend more heavily on pre-empirical theoretical premises, will be referred to at various points throughout but will not be foregrounded.

5.4.   Joint extraction and joint anaphoric reference

Surface structure consideration of **joint extraction** (movement) and **joint anaphoric reference** incorporate implicitly the criterion of **adjacency** (9). To begin with, the various sub-constituents of the VP in a simple clause in English tend to be adjacent to each other. There are some well-known exceptions to this, most conspicuously 'scattered' adverbial, quantifiers, and other optional pragmatic operators. At the grossest level, one hopes to show that the whole verb phrase forms a single constituent, in a sense that the subject plus any sub-part of the verb phrase do not.

We open the discussion of surface-structure criteria for the VP node by citing restrictions on **L-dislocation**, a syntactic process that involves both movement and anaphoric reference. Consider the main options of extracting VP constituents via L-dislocation:[12]

(16)   a. **Simple clause:**
           Joan had left the house in a hurry
           SUBJ AUX V   DO   ADVERB
       b. **Extracting the whole VP:**
           As for [having left the house in a hurry], Joan did it...
       c. **Extracting the VP minus the optional AUX:**
           As for [leaving the house in a hurry], Joan had done it...
       d. **Extracting the VP minus the optional oblique:**
           As for [having left the house], Joan did it in a hurry...
       e. **Extracting the VP minus both optional constituents:**
           As for [leaving the house], Joan had done it in a hurry...

(17)   **Extracting individual daughter nodes:**
       a. **Extracting the object:**
           As for [the house], Joan had left it in a hurry...
       b. **Extracting the verb:**
           *As for [leaving], Joan had done it the house in a hurry...
       c. **Extracting the adverb alone:**
           *As for [in a hurry], Joan had left the house...
       d. **Extracting the AUX alone:**
           *As for [having], Joan left the house in a hurry...

(18) **Extracting discontinuous constituents**:
a. *As for [having the house], Joan left it in a hurry
b. *As for [having in a hurry], Joan left the house
c. *As for [leaving in a hurry], Joan had done it the house

(19) **Joint extraction of subject with obligatory VP sub-nodes**:
a. **Extracting the whole clause**:
As for [Joan having left the house in a hurry], she did it...
b. **Extracting the subject and VP minus the optional AUX**:
As for [Joan leaving the house in a hurry], she had done it...
c. **Extracting the subject and VP minus the optional oblique**:
As for [Joan having left the house], she did it in a hurry...
d. **Extracting the subject and VP minus all optional sub-nodes**:
As for [Joan leaving the house], she had done it in a hurry...

(20) **Joint extraction of the subject without obligatory VP sub-nodes**:
a. **Extracting the subject and VP minus the obligatory DO**:
*As for [Joan having left in a hurry], she had done it the house
b. **Extracting the subject and VP minus the obligatory V**:
*As for [Joan having the house in a hurry], she left
c. **Extracting the subject and verb**:
*As for [Joan leaving], she had done the house in a hurry
d. **Extracting the subject and AUX**:
*As for [Joan having], she left the house in a hurry
e. **Extracting the subject and oblique**:
*As for [Joan in a hurry], she had left the house
f. **Extracting the subject with the obligatory object**:
*As for [Joan the house], she has left it in a hurry

The generalizations emerging out of the data in (16) through (20) can be summarized roughly as follows:

A. **Extracting the VP or its constituents**:
(i)   You can jointly extract — and then refer to — the entire VP node (16b).
(ii) You can jointly extract — and then refer to — all the obligatory constituents of the VP (16c,d,e).
(iii) You can extract alone — and then refer to — only one daughter node of VP, the object NP (17a), but neither the verb (17b) nor the oblique (17c) nor the AUX (17d).

B. **Extracting the subject with VP constituents:**
  (iv) You can jointly extract (and then refer to) the subject with the
        entire VP — i.e. the entire clause — (19a).
  (v)   You can jointly extract (and then refer to) the subject with all
        the obligatory sub-nodes of the VP, excluding either or both the
        AUX and the oblique (19b,c,d).
  (vi) You cannot jointly extract (and then refer to) the subject with
        the VP unless all obligatory constituents are included (20).

The facts surveyed in (16) through (20) and others like them may be taken
as clear motivation for a VP node under certain conditions, with some problems
remaining. First, the extraction of only the obligatory constituents of the VP,
without the optional AUX and OBLIQUE, suggests a tighter bond between the
VP's obligatory components. The traditional way of expressing ("handling")
this would be to posit several VP nodes, the lowest of which governing only
the obligatory constituents. There are at least two alternative configurations of
such a structure, one maximally hierarchic ('subordinating') (21), the other less
hierarchic ('coordinating') (22):

(21) **Maximally hierarchic alternative:**

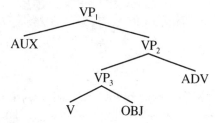

(22) **Less hierarchized alternative:**

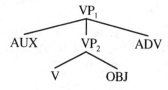

But the data in (16) through (20) do not discriminate between these two
structural alternatives. Further, neither of the two suggests a natural explanation
for the difference between the behavior of the two obligatory constituents, the
verb (not extractable by itself) and the object (extractable by itself).

The constituency structures (21) and (22) are of course not the only ones possible. If one considers extractions that include the subject (19), (20), the data argues just as plausibly for all the obligatory constituents of the clause forming a tighter sub-constituent, excluding both optional constituents, again with two possible interpretations:

(23)   **Maximally hierarchic alternative:**

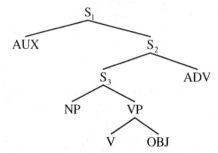

(24)   **Less hierarchic alternative:**

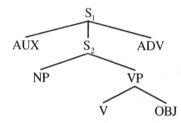

Here again, neither structural interpretation of itself accounts for the special cases, nor for the fact that the subject NP — like the object — can be extracted alone, as in:

(25)   As for **Joan**, she left the house in a hurry

Further, not all auxiliaries behave alike under extraction. Thus 'have' can be jointly extracted with the verb and object (16a,c) but neither modals nor 'be' can be likewise extracted:

(26)   a. She could leave the house.
       b. *As for **can(ing) leave the house**, she did/could (it).
       c. She was leaving the house.
       d. *As for **being leaving the house**, she did/was (it).

One may wish to argue that restrictions (26) are rooted in the morphology, since English modals cannot take inflections and thus cannot be infinitized, while 'have' can. But 'be' can take the -*ing* inflection, though only as a main verb, as in:

(27) a. he is *being* vindictive
      b. as for *being* on time

The special restrictions on extraction — above and beyond the simple principle of adjacency — boil down to three categories:
- The contrast between obligatory vs. optional constituents
- The contrast between "subject" and "object" vs. "verb"
- The contrast between auxiliaries "have" vs. "can" and "be"

Within at least one formal theoretical perspective, one could suggest that all the categories involved in these special restrictions are "syntactic". One then constructs elaborate tree diagrams that "account" for these and other semantically-based exceptions by assigning them different branching locations within the hierarchic structure of the clause. But this is plainly a book-keeping trick, a backhanded infusion of functional categories into syntax. Such a gambit does not make those categories less semantic: What is or isn't an obligatory clausal constituent is fully predicted by the **semantic frame** of the verb. The contrast between NP (subject, object) and verb has little to do with constituency or configuration, but harkens back to the semantic contrast between **entities** (Aristotle's 'substances') and **states/events**, respectively.[13] And the contrast between the three auxiliaries is both syntactic (position, morphology) and semantic (modal vs. perfect vs. progressive).

With semantically-motivated sub-conditions set aside, the restrictions on L-dislocation in English reflect at least two coherent general principles that animate the notion of constituency:

(28) **Most general rules of extraction**:
      a. **Completeness**:
          "Extraction of complete constituents is preferred over extraction of incomplete constituents".
      b. **Adjacency**:
          "Extraction of adjacent constituents is preferred over extraction of non-adjacent constituents".

At first blush, rule (28a) appears to subsumes (28b), given that the sub-components of a complete constituent are likely to be adjacent to each other. It thus seems that adjacency (28b) is the more general principle. To understand why the two restrictions may spring from a common source, it would be useful to couch them in cognitive terms, respectively:

(29) a. **The scattered object constraint**:
          "Scattered — non-adjacent — objects are more likely to be perceived and interpreted as multiple separate entities than as a single entity (28a)".
      b. **The proximity-relevance constraint**:
          "Entities that belong together conceptually should appear adjacent spatio-temporally (28b)".

Principle (29a) is well known in perception and cognition, predicting that entities that are far apart are less likely to be construed as a single entity.[14] But this boils down to (29b): Entities that are mutually relevant are likely to be adjacent. This is one of the best documented natural iconicity principles, widely attested in the organization of linguistic, neurological and in general biological codes.[15] What is natural about syntactic constituency is thus derived, ultimately, from what is natural cognitively, semantically, and pragmatically. This does not mean that one can reduce syntax to cognitive or functional notions, but only that one can understand the naturalness of syntax via such notions.

5.5. The noun-incorporation argument

One possible argument for the VP node — particularly for the "deeper" VP_2 or VP_3 nodes that groups the verb with the direct object as a constituent — is the phenomenon of **object incorporation**. In English, this phenomenon is marginal, a largely lexical pattern found in nominalized VPs:

(30) a. He went **trout-fishing**
      b. They did some **deer-hunting**
      c. She's a **book editor**

There are two sets of facts and one general argument that cast some doubt on the object-incorporation argument. First, optional VP constituents such as instrument and manner are just as easily incorporated into the verb in English and elsewhere:

(31) a. He's an expert at **fly-fishing**
          (> fishing with a fly-rod)
      b. She did some **cross-stitching**
          (> stitching cross-wise)

There is thus no special status for the obligatory direct object in incorporation. The promiscuity of noun incorporation is even clearer in languages where incorporation is an extensive syntactic pattern in main clauses. In Ute, for example, non-referring or non-topical arguments — objects, instruments, manner-adverbs, as well as adjectives and verbs that function as manner adverbs — can all incorporate into the verb. Thus (Givón 1980a):

(32) a. **Referring object**:
kwana-ci   'uway   paqa-pųga
eagle-AN/OBJ DEF/OBJ kill-REM
'(He) killed the eagle'

b. **Non-referring object (antipassive)**:
kwana-paqa-pųga
eagle-kill-REM
'He did (some) eagle-killing'

c. **Referring manner-ADV**:
mama-ci-pani   'uway   paghay-'way
woman-AN/OBJ-like DEF/OBJ walk-PRES
'(He) is walking like that woman'

d. **Non-referring manner-ADV**:
mama-paghay-'way
woman-walk-PRES
'He is walking like a woman' ('He woman-walks')

e. **Referring instrument**:
tųkua-vi   wii-ci-m   'uru   cųkųr'a-pųga
meat-CL/OBJ knife-CL/OBJ-INSTR DEF/OBJ cut-REM
'(She) cut (the) meat with the knife'.

f. **Non-referring instrument**:
tųkua-vi   wii-cųkųr'a-pųga
meat-CL/OBJ knife-cut-REM
'(She) cut (the) meat with a knife' ('She knife-cut the meat')

g. **Incorporated adjective as manner-ADV**:
'umų pia-'apagha-pųga
them sweet-talk-REM
'(She) sweet-talked (to) them'

h. **Incorporated verb as manned-ADV**:
sakų-vǫri-pųga
limp-go-REM
'(He) went limping around'

More damaging to the object-incorporation argument is the fact that noun incorporation in many languages follows an **absolutive pattern**: Both intransitive subjects and transitive objects can incorporate. In English this is again a limited pattern in nominalization:

(33) a. **Intransitive — incorporated subject**:
       Caribou migration is an annual event
      b. **Transitive — incorporated object**:
       Caribou hunting is reprehensible

Subject incorporation into intransitive verbs in main clauses is admittedly less common than object incorporation, but it is attested in some languages. Thus Mithun (1984), in her discussion of classificatory noun incorporation, gives the following examples from Caddo:[16]

(34) a. ná: **kan**-núh-'a'
       that **water**-run.out-FUT
       'That water will run out'
      b. ka'ás háh-**ic'ah**-'í'-sa'
       plum PROG-**eye**-grow-PROG
       'Plums are growing'
      c. wayah hák-**k'uht**-'í'-sa'
       much   PROG-**grass**-grow-PROG
       'A lot of grass is growing'

And similarly from Mohawk (Mithun 1984):

(35) a. n-a-hoti-**ya't**-a'tarihv
       SO-MOD-them-**body**-be.warm
       'in order for them to be warm'
      b. iah árok te-yo-**hy**-á:ri
       NEG yet DU-it-**berry**-be.ripe
       'They (the berries) are not yet ripe'
      c. ka-'sere-ht-í:yo
       it-**drag**-NOM-be.nice
       'the car is nice'

The value of object incorporation as arguments for a VP node is, at the very least, diluted by these facts.

Object incorporation is a well-known structural device used to code the **antipassive** voice function, i.e. to code a semantically-transitive event whose patient is non-referring, non-topical, pragmatically demoted (see chapter 3). Most commonly, the pragmatic demotion of the patient is reflected in its syntactic demotion, whereby it loses its grammatical-object status. As a result, the semantically-transitive clause is now syntactically objectless — thus syntactically intransitive.[17] This syntactic consequence is a bit more striking in ergative languages, where the subject case-marking in the antipassive reverts to the absolutive (or nominative) pattern of the intransitive clause. As illustration of this, consider Chukchee (Comrie 1973):[18]

(36) a. **Intransitive clause**:
         tumg-įt   jegtel-g'et
         friends-NOM escaped
         'The friends escaped'
      b. **Transitive, referring object**:
         tumg-e   na-ntįwat-įn kupre-n
         friends-ERG set   net-DFF
         'The friends set the net'
      c. **Transitive, non-referring object (antipassive)**:
         tumg-įt   kopra-ntawat-g'at
         friends-NOM net-set
         'The friends set a net' ('The friends net-set')

5.6.   Intermezzo: Configurational case-marking

While this in not easy to document, it seems to me that the most persistent motivation for the VP node has been, from the early days of Generative Grammar, formal and pre-empirical. It involves the curious insistence on representing **grammatical relations** (as well as other functional categories that are grammatically relevant) by configurational phrase-structure diagrams. This propensity for down-playing the functional essence of nodes goes back to the Eurocentric dawn of Generative Grammar (Chomsky 1957, 1965), when the entire data-base for theory-development consisted of English. But it also reflects the fundamental insistence that syntactic description be conducted independently of functional considerations. Under prodding from Gruber (1965) and Fillmore (1968), **semantic roles** were conceded some theoretical status. And under various interactions with Relational Grammar and Bresnan's LFG, **grammatical roles** (subject, object) were then ushered into the formal machinery — with a certain residual prejudice. The prejudice is that various rules, processes and constraints, including the very definition of the notions 'subject' and 'object', are still expressed configurationally in formal Chomskian accounts.

Within such a framework, one obvious charm of the VP node is that it allows defining the subject as "the NP directly dominated by S", and the object as "the NP directly dominated by VP". To someone who is not infused with the original formal imperative, and who is interested in formal structures that have relatively direct empirical consequences and thus (hopefully) some mental reality, this aspect of the VP saga is not all that attractive. If subject and direct object are legitimate formal — grammatical — categories, and if they are indeed cognitively real, it is unnecessary and probably undesirable to obscure their significance by deriving them from other formal layers of syntactic description. We will return to a fuller discussion of grammatical relations in chapter 6.

5.7.   The VSO-language argument

One argument that has been used by functionalists to challenge the cross-linguistic validity of the VP node involves the existence of rigid VSO languages. In such languages, the norm is that — whenever both a full-NP subject and a full-NP object are present — the verb and the object are non-adjacent. As illustration, consider transitive clauses in Machiguenga (So. Arawak, Perú; Betty Snell, in personal communication):

(37)   a. **Transitive verb with overt-NP subject:**
o-ma-ig-an-ak-a-tyo   o-ishinto-egi   iroro-ri
3f-do.same-PL-DIR-PERF-TR-EXC 3f-daughter-PL she-CONJ
'...**her daughters** treated her the same way and...'
b. **Transitive verb with anaphoric subject:**
o-nevent-av-aka-**ri**   o-tineri
3f-see/DIST-RECIP-PERF-**3m** 3f-son-in-law
'...**she** saw her son-in-law in the distance...'

One could of course resort to a well known formal gambit, that of positing an "underlying" word-order *cum* configuration for surface-VSO languages, presumably the order VOS with the proper hierarchic configuration and a VP node, and then add a "later" order-scrambling rule for deriving the surface-attested VSO order. That is:

(38)   **underlying structure**   **derived structure**

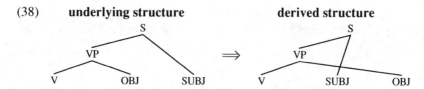

This solution can then be extended to all flexible-order languages ('non-configurational' languages, Hale 1983), or indeed made universal. Word-order thus becomes a relatively trivial 'parameter', excluded from the 'universal base' and 'set' later to achieve full specification. But one has to face then the methodological consequences of such a ploy — a flagrant depletion of the cross-linguistic empirical validity of putative universals.

There is a more compelling argument which suggests that the non-adjacency of object and verb in VSO languages is empirically a non-issue. It is well-known that in coherent, connected discourse the subject tends to be overwhelmingly continuous and anaphoric (see chapter 8). For this reason, the frequency of an actual VSO transitive clause in discourse in a VSO language like Machiguenga is often rather low, while the frequency of VO transitive clauses — or even V clauses with object pronominal agreement on the verb — is rather high. Text-frequency counts of overt vs. unexpressed arguments in continuous narrative in a VSO language (Sacapultec, Mayan) have been reported by DuBois (1987). Consider first the frequency of a 2-overt-NP clauses (VSO), 1-overt-NP clauses (VS or VO) and Ø-overt-NP clauses (V) in the total population of transitive clauses:

(39)   **Frequency of transitive clauses with**
       overt NPs in Sacapultec (Dubois 1987)

number of overt NPs							
2-NP		**1-NP**		**Ø-NP**		**total**	
N	%	N	%	N	%	N	%
/	/	5	27.6	134	**72.4**	185	100.0

The frequency of anaphoric vs. overt-NP subjects and objects in Sacapultec transitive clauses is given in table (40) below.

(40)   **Frequency of overt NP vs. anaphoric arguments
in Sacapultec transitive clauses** (DuBois 1987)

NP type

	anaphoric		indep. PRO		overt NP		total	
argument	**N**	**%**	**N**	**%**	**N**	**%**	**N**	**%**
subj/agent	156	**86.7**	13	7.2	11	6.1	180	100.0
obj/patient	94	**53.1**	2	1.1	81	45.8	177	100.0

This distribution of zero arguments is not unique to VSO languages, but is rather typical of continuous text in general (see chapter 8). Thus, compare the distribution of full NPs in Modern Hebrew, a rigid SVO language, reported by Smith (1992):

(41)   **Frequency of overt NP vs. anaphoric arguments
in Hebrew transitive clauses** (Smith 1992)[19]

NP type

	anaphoric (incl. PRO)		overt NP		total	
argument	**N**	**%**	**N**	**%**	**N**	**%**
subj/agent	252	**93.4**	18	6.6	270	100.0
obj/patient	86	**43.6**	111	56.4	197	100.0

In actual discourse then, fully 86% of Sacapultec transitive clauses and 93% of Hebrew transitive clauses appear without the subject NP, thus with the verb and the object adjacent to each other. At the attested surface-structure level, the VSO argument against the VP node is not much of an argument then, since the difference between VSO and SVO (or VOS) is largely nonexistent. All that speakers — and first language learners — confront at the level of actual language use is a rather uniform — ca. 90% — subjectless VO.

Of course, a Generative Grammarian worth his salt would dismiss these facts as irrelevant to formal structure. This is true especially in regard to language acquisition, which Generative diehards view as guided primarily by an abstract, innate 'Universal Grammar'. Language acquisition within such a framework is largely independent of input and frequency of experience. For functional linguists, on the other hand, frequency of behavior is of paramount importance, since grammatical competence is believed to be both reflected in and shaped by the frequency of experience. Functionally oriented typologists would thus tend to suspect that the typological difference between VSO, VOS and SVO, therefore also between OVS and SOV, is relatively shallow at the level that really counts — actual speech production and comprehension. Typological variability, and its import for both language acquisition and language processing, is only relevant when it translates into actual "performance" facts. The VP node is just as viable in VSO languages as it is in SVO languages, at least as far as the adjacency criterion goes.

5.8.   The VP node in multi-verb clauses

5.8.1.   Preamble

In this section I discuss the implications of multi-verb clauses for the universality of the VP node. Typologically, multi-verb clauses are found in either one of two distinct syntactic configurations — **embedding** (complementation) and **verb serialization**. While the two often reflect the very same semantic patterns of grammaticalization, the syntactic structure employed in them is starkly different. In particular, the two synchronic patterns represent two different diachronic routes to **clause union**.

5.8.2.   Complementation and grammaticalized auxiliaries in embedding languages

One of the areas that best illustrates the differences between hierarchic embedding and verb-serializing languages is the evolution of tense–aspect–modal (TAM) morphology, usually via an intermediate stage of **auxiliary verbs**. The very same lexical verbs can give rise to the very same TAM markers through either grammaticalization strategy; but the syntactic end result is often starkly different. In embedding languages, the most common syntactic configuration through which grammaticalized auxiliaries arise is that of **modality verb plus complement**, as in:

(42)

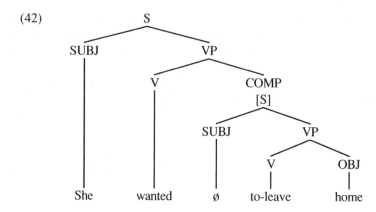

In this process, the finite main verb becomes re-analyzed semantically as a tense-aspect or modal marker, while the less finite complement verb surfaces as the semantic main verb. English auxiliaries, such as 'have' 'be', 'keep' and the various modals have all arisen via this route, which is widely attested elsewhere.[20]

Auxiliaries arising through the embedded complement configuration tend to have strong morpho-syntactic dependency ('control') relations with their complements, a fact that is well documented in the distribution of finite morphology across the complex clause. Finite morphology in embedding languages invariably gravitates to the main verb, while the complement tends to be less finite. This pattern then transfers itself to the auxiliary-cum-main-verb configuration that emerges as the first step of grammaticalization. As an illustration of the point-of-origin of this process, consider the following examples from Spanish. The upward migration of all finite affixes to the main verb is optional with modality verbs:

(43)   a.   **'Want' as a simple transitive verb**:
Juan **la**-quer-**ía**
John **her**-want-**IMPF/he**
'John wanted her/it'

b.   **'Want' as a modality verb with complement**:
la-quer-**ía**   ver   mas tarde
her-want-**IMPF/he**   see/**INF** later
'He wanted to see her/it later'

c.   **'Want' as a modality verb with complement**:
quer-**ía**   ver-**la**,   pero...
want-**IMPF/he**   see/**INF**-**her** but
'He wanted to see it/her, but...'

With some auxiliaries, the very same optional upward-migration of finite morphology is seen:

(44) a. **Auxiliary 'be' (complete migration):**
Ya   **lo**-est-**á** haciendo
Already **it**-be-**he** do/PARTICIP
'He's already doing it'
b. **Auxiliary 'be' (incomplete migration):**
est-**á** haciendo-**lo**   allá
be-**he** do/PARTICIP-**it** there
'He's doing it over there'

And similarly with:

(45) a. **Auxiliary 'go' (complete migration):**
lo-v-**a**   a hacer mañana
it-go-**PRES/he** to do/INF tomorrow
'He's going to do it tomorrow'
b. **Auxiliary 'go' (incomplete migration):**
Juan v-**a**   a hacer-**lo**
John go-**PRES/he** to do/INF-**it**
'John's going to do it tomorrow'

But with other auxiliaries, the upward migration of all finite affixes to the auxiliary it obligatory:

(46) a. **Auxiliary 'have' (complete migration):**
lo-h-**a**   hecho
it-have-**PRES/he** do/PARTICIP
'He has done it'
b. **Auxiliary 'have' (incomplete migration):**
*h-**a**   hecho-**lo**
have-**PRES/he** do/PARTICIP-**it**

The grammaticalization channel of modality verbs to TAM markers does not of course stop at auxiliaries, but most often proceeds toward complete cliticization. To illustrate this in a VO language, consider the Swahili pattern. When the auxiliary is still a main modality verb, it carries all finite affixes except the object pronoun, which is retained on the complement verb:

(47) **Grammaticalized verbs as TAM markers in Swahili**:
  a. **'Want' as modality verb**:
    ni-na-**taka**   ku-**ki**-soma
    I-PRES-**want** INF-it-read
    'I want to read it'
  b. **'Want' as FUTURE**:
    ni-**ta**-ki-soma   (-ta < -*taka* 'want')
    I-FUT-it-read
    'I will read it'
  c. **'Finish' as modality verb**:
    ni-li-**maliza**   ku-**ki**-soma
    I-PAST-**finish** INF-it-read
    'I finished reading it'
  d. **'Finish' as PERF**:
    ni-**me**-ki-soma   (-*me*- < *mel(e)* = 'finish/PERF')
    I-PERF-it-read
    'I have read it'
  e. **'Have' as PRESENT**:[21]
    ni-**na**-ki-soma   (-*na*- < -*na* 'have/be with')
    I-PROG-it-read
    'I'm reading it'
  f. **'Be' as PAST**:[22]
    ni-**li**-ki-soma   (-*li* = *'be')
    I-PAST-it-read
    'I read it'

In embedding OV languages, a mirror image of the same configuration is seen, both in complementation and in the grammaticalization of erstwhile main verbs as TAM markers. As an illustration, consider the pattern of complementation and TAM cliticization in Ute:[23]

(48) a. **Loose modality verb complementation**:
      'uwas-'ura sari-ci tuka-**vaa-ci** 'asti-**kya**
      he-TOP   dog-OBJ eat-**IRR-NOM** want-ANT
      'He wanted to eat (the) dog'
    b. **Bound modality verb complementation**:
      'uwas-'ura sari-ci   tuka-maku-**kwa**
      he-TOP   dog-OBJ eat-finish-ANT
      'He finished eating the dog'

c. **Anterior aspect**:

'was-'ura sari-ci   tụka-**qa**   (-*ka*/-*ga* = 'have'/'be')
he-TOP   dog-OBJ eat-ANT
'He ate (the) dog'

d. **Habitual aspect**:

'uwas-'ura sari-tụka-**miy**   (-*miya* = 'go')
he-TOP   dog-eat-HAB
'He eats dogs'

e. **Future tense**:

'uwas-'ura sari-ci   tụka-**vaa-ni**   (-*va*/*pa* = *'go', 'pass')
he-TOP   dog-OBJ eat-**IRR-FUT**
'He will eat (the) dog'

The less finite form of the complement of the non-implicative 'want' (48a) still involves an irrealis morpheme, in addition to a nominalizer. The implicative 'finish' (48b) is co-lexicalized with its complement, essentially at the same suffixal position as a TAM suffix. An intermediate diachronic stage of finite auxiliary verbs is not attested in Ute.

The fact that auxiliaries tend to be so tightly bound to their main verbs, to the point of retaining all the finite clausal morphology; and the fact they eventually cliticize as TAM affixes on those main verb, are predictable from the hierarchic-embedding structure of the VPs that licensed this grammatical-ization route. Within such a structure, the complement clause is reduced and partially nominalized, and is tightly embedded into the main-clause VP structure — not quite as a grammatical object, but somewhat analogous to it. The tightly-packed, hierarchic embedded structure of the contributory VP, with its "controlled" complement verb, is a syntactic template that virtually guaran-tees eventual **clause union** and the full cliticization of the erstwhile main verb. The migration of finite affixes — particularly pronouns referring to the logical object of the complement verb — to the auxiliary verb is but an intermediate step on the way to full clause union, whereby all arguments now bear grammat-ical relations to a single verb.[24] As we shall see below, serial-verb languages, in which the VP constituent is much more ephemeral, follow a different grammaticalization route.

**5.8.3.   Complementation and grammaticalized auxiliaries
in verb-serializing languages**

In many languages, multi-verb main clauses are attested outside complementation, thus beyond the diachronic rise of main verbs to auxiliaries and
TAM markers. The typological phenomenon of verb serialization has other,
perhaps more general implications to a synchronic account of grammar. But
those more general implications are highlighted by examining the rise of TAM
markers from serial verb constructions.

Compare first the progressive and perfect auxiliary constructions in the
highly embedding English with their equivalents in the serializing Tok Pisin, an
equally rigid SVO language:[25]

(49)   a. **Serial 'be' as PROG:**
       ...em brukim **i-stap**...
       he   break   **PRED-be**
       '...he keeps breaking (it)...'
       b. **Serial 'finish' as COMPL:**
       ...em wokim paya **pinis**...
       she   make   fire   **finish**
       '...she gets the fire started...'

When erstwhile serial verbs are reduced to TAM marker in serial-verb
clauses, nothing of the hierarchic, asymmetrical distribution of finite morphology seems to occur. In part, this may be due to the fact that in transitive clauses,
object NPs intersperse between serial and main verbs and prevent "migration"
of the bound morphology to a single verbal locus in the clause. As illustration
of such "dispersed" TAM morphology, consider the following examples from
Supyire, a Senufu language (Gur, Voltaic; Niger-Congo) from Mali. These are
historically SOV languages, but with post-verbal indirect objects and verbal
complements. Such post-verbal constituents are derived historically from serial-
verb constructions (Carlson 1991). The rigid word-order of Senufu languages
is thus:

(50)   a. S (DO) V IO
       b. S (DO) V COMP

The oldest TAM-marking "auxiliaries" are most commonly post-subject ('second
position') clitics. So that the simple-clause order tends to be:

(51)   S-AUX (DO) V IO/COMP

Further, all TAM markers and/or auxiliaries are probably derived historically from serial verbs. Consider first the serial complementation pattern in Supyire (Carlson 1990):[26]

(52) a. **Simple-clause order**:
        nǫgǫ-lyengi **si**   ngkuu   kan u-a
        man.old-DEF AUX chicken give him-to
        'My father gave him a chicken'

     b. **Serial complement of modality verb**:
        mu **aha' bu**   lyi à   kwǫ...
        you COND MOD eat PERF finish
        '...when you finally finish eating...'
        (Lit.: '...when you finally eat and finish...')

     c. **Serial complement of manipulation verb**:
        mii **à**   u   karima à   pa
        I   PERF him force   PERF come
        'I forced him to come'
        (Lit.: 'I forced him and he came')

     d. **Serial complement of manipulation verb**:
        u   **à**   pi   yyera à   pa
        she PERF them call   PERF come
        'She called them to come'
        (Lit.: 'She called them so that they come')

In addition to the old subject-clitic TAM markers, many of the more recently grammaticalized TAMs in Supyire are still, rather transparently, serial-verbs, often with the overt consecutive prefix *n-*. Some of the more common serial auxiliaries are:

(53) a. **Inchoative aspect with 'come'**:
        kà   u   pyęnge **si**   **m-pa**   **m-pee**
        CONJ his family AUX CONJ-come CONJ-big
        '...and his family became big...'
        (Lit.: 'and his family came and was big')

     b. **Irrealis modal (*'go'?)**:
        mii **sí**   u   lwǫ **n-kan**   yii-a
        I   FUT him take CONJ-give you-to
        'I'll take him to you'
        (Lit.: 'I go take him and give (him) to you')

   c. **The pluperfect aspect with 'be':**
   fyinga **à**   **pyi à**   mpii jo
   python **PERF be** **PERF** those swallow
   '...the python had swallowed those...'
   (Lit.: '...the python was and swallowed those...')
   d. **The repetitive aspect with 'release':**
   ka   **asi laha à**   wu
   CONJ **HAB let.go PERF** pour
   '...and it would again pour out...'
   (Lit.: '...and it would release and pour...')
   e. **The repetitive aspect with 'return':**
   maa '   **nura à**   u   kuntunu-sẹẹge wwu
   CONJ **ASP return PERF** her monkey-skin   take
   '...and she **again** took her monkey-skin...'
   (Lit.: '...and she returned and took her monkey-skin...')
   f. **The quickly aspect with 'hurry':**
   mu **ú**   **fyala à**   pa
   you **MOD hurry PERF** come
   'You must come quickly'
   (Lit.: 'You must hurry and come')
   g. **Progressive copular auxiliaries:**
   caawa **sahana**   **wa** u   mẹẹni-**na na**   n-cee
   warthog **stay PROG be** his song-**LOC PROG CONJ**-sing
   '...Warthog was still singing his song...'
   (Lit.: 'Warthog was still at his song and singing')

Just as serial are the deictic-directional 'come' and 'go':

   (54) a. ka   u   **ú'**   wyẹrẹngi lwọ **à**   **pa**   naha
         CONJ she **AUX** money.DEF take **PERF come** here
         '...then she brought the money here...'
      b. ka   mii **í**   cingikii   lwọ **à**   **kare** pyenga
         CONJ I   **AUX** poles.DEF take **PERF go**   house
         '...then I took the poles (away) home...'

The same dispersed configuration for serial directional can be seen in the SVO-ordered Tok Pisin:[27]

(55) a. ...em tromwey   sospan   **i-go**...
    ...she threw away saucepan **PRED-go**
    '...she threw the saucepan away...'
  b. ...em karim sospan   **i-kam**...
    she carry saucepan **PRED-come**
    '...she brought the saucepan over...'

One must emphasize that there are serial-verb languages where finite inflections gravitate to a single "main" verb. This is clearly the norm in Kalam, an SOV Papuan language:[28]

(56) ...mon konay-nep timb rik tip   pang yok-**sap**...
    wood much-very chop cut chop break throw-**PRES/3s**
    '...he's chopping and cutting and throwing much more wood...'

Only the last of five verbs in clause (56) carries finite inflection, the other four are bare stems.

Other serial-verb languages spread finite morphology to all the verbs in the clause. An example of this may be seen in Akan (Osam 1993a):

(57) a. wo-yi-**i**   no   fi-**i**   Mankesim
    3p-take-**PAST** OBJ/3s leave-**PAST** M.
    'They transferred him from Mankesim'
  b. Kofi á-nantsew á-kọ   Mankesim
    K. **PERF**-walk **PERF**-go M.
    'Kofi walked to Mankesim'
  c. wo-**e-nn**-yi   Kofi **a-mm**-ba   fie
    3p-**PAST-NEG**-take K.   **PAST-NEG**-come home
    'They did not transfer/bring Kofi home'
  d. ọ-**a-nn**-yẹ   edwuma **a-mm**-ma   Ebo
    3s-**PAST-NEG**-do work   **PAST-NEG**-give E.
    'She didn't work for Ebo'

Two tenses in Akan, progressive and future, do not spread across the clause. Rather, they mark only the initial verb in the clause. All other verbs carry a neutral "narrative" prefix:

(58) a. wo-**be**-yi   no   e-fi   Mankesim
         3p-FUT-take OBJ/3s NAR-leave M.
         'They will transfer him from Mankesim'
      b. wo-**ri**-yi   no   e-fi   Mankesim
         3p-PROG-take OBJ/3s NAR-leave M.
         'They are transferring him from Mankesim'

The vagaries of finite marking in serial-verb languages has given consider-able headaches to formal linguists. Thus for example, Byrne (1992) notes the following three options for placing the finite inflection of tense in Saramaccan:

(59) a. **Only on the first verb**:
         Kofi **bi**   bai di buku da di muyee
         K.   TNS buy the book give the woman
         (i) 'Kofi bought the book and gave it to the woman' (non-serial)
         (ii) 'Kofi bought the book for the woman'
      b. **Spread on all verbs**:
         Kofi **bi**   bai di buku **bi**   da di muyee
         K.   TNS buy the book TNS give the woman
         'Kofi bought the book for the woman'
      c. **Only on the last verb**:
         Kofi bai di buku **bi**   da di muyee
         K.   buy the book TNS give the woman
         'Kofi bought the book for the woman'

Byrne makes a valiant attempt to give a configurational account of the fact that only in (59a), where the second verb does *not* carry its own tense marking, can one obtain a non-serial, conjoined-clauses interpretation. But there is no glossing over the fact that morphological finiteness is one of the most reliable correlates of independent main-verb status. So that if anything, on normal iconicity grounds,[29] one would expect (59b) to be the more likely variant that allows a conjoined interpretation.

In Akan, one finds the spreading of two TAM markers to all verbs in the conjoined clause-chains (Osam 1993a):

(60) **Spreading tense-aspects**:
      a. **Past**:
         Araba tọ-ọ   nam, kyew-ee, tọn-ee   nya-a   sika
         A.   buy-PAST fish fry-PAST sell-PAST get-PAST money
         'Araba bought fish, fried it, sold it and got money'

b. **Perfect**:

Araba á-tọ   nam, á-kyew, á-tọn   é-nya   sika
A.   PERF-buy fish PERF-fry PERF-sell PERF-get money
'Araba has bought fish, fried it, sold it and got money'

Other TAM markers do not spread at all, but rather mark only the clause-initial verb, with all subsequent verbs carrying the less-finite and semantically neutral 'narrative' marker:

(61) **Non-spreading tense-aspects**:
   a. **Progressive**:

   Araba **ro**-tọ   nam, a-kyew, a-tọn   e-nya   sika
   A.   PROG-buy fish NAR-fry NAR-sell NAR-get money
   'Araba is buying fish, frying it, selling it and getting money'
   b. **Future**:

   Araba **bọ**-tọ   nam, a-kyew, a-tọn   e-nya   sika
   A.   FUT-buy fish NAR-fry NAR-sell NAR-get money
   'Araba will buy fish, fry it, sell it and get money'

The very same distribution holds for serial clauses (see (57) and (58) above).

5.8.4.   The verb phrase in serial-verb languages

5.8.4.1.   Configurational accounts of serial clauses

The phenomenon of verb serialization has bedeviled generative grammarians for over 20 years now. In the early days, when the only recognized level of conjunction was the clause (S), a universal VP node could be preserved only if multi-verb serial clauses were interpreted as **complex clauses**, either embedded (complementation) or conjoined. And so, many of the formal arguments in the early 1970s centered on selecting the right configurational interpretation — conjoined or subordinated — as the underlying deep structure of serial clauses.[30] The fact that the semantics of serial event-clauses fitted neither deep-structure configuration, and that both configurations thus played havoc with Chomsky's (1965) semantically-supportive deep structure, did not seem a worry at the time.

GB grammarians have only recently joined the fray, albeit with relish.[31] Within the resurrected debate, both Sebba (1987) and Larson (1991) review the range of configurational alternatives and then argue for specific ones. One upshot of the latter-day configurational debate is that it is now permissible to conjoin or subordinate a lower node such as VP. A major conceptual hurdle has thus been dismantled, in that formal descriptions are now re-aligned with the cognitive and rhythmic facts: Multiple-verb serial clauses are single event clauses.[32] Within this new context, Sebba (1987) argues for an analog of the subordination vs. coordination contrast of the 1970s. The theory-laden nature of his approach is acknowledged:

> "... Theoretical paradigms are themselves responsible for the problems researchers have to tackle within them. For Christaller, writing about Twi in 1875, it did not seem to be problematic that some Twi sentences had more than one verb ... Subsequently linguists working within the Chomskyan framework found that this *was* a problem, and tried to argue that serial sentences contained sentences embedded within or conjoined with other sentences ... My own analysis is based on the notion of multiple right-branching VPs ..." (Sebba 1987:211)

Sebba posits both subordinate and coordinate configurations, to account for different types of verb serialization within the same language.[33] Both configurations involve multiple VP nodes. That is, for a VO language (Sebba 1987: 149–170):

(62)   **Coordinate configuration:**

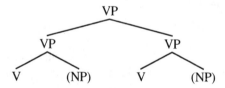

(63)   **Subordinate (right-branching) configuration:**

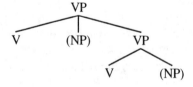

5.8.4.2. Verb serialization and the distribution of finite verbal morphology

Larson (1991) takes a somewhat different formal approach, noting "the general connection between serialization and secondary predication" (1991:207):

"... The distinction between serializing and non-serializing languages would reflect neither a "deep" difference in X-bar theory (as for Baker), nor a difference in the availability of particular lexicalization rules (as for Lefebvre and Li),[34] but instead a rather "shallow" difference in how the inflectional requirements on secondary predicates are met. Such a parameter could presumably be set on the basis of simple sentences involving agreement and inflection ..." (1991:207)

Serial constructions thus contain "secondary" (=serial) predications in addition to the primary (=main) ones. But to Larson this is a "shallow" typological deviation from the 'standard' hierarchic-embedding type. Larson recommends that we look at the rules governing the assignment of finite inflections in single-verb non-serial clauses, then draw from them predictions about what to expect from inflections in multiple-verb serial clauses.

Unfortunately, the rules of finite inflection assignment in single-verb clauses do not extend quite as easily. The most general prediction that can be derived from single-verb clause, regardless of typological variation, is:

(64)   "Attach all finite verbal inflections to the main verb".

In an embedding language, this rule extends rather neatly to multi-verb clauses, with semantic main verbs hogging up most finite verbal inflections. But even in such well-behaved languages, the notion of "semantic main verb" dissolves when that verb is grammaticalized into a TAM marker, directional marker, or causative affix. In embedding languages, grammaticalized auxiliaries retain the syntactic properties of main verbs long after they have lost all vestiges of semantic verbhood. Is the notion "main verb" more secure in a serializing language? If semantic criteria are put aside, can one identify the "main verb" of a serial clause by purely structural criteria? In a non-circular fashion without reference to finite verbal morphology? As we shall see below, the answer is often 'no'.

Finite inflection assignment rules in serial clauses in many languages are neither fully coherent nor fully predictable. To begin with, finite inflections do not always cluster around the semantic main verb. One could probably predict that diachronically the inflections would (eventually) gravitate toward one verb in the clause, as in Kalam and many other serial-verb languages. But in the interim, the facts of Akan, Saramaccan, Tok Pisin etc. suggest that serializing languages can tolerate synchronic states where a less-than-coherent patchwork of rules govern finite inflection assignment. And Larson's (1991) notwithstanding, those rules are not mere extensions of finite inflection assignment in single-verb clauses.

The role of diachrony in predicting the synchronic behavior of verbal inflections is considerable. Thus in Tok Pisin, the verbal inflection *i-*, the so-called 'predicate marker' (PM), is the diachronic offspring of the anaphoric pronoun 'he'. Its synchronic distribution is somewhat reminiscent of that diachronic origin, in that it is almost obligatorily on main verbs in contexts calling for an anaphoric subject; it cannot appear if the subject is the independent pronoun *em*, but may appear when the subject is a full NP:[35]

(65) a. **Zero-anaphoric subject:**
   ...i-wok-im   paya...
   PM-work-TR fire
   '...she makes a fire...'
   b. **Independent pronoun subject:**
   ...em wok-im   paya...
   she work-TR fire
   '...she made a fire...'

The parameter "INFL" in Larson's framework will have to presumably be set separately for each discourse-pragmatic context. And when the subject is overtly expressed, the PM appears only on the serial verb but not on the main verb:[36]

(66) a. **Zero-anaphoric subject:**
   ...i-wakabaut   i-go...
   PM-walk.about PM-go
   '...she walks away...'
   b. **Independent pronoun subject:**
   ...em wakabout i-go...
   she walk   PM-go
   '...she walks away...'

Further, the Tok Pisin PM appears on some serial verbs but not on others:[37]

(67) a. ...i-wakabaut   i-go...
   PM-walk.about PM-go
   '...she walks **away**...'
   b. ...i-wakabaut   i-kam
   PM-walk.about PM-come
   '...she walks **toward** (there)...'

c. ...i-wakabaut   i-stap...
    PM-walk.about **PM**-stop
    '...she **is** walk**ing** around...'
d. ...em wok-im paya **pinis**
    she work-**TR** fire **finish**
    '...she has made a fire...'

In Akan, Kalam, and Misumalpan languages, the inflection rules in serial clauses reflect rather faithfully the rules that govern conjoined same-subject (SS) **chain-medial clauses.** This is so because serial-verb constructions arise diachronically from the condensation of SS-medial clause-chains.[38] Thus in Akan, the same tense-aspect "spreading" rules that govern conjoined clause-chains also governs serial-verb clauses (see (57),(58) and (60),(61) above). In Kalam, the final "main" verb of the SS-chain-medial clause has the least finite morphology of all clause-types, and the morpheme involved is often dispensed with altogether, to the point where only intonation can distinguish an SS-cain-medial verb from a clause-internal serial verb (Givón 1991b). In Miskitu (Misumalpan), SS-chain-medial verbs, equi-subject complement verbs and serial verbs all carry the same non-finite (participial) inflection, reflecting the common origin of all three constructions. The participial suffix -i can be readily interpreted as a **cataphoric SS** marker. Thus (Hale 1991):

(68) a. **SS-chain-medial verb:**
          Baha ulu-ka   pruk-**i**   ik-**amna**
          that wasp-CNS hit-**PAR/SS** kill-**FUT/1**
          'I will hit that wasp and kill it'
      b. **Complement of a modality verb:**
          Naha w-a-tla   mak-**i**   ta alk-**ri**
          this house-CNS build-**PAR/SS** end reach-**PAST/3**
          'He finished building this house'
          (Lit.: 'He built the house and reached the end')
      c. **SS-Serial-verb clause:**
          Baha usus-ka   pali-**i**   wa-**n**
          that buzzard-CNS fly-**PAR/SS** go-**PAST/3**
          'That buzzard flew away'
          (Lit.: 'The buzzard flew and went away')

In rigid SOV languages like Miskitu, the most common rule assigns the most finite verbal inflection(s) to the clause-final verb. But that most-finite verb need not be the semantic main verb (cf. (68c)).

The very same carry-over of chain-medial morphology into complementation and serial clauses is found in switch-subject (DS) concatenations. Here, it is the **cataphoric DS** verbal inflection that is transferred from the DS-chain-medial configuration into the other two syntactic structures. This inflection, here as in other clause-chaining OV languages, is more finite than the cataphoric-SS inflection (Givón 1990, ch. 19; 1991b). Thus, again from Miskitu (Hale 1991):[39]

(69) a. **DS-chain-medial verb**:
Man naha yul-a   pruk-**rika** plap-**bia**
you this dog-CNS hit-**DS/2**   run-**FUT/3**
'You will hit this dog and it will run'

b. **Complement of non-equi verb**:
Yang witin-nani aisi-**n**   wal-**ri**
I   they-PL   speak-**DS/3** hear-**PAST/1**
'I heard them speak'
(Lit.: 'They spoke and I heard (them/it')

c. **DS-serial-verb clause**:
Yang truk-kum atk-**ri**   wa-**n**
I   truck-a   sell-**DS/1** go-**PAST/3**
'I sold the truck off'
(Lit.: 'I sold the truck and it went off')

Other serializing languages such as Kalam and Tairora also display this *resultative* serial structure. And it is in fact the very same structure found in the rigid-SVO Tok Pisin (Givón 1991b) and Mandarin Chinese (Thompson 1973) — but without any switch-reference morphology. Again, the clause-final finite verb in (69c) is not semantically the main verb, unless one interprets the construction literally as, still, a coordinate structure.

Predicting the assignment of finite verbal inflection in serial-verb clauses is just as problematic in Ijo (Niger-Congo). In this rigid-SOV language, the main verbal inflection, the 'past' suffix -*mi*, attaches to the clause-final verb in non-serial clauses (Williamson 1965):[40]

(70) a. **Simple intransitive**:
        eri bo-**mi**
        he come-**PAST**
        'He returned'
      b. **Simple transitive**:
        arau ingo deri-**mi**
        she trap weave-**PAST**
        'She wove a trap'

The most general rule for finite inflection placement is thus the same in Ijo as in Miskitu:

(71) **Finite inflection assignment in an OV language**:
      "Attach the finite verbal inflection to the clause-final verb".

This rule is retained in serial clauses, but other — non-final — verbs sometimes take the "spread" inflection -*ni* and sometimes don't:[41]

(72) a. omini nama tuo fi-**mi**
         they meat cook eat-**PAST**
         'They cooked and ate the meat'
      b. ta-maa   bele seri-**ni**   aki-**mi**
         wife-**DEF** pot remove-**INF** take-**PAST**
         'She took the pot off the fire'

(73) a. eri ogidi   aki-**ni**   indi pei-**mi**
         he machete take-**INF** fish cut-**PAST**
         'He cut the fish with the machete'
      b. arau zu-ye aki buru teri-**mi**
         she basket take yam cover-**PAST**
         'She covered the yam with a basket'

(74) a. eri weni-**ni** ama suo-**mi**
         he walk-**INF** town go-**PAST**
         'He walked to town'
      b. eri weni bo-**ni**   ama la-**mi**
         he walk come-**INF** town reach-**PAST**
         'He walked reaching town'
         'He came walking and reached town'
      c. eri oki   mu toru benin-**mi**
         he swim go river cross-**PAST**
         'He swam away across the river'
         'He went swimming across the river'

Again, the semantic main verb need not be the clause-final one (cf. (74a,b,c)). The problem is just as vexing with Ijo serial causative constructions, where the semantically main verb 'make' is clause-medial, sometimes with and sometimes without the inflection (Williamson 1965):

(75) a. woni u-mie-**ni**   indi die-**mi**
          we   him-make-INF fish share-PAST
          'We made him share the fish'
      b. ari u-mie   mu-**mi**
          I   him-make go-PAST
          'I made him go'
          'She chased him away'
      c. arau tobou mie   bunumo-**mi**
          she child make sleep-PAST
          'She made the child sleep'
          'She soothed the child'
      d. eri bide mie   fumumo-**mi**
          he cloth make dirty-PAST
          'He made the cloth dirty'
          'He dirtied the cloth'

One could argue that a sub-rule for marking the main verb 'make' is clearly discernible in (75). That is:

(76) "The causative main verb 'make' takes the inflection if its complement verb is transitive (cf. (78a)), but not if it is intransitive (cf. (74b,c,d))".

While rule (76) may do the job, it is theoretically both opaque and inelegant; nor is it formulated in terms of the simple clause. Rather, the rule makes inflection assignment on the semantic main verb depend on the transitivity of the semantic complement verb. So that when the main verb 'make' is used alone in a simple transitive clause such as (77) below, the rule is different (obligatory inflection):

(77) eri ogidi   mie-**mi**
      he machete make-PAST
      'He made a machete'

The transitivity hypothesis is further dampened by the alternation found in serial comparison clauses:

(78) a. ari dangai-**ni** u-dengi-**mi**
          I   tall-**INF** him-pass-**PAST**
          'I am taller than he (is)'
      b. eri duma tun-**ni**   i-dengi-**mi**
          he song sing-**INF** me-pass-**PAST**
          'He sang more songs than I did'
      c. eri kure bangi saramo tobou dengi-**mi**
          he can run   fast   child pass-**PAST**
          'He could run faster than a child'

In (78a) the intransitive main verb 'be tall' carries the inflection, while in (78c) the intransitive 'run' does not. And the most likely verb to carry an inflection is still the clause-final, semantically-serial verb.

Finally, modality verbs in Ijo, as in Miskitu and Supyire, also appear in a serial construction;[42] but sometimes they come with and sometime without the inflection:

(79) a. eri kurei-**ni** eke fi-**a** [43]
          he can-**INF** rat eat-**NEG**
          'He could not eat the rat'
      b. eri seri you-**mi**
          he start cry-**PAST**
          'He started to cry'
      c. eri koro-**ni** oki-**mi**
          he start-**INF** swim-**PAST**
          'He started to swim'
      d. ari la   bo-**mi**
          I   succeed come-**PAST**
          'I succeeded in coming'
      e. eri inbali-**ni**   oki-**mi**
          he struggle-**INF** swim-**PAST**
          'He tried to swim'
      f. eri bari-**ni**   inbali koro-**ni** oki-**mi**
          he repeat-**INF** struggle start-**INF** swim-**PAST**
          'He tried to begin to swim again'

Similar problems crop up in the rigid-SVO Akan, for tenses that do not 'spread' beyond the clause-initial verb. The rigid rule for those tenses is the converse of the OV rule (71), and is equally insensitive to the semantic status of the verb:

(80) **Finite inflection assignment in an VO language**:
"Attach the finite verbal inflection to the clause-initial verb".

But some clause-initial, semantically empty serial verbs cannot take TAM inflections at all, having reached a more advanced stage of grammaticalization.[44] The second verb in the clause then carries the inflection, as in (81b) below:

(81) a. Araba **re-yę**   asǫr **a**-ma   Kofi
A.   **PROG**-make prayer **NAR**-give K.
'Araba is praying for Kofi'
b. Araba de   sekan no **re**-twa   ahoma no
A.   take knife the **PROG**-cut rope   the
'Araba is cutting the rope with the knife'

Clearly, one cannot follow Larson's (1991) advice and apply the inflection-attachment rule of simple one-verb clauses to serial clauses. The assignment of finite inflection in many serializing languages is governed by more complex rules, rules that are more subtle, inconsistent, and on occasion also semantically and pragmatically sensitive. These rules often reflect the specific grammaticalization pathways through which the serial clause arose, and often also the diachronic stage of its evolution. What serializing languages do not always reflect is the idealized iconicity principle of finite morphology assignment. This principle, implicit in Larson (1991), is well-attested in hierarchic-embedding languages. It predicts that:

(82) **Finite inflection assignment in embedding languages**:
"Finite verbal morphology will cluster most prominently around the semantic main verb of the clause".

In serializing languages, finite verbal morphology is more scattered across the clause in ways that cannot be derived neatly from principle (82).

5.8.4.3. The typological chasm

As a final illustration of the profound syntactic difference between embedding and serializing languages, compare the benefactive construction in two VO languages that have utilized the very same — near universal — source for benefactive marking, the verb 'give'. The verb-serializing language is Akan; the embedding language is Highlands Ecuadorian Spanish.

(83) **Serial benefactive construction in Akan** (Osam 1993a):

    a. Araba **re**-yɛ   asɔr   **a**-ma   Kofi

       A.   PROG-make prayer NAR-give K.

       'Araba is praying for Kofi'

    b. Esi **ro**-tur-**no**   **a**-ma   Kofi

       E. PROG-carry-**her** NAR-give Kofi

       'Esi carries her (the child) for Kofi'

    c. Esi **ro**-tur   abofra no **a**-ma-**no**

       E. PROG-carry child the NAR-give-**him**

       'Esi carries the child for him (Kofi)'

(84) **Embedding benefactive construction in Highlands Ecuadorian Spanish** (Haboud 1993):

    a. El **le**-dio   preparando el pan a   ella

       He **her**-give/PRET/3s prepare/PAR the bread OBJ her

       'He prepared the bread for her'

       (> instead of her doing it for herself)

    b. **se**-**lo**-dio   preparando

       her-**it**-give/PRET/3s prepare/PAR

       'He prepared it for her'

       (> instead of *her* doing it for herself)

In the hierarchic embedding syntax of Spanish, the semantically empty, grammaticalized 'give' — unattested in other Ecuadorian dialects — follows the normal pattern of Spanish auxiliaries: It persists as the syntactic finite main verb and attracts all finite inflection, including the direct-object pronoun that belongs semantically to the non-finite main verb. In the verb-serializing Akan, the semantically empty grammaticalized 'give' is the second ('serial') verb. It either carries the 'spread' finite inflection, or the less-finite 'narrative' prefix. And object pronouns remain dispersed, following their semantically relevant verbs.

When a semantically empty grammaticalized auxiliary — the syntactic main verb — finally cliticizes in an embedding language, **clause union** most often ensues, and the finite inflections that were carried on the auxiliary now attach themselves, together with the auxiliary, to the growing morphology of the complex verbal word. This can be seen with the causative 'make' in Spanish (VO):

(85)   **Clause union in the Spanish causative:**
se-lo-hizo-comer   el pan   a   su esposa
her-it-make/PRET/3s-eat the bread OBJ his wife
'He made his wife eat the bread'

When the embedding language is OV-ordered, the mirror image construction is obtained. This pattern may be seen with the benefactive suffix -kụ, in Ute. Ute has, strictly speaking, no verb 'give'; the verb 'feed' with an obligatory dative pronoun is used in this sense. The benefactive suffix -kụ, is most likely the grammaticalized verb kụụ, 'take', 'pick up', perhaps through the sense 'take to', thus 'give to'. The benefactive use may be seen in:[45]

(86)   **Clause union in the Ute benefactive:**
mama-ci   'uwa-y tụka-pi   'uni-kụ-xay-'u
woman-OBJ DEF-OBJ food-OBJ make-BEN-ANT-her
'(He) made food for the woman'

    In serial-verb languages like Akan or Ijo, the dispersal of verbs among their logical (or historic) objects makes it much less likely for a gram-maticalized serial verb to stand adjacent to — and thus co-lexicalize with — the 'main' verb. True clause union, in the sense of assembling one finite verb to which all grammatical relations pertain in an erstwhile multi-verb clause, is much harder to affect in serializing languages. While semantically the very same verbs grammaticalize in both configurations, the syntactic consequences of the grammaticalization are rather different. Which is another way of saying that the typological difference between embedded and serial VPs is far from trivial.

5.9.   Discussion

5.9.1.   The generative paradigm as problem generator

> "...Theoretical paradigms are themselves responsible for the problems researchers have to tackle within them..." (Sebba 1987:211)

    The paradigm that engendered the universal VP node, and with it the need to define grammatical relations (and other grammatical phenomena) configura-tionally, marches to a distinct theoretical drummer. It answers to a coherent set of core assumptions about the nature of language **universals** and the balance between universality and diversity:

(87) **Core assumptions of the Generative paradigm**:

    (a) **The abstractness of universals**:
        Universals of language are highly abstract and formal.

    (b) **The uniform application of universals**:
        Universals of language are present in all languages to exactly the same degree.

    (c) **The superficiality of cross-language diversity**:
        Surface typological diversity is superficial.

    (d) **The discreteness of grammatical categories**:
        Grammatical categories are discrete either/or entities.

    (e) **The inviolability of grammatical rules**:
        Grammatical rules are exceptionless and impervious to semantic and pragmatic context.

The conflation of assumptions (87) impels theoreticians within the Generative paradigm to posit one (highest) universal VP node that is unambiguously present in all languages. Cross-linguistic typological diversity that challenges the validity of such a higher node indeed poses a genuine distress within the paradigm. The various formal accounts of verb serialization since the 1970s have been motivated by an implicit need to preserve the paradigm at all costs. Of all the paradigm's salient features, it is assumption (87c) — that cross-language diversity is only superficial — that fairly guarantees successful preservation. The configurational accounts of verb serialization as lower-level branching under the highest VP node (Sebba 1987; Larson 1991) or even all the way down to lexical nodes (Lefebvre, ed. 1991) seem to both take their cue from assumption (87c) and guarantee its preservation. The universal "highest" VP node and a universal configurational rendition of grammatical relations are both central to this preservation effort.

    One formal account that, to my knowledge, has never been entertained, would be to depict serial clauses as lacking a "highest" VP node. Rather, they may have two or more VPs that branch directly under the clause node (S):

(88)

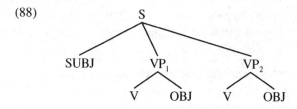

The most substantive argument against (88) would be essentially semantic: It does not provide the same formal configurational account of subject-predicate relations in verb-serializing languages as has been provided for hierarchic embedding languages. But as noted above, the very same argument can be made against the various higher-VP configurational account of verb serialization, whether coordinate or subordinate. To illustrate this, contrast again the Miskitu SS- and DS-serial clauses (68c) and (69c):

(68c)   **SS-Serial-verb clause:**
Baha usus-ka   pali-**i**   wa-**n**
that   buzzard-CNS fly-**PAR/SS** go-**PAST/3**
'That buzzard flew away'
(Lit.: 'The buzzard flew and went away')

(69c)   **DS-serial-verb clause:**
Yang truk-kum atk-**ri**   wa-**n**
I   truck-a   sell-**DS/1** go-**PAST/3**
'I sold the truck off'
(Lit.: 'I sold the truck and it went off')

In the SS-serial clause (68c) a single subject-predicate configurational account can be given, with the single subject pertaining to a single (higher) VP node and thus to its conjoined daughter-VPs. In the DS-serial clause (69c), this account will work only for the first (serial) verb, but not for the second (finite) verb, whose subject is different and is in fact the object of the first (serial) verb.

The problems inherent in (88), and of all other configurational accounts of verb serialization, do not arise from the specifics of the account — deep vs. shallow level of embedding. Rather, the problems are inherent in all configurational accounts of grammatical relations. This approach dates back to Chomsky's (1965) sensible idea that "deep structures must support semantic interpretation". The gist of this disarming observation may be given as the observation that "simple clauses are semantically transparent". Not only is this observation empirically well supported, but it reflects the **markedness** (or meta-iconicity) principle that (chapter 2):

(89)   **Isomorphism between syntactic and semantic markedness:**
"Clauses that are more complex semantically will also
tend to be more complex syntactically"

The semantic opacity that arises via synchronic embedding or synchronic conjunction can always be "handled" transformationally, by mapping complex surface structures back to their semantically-transparent deep structures. But as always, diachronic processes of grammaticalization gum up the works. In this case, they produce various types of semantically-simple clauses that continue to reflect the syntax of their complex precursors. In the case of embedding languages, grammaticalized auxiliaries, directionals and causatives retain main-verb syntactic status long after becoming de-semanticized. So that clauses that are now semantically simple retain the complex **embedding** syntax of multi-verb embedded clauses. In the case of serializing languages, erstwhile conjoined clause-chains have condensed over time into serial-verb clauses. So clauses that are now semantically simple retain, often for quite a while, the complex **coordinate** syntax of conjoined clause-chains. In both instances, a clean synchronic configurational account of grammatical relations is the chief victim of diachronic change.

The configuration (88) does account rather well for the distribution of grammatical **objecthood**,[46] whose scope is restricted to the more concrete ('lowest') VP nodes. The same is of course true of the other configurational accounts. It may well be, however, that to the Generative adept (88) presents a deeper theoretical drawback: It elevates cross-language diversity to much-too-high a level within the hierarchic structure of the clause.

5.9.2. Constituency and the VP node

The facts surveyed above do not contravene the existence of a VP node. Rather, they demonstrate the great complexity of determining constituency on strict empirical grounds without the illicit invocation of pre-empirical assumptions.[47] This complexity is due first to the fact that the VP node — even in embedding languages — requires substantiation by a cluster of semantic, pragmatic, syntactic and morphological criteria. And those criteria do not always mesh. So that a theoretical paradigm that defines its categories in strict either/or terms (cf. (87d)) is ill equipped to deal with this complexity, which fairly cries for a **prototype** approach to categorization.[48]

Ontologically, rule complexity and synchronic-surface mess are almost always the footprints of diachronic change, which scrambles the idealized correspondence between surface syntactic structure and semantic interpretation. Within the Generative paradigm, the iconic principle (89) pertains only to abstract deep structures. In a cognitively oriented, empirically responsible framework, principle (89) is meaningful only vis-a-vis surface structure. Semantically opaque surface structures are real, and they must impel us to concede the real bounds of iconicity.[49]

5.9.3. Alternative means of signalling constituency: Adjacency and morphological binding

Spatio-temporal adjacency is one of the most fundamental, iconic signals of constituency, in that things that belong together cognitively tend to appear adjacent in the speech signal. When adjacency is breached for whatever reason, other means of signalling "belonging together" can often be employed. Morphological agreement between the head noun and its modifiers — in case, gender/class or plurality — is one such means. One of the most striking examples of the use of this device can be seen in Walbiri when NP components are scattered. Head-modifier case agreement is optional in Walbiri and is routinely dispensed with when the head and modifier are adjacent. The case suffix then appears once at the end of the NP. When the head and modifier are scattered, however, case agreement becomes obligatory (Hale 1976):

> (90) a. tjantu wiri-**nki** tji yalku-nu
> dog   big-**ERG** mebite-PAST
> 'The big dog bit me'
> b. tjantu-**nku** tju yalku-nu wiri-**nki**
> dog-**ERG**   me bite-PAST big-**ERG**
> 'The dog bit me (,) the big one'
> c. wirin-**nki** tji yalku-nu tyantu-**nku**
> big-**ERG**   mebite-PAST dog-**ERG**
> 'The big one bit me (,) the dog'

5.9.4. The reality of grammar

Complexity and baffling inconsistencies are the stock in trade of the functionally- and empirically-oriented grammarian. To ignore complexity and abide by the simple strictures of The Paradigm (87) is certainly not a viable option. But complexity need not obviate the fact that grammatical categories do exist, that they are highly though never wholly discrete, and that both their existence and their discreteness have unimpeachable cognitive motivation. All of which boils down, once again, to stating the obvious.

Notes

1) One of the early harbingers of grammatical functionalism, Chafe (1970), was titled *Meaning and the Structure of Language*. An equally eloquent more recent manifesto of the functionalist network, Haiman (ed., 1985), was called *Iconicity in Syntax*.

2) A virtual avalanche of recent literature on grammaticalization describes this "emergence", cf. Traugott and Heine (eds, 1991); Heine *et al.* (1991); Hopper and Traugott (1993), *inter alia*.

3) In epistemology and the philosophy of science, the periodic oscillation between extreme positions is only too well documented; see Givón (1979a, ch. 1; 1989, ch. 8)

4) See chapter 8 below.

5) See chapter 9 below.

6) The connection between rhythmic packaging and what is or is not a single constituent is indeed an abductive hypothesis about the role of intonation and pauses in signalling the boundaries between cognitive units. The experimental support for this hypothesis was reported by Eisler-Goldman (1968); see also Chafe (1987); Givón (1991b).

7) See Keenan-Ochs and Bennett (1977), Ochs (1979), Givón (1979a, ch. 5).

8) We have noted this principle already in the discussion of complementation in chapter 4, and will return to it at various junctures below.

9) For non-verbal predicate, one should of course include here the predicate adjective or noun.

10) For some of the old lore, see Postal (1964).

11) The notions 'subject' and 'predicate' suffuse *The Categories, De Interpretatione* and the *Prior Analytic* (Barnes, ed. 1984, vol. I), forming the very matrix for Aristotle's analysis of meaning, truth and entailment.

12) Other syntactic processes that can illustrate either one or both joint extraction and joint anaphoric reference are relativization, clefting, Y-movement, complementation ('equi') and raising. Of course, one cannot always guarantee that different syntactic tests will yield the very same results. This is a methodological problem with giant theoretical ramifications, going to the very heart of the notion *category* (see chapter 6). The data of L-dislocation cited below is by necessity artificial, due to the need to keep the examples contrastive. The validity of such data rests, of course, on the assumptions that examples of the same *type* can be found in actual text.

13) This contrast predates language and the human mind by a wide margin, being rooted in the primate visual information processing (see chapter 9).

14) Also referred to by Chomsky (1968) citing Hubel's work on vision.

15) See Haiman (1985), Bybee (1985), Givón (1991a); see also (9) above.

16) Mithun's 'classificatory' incorporation involves situations where either a referring noun, a modifier or an anaphoric pronoun appears independently outside the verb, but a more generic 'classificatory' noun is incorporated into the verb. This may be true of both subject *and* object incorporation. In the latter, it may result, over time, in classificatory verbs of the type found in Iroquois and Athabascan.

17) The syntactic arguments for this in ergative languages are well known (see e.g. Dixon 1972). But in most languages the most common antipassive construction remains object-deletion or object incorporation (see chapter 3 as well as Givón 1990b, ch. 14).

18) In nominative languages like English and Ute, the case-marking of the subject is the same for intransitive and transitive clauses.

19) I combined the anaphoric pronoun with zero/agreement for Hebrew because the bulk of pronouns in Modern Hebrew are anaphoric and unstressed, and in that way resembles the functional profile of obligatory subject agreement ("zero") in languages such as Sacapultec or Spanish. The Sacapultec pronouns, on the other hand, are contrastive/stressed pronouns. The Hebrew situation thus closely resemble the current situation of Spoken French, where the subject pronouns have become obligatory subject agreement (Givón 1976). This was already true for object pronouns in Biblical Hebrew (Fox 1983), but has been extended to subject pronoun in Modern Hebrew.

20) See Givón (1971a; 1973a; 1984b, ch. 8); Steele (1978); Heine (1993); *inter alia*.

21) The development of -*na* 'have/be with' as a present tense probably followed an indirect route, most likely first through *perfect* or *immediate past*.

22) The development of -*li* as past tense probably followed an indirect route, most likely with several intermediate steps, with the first one most likely being the *progressive* past.

23) See Givón (1980a). The language currently has pragmatically-controlled ('free') word-order, but most grammaticalization still conforms to the earlier SOV pattern. Subject and object pronominal agreement is optional in Ute. When used, anaphoric pronouns appear as second position clitics.

24) The subject most commonly remains unexpressed on the embedded verb due to coreference with the main-clause subject. It is, of course, already expressed on the main verb.

25) See Givón (1991b).

26) The very same word-order situation (S-AUX-DO-V-IO) is found in Guaymi, a Chibchan language from Panama. The evidence for serial-verb origin of the auxiliaries there is just as compelling (Young and Givón 1990). Serial TAM constructions are also found in SVO languages, such as Tok Pisin, Krio and Kwa languages (see below).

27) See Givón (1991b).

28) See *ibid*.

29) See discussion in Givón (1990b, chapters 13, 19).

30) Most of the early arguments were confined to African linguistics; see Stahlke (1970), Hyman (1971), Awobuluyi (1973), Bamgbose (1973, 1974), Schachter (1974a, 1974b), with Li and Thompson (1973, 1974) the lone areal exception.

31) See Sebba (1987); Byrne (1987, 1992); Lefebvre (ed. 1991); *inter alia*.

32) This hurdle, rooted in the Aristotelian assumption of "one verb, one proposition", is not yet stone dead; see Givón (1991b).

33) In one of the languages he discusses, a dialect of Akan, it turns out that the crucial data of TAM-spreading had been misrepresented by a 19 Century linguist (Christaller; see Osam 1993a).

34) The possibility of *lexical* verb serialization had been suggested by Les Bruce (1985), in the context of a functionalist account of serial verbs in Alamblak. In that Papuan language, some serial verbs are clearly co-lexicalized. A similar suggestion was made for Kalam in Givón (1991b).

Lefebvre's (1991) formal treatment purports to "lower" the scope of serial branching to the level of lexical nodes, at least at some stage of the derivation.

35) See Givón (1991b).

36) See *ibid*.

37) See *ibid*.

38) This diachronic observation was made in Hyman (1971).

39) In these contexts, Hale (1991) labels the participial SS-medial suffix *-i* of Miskitu "proximate", and the DS-medial marker *-ka* "obviative", thus suggesting that a direct vs. inverse contrast is involved (see chapter 3). It is not clear that this is a necessary conclusion, although the two contrasts — proximate/obviate and SS/DS — have a certain functional overlap.

40) The Ijo data cited below dispense with tone and vowel-height markings, with apology to Kay Williamson.

41) Williamson (1991) calls the inflectional suffix *-ni* that appears on some non-final verbs "euphonic".

42) If they were embedded complement constructions, the main verb in a strict SOV language should precede its complement (cf. Young and Givón 1990).

43) In (82c) above the very same modality verb 'can' appears without the inflection.

44) See Osam (1993a) for the gradual grammaticalization of Akan serial verbs.

45) See Givón (1980a).

46) For discussion of this in Akan see Osam (1993b) as well as chapter 6 below.

47) No empirical work is wholly free of such presuppositions, but clear bounds must be imposed on the extent to which they are allowed to proliferate, compete with, and on occasion altogether submerge empirical considerations.

48) See Rosch (1973, 1975), Rosch and Lloyd (eds 1978), Rosch and Mervis (1975), Hyman and Frost (1975), Posner and Keele (1968), Posner (1969, 1986), Tversky (1986), Givón (1989, ch. 2), *inter alia*. This issue comes up again in the discussion of grammatical relations (chapter 6).

49) See chapters 2,3.

6

Taking Structure Seriously, II:
Grammatical Relations

6.1. Introduction*

Grammatical roles, by whatever name, occupy a privileged position in clausal syntax. They form the very matrix of the grammar of simple clauses, as well as of the major grammatical processes[1] associated with syntactic complexity — promotion to direct object, de-transitivization, complementation and causativization, nominalization, relativization, raising, and various types of anaphoric reference. The bulk of functionalist work on grammatical relations has tended to center on documenting and explaining the functional correlates of subjecthood and direct objecthood (see eg. Zubin 1972, 1979; Hawkinson and Hyman 1974; Givón 1976a, 1983 ed., 1984a, 1984b, 1992; Cooreman 1982, 1985, 1988; Rude 1985, 1987; *inter alia*). One important early functionalist volume, Li (ed., 1976), contained a number of papers dealing with more formal aspects of subjecthood. But otherwise functionalists have contended themselves for the most part with the comforting observation that:

- There was a strong ('iconic') correlation between being the subject and being the main clausal topic;
- There was likewise a strong ('iconic') correlation between being the direct object and being the secondary topic.
- One could thus safely ignore grammatical relations, since they mapped so reliably onto pragmatic function(s).

The study of grammatical relation was thus ceded to various formal schools such as Relational Grammar (henceforth RG), Lexical-Functional Grammar (henceforth LFG) or Government and Binding (henceforth GB), where the empirical integrity of the observed facts has become increasingly beclouded by formal, theory-internal considerations.

In the preceding chapter we have dealt with several aspects of grammatical relations, those that pertained to constituency, abstract nodes, and in particular to the status of a single ("highest") VP node. In this chapter we will focus more explicitly on the formal properties associated with grammatical relations: nominal case-marking, verbal agreement, word-order and behavoral constraints. We will embed the rule-governed behavior of subjects and objects in a general theory of human categorization. We will note how such a general theory accommodates some of the more conspicuous off-prototype organization of grammatical relations, such as those found in serializing and ergative languages. We will close by surveying the adjustment in grammatical relation that is inevitably precipitated by clause-union.

6.2. Semantic vs. grammatical case: The dissociation test

Within Generative Grammar, the resurgence of interest in case-roles may be dated back to Gruber (1965) and Fillmore (1968). However, both of those concerned themselves primarily with the grammatical consequences of **semantic roles** (agent, patient, dative, benefactive, location, instrument, etc.). To demonstrate, even in the most superficial way, that a case-role is grammatical rather than semantic, one must demonstrate its **dissociation** from semantic roles. That is, one must show that it admits more than one semantic case-role. For a nominative language such as English, with unmarked subject and direct object, such a demonstration is relatively easy:

(1)　**Multiple semantic roles of the grammatical subject:**
　　a. **Patient of state:**
　　　She is tall
　　b. **Patient of change:**
　　　She is falling
　　c. **Dative:**
　　　She is dreaming
　　d. **Agent:**
　　　She is writing a letter

(2)   **Multiple semantic roles of the grammatical object:**
  a. **Patient of state:**
     He saw her
  b. **Patient of change:**
     He pushed her
  c. **Ablative:**
     He approached her
  d. **Allative:**
     He left her
  e. **Ingressive:**
     He entered the house
  f. **Dative:**
     He gave her a book
  g. **Benefactive:**
     He built her a house

There are, of course, languages where the grammatical role of either subject or direct object is not marked by a unifying morphology. In the most extreme case, that of active-stative languages (Lakota, Choctaw), the nominal morphology of what would pass for subject in the English is split according to semantic roles (agent, patient, dative). Nominal arguments in such a language retain their semantically-sensitive case morphology regardless of whether they are subjects or objects. A less extreme situation may be seen in ergative languages, where subject case-marking is split according to transitivity (see section 6.6. below). In both types, however, other criteria for subjecthood — word-order, behavior-and-control properties — may still reveal the formal unity of the categories subject or direct object. Likewise, in many — perhaps most — languages the nominal morphology of what passes for direct-object in English is confined to mostly the patient semantic role. No morphological provisions are made in such languages for promoting non-patient objects into this case-role.[2] But again, other criteria for direct objecthood, such as word-order and behavioral constraints, reveal the formal unity of the category direct object even when it is not morphologically unified.

6.3.   Empirical criteria for grammatical relations

6.3.1.   The prototype clustering approach to categories

Formal accounts of grammatical case within the generative paradigm, such as those given by RG or GB, have most often backed themselves into a corner by having to define subjecthood and objecthood in totally discrete terms. Such an approach to categories requires the linguist to make painful and sometimes arbitrary choices among the various grammatical properties (membership criteria) that *tend* to cluster around the subject or direct object. When two criteria clash, as is often the case, one of them must be adjudicated as counting more than the other. And NPs with intermediate — borderline — properties are then forced into either one or another discrete category. The universal validity of ranking our multiple criteria for subjecthood or objecthood relative to each other is a thorny issue in the cross-linguistic study of grammatical relations. In typological comparisons, the discrete single-criterion approach to categorization can lead to considerable mischief. The subject in languages that abide by the designated single criterion is counted as subject. The subject in languages that lack that single criterion is counted as non-subject, in spite of the fact that it still abides by many other criteria for subjecthood.[3]

The approach I pursue here owes its cognitive foundations to an alternative theory of human categorization elaborated by Eleanor Rosch.[4] Within this approach, the membership in a natural category need not be determined by a single feature, but rather by a **cluster** of characteristic features. The most typical members of a category are those that display the greatest number of those features, and may be thus considered the category's **prototype**. The majority of members display a great number of the clustered features; they thus closely resemble the prototype. In statistical terms, such members distribute within close proximity of the population's **mean**. But a minority of the membership may display fewer of the characteristic features; they are less like the prototype, and are further away from the population's mean. The prototype approach to categorization allows the cognitive psychologist, the linguist, and presumably the information-processing organism to reconcile two conflicting aspects of natural categories:

- The bulk of the members of a population are easily and unambiguously assigned to distinct categories.
- A certain residual fluidity, flexibility, and context-dependent discrimination is retained, allowing change, variation, and learning to be accommodated.[5]

In such a pragmatic compromise, the ambiguous categorial status of a small minority of a population does not impinge on the unambiguous status and rapid processing of the bulk.

6.3.2.   The clustering approach to grammatical relations

Something resembling a prototype clustering approach to grammatical relations was first suggested in two pioneering papers by Edward L. Keenan. In the first, Keenan (1975) notes that three **overt coding properties** tend to be associated with grammatical subjects:

(a)   word-order
(b)   verb agreement
(c)   nominal case morphology

He further notes that the cross-linguistic study of passive-clause subjects reveals a biased distribution of these three properties: Languages that have (c) tend to also have (b); those that have (b) tend to also have (a); but not vice versa. An implicational hierarchy thus characterizes the cross-linguistic distribution of the three coding properties of passive subjects:

(3)   **Implicational hierarchy of coding properties
       of passive subjects** (Keenan 1975):

       nominal case-marking > verb agreement > word-order

In his second paper, Keenan (1976) extends this approach to a larger cluster of properties. In addition to the overt coding properties (3), two groups of properties are suggested:

• Functional properties: semantic, referential, pragmatic
• Formal properties: rule-governed behavior in relevant syntactic environments

The functional properties considered by Keenan (1976) may be summarized as:

(4)   **Functional properties of grammatical subjects** (Keenan 1976):
       a. independent existence
       b. indispensability
       c. absolute, presupposed or persistent reference
       d. definiteness
       e. topicality
       f. agentivity

With the exception of agentivity (4f), which is probably misplaced on the list,[6] Keenan's functional properties are all reference-related, and can be reduced to (or derived from) a single property — **topicality**. That is, they are all predictable reflections of the fact that the clause's grammatical subject tends to code the current discourse topic at the time when the clause is being processed. This is not to suggest that more formal properties are completely predictable from topicality, nor that they are completely divorced from it. But rather, that the mapping between the formal and the functional properties in grammar is not always obvious, and that even in the best cases such mapping depends in part on an elaborate chain of theoretical reasoning.[7]

In discussing the advantages of his clustering approach to grammatical subjecthood, Keenan (1976: 323–331) notes that such an approach accommodates the well-documented observation that the subjects of complex ("non-basic") clauses tend to display fewer subject properties than the subjects of the simple ("basic") clause. In other words, in the same language the subjects of simple clauses tend to be more prototypical than the subjects of the complex clauses.[8] This observation harkens back to Keenan's earlier paper (1975). Indeed, it is only in the limited context of passive clauses that Keenan (1976) notes the cross-linguistic implications of his clustering approach — that the subject in some languages displays more subject properties than the subject in other languages. Or put another way, that the grammaticalization of the pragmatic function "main clausal topic" is a matter of degree and may thus exhibit typological variation.

Two other papers in the Li (ed., 1976) volume skate near the clustering approach to subjecthood. Li and Thompson (1976) argue for a typology of topic-prominent vs. subject-prominent languages. On further inspection, their suggestion boils down to the fact that topic-prominent languages tend to lack two of the overt morphological coding properties on Keenan's list — case marking and verb agreement. Lacking an explicit clustering framework, Li and Thompson use the term "topic-prominent" as a stand-in for "morphologically less-marked", "less grammaticalized" or "less prototypical" subject.[9] In a somewhat similar vein, Anderson (1976) notes that in "deep" ergative languages both overt-morphological and formal-behavioral properties reveal the same ergative-absolutive split. In "shallow" ergative languages, on the other hand, only the morphology reveals this split, while behavior-and-control properties follow a nominative-accusative pattern. Within a clustering approach, this again boils down to observing that relational categories such as ergative, absolutive, nominative and accusative grammaticalize in different languages to different degrees.

6.4.   Formal properties of subjects and objects

6.4.1.   Preamble

Keenan (1976: 324) divides the formal properties of grammatical subjects into two separate clusters — **overt coding properties** (3) and **behavior-and-control properties**. His analysis can be easily extended to grammatical relations in general. This extension is not only possible but may be unavoidable, because most often it is the *contrast* between subject and object or between direct and indirect object — rather than the single relation itself — that is marked by formal properties (Wierzbicka 1981). A more-or-less exhaustive list of Keenan's behavior-and-control properties includes:

(5)   **Behavior-and-control properties of grammatical roles**:
       a. promotion to direct object
       b. demotion from direct object (antipassive)
       c. passivization
       d. reflexivization
       e. causativization
       f. equi-NP reference in complementation
       g. raising
       h. possessor promotion
       i. anaphoric reference in chained clauses
       j. co-reference in relativization, WH-question,
          cleft constructions and participial clauses

The applicability — or relevance — of formal properties in (3) and (5) to a particular grammatical relation is then determined by answering the question:

"Does one need to mention a particular grammatical relation
 in the definition of a particular grammatical property?"

When the answer is yes, the property is relevant; when the answer is no, it is irrelevant. But the relevance of particular properties to particular grammatical relations is highly selective, both within the same language and cross-linguistically. In the following sections we will illustrate this briefly.

6.4.2.   Overt coding properties

Overt coding properties (3) have always figured prominently in determining the grammatical roles of clausal participants. But an exclusive reliance on these properties is not without problems. To begin with, as Keenan (1976) has pointed out, overt coding properties cluster most reliably around the subject of simple ("basic") clauses, but much less so around the subject of complex ("non-basic") clauses. Further, the applicability of overt coding properties to grammatical relations even in simple clauses varies from one language to another, or within the same language from one case-role to the other. For example, Modern Hebrew has rigid SVO order, a morphologically-unmarked subject, morphologically-marked definite/direct object and indirect objects, and obligatory subject agreement. In such a language, all three overt coding properties are relevant to grammatical relations. But they are not relevant to the same degree. Word-order is relevant to all grammatical relations. Case marking is relevant to objects, and only by contrast to subjects. And grammatical agreement is relevant only to subjects.

In languages with flexible (pragmatically controlled) word-order, word-order is not relevant to grammatical relations. Thus in Spanish and Biblical Hebrew (rigid VO, flexible S), word-order is relevant to the object but not to the subject. And in languages like Papago, Ute, Walbiri or Nez Perce (flexible S,O), word-order is not relevant to any grammatical relation.

In languages with no verb agreement, such as Mandarin, verb agreement is obviously irrelevant to grammatical relations. On the other hand, in languages with both subject and object agreement, such as Swahili or Spanish, verb agreement is relevant to both grammatical relations. Similarly, in languages with partial or altogether absent nominal case morphology, nominal case-marking is obviously irrelevant to grammatical relations. English partially resembles such a language, in that both the subject and direct object are morphologically unmarked, but indirect objects are marked. Other languages may go further along this typological dimension, in having little or no nominal case morphology. In the following section I will describe briefly a more radical example of such a language, in which the bulk of case-marking morphology is loaded on the verb.

6.4.3.   Verb-coding of grammatical roles

A milder case of verb-coding of both the subject and object roles has been described in various Philippine languages, whether interpreted as nominative (Schachter 1976; Givón 1979a) or ergative (Brainard 1994). Similar situations involving only the object role have been described in KinyaRwanda (Kimenyi 1976) and Nez Perce (Rude 1985). In these two languages, direct objects are marked uniformly regardless of their semantic role. For patient direct-objects, this nominal marking suffices. When a non-patient is promoted to direct object status, an added verbal affix marks its semantic role.

Perhaps the most radical example of verb-coding of case-roles is found in the Campa Arawak languages of Peru.[10] In these languages, there is virtually no nominal case-marking of NPs, with the exception of one semantically-bleached locative affix. Subject pronominal agreement by verb prefix is near obligatory. Direct-object pronominal agreement by verb suffix is optional, and is controlled by pragmatic considerations of topicality. Somewhat reminiscent of Kinya-Rwanda and Nez Perce, the semantic role of many non-patient objects is often marked by a verb affix. Thus (from Machiguenga):[11]

(6)   **Intransitive clause:**
impogini **i**-kam-ana-i   o-ime
then   3m-die-DIR-REAL 3f-husband
'...then her husband died...'

(7)   **Transitive clause, DO = topical patient:**
no-nevent-av-aka-**ri**   no-tineri
1-see/DIST-RECIP-PERF-**3m** 1-son-in-law
'...I saw my son in law in the distance...'

(8)   **Transitive, DO = anaphoric topical patient:**
i-kisa-vintsa-vaget-ake-**ro**-tyo
3m-mistreat-DES-DUR-PERF-**3f**-EMPH
'...he was very mean to her...'

(9)   **Transitive, DO = non-topical patient:**
a. **o**-g-unte-ta   onko-shi
3f-eat-DUR-MOM uncucha-leaf
'...she ate *uncucha* leaves...'
b. **i**-aga-vaget-i-ra   o-tineri   i-vatsa
3m-get-DUR-REAL-SUB 3f-son-in-law 3m/CL-meat
'...when her son-in-law got meat...'

(10) a. **Less-topical ASSOC object:**
o-mag-**imo**-ig-a-i   o-ishinto
3f-sleep-ASSOC-PL-HAB-REAL 3f-daughter
'...she lived with her daughters...'

b. **More topical ASSOC object:**
o-mag-**imo**-ta-i-**ri**-ra   o-tineri
3f-sleep-ASSOC-HAB-REAL-**3m**-SUB 3f-son.in.law
'...living with her son-in-law...'

Dative objects are obligatorily promoted to DO, but the verb is not obligatorily coded for their semantic case-role:

(11) a. **Verb unmarked for semantic case-role:**
ga-ra   **pi**-p-aig-i-**ro**   p-iniro
NEG-SUB **2**-give-PL-REAL-**3f** 2-mother
'...(he said:) Don't give your mother (any)...'
b. **Verb marked for trans-locative case-role:**
o-m-p-**u**-te-**na**   no-shinto   kamona
3f-IRR-give-TRSL-IRR-**1** 1-daughter chonta-palm
'...my daughters may give me chonta-palm...'

Among overt coding properties, word-order is obviously important for defining grammatical relations in Machiguenga. But the locus of nominal case-marking has shifted away from the more common location — the noun or NP — to the verb, where pronominal agreement and case-role affixes have become integrated into a complex inflectional system.

6.4.4.   Behavior-and-control properties

6.4.4.1. The problem of applicability

Much like overt coding properties, behavior-and-control correlates of grammatical roles are not always applicable across the board. Within the same language, some rules-governed syntactic processes may be relevant only to the subject, or only to the object. In nominative languages, for example, promotion to direct-object (5a) or demotion from direct-object (antipassive; (5b)) are relevant only to the direct-object, but not to the subject. In ergative languages, on the other hand, grammatical processes that create or destroy direct-objects directly affect transitivity — and thus automatically also the case-role of the agent (ergative vs. absolute). In the same vein, morphological causativization tends to leave the embedded-clause object relatively unaffected, so that it most often retains the same grammatical role it had in the corresponding simple clause. In contrast, causativization is much more likely to affect the grammatical role of the *causee* (embedded-clause subject). And further, a considerable range of cross-language variation exists as to the grammatical role assigned to the causee (Comrie 1976; Cole 1984; see in section 6.8.2.2.1).

Across languages, some rules may be relevant to a particular grammatical relation in one language but not in another. For example, in Turkish, Ute or KinyaRwanda, separate patterns exist for subject vs. object relativization. In other words, relativization is sensitive to both grammatical relations in such languages. At the other extreme, in Japanese and Mandarin Chinese relativization takes the same pattern in all case-roles, and is thus altogether oblivious to grammatical relations. In the same vein, in languages with a promotional passive, passivization is often relevant to both the subject and direct object roles, as in English, KinyaRwanda or Nez Perce. On the other hand, in languages with a non-promotional impersonal passive, passivization is often relevant to only the subject (demoted agent) role, but not to the object, as in the Spanish *se*-passive or in Ute. The applicability of a particular behavior-and-control property to a particular grammatical role must be determined on a case-by-case and language-by-language basis.

6.4.4.2. Conflicts with overt coding properties

The prototype clustering approach to grammatical relations gives rise to one predicament that is not acknowledged in more discrete, either/or approaches to grammatical relations. This has to do with the fact that on occasion an overt coding property of a grammatical relation — say subject — conflicts with one or more behavior-and-control properties. A simple example will illustrate this. In general, the word-order criterion for direct objecthood conforms much better to the behavior-and-control criteria than does nominal case-marking. In English, the direct object in simple transitive clauses is morphologically unmarked, and directly follows the verb. In dative-shifted clauses, both objects appear morphologically unmarked. But only the first of the two unmarked objects, the semantic dative, is accessible to passivization. The second, the semantic patient, is not:

(12) a. **DAT-shifted clause:**
         She showed him a book
      b. **Dative-DO passive:**
         He was shown a book
      c. **Patient-DO passive:**
         *The/A book was shown him

In the corresponding non-shifted clause, on the other hand, word-order and case-marking coincide. The patient in this variant is both post-verbal and morphologically marked as DO, and only the patient is accessible to passivization:

(13) a. **Non-shifted clause:**
         She showed the book **to** two prospective buyers
      b. **Patient-SUBJ of passive:**
         The book was shown **to** two prospective buyers
      c. **Dative-SUBJ of passive:**
         *They were shown the/a book **to**

The same discrimination, this time in both passivization and relativization, is revealed in another "double direct-object" construction in English. Again, the object adjacent to the verb is accessible, the other one is not. Thus compare:

(14) a. **Underlying double-object clause:**
         They elected him president
      b. **First-OBJ relativization:**
         The man they elected president
      c. **Second-OBJ relativization:**
         *The president they elected him
      d. **First-OBJ passivization:**
         He was elected president
      e. **Second-OBJ passivization:**
         *The president was elected him

In the same vein, Keenan's (1975, 1976) cross-language comparisons clearly show that of the overt coding properties of subjects, word-order is the more universal one — it is more likely to persist in "non-basic" clause types such as the passive. That is, the topic of the de-transitive (passive or inverse) clause can occupy the typical subject position without necessarily displaying either the typical case-marking or control of verb agreement. Thus (Nepali):[12]

(15) a. **Active:**
         Ava-**le**   Maya-lay   hirka-y-**in**
         Ava-**ERG** Maya-**DAT** hit-**PAST-3sf**
         'Ava hit Maya'

b. **De-transitive**:
Maya-**lay** Ava-**dwara** hirka-i-y-o
Maya-DAT Ava-OBL   hit-DETRANS-PAST-3sm
'Maya was hit by Ava'

In the de-transitive clause (15b), the patient gains neither subject case-marking nor control of verb agreement. But being now the topical participant, the patient can assume the characteristic clause-initial position of the subject.

A ranking similar to Keenan's (1975) is implicit in Li and Thompson's (1976) typology of "subject prominent" vs. "topic-prominent" languages. The latter turn out to lack subject-related morphology, but not subject-related word-order. A similar ranking — this time of behavior-and-control criteria over morphological criteria — is also evident in Anderson's (1976) treatment of "deep" vs. "shallow" ergative languages. In the latter, the ergative-absolutive split affects only the morphology, while behavior-and-control properties follow a nominative-accusative split. Under their morphological glaze, "shallow" ergative languages are thus really — behaviorally — nominative-absolutive. In "deep" ergative languages, on the other hand, all subject properties are said to follow the ergative-absolutive split. These languages thus exhibit an ergative organization of grammatical relations in a 'deeper' sense. We will return to this issue further below, after surveying a representative sample of behavior-and-control criteria for grammatical relations.

6.4.4.3. Relativization and grammatical relations

In some languages, relativization is irrelevant to grammatical relations, since all case-roles are relativized by the very same strategy. This is true in Japanese, where the same gap strategy (zero anaphora) is used for all case-roles. Thus:[13]

(16) a. **Simple clause**:
otoko-ga onna-ni   tegami-o kaita
man-SUBJ woman-DAT letter-ACC wrote
'The man wrote a letter to the woman'
b. **Subject REL-clause**:
[Ø] onna-ni   tegami-o kaita otoko-wa...
woman-DAT letter-ACC wrote man-TOP
'the man who wrote a letter to the woman...'

   c. **Accusative REL-clause:**
     otoko-ga onna-ni [Ø] kaita tegami-wa...
     man-SUBJ woman-DAT wrote letter-TOP
     'the letter that the man wrote to the woman...'
   d. **Dative REL-clause:**
     otoko-ga [Ø] tegami-o kaita onna-wa...
     man-SUBJ   letter-ACC wrote woman-TOP
     'the woman to whom the man wrote a letter...'

In other languages, relativization strategy differentiates, to various degrees and by varying means, between grammatical roles. This may be seen in Hebrew, where the general relativization strategy is that of anaphoric pronouns. Since verb agreement is obligatory in Hebrew, subject relativization requires only the pronominal agreement on the verb:

(17) a. **Simple clause (anaphoric subject):**
     hi ba-**a**   hena etmol
     she came-**she** here yesterday
     'She came here yesterday'
   b. **Subject REL-clause:**
     ha-isha   **she**-ba-**a**   hena etmol...
     the-woman REL-came-**she** here yesterday
     'the woman who came here yesterday...'

For direct-object relativization, a post-verbal anaphoric pronoun is used — optionally in one-level embedding. That is, the strategy alternates with the Japanese gap strategy and the English word-order strategy:

(18) a. **Simple clause (anaphoric DO):**
     Yoav ohev ot-**a**
     Yoav loves DO-**her**
     'Yoav loves her'
   b. **REL-clause (NP-NP-V order):**
     ha-isha   **she**-Yoav ohev (ot-a)...
     the-woman REL-Yoav loves (DO-**her**)
     'the woman that Yoav loves...'

The anaphoric-pronoun relativization strategy becomes obligatory for indirect objects:

(19)   a. **Simple clause (anaphoric DAT object):**
Yoav natan   l-**a**   et-ha-sefer
Yoav gave-he to-**her** DO-the-book
'Yoav gave her the book'

   b. **REL-clause (anaphoric DAT object):**
ha-isha   **she**-Yoav natan   l-**a**   et-ha-sefer...
the-woman **REL**-Yoav gave-he to-**her** DO-the-book
'The woman to whom Yoav gave the book...'

In KinyaRwanda, relativization discriminates more explicitly among all three grammatical relations. One strategy is used for subjects, essentially the same one as in Hebrew (17).[14] Another one is used for the most common direct object — the patient. It is the same word-order cum gap (zero anaphora) strategy as in English. Thus compare:

(20)   a. **Main clause:**
umugabo **y**-a-kubis-e   abagore
man   **he**-PAST-hit-ASP women
'the man hit the women'

   b. **Subject REL-clause:**
umugabo **u**-a-kubis-e   abagore...
man   **he/REL**-PAST-hit-ASP women
'the man who hit the women...'

   c. **DO REL-clause (patient-DO):**
abagore umugabo y-a-kubis-e...
women man   he-PAST-hit-ASP
'the women that the man hit...

When the object to be relativized is not a patient, it must be first promoted to DO, a process through which it gains verb-marking of its semantic role. Only then can it be relativized. The promotion to DO system in KinyaRwanda is illustrated in:

(21)   a. **DO = patient:**
umugore y-ooher-eje   umubooyi **ku**-isoko
woman   she-send-ASP cook   LOC-market
'The woman sent the cook to the market'

   b. **DO = locative:**
umugore y-ooher-eke-**ho**   isoko umubooyi
woman   she-send-ASP-LOC market cook
'The woman sent to the market the cook'

(22) a. **DO = patient**:
umugabo ya-tem-eje igiti **n**-umupaanga
man   he-cut-ASP tree INSTR-saw
'The man cut the tree with a saw'

    b. **DO = instrument**:
umugabo ya-tem-ej-**eesha**   umupaanga igiti
man   he-cut-ASP-INSTR saw   tree
'The man used the saw to cut the tree'

(23) a. **DO = patient**:
Maria ya-tets-e   inkoko **n**-agahiinda
Mary she-cook-ASP chicken MANN-sorrow
'Mary cooked the chicken regretfully'

    b. **DO = manner**:
Maria ya-tek-**an**-ye   agahiinda inkoko
Mary she-cook-MANN-ASP sorrow   chicken
'Mary regretfully cooked the chicken'

(24) a. **DO = patient**:
umuhuungu ya-riimb-jye ururiimbi **na**-umugore
boy   he-sing-ASP song   ASSOC-woman
'The boy sang the song with the woman'

    b. **DO = associative**:
umuhuungu ya-riimb-**an**-ye   umugore ururiimbi
boy   he-sing-ASSOC-ASP woman song
'The boy sang with the woman a song'

(25) a. ***DO = patient (obligatory promotion)**:
*Yohani y-ooher-eje ibaruwa **ku**-Maria
John   he-send-ASP letter   DAT-Mary

    b. **DO = dative-benefactive**:
Yohani y-ooher-**er**-eje   Maria ibaruwa
John   he-send-BEN-ASP Mary letter
'John sent Mary a letter'

With such a promotional system available, KinyaRwanda exhibits a strong relational constraint on relativization:

(26)   **Relational constraints on relativization (KinyaRwanda):**
       a. Only subjects and direct objects are accessible to relativiza-
          tion.
       b. Non-patient objects must be promoted to DO before they can
          be relativized.

Thus compare:

(27)   a. **Locative REL-clause:**
          isoko   umugore y-ooher-eke-**ho**   umubooyi...
          market woman   she-send-ASP-LOC cook
          'The market the woman sent the cook to...'
       b. **Instrument REL-clause:**
          umupaanga umugabo ya-tem-ej-**eesha**   igiti...
          saw   man   he-cut-ASP-INSTR tree
          'The saw the man cut the tree with...'
       c. **Manner REL-clause:**
          agahiinda Maria ya-tek-**an**-ye   inkoko
          sorrow   Mary she-cook-MANN-ASP chicken
          'the regret with which Mary cooked the chicken...'
       d. **Associative REL-clause:**
          umugore umuhuungu ya-riimb-**an**-ye   ururiimbi...
          woman   boy   he-sing-ASSOC-ASP song
          'The woman with whom the boy sang the song...'
       e. **Dative-benefactive REL-clause:**
          umugore Yohani y-ooher-**er**-eje   ibaruwa...
          woman   John   he-send-BEN-ASP letter
          'the woman that John sent the letter to...'

Another relativization pattern involving strong relational constraints is
found in Philippine languages, such as Bikol. Interpreted as a nominative
language,[15] Bikol has a voice system in which all non-agents can be promoted
to subject/topic of the passive/inverse. In the passive/inverse clause, the promoted subject loses its normal active-clause semantic-role affix, but the semantic
role of the subject/topic is now coded on the verb. Thus consider:

(28)   a. **Agent-topic ('active voice'):**
          nag-ta'o '**ang**-lalake ning-libro sa-babaye
          AGT-give TOP-man   PAT-book DAT-woman
          'The man gave a book to the woman'

b. **Patient-topic ('passive-voice'#1):**
na-ta'o   kang-lalake 'ang-libro sa-babaye
PAT-give AGT-man   top-book DAT-woman
'The book was given to the woman by the man'

c. **Dative-topic ('passive-voice'#2):**
na-ta'o-an   kang-lalake ning-libro 'ang-babaye
DAT-give-DAT AGT-man   PAT-book TOP-woman
'The woman was given a book by the man'

(29) a. **Agent-topic ('active voice'):**
nag-putul 'ang-lalake ning-tubu **gamit**(-'ang)-lanseta
AGT-cut TOP-man   PAT-cane INSTR-knife
'The man cut sugar-cane with a knife'

b. **Instrument-topic ('passive-voice'#3):**
pinag-putul kang-lalake ning-tubu 'ang-lanseta
INSTR-cut AGT-man   PAT-cane TOP-knife
'The knife was used by the man to cut sugarcane'

(30) a. **Agent-topic ('active voice'):**
nag-bakal 'ang-lalake ning-kanding **para**-sa-babaye
AGT-buy TOP-man PAT-goat   BEN-DAT-woman
'The man bought a goat for the woman'

b. **Benefactive-topic ('passive-voice'#4):**
pinag-bakal-**an** kang-lalake ning-kanding 'ang-babaye
BEN-buy-DAT AGT-man   PAT-goat   TOP-woman
'The woman was bought a goat by the man'

This voice system is coupled to relativization by imposing the following relational constraint:

(31) **Relational constraints on Bikol relativization**
(Givón 1979a, ch. 4):
a. Only a subject is accessible to relativization, (i.e. can be the coreferentially-deleted argument in the REL-clause).
b. In order for a non-subject/agent of the active to be relativized, it must be first promoted to subject via inversion/passivization.

Examples of how the various semantic roles are relativized as subjects of the passive/inverse are given below:

(32) a. **Agent REL-clause:**
          marai 'ang-lalake **na**   **nag**-ta'o ning-libro sa-babaye
          good TOP-man   REL AGT-give PAT-book DAT-woman
          'The man who gave a book to the woman is good'
      b. **Patient REL-clause:**
          marai 'ang-libro **na**   **na**-ta'o   kang-lalake sa-babaye
          good TOP-book REL PAT-give AGT-man   DAT-woman
          'The book that was given to the woman by the man is good'
      c. **Dative REL-clause:**
          marai 'ang-babaye **na**   **na**-ta'o-**an**   kang-lalake ning-libro
          good TOP-woman REL DAT-give-DAT AGT-man   PAT-book
          'The woman that was given a book by the man is good'
      d. **Instrument REL-CLAUSE:**
          marai 'ang-lanseta **na**   **pinag**-putul kang-lalake ning-tubu
          good TOP-knife   REL INSTR-cut AGT-man   PAT-cane
          'The knife that was used by the man to cut sugar-cane is good'
      e. **Benefactive REL-clause:**
          marai 'ang-babaye **na**   **pinag**-bakal-**an** kang-lalake ning-kanding
          good TOP-woman REL BEN-buy-DAT AGT-man   PAT-goat
          'The woman that was bought a goat for by the man is good'

6.4.4.4. Passivization and grammatical relations

In principle, passivization can be relevant to all three grammatical relations, in languages where non-subjects of the active are promoted to *bona fide* grammatical subjects of the passive. In languages with a **non-promotional passive**, however, passivization is opaque to grammatical relations. In such languages, all non-subject NPs retain in the passive clause their active-clause case-marking. Most commonly, non-promotional passives impose no relational restrictions on the type of non-agent object that can become topic-of-passive — all non-agent semantic roles, direct and indirect object alike, can become topic-of-passive. As illustration, consider Ute (Uto-Aztecan), where in the passive clause only the non-agent topic can control pronominal agreement on the verb:[16]

(33) **Patient (DO):**
    a. **Active:**   ta'wá-ci̠ siv̠ą́atu-ci pa̠x̂á-qa
                   man-SUBJ goat-OBJ kill-ANT
                   'The man killed the goat'
    b. **Passive:** siv̠ą́atu-ci pa̠x̂á-**ta**-pu̠ga
                   goat-OBJ kill-PASS-REM
                   'Someone killed the goat'
                   'The goat was killed' (by someone)

(34) **Instrumental:**
    a. **Active:**   ta'wá-ci̠ wií-ci-**m**   tu̠ká-qa-'**u**
                   man-SUBJ knife-OBJ-INSTR eat-ANT-he
                   'The man ate with a knife'
    b. **Passive:** wií-ci-**m**   tu̠ká-**ta**-qa-ax̂
                   knife-OBJ-INSTR eat-PASS-ANT-**it**
                   'Someone ate with a knife'

(35) **Locative:**
    a. **Active:**   mamá-ci̠   tu̠vúpu̠-**vwan** 'aví-kya-'**u**
                   woman-SUBJ ground-OBJ-**on** lie-ANT-**she**
                   'The woman lay on the ground'
    b. **Passive:** tu̠vú-pu̠-**vwan** 'aví-ta-qa-ax̂
                   ground-OBJ-**on** lie-PASS-ANT-**it**
                   'Someone lay on the ground'

(36) **Associative:**
    a. **Active:**   máama̠-ci-u   'áapa-ci-**wa** wú̠u̠ka-qa-qa-**amu̠**
                   women-SUBJ-PL boy-OBJ-**with** work-PL-ANT-**they**
                   'The women worked with the boy'
    b. **Passive:** 'áapa-ci-**wa** wú̠u̠ka-qa-**ta**-qa-'**u**
                   boy-OBJ-**with** work-PL-PASS-ANT-**he**
                   'Some persons worked with the boy'

(37) **Manner:**
    a. **Active:**   mamá-ci̠   **pu̠ká**-wú̠u̠ka-qa-'**u**
                   woman-SUBJ **hard**-work-ANT-**she**
                   'The woman worked hard'
    b. **Passive:** **pu̠ká**-wú̠u̠ka-**ta**-qa
                   hard-work-PASS-ANT
                   'Someone worked hard'

Philippine languages such as Bikol,[17] where passivization discriminates between the subject and all object types lumped together (see (28), (29), (30) above), represent an intermediate typological situation. Passivization indeed furnishes evidence for the distinction between subject and non-subject, so that the grammatical relation 'subject' is indeed supported by this rule. But the rule is silent on the distinction between direct and indirect object. In other words, it does not support the grammatical relation 'direct object'.

In KinyaRwanda, finally, the very same promotion-to-DO mechanism used in relativization is also used in passivization. And this mechanism licenses a similar relational constraint on passivization as on relativization (see (26), (27) above):

(38)   a. Only direct objects can be made subjects of the passive.
       b. Before a non-patient object can be promoted to subject
          of the passive, it must be first promoted to DO.

In other words, promotion to DO in KinyaRwanda is an obligatory "feeder" to passivization. Thus compare:

(39)   a. **Patient subject-of-passive**:
          umubooyi y-ooher-ej-**we**   **ku**-isoko
          cook/SUBJ he-send-ASP-PASS LOC-market
          'The cook was sent to the market'
       b. **Locative subject-of-passive**:
          isoko   ry-ooher-ej-**we-ho**   umubooyi
          market/SUBJ it-send-ASP-PASS-LOC cook
          '*The market was sent the cook to'
          'Someone sent the cook to the market'
       c. **Instrument subject-of-passive**:
          umupaanga wa-tem-**eesh**-ej-**we**   igiti
          saw/SUBJ   it-cut-INSTR-ASP-PASS tree/OBJ
          'The saw was used to cut the tree'
       d. **Manner subject-of-passive**:
          agahiinda   ga-tek-**an**-w-e   inkoko
          sorrow/SUBJ it-cook-MANN-PASS-ASP chicken
          '*Regret was cooked the chicken with'
          'Someone cooked the chicken regretfully'

e. **Associative subject-of-passive:**
umugore   ya-riimb-**an-w**-e   ururiimbi
woman/SUBJ she-sing-ASSOC-PASS-ASP song/OBJ
'*The woman was sung a song with'
'Someone sang a song with the woman'

f. **Dative-benefactive subject-of-passive:**
Maria   y-ooher-**er**-ej-**we**   ibaruwa
Mary/SUBJ she-send-BEN-ASP-PASS letter/OBJ
'Mary was sent a letter'

6.4.4.5. Equi-NP deletion and grammatical relations

On a graded scale, the control of coreference in embedded complement
clauses — equi-NP deletion (henceforth equi) — comes as close as any syntactic
rule to being uniformly applied cross-linguistically as any relationally-governed
syntactic process. But even this process is not immune to some typological
variability. Within the same language, equi applies differentially to grammatical
relations in different types of complement-taking verbs. In modality verbs
('want', 'start', 'try' etc.), equi is relevant to the subject of both clauses:

(40)   **She** wanted [Ø] to leave

In manipulation verbs ('force', 'tell', 'make'), on the other hand, equi is relevant
to the subject of the complement and the object of the main clause:

(41)   She told **him** [Ø] to leave

In English and many other languages, the human object of manipulative
verbs (41) is unmistakably a direct object, so that equi can be formulated in
terms of the subject of the complement and the direct object of the main clause.
Equi is here relevant to both grammatical relations. In other languages, equi in
manipulative-verb complements is more problematic. In Hebrew, for example,
the manipulee takes different case-roles following different manipulation verbs:

(42)   a. hixrax-nu   **ot**-a   la-avor   dira
         force/PAST-we **DO**-her INF-move apartment
         'We forced her to switch apartments'
      b. amar-nu   **l**-a   la-avor dira
         tell/PAST-we **DAT**-her INF-move apartment
         'We told her to switch apartments'

    c. azar-nu   l-a   la-avor dira
       help/PAST-we DAT-her INF-move apartment
       'We helped her switch apartments'
    d. mana-nu   **mi**-mena la-avor dira
       prevent/PAST-we **from**-her INF-move appartment
       'We prevented her from switching apartments'

The *et*-marked object in Hebrew is not quite a direct object, but rather a semantic — albeit grammatically restricted — role, that of **definite patient**. Equi in manipulative verb complements in Hebrew thus applies to a certain class of semantic roles, rather than to the grammatical direct-object role.

6.4.4.6. Reflexives and grammatical relations

Another behavior-and-control property that is applicable to one grammatical relation — the subject — is reflexivization. The 'true' reflexive is invariably controlled by the subject, although the coreferentially-deleted argument may be either direct or indirect object:

(43) a. **Direct-object reflexive**:
       She hurt **herself**
    b. **Indirect-object reflexive**:
       She was thinking about **herself**

Equally applicable to grammatical subjecthood is the possessive reflexive, as in:

(44) a. **Direct-object reflexive**:
       He shunned **his own** mother
    b. **Indirect-object reflexive**:
       She didn't go to **her own** mother, but rather...

6.5.   Gradations and indeterminacy of grammatical relations

6.5.1. Preamble

The ambiguous status of the Hebrew direct object — neither a purely semantic patient nor a purely grammatical direct-object (see section 6.4.4.5. above) — is indicative of a broad range of facts that a prototype clustering approach to grammatical relations cannot ignore. In various formal approaches to subjecthood and objecthood, this problem is dispatched with single-trait definitions that produced unambiguous discrete classes. But a responsible empirical account of grammatical relations has no recourse to this taxonomic luxury. It must own up to indeterminancy and gradation, and then strive to explain them in a principled way.

6.5.2. Gradation of direct objecthood

There is a well-documented semantic and pragmatic overlap between the categories definite patient (Hebrew), dative and human patient (Spanish), dative and pronominal patient (Provencal), dative and topical patient (Newari, Nepali). The pragmatic common denominator is transparent — **topicality**. The semantic common thread is equally transparent — an **affected human** participant.[18] A truly grammatical direct-object role, fully independent of semantic roles so as to pass the dissociation test (see section 6.3.), most commonly arises diachronically from the reanalysis of an erstwhile dative or associative case. Both semantic roles are typically human and thus inherently topical. But different languages are synchronically at different stages along this grammaticalization — de-semanticization — continuum. Table (45) below scales some languages along this diachronic continuum.

(45)   **The continuum toward a grammaticalized DO:**

language	type of object-role	freedom of promotion to direct-object
	most semantic	
a. Japanese	patient	no promotion
b. Hebrew	definite patient	no promotion
c. Spanish	dative, human patient	no promotion
Provençal	dative, pronoun patient	no promotion
Newari	dative, topical patients	no promotion
d. Ute	patient, dative, benefactive	no promotion[19]
e. Tzotzil	patient, dative, benefactive, possessor of object	obligatory promotion
f. English	direct object	some promotion[20]
g. Nez Perce, KinyaRwanda	direct object	fully promotional
	most grammatical	

6.5.3. Gradation of subjecthood

The universality of formal subject properties (cf. Keenan 1976) is always complicated by the fact that many behavior-and-control syntactic processes are not equally distributed across languages. For example, few languages display much if any **raising**, so conspicuous in English. Many languages exhibit no morphological promotion to direct object (Sherpa, Japanese, Hebrew, Ute). Many have a non-promotional passive (Uto-Aztecan, Tibeto-Burman), a non-promotional inverse (Plains Cree, Modern Greek, Maasai). Many serial-verb languages have no embedded complements, and thus no strong syntactic difference between equi and zero anaphora (Supyire, Akan, Miskitu). The subject of one language may thus display one sub-set of properties, while that of another language another. This variability does not automatically mean that the subject of language A is less subject-like than that of language B. But Keenan's large basket of subject properties is not quite easy to apply uniformly across languages. And the apparent variation raises two important issues of interpretation:

• degree of grammaticalization
• relative ranking of subject properties

As a brief illustration of the potential magnitude of the ensuing cross-language variability, consider the following table of the availability of various formal subject properties in a number of nominative languages.

(46) **Distribution of formal subject properties in a sample of nominative languages**

properties

	overt coding prop.			behavior-and-control prop.		
	word order	**verb agreement**	**case marking**	**Equi**	**reflexive**	**zero anaphora**
English	+	+/–	–	+	+	+
Mandarin	+	–	–	+	+	–
Japanese	+	–	+	+	+	–
Spanish	–	+	–	+	+	+
Bibl. Hebrew	–	+	–	+	+	+
Ute	–	+/–[21]	–	+	+	–
Early Latin	+	+	+	+	+	+
Late Latin	–	+	+	+	+	+
Krio	+	–	–	+	+	+

The only language in our sample (46) that exhibits all six subject properties on the list is Early Latin. Other languages miss between one and three. A simple-minded approach to prototype clustering would invoke **degree of grammaticalization** at this juncture: Languages with fewer subject properties have a less prototypical — less grammaticalized — subject. Such an approach is implicit in Li and Thompson's (1976) typology, which took into account only overt morphological features. But the problem is a bit more complex.

The only properties on the list that are unambiguously present in all the languages in our sample are two behavior-and-control properties — equi and reflexivization. The third behavioral property, zero anaphora in clause-chaining, is subject-controlled in six of the languages, but not in Mandarin, Japanese and Ute. In those three, zero anaphora does not discriminate between the subject and the object.[22] Is there a principled **relative ranking** by which some formal subject properties can be shown to count more than others?

6.5.4. A functional account of cross-language variability: The ranking of formal subject and object properties

Full documentation of formal subject and object properties in all languages is not yet available. Most conspicuously missing is fuller documentation of behavior-and-control properties. The vast majority of these are transparently linked to topicality and referential continuity.[23] Of the entire list, only three — reflexivization, causativization and equi — have stronger semantic components. But referential continuity remains an important ingredient in these three as well. The more-or-less full list includes:

(47)   **Behavior-and-control properties of grammatical relations**:
  a. promotion to direct object
  b. demotion from direct object (antipassive)
  c. passivization
  d. inversion
  e. reflexivization
  f. causativization
  g. equi-NP in complementation
  h. raising
  i. possessor acention
  j. anaphoric reference in chained clauses
  k. co-reference in relativization, WH-question
     and cleft constructions.

Can these formal properties be ranked, in a principled way, relative to Keenan's (1975) ranking of overt coding properties?

My hunch is that Keenan's (1975) intuition was essentially sound, and that his ranking — case marking least universal, pronominal agreement more universal, word order most universal — can be easily and naturally extended. This can be done my observing that of those three overt coding properties, word-order correlates most closely to topicality (Givón 1988), to subjecthood (Keenan 1976), and to direct objecthood (Givón 1984a). Pronominal agreement is heavily associated with topicality (Givón 1976a). And morphological case is the least associated with topicality. A principled relative ranking of the formal properties of grammatical relations springs out of a transparent fuctional principle:

(48)   **Correlation between universality and functional transparency of subject and object properties**:
       "The more closely a formal property of subjects and objects is associated with their pragmatic function of topicality, the more universal it is likely to be in its cross-language distribution".

The relative ranking is then:

(49) **Ranking of all properties of grammatical roles according to universality and functional transparency:**

most universal
a. Functional reference-and-topicality properties
b. Behavior-and-control properties
c. Word-order
d. Grammatical agreement
e. Nominal case-marking

least universal

This ranking, if valid, suggests an underlying general principle: Morphology, and in particular nominal case morphology, is the least universal trait of grammatical relations. Being the most grammaticalized, ritualized or automated feature in grammar,[24] morphology has a higher potential for dissociation from semantic pragmatic function, in this case the topicality function of subjects and objects. Syntactic behavior-and-control properties of grammatical relations, at the other extreme, are more universal precisely because they are more transparently motivated by the pragmatic function of subjects and objects. The most universal properties of grammatical relations are their functional properties, i.e. those listed by Keenan (1976) as "reference properties".

Whether principle (48) can serve as a basis for weighting various subject properties in cases of conflict remains to be seen. One highly conspicuous such conflict, "surface" ergative languages (Anderson 1976), will be discussed in section 6.6. below. But the effect of diachronic change in introducing functional opacity into both morphology and syntax is well documented.[25]

6.6.   Grammatical relations in ergative languages

6.6.1.   Overt coding properties in ergative languages

6.6.1.1.   Nominal morphology: Split subject marking

The nominal case-marking morphology of nominative-accusative languages is maximally aligned with the discourse-pragmatic function of subjects and objects, i.e. their topicality. Regardless of transitivity, the claus's main topic it marked morphologically in a unified way — as nominative. What stands out immediately about ergative languages is the split morphological marking of the clause main topic — the subject/agent of the transitive clause is marked as ergative, the subject of the intransitive clause as absolutive. And in many ergative languages the object/patient of the transitive clause is also marked as absolutive case. As illustration of this nominal case-marking pattern, consider first the pattern of Nepali:[26]

(50) a. **Intransitive:**
          kita:b   tebul-ma   thi-y-o
          book/ABS table-LOC be-PAST-1sm
          'The book is on the table'
      b. **Transitive (non-human patient):**
          Raj-**le**   kukhura   pǫka-y-o
          Raj-ERG chicken/ABS cook-PAST-1sm
          'Raj cooked the/a chicken'

A human patient/object, however, is marked as dative rather than absolutive in Nepali:

(51) **Transitive (human patient):**
        Omi-**le**   Raj-**lay** hirka-y-in
        Omi-ERG Raj-DAT hit-PAST-1sf
        'Omi hit Raj'

In Nepali, the split in marking the absolutive NP is only partial. In Nez Perce this split is complete, with absolutive subjects being zero-marked and absolutive direct objects being suffixally marked (Rude 1985):

(52) a. **Intransitive:**
          hi-páayna   háama
          3/ABS-arrived man/ABS
          'The man arrived'
      b. **Transitive:**
          yu's-**ne** **pu**-ut'eye   piyée-**pim**
          poor-DO 3/ERG-whipped brother-ERG
          'The older brother whipped the poor one'

6.6.1.2. Control of verb agreement

In both Nepali and Nez Perce, pronominal agreement on the verb is controlled by the subject — regardless of whether it is absolutive or ergative. However, in Nepali the same set of pronominal verb-suffixes is used with either absolutive and ergative subjects. Verb agreement is thus fully controlled by the nominative NP. Such an agreement pattern is also reported in Walbiri (Hale 1973), and is probably the most common pattern in Ergative languages (Anderson 1976; Comrie 1977). The situation in Nez Perce is actually more complex. Verb agreement is indeed controlled by the subject in both transitive and intransitive clauses. But the actual pronominal form used is selected according to transitivity: One set of verb-prefixed pronouns is controlled by absolutive subjects (52a), the other by ergative subjects (52b).

A third type of agreement in an ergative language is reported in many Mayan languages, where in the intransitive clause the verb agrees only with the absolutive subject. In the transitive clause, however, the verb agrees with both the absolutive object and the ergative subject. Thus, from Jacaltec (Craig 1977):

> (53) a. **Intransitive clause (ABS agreement):**
>   ch-**in**   axni
>   AUX-ABS/**1** bathe
>   'I bathed'
>   b. **Transitive clause (ABS and ERG agreement):**
>   ch-**in**   **haw**-ila
>   AUX-ABS/**1** ERG/**2**-see
>   'You saw me'

A similar agreement pattern is also reported in Inuit Eskimo (Kalmár 1980) and in Basque (Mejías-Bikandi 1991). And likewise in Kapampangan, when interpreted as an ergative language (from Keenan 1976):[27]

> (54) a. **Antipassive intransitive (ABS agreement):**
>   s-**um**-ulat-**ya**   **ing**-lalaki **ng**-poesia
>   AGT/IRR-write-**he** ABS-boy   OBL-poetry
>   'The boy will write poetry/a poem'
>   b. **Ergative-transitive (ABS and ERG agreement):**
>   i-sulat-**na-ya**   **ning**-lalaki **ing**-poesia
>   PAT-write-**it-he** ERG-boy   ABS-poetry
>   'The boy wrote the poem'

One way of interpreting the naturalness of the double-agreement pattern in these ergative languages could be to suggest that the ergative clause arose via re-analysis of an erstwhile *inverse*, where a double agreement — with both the subject and topicalized object — is indeed natural.[28]

Only rarely does verb-agreement in an ergative language display clear absolutive control, i.e. a clear non-nominative pattern. This pattern is reported in

Khinalug, a N.E. Caucasian language, where the verb agrees with the class/gender of the absolutive NP. Thus (Comrie 1977):

(55) **Intransitive subject agreement**:
   a. ligild   sacax-ø-q'iqomä
      man/ABS silent-M
      'The man is silent'
   b. xnímk'ir   sacax-z-q'iqomä
      woman/ABS silent-F
      'The woman is silent'

(56) **Transitive object agreement**:
   a. bij-i   shi   ti-ø-k'í
      father-ERG son/ABS awaken-M
      'The father awakened the son'
   b. bij-i   rishi   ti-z-k'í
      father-ERG daughter/ABS awaken-F
      'The father awakened the daughter'

A purely ergative-absolutive control of verb agreement, as in Khinalug, is indeed rare. Verb agreement thus seems to be more universally predictable than case-marking, in that it tends to abide by the pragmatic function of the subject as the main topical argument in the clause.

One must note, finally, that the verb-agreement pattern in both nominative and ergative languages is to quite an extent the product of the particular grammaticalization pathway through which particular constructions — nominative or ergative — arose. This is a rather involved subject that will not be pursued further here.[29]

6.6.1.3. Word order in ergative languages

As is to be expected from the preceding discussion and hierarchy (49), word order is most commenly insensitive to the difference between nominative and ergative organization. Thus, in SOV-ordered ergative language such as Basque, Eskimo or Nepali, both the ergative subject of the transitive and the absolutive subject of the intransitive occupy the same clause-initial position. Similarly, in VSO-ordered ergative languages such as Jacaltec, Chamorro, Bikol or Maori, both ergative and absolutive subjects claim the post-verbal position. Likewise in pragmatically-controlled ('free-order') ergative languages such as Nez Perce, Walbiri or Dyirbal, word-order is equally irrelevant to the absolutive

or ergative status of agents and patients. Put another way, word-order —
whether grammaticalized or not — tends to follow the pragmatics of topicality
rather than the semantics of transitivity.[30] In an ergative language, the absolutive
subject of an intransitive clause and the ergative subject of an transitive clause
are both topical. And they are just as topical as, respectively, nominative subject
of an intransitive and transitive clause in a nominative language. In the same
vein, the absolutive patient in an ergative language is much less topical than the
ergative agent, much like the accusative patient in a nominative language is less
topical than the nominative agent.[31]

6.6.2.   Behavior-and-control properties in ergative languages

6.6.2.1.   Preamble

As both Anderson (1976) and Comrie (1977) note, in most ergative
languages, behavior-and-control properties are controlled by the same nominative-accusative split that governs them in nominative languages. The ergativity
of such languages is thus purely morphological or "shallow". In a few languages, the ergative-absolutive contrast goes beyond case-marking morphology,
affecting rule-governed syntactic behavior. Implicit in the distinction between
"shallow" and "deep" ergative languages is the very same **weighting** of relation-
related properties seen in (49) above, by which behavior-and-control are ranked
higher — i.e. more universal — than surface morphology. "Shallow" ergative
languages are thus, deep down, nominative languages with misleading surface
morphology (Anderson 1976).

As noted above (49), the privileged status of behavior-and-control properties, as somehow reflecting grammatical relations more faithfully, has considerable factual support even apart from ergativity. The feasibility of this idea is
further supported by the cross-linguistic distribution of the four logically-
possible types of association between case-marking morphology and behavior-
and-control properties:

(57)   Types of association between morphological
       and behavior/control features

morphology	behavior/control	languages
a. nominative	nominative	(English, Hebrew, Ute)
b. nominative	ergative	/ / / / /
c. ergative	nominative	(Basque, Jacaltec, Nepali)
d. ergative	ergative	(Dyirbal, Eskimo, Karao)

There is a conspicuous gap in the attested distribution of the four logically-possible types — type (57b) is unattested. In addition, there is also an equal if less visible gap in frequencies: The number of languages of type (57d) — "deep" ergative languages — is extremely small.[32] The biased distribution of the four possible types in (57) suggests a strong tendency for syntax to follow nominative-accusative control. Only a small sub-set of ergative languages ever violate this tendency. In the following sections we will survey some of the most conspicuous examples of ergative-absolutive control of syntactic behavior.

6.6.2.2. Control of equi

The control of equi-NP deletion (or coreference) in complement clauses is one of the least likely behavior-and-control feature to show ergative-absolutive control. But occasionally one finds such cases, as in Khinalug (Comrie 1977). In complements of manipulative verbs in Khinalug, the manipulee is coded as absolutive if the complement is intransitive, but as ergative if the complement is transitive:

(58)   a. **Intransitive complement**:
           as-ir   gada   tochkwi   jukwathmä
           I-DAT boy/ABS get.up/INF want
           'I want the boy to get up'
       b. **Transitive complement**:
           as   jukwathmä hin-i   phshä   q'izi
           I/ABS want   she-ERG bread/ABS bake/INF
           'I want her to bake bread'

This is a limited phenomenon in Khinalug, so that equi in the complements of modality verbs reveals no trace of ergative-absolutive control (Comrie 1977):

(59) a. **Intransitive complement**:
       hin-**u**   lik'úvri muxwizhmä
       she-DAT sing/INF can
       'She can sing'
      b. **Transitive complement**:
       hin-**u**   phshä q'izi   muxwizhmä
       she-DAT bread bake/INF can
       'She can bake bread'

One must point out, however, that there is another way of interpreting the data in (58): The complement of 'want' may not be an infinitive but rather a **subjunctive** complement. The absolutive (58a) and ergative (58b) manipulee is thus not the object of the main verb, but rather the undeleted subject of the complement. Indeed, an ergative-marked manipulee is just as bizarre and unprecedented in ergative languages as would a nominative-marked manipulee in a nominative language (see Comrie 1976; Cole 1984; or Givón 1990b, ch. 13). But marking the manipulee as subject would be natural in subjunctive complements, as in Spanish:

(60) a. **Intransitive complement**:
       Quiere   que Juan   se-vaya
       wants/3S SUB Juan/NOM REF-go/SUBJUN
       'She wishes that John would leave'
      b. **Transitive complement**:
       Quiere   que Juan coma   su bocadillo
       wants/3S SUB Juan eat/SUBJUN his sandwich
       'She wishes that John would eat his sandwich'

As we shall see further below, even the most extreme "deep" ergative language retains nominative control of equi.

6.6.2.3. Control of reflexivization

Reflexivization is another syntactic process that even in the most "deep" ergative languages displays nominative control. That is, the non-subject NP becomes the reflexive pronoun regardless of transitivity:

(61) **Intransitive clause**:
      a. Mary talks to **herself**
      b. *__Herself__ talks to Mary

(62) **Transitive clause:**
   a. Mary shot **herself**
   b. ***Herself** shot Mary

An absolutive-controlled pattern of reflexivization would be:

(63) a. **Intransitive clause:**
      Herself talked to Mary
   b. **Transitive clause:**
      Mary shot **herself**

To my knowledge no language, ergative or nominative, displays this pattern. As an illustration of nominative control of reflexivization in an ergative language, consider Tagalog (Philippine):[33]

(64) a. **Intransitive clause (ABS subject):**
      nag-trabajo **ang**-lalaki para **sa**-babae
      AGT-work   ABS-man   for   OBL-woman
      'The man worked for the woman'
   b. **Reflexive (ABS subject control):**
      nag-trabajo **ang**-lalaki para **sa**-sarili   **niya**
      AGT-work   ABS-man   for   OBL-SELF **his**
      'The man worked for himself'
   c. **Transitive clause (ERG subject):**
      p-**in**-atay **ng**-lalaki **ang**-aso
      PAT-kill   ERG-man ABS-dog
      'The man killed the dog'
   d. **Reflexive (ERG subject control):**
      p-**in**-atay **ng**-lalaki **ang**-sarili **niya**
      PAT-kill   ERG-man ABS-self   **his**
      'The man killed himself.

There is a variant of (64d) where, seemingly, the controlling agent reverts to absolutive, thus appearing in an intransitive **antipassive** construction. In that construction, the reflexive morpheme incorporates into the verb:[34]

(65) a. **Antipassive clause (ABS subject/agent):**
      nag-patay **ang**-lalaki (**ng**-aso)
      AGT-kill   ABS-man   OBL-dog
      'The man killed (a dog)'

b. **Reflexive (ABS subject control):**
nag-p-**akam**-atay **ang**-lalaki
AGT-REFL-kill   ABS-man
'The man self-killed'

However, antipassivization is not obligatory for reflexivizing a transitive clause. Most commonly antipassive clauses are objectless and thus syntactically intransitive. One can thus interpret the reflexive in (65b) the same way as the reflexive in (64b) — control by the absolutive subject of an intransitive clause.

6.6.2.4. Control of zero anaphora in chained clauses

Probably the most startling example of ergative-absolutive control of a syntactic process was Dixon's (1972) report of the control of zero anaphora in Dyirbal. In nominative languages, the nominative (subject) tends to control zero-anaphora in clause-chaining. That is:

(66) a. **Nominative INT to nominative TR:**
The man came and [Ø] hit the woman
b. **Nominative TR to nominative INT:**
The man hit the woman and [Ø] left

In Dyirbal, Dixon (1972) reported an absolutive control of zero-anaphora. To translate this pattern into English meaningfully would require passivization of the transitive clause:

(67) a. **Absolutive INT to absolutive TR:**
The man came and the woman hit [Ø]
(**The man** came and [Ø] was hit by the woman)
b **Absolutive TR to absolutive INT:**
The man hit the woman and [Ø] left
(**The woman** was hit by the man and [Ø] left)

Since Dyirbal exhibited both patterns, it was of interest to see which one predominated. A text-frequency study by Cooreman (1988) revealed that the nominative pattern (66) predominated in Dyirbal discourse. A similar result was reported for Tagalog by Cooreman *et al* (1984). But at least in one Philippine language, Karao (Brainard 1994a), the absolutive control of zero anaphora — pattern (67) — predominates in text.

6.6.2.5. Control of relativization

If one interprets Philippine languages as nominative (Schachter 1976; Givón 1979a), then relativization is controlled by the nominative (subject) relation, as noted in (31):

(31)   **Relational constraints on relativization (Bikol)**
       (Givón 1979a, ch. 4):
       a. Only a subject is accessible to relativization, (i.e. can be the coreferentially-deleted argument in the REL-clause).
       b. In order for a non-subject/agent of the active to be relativized, it must be first promoted to subject via inversion/-passivization.

If a Philippine language is interpreted as an ergative language, however,[35] relativization automatically turns out to be controlled by the absolutive argument. Thus, in re-interpreting Bikol as an ergative language, the absolutive subject of the intransitive clause is directly accessible to relativization:

(68)   a. **Simple intransitive clause:**
          nag-turog 'ang-babaye
          AGT-sleep ABS-woman
          'The woman slept'
       b. **Absolutive subject relativization:**
          marai 'ang-babaye na   nag-turog
          good ABS-woman REL AGT-sleep
          'The woman who slept is good'

A semantically-transitive event may appear either as a direct-active (ergative) clause, where the agent is ERG-marked and the patient ABS-marked; or as an antipassive clause, where the agent is ABS-marked and the patient takes an oblique-patient case:

(69)   a. **Ergative clause:**
          na-pakul kang-lalake 'ang-kanding
          PAT-hit   ERG-man   ABS-goat
          'The man hit the goat'
       b. **Antipassive clause:**
          nag-pakul 'ang-lalake ning-kanding
          AGT-hit   ABS-man   PAT-goat
          'The man hit a/some goat'

The agent cannot be relativized from the ergative pattern (69a), only from the antipassive pattern (69b). That is, it must be demoted to absolutive before it is accessible to relativization. The patient, on the other hand, is accessible to relativization from the ergative pattern (69a), in which it is the absolutive argument:

(70)   a. **Agent relativization (antipassive pattern)**:
           marai **'ang**-lalake **na   nag**-pakul **ning**-kanding
           good ABS-man   REL AGT-hit   PAT-goat
           'The man who hit the goat is good'
       b. **Patient relativization (ergative pattern)**:
           marai **'ang**-kanding **na   na**-pakul **kang**-lalake
           good ABS-goat   REL PAT-hit   ERG-man
           'The goat that the man hit is good'

Finally, all oblique arguments must be promoted to absolutive — thus to direct object — as pre-condition to relativization. The re-interpretation of a Philippine language as an ergative language thus converts the promotion-to-subject system into a promotion to direct-object system reminiscent of the one seen in Kinya-Rwanda. As in KinyaRwanda, the semantic role of the absolutive non-patient DO is morphologically coded on the verb. Thus compare:

(71)   a. **Patient ABS/DO:**
           na-ka'ag **kang**-lalake **'ang**-libro **sa**-lamesa
           PAT-put ERG-man   ABS-book LOC-table
           'The man put the book on the table'
       b. **Locative ABS/DO:**
           pinag-ka'ag-**an kang**-lalake **'ang**-lamesa **ning**-libro
           LOC-put   ERG-man   ABS-table   PAT-book
           'The man put on the table a book'

The patient is accessible to relativization only via pattern (71a), where it is the absolutive DO. The locative is accessible to relativization only via pattern (71b), where it has been promoted to absolutive DO:

(72)   a. **Relativization of ABS/DO patient**:
           marai **'ang**-libro **na   k-in**-a'ag **kang**-lalake **sa**-lamesa
           good ABS-book REL PAT-put   ERG-man   LOC-table
           'The book that the man put on the table is good'

b. **Relativization of ABS/DO locative**:
marai 'ang-lamesa na pinag-ka'ag-an kang-lalake ning-libro
good ABS-table   REL LOC-put   ERG-man   PAT-book
'The table that the man put a book on is good'

Other obliques must likewise be promoted to absolutive DO before they are accessible to relativization.

The relational constraints on Bikol relativization can be thus given in terms of the absolutive grammatical relation:

(73) **Relational constraints on relativization in Bikol interpreted as an ergative language**:
   a. Only an absolutive NP can be the coreferentially-deleted argument in the REL-clause.
   b. The subject of a transitive clause must be demoted to absolutive status — via antipassivization — in order to become accessible to relativization.
   c. Oblique non-patient arguments of the active must be promoted to absolutive — to direct-object — in order to become accessible to relativization.

6.6.2.6. Raising to object

Raising is a rare phenomenon outside English and relatively few like-minded languages. In the few nominative languages that tolerate raising, raising-to-object applies only to the subject — nominative — of the complement clause.[36] But in at least one ergative language, Karao (Philippine), raising an absolutive direct object is possible.[37] Raising in Karao is attested for only one verb, and is a sub-pattern of equi in modality-verb complementation. Thus (Brainard 1994a):[38]

(74) a. **Simple intransitive clause**:
   man-pasiyal 'i-bi'i
   AGT-visit   ABS-woman
   'The woman will go visiting'
   b. **Equi with intransitive complement**:
   piyan na-bi'i   'a man-pasiyal
   want ERG-woman SUB AGT-visit
   'The woman wants to go visiting'

    c. **Simple ERG-transitive clause:**
        basa-**en**   **na**-bi'i   **'i**-dibcho
        read-PAT ERG-woman ABS-book
        'The woman will read the book'
    d. **Equi with ERG-transitive complement:**
        piyan **na**-bi'i   **'a**   basa-**en**   'i-dibsco
        want ERG-woman SUB read-PAT ABS-book
        'The woman wants to read the book'
    e. **Equi ERG subject plus raising ABS object:**
        'on-semesemek **na**-bi'i   **'i**-dibcho   **'a**   basa-**en**
        IMPFV-love   ERG-woman ABS-woman SUB read-PAT
        'The woman would love to read the book'
        (Lit.: 'The woman would love the book to read')

This pattern is probably marginal.

6.6.2.7. Overview: Mixed control of syntactic processes and gradation in grammatical relations

    In her summary of the behavior and control properties of grammatical relations in Karao, Brainard (1994a) presents the distribution in (75):

(75) **Relational control of subject properties in Karao**
      (Brainard 1994a)

property	nominative	absolutive
	type of control	

property	nominative	absolutive
case morphology		ERG/ABS
word-order	NOM	
verb agreement	(irrelevant)	
equi	NOM	
relativization	NOM/ACC	
pseudo-cleft		ABS
zero anaphora		ABS
raising	ACC ?	ABS
passivization	ACC	
promotion to DO	ACC	
antipassive	ACC	
reflexivization	NOM	

The summary suggests that even in a language as syntactically — "deeply" — ergative as Karao, the majority of syntactic behavior-and-control properties are controlled by either the nominative or by the accusative. Only two syntactic processes — zero anaphora and pseudo-cleft — show clear absolutive control.[39] In the diachronic shift from nominative to ergative in Philippine languages, the correspondence of clause-types is as given in (76):

(76) **Diachronic correspondence of clause-types along the NOM-to-ERG shift in Philippine languages:**

construction	nominative	⟹	ergative
(a) AGT-focus	direct-active		antipassive
(b) PAT-focus	inverse/passive		ergative/patient-DO
(c) OBL-focus	inverse/passive		ergative/oblique-DO

That this correspondence is diachronically valid is supported by the suggestion of similar correspondences in Indonesian languages (Rafferty 1982; Verhaar 1985). It is also mirrored by similar correspondence in Sahaptian between the nominative organization of Sahaptin and the ergative organization of Nez Perce

(Rude 1991; see Chapter 3). Brainard's results also support the validity of our extension of Keenan's (1975, 1976) hierarchic prediction. Relational properties can be ranked in terms of the degree of their association with the pragmatic function of grammatical relations (49). Properties that are more transparently associated with the pragmatic function of grammatical relations distribute more uniformly — thus more universally — across languages (principle (48)).

A more general conclusion concerns the validity of a discrete approach to grammatical relations. Such approach is intrinsically incapable of capturing either the typological generalizations or the typological variability seen in ergative languages. The tendency of case-marking to be controlled by one set of grammatical relations (ERG/ABS) while the rest of the grammar marches to the drum of another set (NOM/ACC) is impenetrable to a discrete approach. Nor is the fact that even in "deep" ergative languages, the degree and manner to which differant syntactic processes are controlled by the ERG/ABS relations may vary considerably. A theoretical framework that does not recognize **degree of grammaticalization** of what are essentially universal functional domains — in this case universals of discourse-pragmatic notions such as primary and secondary topic — will gloss over these typological differences as 'superficial' or 'uninteresting'.[40]

A final word of caution is due concerning the relationship between grammatical and cognitive universals. Our survey thus far has tended to support Anderson's (1976) suggestion that behavior-and-control properties of subjects and objects are more universal, and that morphology — or at least nominal case-marking — is a more superficial property of grammatical relations. But three facts about behavior-and-control properties must be born in mind:

- The evidence for these syntactic processes tends to be available primarily in **complex clauses**.
- Complex clauses are **infrequent** in human discourse, appearing roughly at a ratio of 1:10 as compared to simple (main, declarative, affirmative, active) clauses (chapter 2).
- Complex syntax is acquired much later by children.

In both language acquisition and everyday language use then, the overt coding properties of subjects and objects are much more frequently encountered than "deeper" syntactic properties. When children acquire a "shallow" ergative language, do they first acquire ergative-absolutive grammatical relations? And do they then modify this early relational organization after acquiring complex constructions that reflect a contradictory — nominative-accusative — relational organization? Or do children somehow, because of an innate pre-disposition toward nominativity, impose a "deep" nominative-accusative interpretation on the surface facts of simple clauses even before encountering any syntactic complexity? Even more perplexing, when acquiring a "deep" ergative language, are children so closely guided by "deep" innate universals that they first reject the superficial ergative morphology and adopt a "deep" nominative organization? And do they then, when complex syntax comes on line, modify their grammar toward an equally "deep" but conflicting ergative-absolutive organization, one that now meshes well with the superficial morphology? At the moment I see no clear answer to these questions, though I suspect they should be equally challenging to functionalists and formalists.

6.7. Grammatical relations in serial-verb languages

6.7.1. Preamble

In the preceding chapter we have introduced serial-verb languages as a nagging problem for a syntactic analysis that insists on a universal, abstract VP constituent. From our survey there, it emerged that all current formal accounts of the verb phrase in serial-verb languages — including my own (77c) — allowed for multiple 'lower' VP nodes, differing only on the 'higher' hierarchic organization that dominates those multiple nodes.[41] That is:

(77) a.

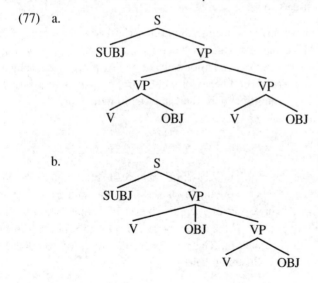

b.

c.

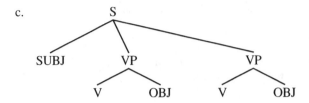

Accepting a formal multiple-VP model, with each 'lower' VP comprising of a verb and a possible object, amounts to a tacit concession that a single clause need not have a unified set of grammatical relations. At least as far as grammatical objecthood is concerned, each object in the serial clause need not bear its grammatical relation to the highest VP, but only to the lower VP directly dominating it.

In this section we will re-examine the status of grammatical relations in seria-verb languages more closely, beginning with the grammatical object. We will then turn to the seemingly less controversial relation, that of the grammatical subject, surveying constructions in which subjecthood is also problematic. The predicament of subjecthood in serial-verb languages turns out to be a predicament only within the confines of a certain formal approach. The predicament is thus, in a large measure, self-inflicted.

6.7.2.   Multiple objects in serial clauses

The most extensive analysis of objecthood in serial-verb languages can be found in Byrne's (1987) exhaustive syntactic description of Saramaccan, *Grammatical relations in a Radical Creole*. In addition to overt coding properties of objects and verbs, Byrne examines several behavior-and-control properties to assess the grammatical status of the multiple verbs and objects, in particular:

* relativization
* WH-movement
* clefting

These tests reveal that the multiple verbs in Saramaccan serial clauses behave syntactically like the single verbs of simple clauses. And the multiple objects in serial clauses likewise behave like the single objects of simple clauses. This syntactic fact stands regardless of the diversity of the semantic function of the serial constructions in Saramaccan. The main semantic types of serialization Byrne (1987) examines are illustrated below:

(78) Main multi-object serial constructions in Saramaccan
(Byrne 1987)

a. **Instrumental case with 'take':**
   di mii **tei** di pau naki di dagu
   the child **take** the stick hit   the dog
   'The child hit the dog with a stick'

b. **Dative/benefactive with 'give':**
   a sei di wosu **da** di womi
   he sell the house **give** the man
   'He sold the house **to/for** the man'

c. **Directional-deictic with 'go'/'come':**
   a tsa di meliki **go/ko**   a   di konde
   he carry the milk   **go/come** LOC the village
   'He **took/brought** the milk to the village'

d. **Directional-deictic with 'go'/'come':**
   a waka **go/ko**   a   di opolani
   he walk **go/come** LOC the airplane
   'He walked **to/from** the airplane'

e. **Directional-deictic complementizers 'go'/'come':**
   de ke   **go/ko**   wasi di wagi
   they want **go/come** wash the car
   'They want to **go/come** (and) wash the car'

f. **Perfective aspect with 'finish':**
   Kofi bi-fefi   di wosu **kaba**
   Kofi PERF-paint the house **finish**
   'Kofi had painted the house'

g. **The comparative 'pass':**
   a bigi **pasa** di mii
   he big **pass** the child
   'He is bigger than the child'

h. **The comparative 'more':**
   a bigi **moon** di mii
   he big **more** the child
   'He is bigger than the child'

Byrne's (1987) conclusions are well worth citing:

"... in most serial types a particular serial string is best looked at as **a series of finite subordinate clauses** .... That is, because of [overt coding and behavior-and-control properties; TG] most of the serial verbs in this chapter are finite Ss ... " (1987: 242; emphases added)

While reaching this conclusion, Byrne does not ignore the problem of gradual grammaticalization:

"... if the analysis of *moon* 'more' is correct, then it represents the most radical change of the serials studied in this chapter; while all the serials analyzed show at least some minimal indications of change towards non-finite status for some speakers, only *moon* 'more' has categorically achieved this result for all speakers ... " (1987: 242)

It is important to emphasize that the finite syntactic properties of Saramaccan serial verbs observed by Byrne (1987) reveals once again the strong dissociation between semantic and syntactic components of grammaticalization. While semantically grammaticalized, most serial verbs in (78) retain their syntactic verbal properties. Consequently, their objects retain their direct-objecthood relation vis-a-vis the verb.[42] Byrne's conclusion — that serial-verb clauses are best looked at "as a series of finite subordinate clause" — is forced upon him by the pre-empirical — Aristotelian — demands of the early trans-formational:

"One verb = one clause"

Combined with an extreme configurational approach to grammatical relation, this account demands that only a VP dominated by S can harbor a grammatical object.[43]

Similar general conclusions — multiple VPs with multiple DOs — were reached by Osam (1993b) in his study of grammatical objecthood in Akan. The bi-transitive 'give' in Akan can take two syntactic frames, one non-serial, the other serial:

(79) a. **Non-serial variant (dative more topical)**:
         Kofi ma-**a**   papa-no sika
         Kofi give-PAST man-the money
         'Kofi gave the man money'
      b. **Serial variant (patient more topical)**:
         Kofi **de**   sika-no   ma-**a**   papa-no
         Kofi **take** money-the give-PAST man-the
         'Kofi gave the money to the man'

The patient object is more naturally definite when topicalized in (79b), but more naturally indefinite when de-topicalized (79a). When testing for object pro-nominalization, only the topicalized dative can be pronominalized in the non-serial (79a):[44]

(80) a. Kofi ma-a   **no** sika
          Kofi give-PAST **him** money
          'Kofi gave him money'
      b. *Kofi ma-a   papa-no Ø
          Kofi give-PAST man-the **it**
          '*Kofi gave the man it'

In the serial construction (79b), on the other hand, both objects can be pro-nominalized:

(81) a. Kofi **de** Ø ma-a   papa-no
          Kofi **take it** give-PAST man-the
          'Kofi gave it to the man'
      b. Kofi **de** sika-no   ma-a   **no**
          Kofi **take** money-the give-PAST **him**
          'Kofi gave the money to him'

The same discrimination occurs in relativization. Only the dative object can be relativized out of the non-serial (79a):

(82) a. papa-no **a**   Kofi ma-a   **no** sika no[45]...
          man-the **REL** Kofi give-PAST **him** money the...
          'The man Kofi gave money to...'
      b. *sika-no **a**   Kofi ma-a   papa-no...
          money-the **REL** Kofi give-PAST man-the

But both objects can be relativized out of the serial variant (79b):

(83) a. papa-no **a**   Kofi **de** sika-no   ma-a   **no** no...
          man-the **REL** Kofi **take** money-the give-PAST **him** the
          'The man to whom Kofi gave the money...'
      b. sika-no **a**   Kofi **de** Ø ma-a   papa-no...
          money-the **REL** Kofi **take it** give-PAST man-the
          'The money that Kofi gave (to) the man...'

Osam (1993) concludes that by all three criteria for direct objecthood — word-order, control of object pronominalization, and control of object relativization —

the serial clause (79b) has two grammatical objects, one per verb. This is true in spite of the fact that the serial verb *de* 'take' is morphologically the most grammaticalized in Akan, never taking any finite inflections; and in spite of the fact that *de* is also semantically grammaticalized and does not mean 'take' in these serial constructions.

Other bi-transitive verbs in the 'give' class may vary in their syntactic behavior. Thus, 'teach' has no corresponding serial variant and allows no word-order variation; and its patient object cannot be pronominalized. But 'teach' allows the patient to be definitized (within the fixed DAT-PAT order) and relativized:

(84) a. **Indefinite patient**:
          Kofi kyerę-ę   mbofra-no ndwom
          Kofi teach-PAST children-the song
          'Kofi taught the children a song'
      b. **Definite patient**:
          Kofi kyerę-ę   mbofra-no   ndwom-no
          Kofi teach-PAST children-the song-the
          'Kofi taught the song to the children'
      c. ***Fronted patient**:
          *Kofi kyerę-ę   ndwom-no mbofra-no
          Kofi teach-PAST song-the   children-the
      d. **Pronominalized dative**:
          Kofi kyerę-ę   **họn** ndwom
          Kofi teach-PAST **them** song
          'Kofi taught them a song'
      e. ***Pronominalized patient**:
          *Kofi kyerę-ę   mbofra-no **Ø**
          Kofi teach-PAST children-the **it**
          ('Kofi taught it to the children')
      f. **Relativized dative**:
          mbofra-no   **a**   Kofi kyerę-ę   **họn** ndwom...
          children-the **REL** Kofi teach-PAST **them** song
          'the children that Kofi taught a song (to)...'
      g. **Relativized patient**:
          ndwom-no **a**   Kofi kyerę-ę   mbofra-no **Ø**...
          song-the **REL** Kofi teach-PAST children-the **it**
          'the song that Kofi taught (to) the children...'

The patient object of 'teach' thus passes two objecthood tests — definitization and relativization. It fails two others — post-verbal position and pronominalization.

Akan bi-transitive verbs with non-human indirect objects ('put on', 'take off', 'put in', 'take out', 'cover with', 'spread on') also require the use of serial verbs. While the two VPs appear in a fixed order, both objects are accessible to definitization, pronominalization and relativization. And the semantically grammaticalized verb may be either the first or the second in the clause:

(85) a. Esi **de** ekutu-no to-o famu
         Esi **take** orange-the put-PAST floor
         'Esi put the orange on the floor'
     b. Esi yi-i tam-no **fi-i** pon-no-don...
         Esi take-PAST cloth-the **leave-PAST** table-the-on
         'Esi took the cloth off the table'
     c. Esi hue-e nsu **gu-u** ankora-no-mu
         Esi pour-PAST water **put-PAST** barrel-the-in
         'Esi poured the water into the barrel'

(86) a. **Pronominalized patient:**
         Esi yi-i   Ø **fi-i**   pon-no-don
         Esi take-PAST **it leave-PAST** table-the-on
         'Esi took it off the table'
     b. **Pronominalized locative:**
         Esi yi-i   tam-no **fi-i**   Ø-don
         Esi take-PAST cloth-the **leave-PAST** it-on
         'Esi took the cloth off it'
     c. **Relativized patient:**
         tam-no   **a** Esi yi-i   Ø **fi-i**   pon-no-don...
         cloth-the **REL** Esi take-PAST **it leave-PAST** table-the-on
         'the cloth that Esi took off the table...'
     d. **Relativized locative:**
         pon-no   **a** Esi yi-i   tam-no **fi-i**   Ø-don...
         table-the **REL** Esi take-PAST cloth-the **leave-PAST** it-on
         'the table off which Esi took the cloth...'

By the four tests for direct objecthood in Akan — post-verbal position, word-order, pronominalization and relativization — both objects in these serial clauses are bone fide direct objects.

6.7.3. The grammatical subject in serial clauses

Most serial verb constructions arise diachronically from an equi-subject (SS) clause-chain, so that the problems they create for grammatical relations tend to involve multiple objects in the condensed, grammaticalized clause. The single subject NP of the clause is semantically the subject of both verbs, thus formally of both lower-level VPs — or even of the higher VP node. Some serial clauses, however, arise diachronically from the condensation of a switch-subject (DS) clause-chain. This type of clause-chaining is well recognized, at least semantically, even in a language with no switch-reference morphology. Compare the following serial clauses in Akan, one SS-serial, the other DS-serial (Osam 1993):

> (87) a. **Equi-subject (SS) serial clause**:
>   Kofi tur   abofra-no **ma**-a   Esi
>   Kofi carry/PAST children-the **give**-PAST Esi
>   'Kofi carried the children for Esi'
>   (*Historically*: 'Kofi carried the children and (*he*) gave
>   them to Esi')
>   b. **Switch-subject (DS) serial clause**:
>   Esi yi-i   tam-no   **fi**-i   pon-no-don
>   Esi take-PAST cloth-the **leave**-PAST table-the-on
>   'Esi took the cloth off the table'
>   (*Historically*: 'Esi took the cloth and *it* left the table')

As a chain-medial clause prior to condensation, the second clause in (87a) was an equi-subject (SS) clause, while the second clause in (87b) was a switch-subject (DS) clause. As noted in Chapter 5, this phenomenon is common in serializing languages. But is there any indication that 'cloth' in (87b) bears a subject grammatical relation to the serial verb 'leave'? By Osam's (1993b) syntactic criteria — word-order, pronominalization, relativization — 'cloth' bears only an object relation (to 'take') but no relation whatever — subject or object — to 'leave'.

Similar resultative-causative DS-serial clauses are found in most serializing languages. Thus, recall the contrast between SS and DS serial clauses in Miskitu, where the SS/DS morphology of clause chaining is retained in serial clauses (Hale 1991):

(88) a. **SS serial clause**:
    Baha usus-ka   pali-**i**   wa-**n**
    that buzzard-CSN fly-**PAR/SS** go-**PAST/3**
    'The buzzard flew away'
    (*Historically*: 'The buzzard flew and (*he*) went'
   b. **DS serial clause**:
    Yang truk-kum atk-**ri**   wa-**n**
    I   truck-a   sell-**DS/1** go-**PAST/3**
    'I sold the truck away'
    (*Historically*: 'I sold the truck and *it* went')

Byrne (1987, 1992) proposes an **embedded clause** analysis of all serial clauses in Saramaccan. He posits the — syntactically embedded but semantically chained — 'deep structure' (89b) as the underlying syntactic structure of the serial clause (89a). That is (Byrne 1992: 203):

(89) a. a bi   fefi di wosu **kaba**
      he TNS paint the house **finish**
      'He **had** painted the house'

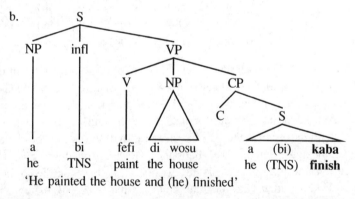

'He painted the house and (he) finished'

Since (89a) arose from an equi-subject (SS) chained construction, (89b) is a deceptively adequate account of its semantic and syntactic properties.[46] For a switch-subject (DS) serial constructions, Byrne's account would be more problematic. Thus consider such an account of the Akan clause (87b):

(90) a. **Switch-subject (DS) serial clause:**
Esi yi-i   tam-no   fi-i   pon-no-don
Esi take-PAST cloth-the **leave**-PAST table-the-on
'Esi took the cloth **off** the table'

b.

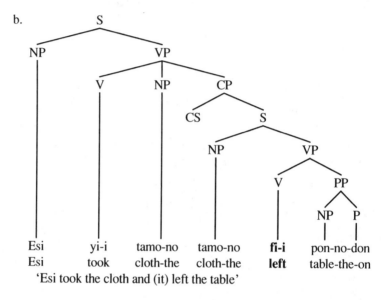

'Esi took the cloth and (it) left the table'

By all available formal criteria, 'cloth' in (87b)/(90) and 'truck' in (88b) bear only an object grammatical relation — to the first verb in the clause, but no grammatical relation whatever — subject or otherwise — to the second (serial) verb. As underlying semantic structures, (89b) and (90b) do not fare much better. This is because the current meaning of (89a) is not the historical 'He painted the house and *finished*', but rather 'He *had* painted the house'. Likewise, the current meaning of (90a) is not the historical 'Esi took the cloth and it *left* the table' but rather 'Esi took the cloth *off* the table''. Byrne's (1987, 1992) proposal thus glosses over the fact that both **grammaticalization** and **clause-union** have taken place. Both processes are diachronic mappings from older to newer structures — and meanings, rather than synchronic mappings from deep to surface structure.

6.8.   Grammatical relations and clause union

6.8.1.   Preamble

The problem of both syntactic and semantic representation of serial-verb clauses is rooted in our notion of **clause union**. In both embedding and serializing languages, what started historically as two verbal clauses, each with its own verb and set of relation-bearing grammatical arguments, can condense over time into a single event clause with a unified set of grammatical roles. Clause union, viewed diachronically, may be thus defined as:

(91)   "The process by which two (or more) clauses with two
        (or more) sets of arguments, with each set bearing gram-
        matical relations in its proper clause, are merge to yield a
        single clause, within which the arguments of both sets
        now bear grammatical relations in the unified clause".

The two major venues for obtaining syntactic complexity — embedding and serialization — involve starkly different diachronic strategies to create complex multi-verb structures, i.e. clause union. Embedding languages arrive at clause union via the route of **verb complementation**. Serializing languages arrive at clause union via the route of **clause chaining**. We have surveyed this major typological contrast briefly in the preceding chapter. In this section we will review its ramifications for grammatical relations.

6.8.2.   Syntactic constraints on clause union

In both embedding and serializing languages, two major types of relational configurations can partake in clause union — equi-subject (SS) and switch-subject (DS). The two types have somewhat different consequences for clause union, so that we will consider them separately.

6.8.2.1.   Clause union in equi-subject (SS) configurations

6.8.2.1.1. Embedding languages

Clause union of equi-subject (SS) configurations is the main diachronic source of grammaticalized auxiliaries and eventually of tense-aspect-modal and directional markers in language (Givón 1971a, 1973a; Heine 1893). In embedding languages, the initial syntactic configuration for SS clause-union is equi-subject (SS) **complementation**. The V-plus-COMP verb phrase in an embedding language is constructed by analogy to the V-plus-OBJ verb phrase of the simple clause. The main verb retains all finite inflections, such as tense-aspect-modality and pronominal affixes. The complement verb is either partially or fully nominalized, exhibiting less-finite form.

In both VO and OV languages, SS-complementation places the complement verb directly adjacent to the main verb. Thus compare the VO complementation pattern of English (92a) with the OV pattern of Ute (92b):

(92) **Equi-subject (SS) in embedding languages**:

a. **English (VO)**

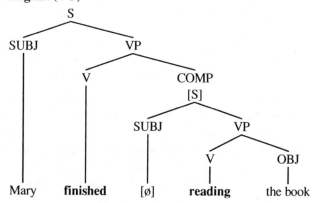

b. **Ute (OV)**:

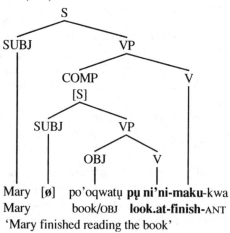

Mary [ø] po'oqwatụ **pụ ni'ni-maku**-kwa
Mary   book/OBJ **look.at-finish-**ANT
'Mary finished reading the book'

When the main verb 'finish' grammaticalizes into a perfect(ive) aspect, it becomes — at least initially — a finite **auxiliary verb**; and it remains morpho-syntactically the main verb of the complex two-verb clause. This is the case with the English example (92a). When the auxiliary cliticizes, it becomes a prefix (VO) or a suffix (OV) on the complement verb, which is now the main verb. With cliticization, the erstwhile auxiliary now brings all its finite morphology to the new main verb, as in the Ute example (92b).

6.8.2.1.2. Serializing languages

In serial-verb languages, two independent factors conspire against the completion of clause union. First, the chained structure most commonly prevents verb adjacency, by scattering the verbs on the opposite sides of object NPs. One of the verbs in the clause may have grammaticalized semantically, but the two non-adjacent verbs cannot co-lexicalize. As an illustration of this, compare the embedding languages in (92) above with the verb-serializing Saramaccan (VO) and Supyire (OV) in (93):

(93)   **Equi-subject (SS) in a serializing language**:
       a. **Saramaccan (VO)** (Byrne 1987):

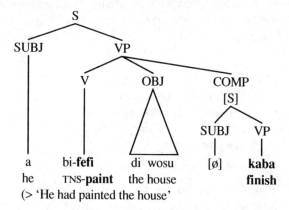

       a   bi-**fefi**   di wosu   [ø]   **kaba**
       he   TNS-**paint**   the house   **finish**
       (> 'He had painted the house'

b. **Supyire (OV)** (Carlson 1990):

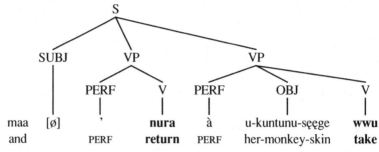

maa	[ø]	'	**nura**	à	u-kuntunu-sęęge	**wwu**
and		PERF	**return**	PERF	her-monkey-skin	**take**

'...and she again took her monkey-skin ...'

When 'finish' in (93a) and 'return' in (93b) grammaticalize as aspect markers, they have no adjacent main verb to cliticize on.[47]

The second factor is tangentially related to the first. As noted above, the complementation structure that eventually gives rise to clause-union in an embedded language is structured by analogy with a verb-object configuration. In such a configuration, the main verb retains all finite verbal features, while the complement verb becomes nominalized, non-finite or less-finite. When clause union occurs under such a configuration, the grammaticalized main verb — now co-lexicalized with the complement verb — contributes all its finite inflections to the combined single lexical verb. As an illustration of this, consider again the Spanish auxiliaries:

(94) a. **se-lo-est-amos**   explicando
       DAT/3s-ACC/3sm-be-1p explain/PART
       'We are explaining it to him/her'
    b. **se-la-h-an**   dado
       DAT/3s-ACC/3sf-have-3p give/PART
       'They have given it to her/him'

The gravitation of all finite morphology to the main verb can, on occasion, yield strange temporary results. As illustration, consider Acatec (Mayan), an ergative language in which ergativity expressed only in the pronominal agreement on the verb. As in Jacaltec (see earlier above), intransitive verbs in Acatec display absolute subject agreement, while transitive verbs display double agreement — with both the ergative subject and absolutive object (Zavala 1993):

(95) a. **ABS agreement (intransitive clause):**
          sep   oj-Ø-to-j   'ix y-awal
          early IRR-ABS/3-go-IRR   she 3-cornfield
          '...She'll go to her cornfield...'
      b. **ERG & ABS agreement (transitive clause):**
          Ø-y-i'-on-ab'   pax-aa-tej   jun sq'an juun
          ABS/3-ERG/3-take-AGTV-EVID DIR-DIR-DIR   one yellow paper
          '...that one also took a cigarette...'

Motion verbs in Acatec have been grammaticalizing into directional auxiliaries (eventually directional clitics), along the familiar route of equi-subject complementation. When the complement clause is intransitive, the absolutive subject agreement gravitates to the auxiliary alone, with the complement verb now marked only by a non-finite irrealis marker:

(96) x-**ach**-jul   wey-oj
      AUX-ABS/s2-come sleep-IRR
      'You're coming to sleep'

When the complement clause is transitive, several agreement patterns are possible. In one type, when the main verb 'go' is not yet semantically grammaticalized, the intransitive auxiliary retains agreement with its absolutive logical subject, and the transitive complement agrees with both its ergative subject and absolutive object. Both verbs thus retain the agreement pattern they would have had in the simple-clause:

(97) ch-**in**-b'et-ey   Ø-**in**-tx'a-on   'el ko-pichil ti'
      INC-ABS/1-go-DIR ABS/3-ERG/1s-wash-AGTV DIR 1p-clothes PROX
      '...I went to wash our clothes...'

But another, more grammaticalized, pattern also exists, in case when 'go' is semantically grammaticalized as a 'future' marker. In this pattern, the agreement splits in a way that defies the logic of simple-clause grammatical relations. The auxiliary now agrees with the absolutive object of the embedded transitive verb, while the embedded verb agrees only with its ergative subject:

(98) oj-**ach**-to-j   w-il   an
      IRR-ABS/2s-go-IRR ERG/1-see 1s
      'I'm going to see you'

Modal verbs in Acatec display another grammaticalization pattern yet, whereby the grammaticalized modal auxiliary loses its absolutive agreement altogether, while the embedded verb retains its simple-clause agreement pattern (ABS agreement for intransitives, ERG-ABS agreement for transitives):

(99) a. **Intransitive complement (ABS agreement):**
      chi-ske' **in**-b'ey   an
      INC-can ABS/1s-walk 1s
      'I can walk'

   b. **Transitive complement (ERG-ABS agreement):**
      chi-ske' **ach-w**-il-on   an
      INC-can ABS/2s-ERG/1s-see-AGTV 1s
      'I can see you'

This modal pattern is also found when 'go' is fully grammaticalized as future marker, as in:

(100) a. **Intransitive complement (ABS agreement):**
      to-j   **in**-jul-oj
      go-IRR ABS/1s-come-IRR
      'I'm going to come (here)'

    b. **Transitive complement (ERG-ABS agreement):**
      to-j   Ø-**w**-a'   lo-w   naj an
      go-IRR ABS/3-ERG/1s-give eat-INT 3s 1s
      'I'm going to let him eat'

In all clause-union patterns in Acatec, the auxiliary and complement verbs are adjacent. When they finally co-lexicalize, the combined new main verb carries all the finite verbal inflections of the clause. But the inflectional pattern is often morphotactically scrambled, thus at odds with the pattern of the simple clause.

In serializing languages, the diachronic precursor of clause union (clause chaining) tends to disperse the verbs among the object NPs. Further, in many serial-verb language (Akan, Saramaccan, Ijo), the verbs in the precursor chained structure are all equally finite (or equally non-finite). Thus when an erstwhile chain condenses into a single serial clause, the verbs in it do not diverge in finite marking. A serial verb may have grammaticalized semantically, but it continues to carry its verbal morphology long after losing verbal meaning. What is more, even in languages where finite verbal morphology had consolidated on a single verb in the precursor chain — and thus on single verb in the resulting serial clause, that verb could just easily be the semantically-bleached grammaticalized verb. Thus, in Miskitu (OV) the grammaticalized chain-final 'go' in (101) displays all finite marking, while the semantic main verb 'fly' is non-finite (Hale 1991):

(101) Baha usus-ka   pali-**i**   wa-**n**
     that   buzzard-CNS fly-INF go-PAST/**3**
     'That buzzard flew away'

Similarly in Saramaccan (VO) the grammaticalized chain-final 'give' in (102) carries the finite inflection, while the semantic main verb 'buy' goes unmarked (Byrne 1992):

(102) Kofi bai di buku **bi**-da   di muyee
     Kofi buy the book TNS-give the woman
     'Kofi bought the book for the woman'

The conflation of both factors — verb dispersal and lack of consolidated single locus for finite verbal morphology — renders clause-union in serializing languages a radically different syntactic affair than in an embedding language. Even in equi-subject clauses, serializing languages tend to preserve much of the original morpho-syntax of the erstwhile chained structure, retaining multi-VP structures and multi-object relations.

6.8.2.2. Clause union in switch-subject (DS) configurations

6.8.2.2.1. Embedding languages

Switch-subject (DS) clause unions involve a family of broadly **causative** or **resultative** constructions. In embedding languages, these structures are broadly patterned on DS complementation of manipulative verbs ('make', 'cause', 'force', 'let' etc.).[48] This pattern concentrates all finite marking on the main manipulative verb, leaving the complement verb nominalized, non-finite or less-finite. Semantically, the co-reference constraint on such structures is as follows:

"The agent of the complement is the manipulee of the main verb".

Syntactically, the manipulee bears an object relation to the main verb. But there is no syntactic evidence that the manipulee retains subject relation to the complement verb:[49]

(103) a. She **told** Marvin **to wash** the dishes
     b. He **made** Susan **quit** her job

In SOV languages, the main causative verb in DS complementation always winds up adjacent to the complement verb. As an illustration of this, consider the following from Ute (Givón 1980a):

(104)

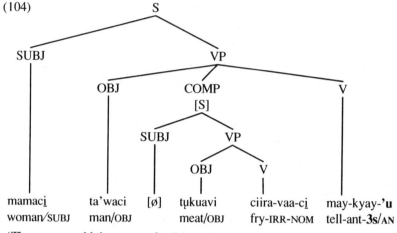

mamacį   ta'waci   [ø]   tųkuavi   ciira-vaa-cį   may-kyay-'u
woman/SUBJ   man/OBJ   meat/OBJ   fry-IRR-NOM   tell-ant-3s/AN

'The woman told the man to fry the meat'

The adjacency of the main and complement verbs makes co-lexicalization and thus clause union only a matter of time — provided the main verb grammaticalizes semantically.[50] This has in fact occurred in the morphological causative of Ute:

(105)

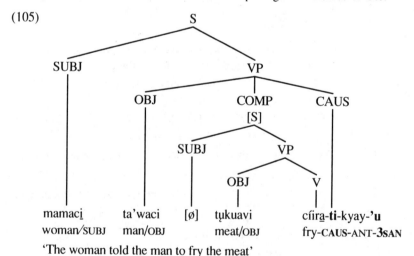

mamacį   ta'waci   [ø]   tųkuavi   cíira-ti-kyay-'u
woman/SUBJ   man/OBJ   meat/OBJ   fry-CAUS-ANT-3sAN

'The woman told the man to fry the meat'

The syntactic structure given in (105) is actually too abstract, since clause-union leaves us a complex bi-transitive verb with two objects — one the causee, the other the patient of 'fry':

(106)

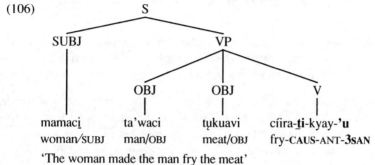

'The woman made the man fry the meat'

Neither overt-coding nor behavior-and-control tests can show that the two objects bear their respective object relations to anything but a single — if semantically complex — verb.

By several syntactic criteria, the two surface objects in Ute are not on a par, neither in causative constructions nor in other double-object constructions. First, their order is rigid, with the more topical human causee preceding the inanimate patient. Second, the more topical, fronted causee lays claim to object agreement. Thus compare:

(107) *mamac<u>i</u>   tu̞kuavi ta'waci   cíir<u>a</u>-ti-kyay-ax
      woman/SUBJ meat/OBJ man/OBJ fry-CAUS-ANT-3s/INAN

The same constraint is seen in another two-object construction in Ute, involving an obligatorily-promoted benefactive NP. That NP must be the direct object, commands object agreement, and must precede the patient object:

(108) a. **Simple transitive clause**:
         mamac<u>i</u>   tu̞kuavi cíir<u>a</u>-qa-ax
         woman/SUBJ meat/OBJ fry-ANT-3s/INAN
         'The woman fried the meat'
      b. mamac<u>i</u>   ta'waci tu̞kuavi cíir<u>a</u>-ku̞-qay-'u
         woman/SUBJ man/OBJ meat/OBJ fry-BEN-ANT-3s/AN
         'The woman fried the meat for the man'
      c. *mamac<u>i</u>   tu̞kuavi ta'waci cíir<u>a</u>-ku̞-qay-ax
         woman/SUBJ meat/OBJ man/OBJ fry-BEN-ANT-3s/INAN

In embedding SVO languages, the situation is compounded a bit by the fact that there is no automatic provision for adjacency in DS-complementation. But over time, a VO language can affect **predicate raising** to remedy the situation. This can be seen in Spanish, where in a sense the two verbs are ready to co-lexicalize:

(109) María se-la-hizo   comer la manzana a   Juan
     Mary **him-it**-make/PRET/3s eat/INF the apple   DAT John
     'Mary made John eat the apple'

The pronominal clitics agreeing with the two objects now appear at the beginning of the verbal complex, regardless of the fact that 'apple' is the patient of 'eat'. And there is no morpho-syntactic evidence that the two objects bear their respective grammatical relations to two different verbs, or partake in two different VPs.

Clause-union in embedding languages is sometimes a matter of degree. In general, the syntactic integration of the complement clause into the main clause involves four structural features:

(110) **Structural features of clause integration** (Givón 1990a, ch. 13):
   a. co-lexicalization of the two verbs
   b. relational integration of the agent-of-complement (causee) into the main clause
   c. the morphology — finite/non-finite — of the complement verb
   d. separation between the clauses by a subordinator or pause

These sub-components tend to exhibit strong association, so that creating a clear grammatical case-role for the causee — agent of the complement clause — inside the main clause is but one facet of clause union. In general, implicative verbs of manipulation ('make', 'cause', 'force'), whose complement event is co-temporal with the main event, are more likely to be co-lexicalized with their complements; while non-implicative verbs ('tell', 'order', 'ask') are less likely. On the scale of event-and-clause integration, causative and resultative constructions are ranked at the very top. And **morphological causatives** arise as the natural clause-union consequence of the complementation of causative verbs.

While the causee in morphological causatives indeed bears a grammatical object relation to the combined causative verb, its exact case-role is open to considerable cross-language variation. Comrie (1976) has suggested a universal syntactic **bumping hierarchy** by which the causee occupies the highest available object relation that is not yet occupied by semantic objects of the complement verb:

(111) DO > IO > OBL

Thus in French, if the complement is intransitive, the causee is marked as DO. If the complement is transitive, the causee is marked as dative. And if the complement is bi-transitive, the causee is marked as an oblique agent-of-passive (Comrie 1976):

(112) a. Je ferai   courir **Henriette**
         I   make/FUT run/INF **Henriette/DO**
         'I'll make H. run'
      b. Je ferai   manger les gateaux à   **Henriette**
         I   make/FUT eat/INF   the cakes   DAT **Henriette**
         'I'll make H. eat the cookies'
      c. Je ferai   écrir une lettre   au   directeur **par Jean**
         I   make/FUT write a   letter/DO DAT/the director **by   Jean**
         'I'll make Jean write a letter to the director'

But as both Comrie (1976) and Cole (1984) point out, many other variants of causee case-marking are possible, including doubling on the direct-object case, doubling on the dative case, and more. A well known case in Japanese illustrates semantic control over the choice of case-role: accusative when the causee has no control, dative when it retains some control:[51]

(113) a. Oji-ga   Odette-**o**   odor-**ase**-ta
         Prince-SUBJ Odette-ACC dance-CAUS-PAST
         'The prince made Odette dance'
      b. Oji-ga   Odette-**ni** odor-**ase**-ta
         Prince-SUBJ Odette-DAT dance-CAUS-PAST
         'The prince let Odette dance'

Less acknowledged is the fact that when case-doubling occurs, the behavior-and-control properties of the like-coded objects are rather different. As noted throughout, surface morphology does not disclose the entire story of grammatical relations. We have already seen one such a case in Ute (examples (106), (107), (108) above). A more extensive example may be seen in the double-object bi-transitive clauses in Bantu. In such clauses, only one of the objects — the more

topical human dative/benefactive — can occupy the post-verbal DO position,
and only that object controls object agreement. Thus (Swahili):

(114) a. Watoto   wa-li-**m**-p-ia   Juma kitabu
       children they-PAST-**him**-give-BEN Juma book
       'The children gave Juma a book'
   b. *watoto   wa-li-**m/ki**-p-ia   kitabu Juma
       children they-PAST-**him/it**-give-BEN book   Juma
   c. *watoto   wa-li-**ki**-p-ia   Juma kitabu
       children they-PAST-**it**-give-BEN Juma book

Further, only the dative/benefactive object is accessible to passivization, which
is promotional in Bantu. And once the dative/benefactive becomes the subject,
the patient DO controls object agreement, and the agent is demoted to *chômeur*:

(115) a. Juma a-li-**ki**-p-i-**wa**   kitabu (kwa watoto)
       Juma he-PAST-**it**-give-BEN-**PASS** book   (by children)
       'Juma was given the book (by the children)'
   b. *kitabu **ki**-li-**m**-p-i-**wa**   Juma (kwa watoto)
       book   **it**-PAST-**him**-five-BEN-**PASS** Juma (by   children)
   c. *Juma a-li-**wa**-p-i-**wa**   kitabu (kwa watoto)
       Juma he-PAST-**them**-give-BEN-**PASS** book   (by   children)

When a double-object construction arises in Swahili via morphological
causativization, exactly the same discrimination between the two objects is
observed, with the human causee claiming both the post-verbal position and
control of object agreement:

(116) a. Juma a-li-**ki**-soma   kitabu
       Juma he-PAST-**it**-read book
       'Juma read the book'
   b. wa-li-**m**-som-**esha**   Juma kitabu
       they-PAST-**him**-read-CAUS Juma book
       'They made Juma read a/the book'
   c. *wa-li-**ki**-som-**esha**   Juma kitabu
       they-PAST-**it**-read-CAUS Juma book
   d. *wa-li-**ki/m**-som-**esha**   kitabu Juma
       they-PAST-**it/him**-read-CAUS book Juma

And again, only the causee is now accessible to passivization:

(117) a. Juma a-li-**ki**-som-esh-**wa**   kitabu (kwa watoto)
          Juma he-PAST-**it**-read-CAUS-PASS book   (by   children)
          'Juma was made to read a book (by the children)'
     b. *Kitabu a-li-**m**-som-esh-**wa**   Juma (kwa watoto)
          book   he-PAST-**it**-read-CAUS-PASS Juma (by   children)
     c. *Juma a-li-**wa**-som-esh-**wa**   kitabu (kwa watoto)
          Juma he-PAST-**them**-read-CAUS-PASS book   (by   children)

Clause union in embedding languages thus forces the same kind of hierarchized grammatical relations as one finds in such languages in multi-object main clauses. Having a single co-lexicalized verb and having an integrated set of grammatical relations seem to go hand in hand.

Note, finally, that clause union is fundamentally a diachronic process. As alsewhere in grammaticalization, the semantic component of clause union — grammaticalized verb and event integration — come on line first and rapidly, outpacing the much slower and gradual syntactic realignment (Givón 1975, 1991b; Heine *et al.* 1990). During this gradual process, intermediate stages can display considerable sensitivity to various semantic factors. An example from Spanish causative clause-union may illustrate this. When the underlying patient of the complement verb is non-human, predicate raising and thus full clause-union proceed seemingly to full co-lexicalization of the two verbs:

(118) **se-la**-hizieron   comer la   manzana **a**   Juan
      him-it-made/3p eat/INF the apple   DAT Juan
      'They made John eat the apple'

When the underlying patient is human, the potential for case-role confusion is apparently real enough to block full clause union. The causee is now placed between the two verbs, thus effectively nullifying predicate raising. In the resulting construction, each object follows its semantically-proper verb, with object agreement likewise dispersing:[52]

(119) a. **le**-hizieron   **a**   María pergar-**le**   **a**   Juan
         her-made/3p DAT María hit/INF-**him** DAT Juan
         'They made María hit Juan'
     b. *se-**le**-hizieron   pegar   **a**   María **a**   Juan
         her-him-made/3p hit/INF DAT María DAT Juan

6.8.2.2.2. Serializing languages

In a rather obvious way, serializing languages again fail to create true clause union. Of the four syntactic devices universally used to code clause-integration (110), serializing languages skip three:

- They tend to keep the multi-verbs in the serial clause apart, so that they do not co-lexicalize (110a)
- They tend to keep the objects apart with their respective verbs or even VPs, so that several object may bear the same grammatical relation within the clause — each to its own verb or VP (110b)
- They often do not concentrate all finite morphology on one verb and mark the rest as non-finite (110c).

The only structural device serializing languages use consistently to indicate clause integration is the lack of subordinator or pause (110d).

With respect to the subject relation, serializing languages stand on a par with embedding languages, facing the same problem in the analysis of switch-subject (DS) marged clauses. Thus, consider again the resultative DS-serial construction:

(120) a. **Akan** (Osam 1993):

Esi yi-i   tam-no **fi-i**   pon-no-don
Esi take-PAST cloth-the **leave-PAST** table-the-on
'Esi took the cloth **off** the table'
(*Historically*: 'Esi took the clause and *it* left the table')

b. **Miskitu** (Hale 1991):

Yang truk-kum atk-**ri**   wa-**n**
I   truck-a   sell-DS/1 go-PAST/3
'I sold the truck away'
(*Historically*: 'I sold the truck and *it* went')

c. **Tok Pisin** (Givón 1991b):

...em layt nau paya i-kamap...
she light now fire PRED-come.up
'...She lights the fire...'
(*Lit.*: 'She lights the fire and *it* comes up')

d. **Tok Pisin** (Givón 1991b):

...em tromwey   sospan   i-go...
...she threw.away saucepan PRED-go
'...She threw the saucepan away...'
(*Lit.*: 'She threw the saucepan and *it* went')

e. **Kalam** (Givón 1991b):
...mon d-angiy-**ek**   yin-**ip**...
wood take-light-PAST/SEQ/DS/3s burn-**PERF**/3s
'...She lights the wood...'
(*Lit*.: 'She takes and lights the wood and *it* burns')

In all of these examples, the object of the first verb is semantically the subject of the second. But no syntactic test can show that the object NP is anything but a grammatical object in the serial clause.

The same also applies to causative constructions in serializing languages:

(121) a. **Supyire** (Carlson 1989):
mii à   u   **karima** à   ngukuu **lyi**
I   PERF him **force** PERF chicken **eat**
'I forced him to eat the chicken'
(*Lit*.: 'I forced him and *he* ate the chicken')

b. **Ijo** (Williamson 1965):
woni u   mie-**ni**   indi die-**mi**
we   him make-ASP fish share-ASP
'We made him share the fish'
(*Lit*.: 'We made him and *he* shared the fish')

c. **Ijo** (Williamson 1965):
ari u   mie   mu-**mi**
I   him make go-ASP
'I chased him away'
(*Lit*.: 'I chased him and *he* went')

And likewise with the limited serial-resultative pattern in English:

(122) a. They shot him dead
('They shot him and *he* is dead')
b. It struck him dumb
('It struck him and *he* became dumb')
c. She broke the box open
('She broke it so that *it* opened')
d. He packed/stuffed it full of rocks
('He packed/stuffed it and *it* is full of rocks')
e. She wiped/rubbed it dry/clean
('She wiped/rubbed it and *it* is dry/clean')
f. They pried the door open
('They pried the door and *it* is open')

A 'deep' syntactic representation of such DS-serial clauses as embedded
subordinate structures, along the lines proposed by Byrne (1987, 1992), would
be (from Akan):

(123) a. **Switch-subject (DS) serial clause:**
Esi yi-i   tam-no   fi-i   pon-no-don
Esi take-PAST cloth-the **leave-PAST** table-the-on
'Esi took the cloth **off** the table'

   b. **'Deep' syntactic representation:**

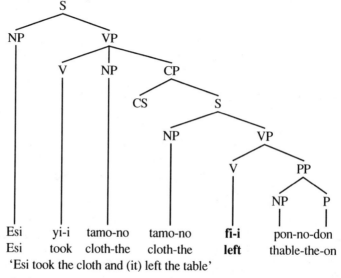

Esi   yi-i   tamo-no   tamo-no   **fi-i**   pon-no-don
Esi   took   cloth-the   cloth-the   **left**   thable-the-on
'Esi took the cloth and (it) left the table'

But what exactly does structure (123b) represent? Surely it could not represent
the synchronic syntactic structure, since synchronically (123a) is a single clause
with a single subject. Neither could it represent the synchronic semantic
structure, since — with the exception of true causative constructions like (121)
— the second verb in all our DS-serial clauses is semantically grammaticalized;
it has no verbal meaning but rather prepositional meaning. And there is no sense
in which any NP in the clause is the semantic subject of such a grammaticalized
verb. Finally, structure (123b) cannot represent the diachronic precursor structure
— syntactic *or* semantic — of the DS-serial clause (123a) because that precursor
was a chained (coordinate) structure rather than embedded (subordinate) one.

One must conclude, however reluctantly, that grammatical relations in serial
clauses cannot be squeezed into the syntactic mould of embedding languages.

The two types exhibit genuine differences in their syntactic organization. Complete clause union, with co-lexicalized verbs and total re-alignment of grammatical relations, often does not occur in serializing languages, or at least not to the same extent as it does in embedding languages. At the very least, multiple object relations survive the condensation into a single clause. By all available syntactic tests, serial clauses tend to display multiple verbs, multiple direct-objects, and thus multiple VPs (Sebba 1987) long after one or more of the verbs have grammaticalized, semantically or even morphology.

As for the subject relation, clause union in serializing languages does indeed occur. So that by all available syntactic tests serial clauses have a single grammatical subject. In the case of DS-serial clauses, this single grammatical subject is the 'underlying' semantic subject of only the first verb. It bears its grammatical relation — and the pragmatic function of main clausal topic — not to individual verbs or VPs in the complex clause, but rather to the entire merged clause. Which makes a considerable amount of sense in light of the strong parsimonious tendency in human discourse to have only one topical referent per clause.[53]

6.8.3. Degree of grammaticalization and re-analysis of grammatical relations

There is a certain correlation, albeit not a perfect one, between the degree of semantic grammaticalization of the main verb and the re-alignment of grammatical relations in clause union. Consider first the contrast between the non-grammaticalized verb 'want' and the grammaticalized modal 'will' in English:

> (124) a. I **want to** eat the apple
> b. *The apple **wants to** be eaten
> c. I **will** eat the apple
> d. The apple **will** be eaten

Historically, 'will' meant 'want' and selected a dative subject. It also had the same syntactic properties as 'want', so that (124d) would have been equally implausible then. Only when 'will' became semantically bleached and lost its earlier selectional restrictions could the patient/object of the complement verb be promoted to the subject of the passive clause (124d). But now it is not a selected dative subject of the modal 'will', but rather a selected patient-subject of the passive 'be eaten'. In the same vein, compare the behavior of the grammatical-ized modal 'can' with its non-grammaticalized semantic equivalent 'be able to':

(125) a. She **was able to** eat the apple
     b. *The apple **was able to** be eaten
     c. She **can** eat the apple
     d. The apple **can** be eaten

Similarly, compare the long-grammaticalized progressive auxiliary 'be' with the more recently grammaticalizing 'keep', 'finish', 'stop' and 'resume':

(126) a. He **was** fixing the roof
     b. The roof **was** being fixed
     c. He **kept** fixing the roof
     d. ??The roof **kept** being fixed
     e. He **finished** washing the dishes
     f. ??The dishes **finished** being washed
     g. She **stopped** writing her memoirs
     h. ??Her memoirs **stopped** being written
     i. She **resumed** writing her memoirs
     j. ??Her memoirs **resumed** being written

Likewise, consider the slightly less clear contrast between the long-grammatic-alized modal 'should' and its close semantic equivalent 'need to':

(127) a. They **should** build the house there
     b. The house **should** be built there
     c. They **need to** build the house there
     d. ?The house **needs to** be built there

Though creeping grammaticalization of 'need' is in progress, as is evident from the seeming acceptability of passive expressions such as:

(128) a. It **needs to** be done
     b. This paper **needs to** be carefully edited
     c. His room **needs to** be cleaned

What we observe here is a correlation between the degree of grammaticali-zation of an erstwhile main verb and the completion of clause-union. When a main verb is not fully grammaticalized, it continues to exert strong semantic — animacy — restrictions on its subject. The lower-clause patient is semantically inadmissible as subject of the main verb. Nor is it admissible as patient of the main verb, because the main verb does not take that type of a patient. Being inadmissible as a patient, the lower-clause object is also inadmissible as a main-clause object. It thus cannot be promoted to subject-of-passive in the main clause for two related reasons, one semantic, the other syntactic:

- The main verb will not tolerate it semantically, neither as its agent nor as its patient.
- As grammatical object of an embedded clause, it cannot be promoted to subject-of-passive in another clause.

When the erstwhile main-verb reaches full semantic grammaticalization, so that it exerts no selectional restrictions of its own, the erstwhile complement verb becomes semantically the main (and only) verb. Only now can the lower-verb patient bear an object relation within the unified clause — and thus become accessible to passivization.

6.8.4. Clause union, reflexivization and grammatical relations

Like the promotional passive, reflexivization is defined by grammatical relations within the same syntactic clause. This is true of both "true" reflexive and possessive reflexives. In English as in most other languages, neither the subject not the object of the main clause can control reflexivization in a loosely-bound complement clause, one that retains its own independent relational structure. That is:

(129) **Subject control of "true" reflexives:**
    a. John saw Mary in the mirror
    b. John saw **himself** in the mirror
    c. I told John that Mary saw **herself** in the mirror
    d. *I told John that Mary saw **himself** in the mirror
    e. *I told John that Mary saw **myself** in the mirror

(130) **Subject control of possessive reflexives:**
    a. Mary hit **her** mother
    b. Mary hit **her own** Mother
    c. I told John that Mary hit **her** mother
    d. I told John that Mary hit **his** mother
    e. I told John that Mary hit **her own** mother
    f. *I told John that Mary hit **his own** mother
    g. *I told John that Mary hit **my own** mother

At first glance, the control of reflexivization appears to shift to the main-clause in more tightly-bound equi-subject (SS) and switch-subject (DS) complements:

(131) a. John wanted to hit **his own** mother
    b. John wanted to hit **himself**
    c. John told Mary to hit **her own** mother
    d. John told Mary to hit **herself**
    e. ?John told Mary to hit **his own** mother
    f. *John told Mary to hit **himself**

However, in the equi-subject structures (131a,b) 'John' is also the subject of the complement. Likewise in the switch-subject structures (131c,d) 'Mary' is also the subject of the complement. Control of reflexivization thus remain vested properly within the same clause.

In Ute, unlike English, possessive reflexivization is obligatory. If the normal possessive pronoun is used, the object could only be possessed of someone other than the subject. If the subject possesses the object, the invariant reflexive suffix -*av* must be used:[54]

(132) a. mamac̲i̲   tuaci-'**u**   pu̲nikyay-kya
    woman/SUBJ child/OBJ-**3s/AN** see-ANT
    'The woman saw *his/her* child' (= not her own)
    b. mamac̲i̲   tuaci-**av**   pu̲nikyay-kya
    woman/SUBJ child/OBJ-**REFL** see-ANT
    'The woman saw *her own* child'

Surprisingly, subjects of main-clause in Ute retains control of possessive reflexivization in their complements. This is least shocking in morphological causativization, where full clause-union has taken place:

(133) a. mamac̲i̲   ta'waci tuaci-'**u**   magha-**ti**-kya
    woman/SUBJ man/OBJ child/OBJ-**3s/AN** feed-**CAUS**-ANT
    'The woman made the child feed *his* child'
    '*The woman made the child feed *her* child'
    b. mamac̲i̲   ta'waci tuaci-**av**   magha-**ti**-kya
    woman/SUBJ man/OBJ child/OBJ-**REFL** feed-CAUS-ANT
    'The woman made the man feed *her* child'
    '*The woman made the man feed *his* child'

But main-clause subject control persists in looser switch-subject (DS) complements of manipulation verbs, as in:

(134) a. mamac_i   ta'waci may-kyatuaci-**'u**   magha-vaa-**ku**
woman/SUBJ man/OBJ tell-ANT child/OBJ-**3s/AN** feed-IRR-NOM
'The woman told the man to feed *his* child'
'*The woman told the man to feed *her* child'
   b. mamac_i   ta'waci may-kyatuaci-**av**   magha-vaa-**ku**
woman/SUBJ man/OBJ tell-ANT child/OBJ-**REFL** feed-IRR-NOM
'The woman told the man to feed *her* child'
'*The woman told the man to feed *his* child'

And this pattern persists in the loosest complements of perception and cognition verbs:

(135) a. mamac_i   pu̲cucugwa-y 'áapaci sarici-**'u**
woman/SUBJ know/IMM   boy/GEN dog/OBJ-**3s/AN**
táa-ka-**na-y**
kick-**ANT-NOM-OBJ**
'The woman knows that the boy kicked *his* dog'
'*The woman knows that the boy kicked *her* dog'
   b. mamac_i   pu̲cucugwa-y 'áapaci sarici-**av**
woman/SUBJ know/IMM   boy/GEN dog/OBJ-**REFL**
táa-ka-**na-y**
kick-**ANT-NOM-OBJ**
'The woman knows that the boy kicked *her* dog'
'*The woman knows that the boy kicked *his* dog'

What is it in the grammar of Ute that makes the subject of a main clause extend its relational control into the loosest type of complement clause? A tentative answer is that diachronically all Ute of complement clauses are **nominalized**. In the case of equi-subject (SS) (133) or switch-subject (DS) complements (134), only one surface subject appears in the complex clause, much like in English. But in Ute this is also true in the case of the seemingly looser complements of cognition/perception verbs (135). The semantic subject of such complements appears in the **genitive** case, so that the diachronically-more-faithful rendition of their meanings could have been:

(136) a. The woman knows of the **boy's** killing **of** his dog (135a)
   b. The woman knows of the **boy's** killing **of** her dog (135b)

One way of explaining the control of reflexivization in Ute would be then to suggest that nominalized complements in an embedding language are themselves object-like. Their genitive subject — whatever its semantic status — has apparently not yet regained syntactic subject status. Not being a syntactic subject, it cannot control reflexivization.

One must note, finally, that a possessive reflexive pronoun can also replace the subject of a complement clause. In this configuration, English now seems to adopt, at least to a degree, the same bias as Ute — control of reflexivization by the subject of the main clause:

(137) a. Joe told Mary that **his own** mother was sick
      b. ??Joe told Mary that **her own** mother was sick

(138) a. mamac<u>i</u>   ta'waci may-kya tuaci-'**u**
          woman/SUBJ man/OBJ tell-ANT child/GEN-**3s/AN**
          nagham<u>i</u>-kya-**na**-y
          sick-ANT-**NOM-OBJ**
          'The woman told the man that *his* child was sick'
          ('The woman told the man of *his* child's being sick')
          '*The woman told the man that *her* child was sick'
      b. mamac<u>i</u>   ta'waci may-kya tuaci-**av**
          woman/SUBJ man/OBJ tell-ANT child/GEN-**REFL**
          nagham<u>i</u>-kya-**na**-y
          sick-ANT-**NOM-OBJ**
          'The woman told the man that *her* child was sick'
          ('The woman told the man of *her* child's being sick')
          '*The woman told the man that *his* child was sick'

To some extent this is not surprising, given that the subject of the complement has effectively dropped from competition for controlling reflexivization, being itself the reflexive pronoun.

Nominalization of embedded clauses, it seems, brings a complex clause come nearer clause-union. And one predictable consequence of clause-union is that subject properties are more fully concentrated in a single NP; so that a more unified relational structure has been affected. As noted earlier, embedding languages construct their complement structures via a syntactic analogy with the V-OBJ configuration. Among embedding languages, those that fully nominalize their complements are thus likely to present the most extreme case of clause union.

6.9.   Recapitulation

6.9.1.   The clustering approach to grammatical relations

In spite of the immense cross-language diversity in the treatment of grammatical relations, a coherent set of general principles can be discerned. Those principles seem paradoxical until one adopts a **prototype** approach to grammatical categories. This approach recognizes the **clustering** of many features to determine subjecthood and objecthood, even when none of the features is by itself necessay or sufficient. Some of these features involve concrete (overt) coding properties; others involve more abstract behavior-and-control properties. In spite of the considerable potential for incoherent results inherent in this approach, the cross-language clustering of subject and object properties in fact yields strong generalizations:

(i)   The degree of overt coding of subject and object may vary, and this variation may be described as **degree of grammaticalization**.

(ii)   Subject or object features that are more directly associated with underlying **pragmatic function** (topicality) are more likely to be universal, with an implicational hierarchy that extends Keenan's (1975, 1976) predictions:

- nominal case-marking
- grammatical agreement
- word order
- behavior-and -control features

(iii)   A configurational account of grammatical relations, especially of grammatical subjecthood, is a woefully inadequate formal means of accounting for the syntactic facts.

6.9.2.   Ergativity and grammatical relations

In most ergative languages, the discrepancy between universal predictions and language-specific facts is confined to nominal case-marking, the least universal feature of our cluster of relational properties. Even in the small number of "deep" ergative languages, where some behavior-and-control features deviate from the nominative organization principle, the deviations are partial, and the majority of syntactic rules still display nominative-accusative control. This reinforces our observation concerning the more universal nature of relational properties that are associated with the pragmatic functions of subjects and objects.

6.9.3. Serial verbs and grammatical relations

There is no skirting the fact that verb-serializing languages retain, for a long time after clause-chains have condensed into single serial clauses, multi-object relational structure. In this sense, the multi-VP analysis of Sebba (1987) and Larson (1991) is indeed correct — with one glaring exception: The syntactic facts do not support a single VP-node analysis. A more abstract syntactic analysis, the one that attempts to view serialization as clausal embedding (Byrne 1987, 1992), turns out to account well for neither meaning nor syntax nor diachrony.

6.9.4. Clause union and grammatical relations

The difference between clause embedding vs. clause chaining represents a profound typological dichotomy in the diachronic pathways languages can take toward clause-union. In embedding languages, clause union is achieved much more completely, with a single, integrated set of grammatical relations and a single lexical verb that bears all finite verbal inflections. In serializing languages, clause-union remains weaker and partial, allowing for the retention — often for a long time — of multi-verb, multi-object, and thus multi-VP structure. This **syntactic scattering**, however, does not affect the grammatical subject, for a reason that is partially diachronic: Clause-chains are overwhelmingly **equi-topic**, even when interlaced with an occasional switch-topic (DS) clause. The condensation process in clause-union thus tends to yield a single-topic clause, and therefore also a single-subject clause.

Notes

*) I am indebted to Sheri Brainard and Emmanuel K. Osam for sharing their findings on Karao and Akan, respectively; to Marlene Haboud for comments on the Spanish data; to Jiffi Arboleda for the Tagalog data. And last but not least, to John Haiman for a critical reading of an earlier draft of this chapter and many insightful comments.

1) I use the term "processes" in a lame attempt to circumvent the naive cognitive interpretation of complex structures as "derived" — by various "transformations" — from underlying simple structures. Chomsky's distinction between performance and competence makes it relatively easy to view the derivational metaphor as a formal convenience, an entity in the realm of competence with no implied consequences in the realm of performance. Still, the tendency to extend the reach of the derivational metaphor beyond the realm of the formal model persists. This is, one suspects, a natural outcome of taking theoretical models seriously, i.e. assuming that they have real empirical consequences.

2) See Givón (1984a).

3) The mischief is by no means limited to formal grammarians. Thus, Li and Thompson's (1976) much cited typology of "topic prominent" vs. "subject prominent" languages is founded on the selection of morphology — nominal case-marking and grammatical agreement — as the criteria for subjecthood, relegating all other criteria to irrelevance. In a similar vein, Bresnan (1993), following Bresnan and Kanerva (1988), argues that the fronted locative argument of presentative constructions ("To the village came the visitors") is the grammatical subject in ChiChewa (Bantu), since such a locative is pre-verbal and controls subject agreement. The 'logical' subject ('the visitors') is then assigned the grammatical relation of *object*, since it is post-verbal and does not control subject agreement. The fact that it does not control object agreement either — a reliable test for direct objecthood in Bantu (Hawkinson and Hyman 1974) — is not deemed relevant.

4) Most immediately relevant are Rosch (1973, 1975), Rosch and Mervis (1975), Rosch and Lloyd (eds) 1978. But see also Posner and Keele (1968), Tversky (1969, 1975), Hyman and Frost (1975), Posner (1986), or Givón (1986), *inter alia*.

5) This predicament has plagued the study of categories at least since Aristotle, who attempted a less-than-elegant solution to the problem by assigning categorial rigidity to the synchronic medium of "forms", while relegating inter-categorial diachronic flux to another medium, the *synolon* (Tweedale 1986). Another reflection of this problem is seen in the distribution of attended vs. automated processing (see Chapter 8 as well as Givón 1989, ch. 7). Automated processing is more heavily dependent on rigid catetegories, and is in general faster, less error-prone, and less context sensitive.

6) The fact that the majority of verbs in a language may require an agentive subject is not a good argument for suggesting that agentivity is a diagnostic subject-property, and the opposite is in fact expected if one is to adopt our criterion of dissociation (cf. (1), (2) above). The subjects of non-agentive verbs in either nominative or ergative languages do not display fewer of subject properties — either functional or formal — than the subjects of transitive verbs. If anything, in some ergative language the absolutive subjects of intransitive clauses display *more* subject properties than the ergative subjects of transitive clauses (see section 6.6. below).

7) See Hawkinson and Hyman (1974); Givón (1976a; 1979a, ch. 4; 1992); *inter alia*. This more elaborate chain of theoretical arguments resembles an **explanation** more than it does a **reduction**, although the difference between the two is often a matter of degree.

8) See discussion of markedness of clause-types in Chapter 2. Obviously not all "non-basic" clauses have reduced subject properties. Most typical in this respects are passives (Keenan 1975), inverses (see Chapter 3), and existential-presentatives (Hetzron 1971; Bresnan and Kanerva 1988; Bresnan 1993).

9) The substantive claim that the subject in any language is somehow less "topic prominent" has never been defended, nor is it likely to stand, given the mountain of data suggesting that the functional correlates of grammatical subjecthood — Keenan's "reference properties" — are the most universal of all subject properties; see Givón (ed. 1983), Cooreman (1988), as well as Chapter 3 above.

10) For the classification of Machiguenga and Arawak see David Payne (1991).

11) The Machiguenga examples below are all taken from texts collected and analyzed by Betty Snell (in personal communication).

12) Raj Shresta (in personal communication).

13) For a comprehensive discussion of the typology of REL-clauses see Givón (1990b, ch. 15), where sources for all the data in this section are cited.

14) The slight difference involves the fact that in KinyaRwanda the subject pronominal agreement on the verb for 3rd-person singular human takes one form in main clauses (y-) and another form in subject REL-clauses (u-). For other genders, the difference is only in tone. In Hebrew, on the other hand, the same pronominal form is used on the verb in both main and relative clauses.

15) One can assume that the nominative interpretation of Philippine grammar, as in Schachter (1976) or Givón (1979a, ch. 4), represents an earlier diachronic stage. An ergative interpretation (cf. Brainard 1994a,b) converts the Philippine promotional system from promotion to subject (i.e. inversion) to promotion to DO; in which case the interaction between promotion and relativization now resembles that of KinyaRwanda.

16) For further discussion of Ute relativization see Givón (1990b, ch. 14), where the sources for all the data in this section are cited.

17) Again interpreted as a nominative language.

18) See Givón (1976a).

19) One may argue that datives and benefactives in Ute are "obligatorily promoted" to direct object, a situation reminiscent of that in Bantu and Mayan.

20) In English, promotion to DO is optional and applicable primarily to dative and benefactive objects. In terms of text frequency, however, the vast majority of datives and benefactives appear as direct objects (Givón 1984a).

21) Pronominal agreement in active clauses in Ute can be controlled by either the subject or the object, so that it is irrelevant to grammatical relations. But plural agreement on the verb is controlled by the subject, and is thus relevant.

22) The story is a bit more complicated, since in all three the frequency of zero subjects is no doubt much higher than that of zero objects, due to the much higher probality of subject continuity (Givón, ed. 1994; Pu, forthcoming).

23) See Keenan (1976) and, more explicitly, Givón (1979a, ch. 4; 1984b; 1990b).

24) For identifying the 'ritualization' and 'emancipation' of grammar with grammaticalization see Haiman (1991). For the connection between grammaticalization and automaticity see Givón (1979a, ch. 5; 1989, ch. 7). Haiman tends to over-estimate the degree to which grammar can become emancipated from function.

25) See e.g. Givón (1979a, ch. 6: "Where does crazy syntax come from?").

26) From Raj Shresta (in personal communication).

27) When interpreted as a nominative pattern, this Philippine language then exhibits subject agreement in the active and double agreement in the passive/inverse (Keenan 1976: 330).

28) See discussion of Kimbundo in Chapter 3.

29) For the rise of verb-agreement from independent pronouns see Givón (1976a). Many ergative clauses arise diachronically from erstwhile inverse constructions, as was probably the case in Kapampangan and Nez Perce. Their verb-agreement pattern thus often reflects the morphology of the source inverse clause (see again Chapter 3).

30) For the pragmatics of word-order see Givón (1988, 1992). However, Spike Gildea (in personal communication) notes the existence of some carib languages with an ergative-absolutive distribution of word-order:

Intransitive: ABS-V (SV)
Transition: ABS-V-ERG (OVS)

31) This was for a while challenged for "deep" ergative languages such as Dyirbal (Dixon 1972, who claimed that the absolutive object is the clausal topic in Dyirbal). However, a text-based measure of the topicality of the agents and patients in Dyirbal transitive clauses (Cooreman 1988) settled the issue, as it was settled for another Australian ergative language (Tsunoda 1985, 1987), as well as for several Philippine languages such as Tagalog (Cooreman *et al.* 1984), Cebuano (T. Payne 1994) or Karao (Brainard 1994b).

32) This cannot be supported by a hard count, but the most common examples mentioned are Dyirbal, Eskimo and Philippine languages. One could probably add to this at least some Indonesian languages. My own impression is that the common denominator here is a relatively recent shift to ergativity, whereby the absolutive-controlled behavior-and-control properties of ergative clauses are really leftovers of *nominative*-control in an inverse/passive clause, i.e. a patient-topicalizing clause. The absolutive control of grammatical properties in a "deep" ergative clause makes perfect sense as an instance of nominative pattern in a passive/inverse clause. See further below.

33) Jiffy Arboleda (in personal communication).

34) *Ibid.*

35) For ergativity in Philippine languages see T. Payne (1982, 1984), Cooreman *et al.* (1984), Brainard (1984a,b) *inter alia.*

36) The lone exception to that has been reported in ChiChewa (Trithart 1977), where an L-dislocated — topicalized — object of the complement can be raised to object of the main clause.

37) Brainard (1994a) reports no raising of a subject of any kind — ergative or absolutive. But this may be an accidental gap, given that all her examples are text-derived.

38) The Karao data are somewhat simplified below in terms of morphophonemics and cliticization. All verbs are in the imperfective (irrealis) mode.

39) Since pseudo-cleft is a relative-clause pattern, one could surmise that relativization in Karao may have also been absolutive-controlled till recently. In Bikol this is still the case. If Bikol turns out to behave like Karao in zero anaphora control, that would make it a "deeper" ergative by one more syntactic property (relativization). In Tagalog, on the other hand, zero-anaphora can be controlled by either the absolutive or the nominative, with nominative control predominating in text (Cooreman *et al.* 1984).

40) These two epithets are the ones most frequently used for dismissing recalcitrant facts in current GB and in the early 1960's GG, respectively.

41) Rather than the multiple-clause accounts of the 1970s discussion.

42) In a subsequent paper, Byrne (1992) recognizes this discrepancy formally by proposing two separate tree-diagrams for some serial constructions, one to account for the syntax, the other for the semantics. In both diagrams, however, each verb must be dominated by a clausal (S) node.

43) As noted in Chapter 5, Larson (1991) dropped the necessity for a clause node for each serial phrase, retaining a lower VP node for it, along the lines suggested in (77a,b) above.

44) Inanimate pronouns are *zero* in Akan, with minor exceptions.

45) The scope of the final *no* 'the', which must bracket the REL-clause, is the entire relative clause rather than the indefinite 'money'.

46) This semantic account captures only the diachronically-prior meaning of the grammaticalized 'finish', but not the diachronically-prior chained (coordinate) structure. Both the meaning of the verb (verb to aspect) and the structural configuration (chained to single-clause) have been modified by grammaticalization. Byrne's account is neither semantically not syntactically adequate (see further below).

47) These are of course not the only possible configurations in serializing language, so that in some cases verb-adjacency can occur — when a single-verb serial phrase precedes the semantic main verb in a VO language, or follows it in an OV language. Thus compare for Saramaccan (VO) (Byrne 1987):

<blockquote>
de ke   **go wasi** di wagi
they want **go wash** the car
'The want to go (ahd) wash the car'
</blockquote>

And for Supyire (OV) (Carlson 1990):

<blockquote>
fyinga à   pyi à   mpii **jo**   à   **kwo,**
python PERF be   PERF those **swallow** PERF **finish**
'The python had finished swallowing those...'
</blockquote>

48) See Givón (1990b, ch. 13).

49) The seeming exceptions turn out to be non-reduced subjunctive complements, where no clause-union is involved, as in Spanish:

<blockquote>
María dijo a Juan que se-**fuera**
Maria said to Juan SUB REFL-go/SUBJUN/3s
'Mary told John that he should leave'
</blockquote>

Or Hebrew:

<blockquote>
Hi amra lo   she-hu **ye-lex**   lo
she told   DAT/3sm SUB-he **3sm**-go/**IRR** DAT/3sm
'She told him that he should leave'
</blockquote>

50) In Yaqui, another Uto-Aztecan language, all complement-taking main verb co-lexicalize with their complement verbs (Givón 1990b, ch. 13).

51) Atsuko Hayashi (in personal communication); see general discussion in Cole (1984).

52) Marlene Haboud (in personal communication).

53) See Chapter 8 below as well as Givón (1992).

54) See Givón (1990b).

7

The Distribution of Grammar in Text:
On Interpreting Conditional Associations

"...When everything else is impossible, that which
remains, however improbable, must be the case..."
Sherlock Holmes

7.1. Introduction*

Tracking the communicative use of grammar via the distribution of
grammar in text has been the central tool in the methodological arsenal of the
functional grammarian. In the protracted evolution of the functional approach
to grammar — from a mere expression of faith, through an intuitive assignment
of functional-sounding labels to grammatical constructions, and on to an increasingly responsible empirical endeavor — no other tool has been as indispensible.
No other tool has set the communicative approach to grammar quite as vividly
apart from both its structuralist and functionalist counterparts. Yet paradoxically, no other tool in the functionalist's arsenal has engendered more theoretical
confusion and methodological mischief. The reasons for this paradoxical impact
of the grammar-in-text distributional method can be viewed from two perspectives.

At the theoretical end, there is first the delicate question of how one
defines **communicative function**, and what is the ultimate theoretical status of
heuristic definitions. As the heuristic nature of our definitions becomes more
apparent, they turn out to be at considerable remove from the real arena where
all communicative functions play their role — the mental arena of categories
and operations, where what we call "grammar" is but a set of mental processing
instructions, part and parcel of the complex mapping between thought and
speech.

At the methodological end, there remains the equally delicate question of how one constructs a viable empirical methodology to investigate heuristically-defined communicative functions: How to make hypotheses about form-function association explicit enough so that they generate explicit **factual predictions**; and how to subject such factual predictions to falsificatory testing. Within this context, the role of quantification and induction in falsificatory testing must be confronted, so that the balance between variability and categoriality in linguistic behavior can be discovered — rather than presupposed.

The role of deductive reasoning in interpreting **conditional associations** must also be clarified and perhaps reasserted. And the reason for the residual imperfections in form-function correlations — correlations that are always high but never quite perfect — must be sought. Whereby one most often must adjudicate between two competing explanations: (a) Unavoidable methodological garbage, the penalty we pay for exploring complex multivariant environments; and (b) some theoretically predicted, inherent processing slop.

In the evolution of empirical methodology in linguistics, it is important to understand the intermediate position of the text-distribution method, midway between the traditional field techniques of the descriptive linguist and the tightly-constrained procedures of the experimental psycholinguist. The choice of appropriate method turns out to hinge on two elusive questions:

• the accessibility of mental categories to conscious reflection
• the cross-subject reliability of the proverbial native intuition.

Both are core questions at the intersection of theory and methodology.

7.2.   The problem of access

7.2.1. The limits of conscious reflection

The traditional descriptive method, however intuitive, has always rested on unimpeachable empirical foundations. To determine the semantic correlates of a form, you hold all variables constant but one. You then manipulate that one variable, and record the semantic effect of the manipulation. As a quick illustration of this method, consider the elicitation of Swahili verbal paradigms:

(1)   a. **Manipulating variable *a* (subject pronoun):**
      ni-limuona   =   '**I** saw him/her'
      ku-limuona   =   '**You** saw him/her'
      a-limuona   =   '**S/he** saw him/her'

b. **Manipulating variable b (tense-aspect):**

ni-**li**-muona	=	'I **saw** him/her'
ni-**na**-muona	=	'I **see** him/her'
ni-**ta**-muona	=	'I **will see** him/her'
ni-**me**-muona	=	'I **have seen** him/her'

c. **Manipulating variable c (object pronoun):**

a-li-**ni**-ona	=	'S/he saw **me**'
a-li-**ku**-ona	=	'S/he saw **you**'
a-li-**mu**-ona	=	'S/he saw **him/her**'
a-li-**ki**-ona	=	'S/he saw **it**'

d. **Manipulating variable d (verb stem):**

a-li-ki-**ona**	=	'S/he **saw** it'
a-li-ki-**piga**	=	'S/he **hit** it'
a-li-ki-**amba**	=	'S/he **said** it'

e. **Manipulating variable e (transitivity):**

a-li-mu-on-**a**	'S/he saw him/her'
a-li-mu-on-**ea**	'S/he saw something for him/her'
a-li-on-**ewa**	'S/he was seen'
a-li-on-**eka**	'S/he was visible'
a-li-mu-on-**esha**	'S/he showed him/her something'
wa-li-on-**ana**	'They saw each other'

Our manipulations have yielded rich data concerning the various form-meaning associations along the verb-inflectional paradigm. But the validity of our results rests upon the two related assumptions:

(a) The meaning of the manipulated forms is accessible to conscious reflection.

(b) All speakers will respond uniformly.

The grammar-in-text methodology is designed to take over precisely where assumption (a) is weak and assumption (b) thus becomes untenable. But under certain conditions — and given another set of goals — the grammar-in-text method too is likely to reach its natural limits. Whereby one must let go and reach for other methods.

One of the most striking facts that all grammarians — be they Aristotle, Bopp, Jespersen, Bloomfield, Tesnière, Harris, Halliday or Chomsky — could not but notice is that roughly the same informational contents can be packaged into a wide array of different syntactic clausal structures. That is:

(2)   a. Marla saw Henry
      b. **Marla** didn't **see Henry**
      c. Go **see Henry, Marla**!
      d. Who **saw Henry?**
      e. Did **Marla see Henry?**

(3)   a. Marla saw Henry
      b. She **saw Henry**
      c. **Marla saw** him
      d. **Henry** was **seen** (by **Marla**)
      e. The woman who **saw Henry** was **Marla**
      f. The man **Marla saw** (was **Henry**)
      g. We told **Marla** to **see Henry**
      h. We suspected that **Marla saw Henry**
      i. We suspected **Marla** of **seeing Henry**
      j. As for **Henry, Marla saw** him
      k. Having **seen Henry,** (**Marla** left)
      l. After **Marla saw Henry**...

Harris' (1956) early transformational observations hinged on noting these **co-occurrences** of meaningful units. That is, all the clauses in (2) and (3) seem to more-or-less involve the same agent/subject, patient/object and verb, and thus in a sense "refer to the same event". The variation in syntactic structure in (2)/(3) — with all lexical variables held constant — must surely map onto a parallel variation in meaning.

So far, the analytic task seems to parallel the verb-paradigm manipulations in (1). And indeed, in the case of negation (2b) and non-declarative speech-acts (2c,d,e), the functional correlates of structural variation seem obvious and accessible.[1] However, both the speakers' and the linguist's intuitions about the functional correlates of syntactic structure are much harder to nail down with any degree of cross-subject reliability in the case of manipulations (3) — pronouns (3b,c), passives (3d), relative clauses (3e,f), verb complements (3g,h), raising to object (3i), L-dislocation (3j), adverbial clauses (3k,l). Our **propositional semantic** intuition about agents, patients and verbs seems both accessible and replicable. But our **discourse-pragmatic** intuition about the communicative function of grammar turns out to be rather fickle.

7.2.2. Definitions and observations

In attempting to understand how the same information-bearing clause mutates through so many different syntactic structures, our natural instinct is to look for different **communicative uses** that co-occur systematically with different structures. But in order to accomplish this in a responsible way — given the manifest limits of our intuition — functionalists must find some means of observing the use of grammar in its natural habitat — in natural communication.[2]

Suppose we go and observe ongoing communication and record it for future analysis on tape or paper. We have got a text now, but how do we identify "communicative functions" in it? This question, a subversive silent partner of the working text linguist, has given rise to two radical responses, both of which contrived to bypass the question. One radical bypass is that of **functional intuitionism,** as seen in the Praguean notion "communicative dynamism" or the Hallidayan "theme". The other radical bypass is that of **naive iconism,** the practice of conferring functional-sounding labels on grammatical structures.[3]

However important these two extreme approaches have been in the history of discovering the functional correlates of grammar, they both turn out to bog down in methodological circularity. The inaccessibility of communicative function to conscious reflection eventually compels the intuitionist to fall back on structure as means of discovering function. The Prague ans' automatic equation of "fronted clausal position" with "theme" is a glaring case in point. At the other extreme, naive iconism is susceptible to the same circularity. Structures are seldom 100% iconic (see Chapter 2); but even if they were, in the absence of a structure-independent definition of "function", iconism decays into tautology.

The only viable alternative to both extreme bypasses is to define communicative functions independently of both structure and intuition. The fundamental justification for such a procedure is essentially logical:[4]

(4)   **Correlation vs. tautology**:
      "If two entities A and B are said to correlate, then nei-
      ther can partake in the other's definition; otherwise
      stating that they 'correlate' is stating a tautology".

7.2.3.   Discourse context as a heuristic

For the grammar-in-text linguist, the task of defining communicative function independent of both structure and intuition boils down to roughly the following procedure:

(5)   a. Define, independently of both structure and intuition, a set of **discourse contexts**.
   b. Study the **distribution** of the various grammatical structures in — or their **association** with — these discourse contexts.
   c. When significant **correlations** are observed, seek explanatory hypotheses about why the correlations are the way they are.
   d. Argue — in a principled, theory-guided fashion — that the observable discourse contexts indeed correspond to some unobservable **communicative functions**.

The Achilles heel of procedure (5) is of course step (5d) — the *sine qua non* link in the chain of scientific reasoning, whose absence sooner or later yields devastating consequences. This link rests on vital theoretical connections to other empirical domains, as well as on further theoretical reasoning about the text-distribution facts. This is where the linguist's grammar-in-text distributional study link up with relevant theories of face-to-face interaction, information processing and mental representation; that is, with the social, cognitive and neurological underpinning of language.

7.3.   Methodological perspective

The distributional study of grammar in text can also be viewed from a methodological perspective, that of linguistics as a would-be empirical science. From this perspective, any pairing between a particular grammatical structure and a proposed communicative function is only a **hypothesis** to be tested inductively. Like most hypotheses in a complex domain, suggested form-function associations cannot be tested directly. Rather, one tests their deduced **logical consequences.**

In both the functional intuitionist and naive iconist approaches to communicative function, the question of testing is bypassed. What is true of one observed instance of a grammatical construction, in or out of text, must presumably be true of all other (yet unobserved) instances of the same construction. As in the case of Chomsky's idealized "competence", the questions of **population variation, sampling** and **induction** are moot.

For the grammar-in-text linguist, population variation, sampling and induction are harder to ignore. Hypotheses may indeed be reached by diverse routes — intuition, analogy, common sense, divine guidance. Still, hypothesis formation is probably best viewed in terms of Hanson's (1958) schema of **abductive reasoning** (following Peirce 1934: 134):

(6)   **Hypothesis about the communicative function of syntactic structures:**

    a. **Puzzling facts:** Various facts about the behavior of syntactic structures A and B do not make sense given our current theoretical perspective.

    b. **Hypothesis:** But if structure A turned out to have the communicative function X, and structure B the communicative function Y, their behavior would now make perfect sense.

    c. **Abduction:** Therefore hypothesis (6b) must be the case, and our current theoretical perspective must be expanded to incorporate (6b) as an integral part.

Since communicative functions X and Y are unobservable mental entities, one must now deduce some **logical consequences** of X and Y that can be observed more directly. In this case, one argues for a stable association between the invisible X and Y and two observable discourse contexts P and Q:

(7)   **Deduced logical consequences of hypothesis (6b):**
"Unimpeachable theoretical grounds compel us to assume that communicative functions X and Y must be strongly associated with discourse contexts P and Q, respectively".

The exact strength of the predicted association (7) must for the moment remain open. At the very least, the association must be a **one-way conditional** association, that is:

(8)   "If context P, then function X (but not necessarily vice versa);
    if context Q, then function Y (but not necessarily vice versa)".

A **bi-conditional** association would be more desirable on theoretical ground,[5] but is probably unrealistic at this juncture, given the strong heuristic residue in prediction (7).

It is only the deduced logical consequences of hypothesis (6b) — prediction (7) — that can now be tested inductively, following the standard procedure of **falsificatory testing** (Popper 1959):

(9)   **Falsificatory testing of the association between syntactic structures A,B and discourse contexts P,Q, respectively**:

a. **Sampling**: Collect all instances of structures A and B and discourse-contexts P and Q in a large enough body of text.[6]

b. **Descriptive statistics**: Express the distribution of structures A and B in contexts P and Q as percents of their total populations.

c. **Observing correlations**: Decide whether the numerical distributions match prediction (7).

d. **Inferential statistics**: Apply statistical tests to the observed distributions to see whether the correlations are not simply due to random fluctuation in sampling.

Our testing procedure of course does not guarantee that the tested prediction (7) is verified, but — at best — that the results of testing are compatible with the tested hypothesis; i.e. that for the moment we have **failed to falsify** one deductive consequence of our original hypothesis (6).[7] Nor does repeated failure to falsify (7) guarantee that the original hypothesis (6b) is non-trivial, theoretically interesting, or central to the investigation at hand. Such guarantees, such as they are, must come first from the initial process of hypothesis formation. That is, they must come from the complex chain of — first abductive, then deductive — theoretical reasoning that associated visible structures A,B with putative, invisible functions X,Y (6), and then associated the invisible functions X,Y with the visible discourse contexts P,Q (7). But when proper theoretical reasoning has driven the formulation of hypotheses and deduction of their testable consequences, then the text-distributional study of the communicative function of grammar can be, at least in principle, an viable empirical undertaking.[8]

7.4.   Conditional associations

The bulk of this chapter involves trying to understand a phenomenon that crops up, invariably, when one studies the distribution of grammar in text — **biased conditional associations**. On the face of it, the phenomenon involves the deductive logic of the correlation between two entities that are said to "associate". Such associations are most often biased, resembling the one-way conditional (⊃) of logic (10), rather than the bi-conditional (=) (11):

(10)   **One-way ('biased') conditional:**
       B ⊃ A
       "If B, then A"as (but not necessarily vice versa)

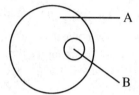

(11)   **Bi-conditional ('unbiased'):**
       A = B
       "If A, then B; and if B, then A"

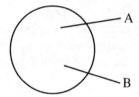

While deductive logic takes the two patterns of associations (10) and (11) to be discrete and incompatible, it is easy to show that there is an inductive continuum between them. Consider for example the pattern of association in (12):

(12)

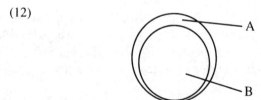

On purely logical grounds, (12) is a biased, one-way conditional association akin to (10). Probabilistically, however, it is much closer to the bi-conditional association in (11), since only in an extremely small fraction of the population A could one find individuals that are not also members of B. This observation may of course be irrelevant to the logician, but it turns out to be extremely important in cognition and language.

What the case-studies below suggest is that many of us who practice the text-distribution method fall prey to a common fallacy — ignoring the directional bias of conditional associations. We will observe a number of cautionary tales where this has led to theoretical confusion or methodological murk. I will also try to outline two separate reasons why grammatical forms and discourse contexts should exhibit a biased one-way conditional association. At the bottom of the phenomenon, I suggest, lie two by-now-familiar issues:

- **Methodological**: A discourse context is only a heuristic stand-in for some cognitively-significant communicative function, so that its association with any particular function — and thus with its correlated structure — is imprecise.
- **Theoretical**: The same form may ambiguously map onto more than one function, but the same function always maps unambiguously onto only one form.[9] The cognitive processor may thus tolerate a certain level of slop in one mapping direction — from form to function (i.e. in speech perception).

When we observe biased conditional associations between grammatical forms and discourse context, we should attempt to determine whether the observed bias is due to a methodological or a theoretical source, or both.

7.5. Case studies

7.5.1. Word-order in Mandarin Chinese

7.5.1.1. Background

In a well known classic, Li and Thompson (1975) proposed that the preverbal position of NPs in Mandarin — both subjects and objects — signalled definiteness, and the post-verbal position signalled indefiniteness. Their conclusions were given as the following two tendencies, the first synchronic, the second diachronic:

(13) *Tendency A*: Nouns preceding the verb tend to be definite, while those following the verb tend to be indefinite. (Li and Thompson 1975: 170)

Tendency B: Mandarin is presently undergoing a word order shift from SVO to SOV. (*ibid*, 185)

In a subsequent quantified text-based study of Mandarin word-order, Sun and Givón (1985) arrived at the exact opposite conclusions:

(14) a. It could not possibly be the case that OV vs. VO word-order contrast in Mandarin Chinese is used to code the functional contrast of definite vs. indefinite, respectively.

b. Rather, there is a near-categorial correlation between the OV word-order in Mandarin and the feature of **contrastive topicalization**.

c. It is most unlikely that Mandarin Chinese shows any dia-chronic drift from predominantly VO to predominantly OV syntax.

The text-distributional results on which conclusions (14a-c) were based are reproduced, in a slightly compressed form, in Tables 1 and 2 below.

TABLE 1: **Distribution of Word-Order in Written Mandarin**
          (after Sun and Givón 1985)

	word order					
	vo		**ov**		**total**	
category	N	%	N	%	N	%
REF-INDEFINITE	276	99.0	3	1.0	279	100.0
NON-REF INDEF.	45	93.1	3	6.9	48	100.0
DEFINITE	870	92.2	73	7.8	943	100.0
TOTAL:	1191	93.8	79	6.2	1270	100.0

TABLE 2: **Distribution of Word-Order in spoken Mandarin**
(after Sun and Givón 1985)

word order

category	vo		ov		total	
	N	%	N	%	N	%
REF-INDEFINITE	109	99.0	1	0.0	110	100.0
NON-REF INDEF.	41	87.2	6	12.8	47	100.0
DEFINITE	289	90.3	31	9.7	320	100.0
TOTAL:	439	92.0	38	8.0	477	100.0

In a subsequent commentary on Sun and Givón (1985), Johanna Nichols (unpubl.) challenged our conclusions, specifically their synchronic portions (14a,b). The issues raised by Nichols go to the very heart of how one should interpret the distributional results of grammar-in-text studies, i.e. the frequency association of grammatical structures and communicative functions or discourse contexts.

7.5.1.2. The Mandarin facts

In her paper, Nichols observed that a *Chi*-square analysis shows that there is indeed a strong statistical correlation between definiteness and OV syntax in Mandarin Chinese. The correlation is in fact visible to the naked eye surveying the distributional Tables 1, 2. It is a biased one-way conditional association: The predictability from the function definite to the form OV is exceedingly low, roughly at the level of **8 percent**. This was the gist of our empirical claim (14a). But the predictability in the opposite direction, from the form OV to the function definite,[10] is around **90 percent**. Or, as we noted at the time:

> "...Thus in Spoken Mandarin (Table 2), out of the total of 38 tokens of OV order, 31 (82%) involve definite objects... The same can be seen for the written language (Table 1): out of 79 tokens of OV order, 73 (92%) involve definite objects..." (Sun and Givón 1985: 344)

This striking directional bias in strength of association impelled us to make our empirical claim (14b). The facts of the one-way conditional association between the function definite and the form OV may be summarized roughly as follows:

(15)   a. **From function to form**: if DEF then OV = 8%
      b. **From form to function**: if OV then DEF = 90%

This skewed distribution can be represented in the Ven diagram:

(16)

In other words, almost all members of the form-class OV are also members of the function-class definite. But the vast majority of the members of definite are not members of OV; rather, they are members of the form-class VO.

How come then the *Chi*-square test, as reported by Nichols (unpubl.), shows a significant statistical association between the function definite and the form OV? The answer is simple: The *Chi*-square test of association is blind to directional bias. All it can tell you — as it told Nichols — is that there is a strong association between definite and OV. It is impervious to the fact that the association is skewed, that it is only a one-way conditional. But what does such a skewed correlation mean?

7.5.1.3. Interim explanation

In Sun and Givón (1985: 345-348) we went ahead and proposed an explanation for the biased association between *definite* and OV in Mandarin. Our explanation — or hypothesis — may be summarized as follows:

(17)   a. The skewed conditional association is due to an **indirect** correlation between OV order and definite in Mandarin; in other words, some other discourse-functional feature mediates the correlation.

      b. That mediating feature is **contrastive topicalization**. That function correlates at a near-categorial level — roughly 90% — with the OV order in Mandarin.

      c. It is well known that contrastive movement is a topicalizing device.[11]

      d. Topical NPs in normal human-oriented narrative are overwhelmingly definite, with a small residue of generic NPs, but no referring-indefinite NPs.[12]

e. Thus, the near-categorial uni-directional association of OV
⊃ definite was due to the equally high — but undoubtedly
less skewed — association of topical ⊃ definite.

7.5.1.4. Falsificatory testing

In support of hypothesis (17), we raised several arguments. We first noted
that Y-movement shares systematic restrictions with other topicalizing constructions, such as L-dislocation and cleft-focus. One of the restrictions is a shared
aversion for REF-indefinite NPs. Thus compare:

(18) **Y-movement:**
    a. **NON-REF:**   (I don't like tomatoes.) **Potatoes** I like.
    b. **REF-DEF:**   (I didn't see Mary.) **John** I saw right away.
    c. **REF-INDEF:**   *(I didn't see a horse.) **A cow** I saw.

(19) **L-dislocation:**
    a. **NON-REF:**   As for **potatoes**, I seldom eat any.
    b. **REF-DEF:**   As for **Mary**, I saw her yesterday.
    c. **REF-INDEF:**   *As for **one man**, I saw him yesterday.

(20) **Cleft:**
    a. **NON-REF:**   It's **potatoes** I like, not tomatoes.
    b. **REF-DEF:**   It's **Mary** I saw, not John.
    c. **REF-INDEF:**   *It's **one man** I saw, not one woman.

While not a conclusive proof by any means, the facts in (18)-(20) are compatible with our hypothesis, reinforcing our interpretation of the Mandarin OV order as
a topicalizing device. Our initial distribution tables show the OV category to
consist of a majority of definite-referring NPs, a significant minority of non-
referring (generic) NPs, and a minute trace of REF-indefinite NPs.

Second, we showed (Sun and Givón 1985, Tables 6,7,8,9, pp. 340-343)
that two discourse-based measures that have correlated well in other languages
with contrastive devices (see Givón, ed. 1983a) — low referential distance
(RD) and high potential interference (PI) — indeed characterize the OV
construction in Mandarin.

In this connection, we also showed (Sun and Givón 1985, Table 12, p.
345) that the OV construction in Mandarin compares rather well with Y-
movement in at least one other rigid-VO language (Biblical Hebrew; A. Fox
1983), in terms of the two text-based measures (RD, PI). What is more, the OV

constructions in Mandarin and Biblical Hebrew also compare well in their text frequency. The three comparisons are summarized in Table 3 below.

TABLE 3: **Text frequency, referential distance (RD) and potential inter-ference (PI) of pre- and post-verbal objects in Mandarin Chinese and Biblical Hebrew** (after Sun and Givón 1985)

measure	written Mandarin		spoken Mandarin		biblical Hebrew	
	VO	OV	VO	OV	VO	OV
% in text	94%	6%	92%	8%	97%	3%
average RD	10.0	3.0	4.0	2.0	12.1	2.5
average PI	1.09	1.47	1.14	1.80	1.69	2.00

Fourth, we took the entire sample of OV constructions from our spoken Mandarin text and showed that in most cases some type of contrast was involved (Sun and Givón 1985: 346–34), and that most OV cases also involved other contrastive items, such as negation or contrastive quantifiers ('all', 'only', 'even', 'really'). To be sure, we had not proved our hypothesis, we had only failed to falsify it. But this is only to be expected, as suggested by Karl Popper:

"... The game of science is, in principle, without end. He who decides one day that scientific statements do not call for any further [falsificatory; TG] test, and that they can be regarded as finally verified, retires from the game ..." (Popper, 1959: 53)

In a subsequent correspondence over these issues, Nichols (in personal communication) chided us for having offered only a hypothesis:

"... Your claim that OV order responds to contrast is only a hypothesis. The survey in S&G (1985) cannot possibly test this hypothesis, since you did not independently code for contrast. Your paper makes it clear that this is only a hypothesis ... I have no quarrel with your hypotheses, and no grounds for proposing any of my own ..." (Nichols, *ipc,* pp. 2-3)

Nichols' comment indeed raises an issue in text-distribution studies that has already been alluded to above: The communicative function of grammatical form is seldom if ever measured — or even observed — directly. Rather, one makes a hypothesis about some form-function pairing and then deduces some of its logical consequence, and only those are then tested (cf. Popper 1959). Which is the procedure we followed in Sun and Givón (1985), testing several logical consequences of hypothesis (17). And in principle we could have gone and tested more and more *ad infinitum*.[13]

7.5.1.5. A broader theoretical context

7.5.1.5.1. The cognitive basis of word-order pragmatics

Most empirical cycles of investigation in so-called **normal science**[14] take place in a broader theoretical context, one which illuminates both the theoretical reasoning that went into formulating particular hypotheses and the methodological reasoning that prompted specific falsificatory tests.[15] The Sun and Givón (1985) text-based study of Mandarin word-order was deeply embedded in such a context. In a number of studies on the pragmatics of word-order flexibility, covering a range of unrelated and typologically diverse languages, it has been observed that the **pre-posing** of NPs (subjects, objects) occurred in a rather consistent array of discourse contexts. To summarize (Givón 1988):

(21) a. Constituents tend to be fronted in contexts of either low anaphoric **accessibility** ('low continuity') or high thematic **importance** ('high topicality').

 b. In most cases when the two principles come in conflict, thematic importance wins over anaphoric predictability.

 c. Most of the cases where low accessibility seems to be the motivation for fronting turn out to involve a combination of both principles; that is, less accessible NPs that are also topical.

It is now easy to see why the Mandarin Chinese distribution of OV vs. VO order was of great interest to us. A definite NP is by definition more accessible in the preceding (anaphoric) discourse. An indefinite NP is by definition less accessible, since it appears in the discourse for the first time. In all the previous text-based studies where the DEF vs. INDEF contrast was investigated, a strong tendency had been observed for definite NPs to be *post*-posed, and for indefinites to be *pre*-posed. If it turned out that Li and Thompson (1975) were right in their claim about Mandarin Chinese, that language would have constituted a disturbing counter-example to the otherwise universal applicability of principles (21). In the same text-based studies summarized in Givón (1988) it was also noted that a very strong correlation existed between the pre-posing of

NPs and contrastiveness.[16] The text-distributional data on the Mandarin OV construction reported in Sun and Givón (1985), and our explanation of those data, were again compatible with the rest of the cross-linguistic evidence.

7.5.1.5.2. The inherent bias in form:function correlations

There is another theoretical context within which our findings about Mandarin word-order must be considered. As noted earlier,[17] functionalists in linguistics often tend to over-represent or idealize the principle of "one form, one function". This may be seen in the well-known quote from Dwight Bolinger (1977):

> "... the natural condition of language is to preserve one form
> for one meaning and one meaning for one form ..."
> (Bolinger 1977: x)

Put another way, Bolinger suggests that the association between form and meaning is equally strong in both directions, thus a bi-conditional association. But as Haiman has pointed out (1985: 21–22; see also Marchand 1968), Bolinger's assumption was over-extended. In human language **polysemy** ('ambiguity') is quite common, but its converse, **synonymy**, is rare. What is more, the iconicity (fidelity) of the linguistic code, particularly the grammatical code, is subject to corrosive diachronic pressures from both ends of the semiotic equation. The code (form) is constantly eroded by **phonological attrition,** leading to increased ambiguity. And the message (function) is constantly reshaped by **creative elaboration,** so that a form is extended to different (though initially similar) functions — again yielding increased ambiguity. Both diachronic processes thus create the same pressure toward a biased form-meaning correlation: lower predictability from form to function (one-to-many), but higher predictability from function to form (one-to-one).

The systematic bias in the linguistic code may be understood in terms of the different processing demands on speech production and speech perception. The task confronting speakers in mapping function into form is more deterministic, since speakers presumable know — or have a higher probability of knowing[18] — what they have in mind. There is no adaptive reason for them to employ anything but a one-to-one mapping procedure. In contrast, hearers, in decoding from form to function, can tolerate a certain level of ambiguity in code-meaning associations, ambiguity that can be resolved by recourse to context. A lower predictability in mapping from form to function is thus theoretically feasible.

On the face of it, the theoretical consideration outlined above clashes with the Mandarin facts. The mapping predictability from function to form (speaker's perspective; definite ⊃ OV) appeared very weak — 8% only. The mapping predictability from form to function (hearer's perspective; OV ⊃ definite) appeared much stronger — 90%. This contradiction however, is only apparent, and this illustrates another conundrum. We have already noted that the relevant function associated with OV in Mandarin is not definite but probably contrastive topic. When the relevant function is thus re-defined, the predictability in the direction function-to-form (contrastive topic ⊃ OV) is much stronger, probably approaching categoriality.[19] And the predictability in the opposite direction, form-to-function (OV ⊃ contrastive topic), is probably weaker, given that the OV construction in Mandarin may serve some non-contrastive functions as well.[20]

Our apparent conundrum is rooted in the fact that most of our structure-independent definitions of communicative function — "definite", "contrastive", "object topicalizing", "inverse" etc. — are at best heuristic stand-ins. They are intermediate theoretical constructs that will carry us only part of the way toward understanding communicative function. Gradually, we must discard such intermediate constructs and replace them with theoretical entities that are more in line with mental categories; that is, with theoretical constructs that are closely aligned to specific cognitive operations in the mind/brain of speech producers and speech comprehenders.

7.5.1.5.3. Searching for structures vs. searching for functions

There is another, procedural lesson to be learned from the history of the Mandarin OV debate. Why did Li and Thompson (1975) arrive at the more valid part of their synchronic conclusions (OV ⊃ definite) so naturally? And why did they just as naturally ignore the invalid part (definite ⊃ OV)? The answer is probably that they looked only in one direction. Their search procedure involved identifying the population of pre-verbal objects (OV), rather than the population of definite objects. This methodological bias, a propensity for searching for the visibles and taking the invisibles for granted, may or may not be a legacy of structuralism. But it may just as well be the legacy of naive iconism — correlations are expected to be strong in either direction, so we assume they will be. Our propensity for making this assumption drives home once again the need for a structure-independent definition of communicative function.

7.5.1.5.4. The cross-language validity of "same function"

As noted earlier, grammatical typology is both circular and meaningless without an independent functional definition of the domains to be "typologized".[21] However tentative and heuristic, our progressively refined text-based functional definitions make it possible to arrive at more precise cross-language typological comparisons of constructions that perform "the same function". As an example of how a functional definition may be progressively refined, consider the family of syntactic constructions that code de-transitive voice. The most permissive definition will incorporate at least the following semantic restriction:

(22)   "Allow only semantically-transitive de-transitive clauses (i.e. those with a verb that *can* take both an agent and a patient)".

Definition (22) would admit into the de-transitive domain a large family of detransitive constructions in English:

(23)   **De-transitive voice:**
   (i)   **Pragmatic de-transitives:**
      a. **BE-passive:**   Mary was hurt (by Bill)
      b. **GET-passive:** Mary got hurt (in an accident)
      c. **Impersonals:** They hurt you (real bad this way)
                          We hurt people (right and left here)
                          You can hurt people (this way)
      d. **L-dislocation:** As for Mary, they didn't hurt her
      e. **Y-movement:** Mary they didn't hurt
      f. **Antipassives:** (When she hits), she hurts (you)
                          She's a people-hurter
   (ii)   **Semantic de-transitives:**
      g. **Adjectival:**   (When she finally found it,)
                          the car was painted (bright yellow)
      h. **Middle voice:** She hurts real easy
                          She's vulnerable
                          She get's hurt real easy

Definition (22) is obviously lax and cannot guarantee 100% predictability from function to form. But it narrows the domain of clause types considerably, yielding a coherent set of syntactic constructions in which, in one way or another, the prototype active-clause's balance between agent and patient is disrupted. One may next narrow down the definition with an added semantic condition, as in (24a):

(24) "Allow only semantically-transitive clauses that
    (a) refer to an actual event".

Substituting definition (24) would bar from the domain all the semantically-stative adjectival and middle-voice constructions (23g,h), and will leave only pragmatic voice construction (23a-f).

One may now add another semantic condition that will further narrow down the definition, as in (25b):

(25) "Allow only semantically-transitive clauses that
    (a) refer to an actual event; and
    (b) have a non-agentive patient".

Definition (25) will now exclude the GET-passive (23b), whose subject-patient tends to be human, volitional, agentive.[22] This definition may be narrowed down further with a discourse-pragmatic condition, as in (26c):

(26) "Allow only semantically-transitive clauses that
    (a) refer to an actual event;
    (b) have a non-agentive patient; and
    (c) have a topicalized patient".

Definition (26) will now eliminate both the patient-demoting antipassives (23f) and the impersonal clauses (23c). And this definition may now be narrowed once more with another discourse-pragmatic condition (27d):

(27) "Allow only semantically-transitive clauses that
    (a) refer to an actual event;
    (b) have a non-agentive patient;
    (c) have a topicalized patient; and
    (d) have a de-topicalized ('demoted') agent".

Definition (27) will rule out the two inverse-like constructions, L-dislocation (23d) and Y-movement (23e), both of which tend to retain a topical agent.[23]

Our definition now admits only one English construction, the BE-passive (23a). But in other languages it may well turn out that more than one construction abides by definition (27), so that further refining of the definition may be necessary. For English, we have arrived at a useful, unambiguous (if not cognitively ultimate) functional definition of one grammatical construction. Our exercise illustrates a number of useful methodological lessons:

• The point where one can stop refining one's definition of "communicative function" for the purpose of conducting a text-distributional study of some form-function correlation in a particular language is, in principle, a heuristic matter. The decision is, to some extent, a matter of methodological convenience.

• The theoretical assumption that predictability from function to form must be 100% — and thus a unique path from a well-defined function to a single construction can be found — leads us to seek a natural cutoff point where the definition could in fact be narrow enough so that it applies to a single construction.

• In constructing a grammatical typology of constructions that perform the same communicative function in different languages, one does not always find ideal correspondences. One construction in language A may match the functional definition of two constructions in language B. Language B, it turns out, sub-divides the domain more narrowly than language A. But the same construction in language A may correspond to *no* precisely-matched construction in language C. That is, language C sub-divides the domain more broadly than language A.

7.5.2.   Word-order in Tagalog

As noted above, the skewed correlation between OV and DEF in Mandarin was probably due to their indirect ('mediated') association, or to imprecision in identifying the relevant function. The next case study illustrates a related problem, where one form seems to code several sub-functions — at least as heuristically defined. In her study of pragmatic word-order in Tagalog, Barbara Fox (1985) observed the text-distribution of **pre-posed** NPs in this largely V-first language. A cluster of communicative functions — again translated into discourse contexts — seem to correlate with this grammatical device, all coming under the general heading of **discontinuity** relative to the preceding (anaphoric) text. The four discourse contexts — heuristic measures of continuity — used by Fox to assess continuity may all be viewed as reasonable deductive consequences of the hypothesis that pre-posing is associated with — or 'codes' — discontinuity. They are (B. Fox 1985):

(28)   **continuous**   **discontinuous**

   a. paragraph medial   paragraph initial
   b. following a comma   following a period
      or zero punctuation
   c. temporally continuous   temporally discontinuous
   d. continuing referent (SS)   changing referent (DS)

The text-distribution of each of the four textual contexts (28a-d) was measured independently, and the *Chi*-square test showed a statistically significant correlation between the syntactic feature "pre-posed NP" and each of the discontinuity measures in (28). However, the correlation was much more dramatic when expressed as a predictability from function to form (discontinuity ⊃ fronted-NP) than as a predictability from form to function (fronted-NP ⊃ discontinuity). To illustrate this directional bias, consider B. Fox's results concerning the paragraph position measure (28a), given as Table 4 below.

TABLE 4: **Pre-posing and position in the paragraph:**
Percent distributions of structure in function
(from Fox 1985, Table 1)

	position in the paragraph					
	initial		non-initial		total	
syntax	N	%	N	%	N	%
pre-verbal NP	61	27%	165	73%	226	100%
post-verbal NP	50	13%	338	87%	388	100%

The distributional contrast in Table 4 — a 27-73 ratio vs. 13-87 ratio — is not exactly dramatic. The categorial tendency in both is in the very same general direction: The bulk of both pre-posed and post-posed NPs still appear at the paragraph medial context. Nonetheless, the *Chi*-square test yielded a highly significant correlation between the syntactic structure pre-posed-NP and the discourse context paragraph-initial (*Chi*-square 18.24, significant at the respectable level of $p < 0.01$).

The very same data in Table 4 can be re-computed, as correlations from function to form. And when this is done, with the *Chi*-square test showing the same values, the correlation looks much more dramatic, as may be seen in Table 5.

TABLE 5: **Re-computed correlations: Percent distributions of function in structure** (recomputed from Fox 1985, Table 1)

position in the paragraph	pre-verbal NP		post-verbal NP		total	
	N	**%**	**N**	**%**	**N**	**%**
paragraph initial	61	55%	50	45%	111	100%
paragraph non-initial	165	32%	338	68%	503	100%

(syntax, spanning the three NP columns)

While the distributions in Table 4 are not fully categorial in either direction, the numerical ratios for the two 'functions' now go in the opposite direction — 55-45 vs. 32-68. In other words, the distribution begins to creep toward categoriality.

With minor variations, similar results can be shown with B. Fox's (1985) three other heuristic measures of discontinuity. In each case, the correlation — or predictability — from function to form looks much more dramatic than the predictability from form to function. But why should this be the case? One general theoretical answer to this question has already been suggested above: The general preference is for one-to-many association from form to functions (decoding ambiguity) but only for one-to-one association from function to form (coding uniqueness). This general tendency seems supported by more specific studies of word-order variation. For example, many of the studies of word-order pragmatics surveyed in Givón (1988) show that the very same syntactic device — pre-posing — is consistently used in one language after another to code discontinuity (or unpredictability) in discourse regardless of the source of that discontinuity — referential, temporal, spatial, modal, thematic. What we may be dealing with, it seems, is a complex one-to-many association between form (pre-posed constituent) and function (discontinuity), with each sub-type of discontinuity correlating significantly with the same syntactic device.

But are these sub-measures of continuity really different functions? And are the measures really independent of each other? The answer to both questions is probably *no*. What I suspect we have here are four heuristics measures that tap into a single complex function — **thematic coherence**. The paragraph (or clause-chain) boundary in discourse is a textual environment where all types of discontinuity cluster together — discontinuities of reference, spatiality, temporality, aspectuality, modality, perspective, etc. Taken together, these are the visible, measurable manifestations of a single epiphenomenon — thematic coherence.[24] While we study the text distribution of visible elements of text continuity, we need to keep in mind that they are but the heuristic measures through which we probe an underlying but alas invisible theoretical-cognitive entity.

7.5.3.   Scalarity vs. discreteness of "topic"

The next case illustrates another pitfall of text-distribution studies of the functional correlates of grammar. The pitfall again traces back to the use of discourse contexts as heuristic stand-ins for communicative functions. In a collection of text-based studies of referential continuity in discourse (Givón ed. 1983) I suggested that one anaphoric measure of topic continuity — **referential distance** — revealed that a host of anaphoric, definite referent-coding devices distributed along a scalar functional dimension of topic continuity, or **topic accessibility**. The *prima facie* evidence for this graduated scale was the apparent scalar distribution of the mean values of referential distance (RD) of NPs coded by the various grammatical devices. These means seemed reasonably stable, and a *Chi*-square test applied to pair-wise comparisons of constructions would have shown the difference between means to be highly significant. Nevertheless, my theoretical conclusions were dead wrong.

The first hint of trouble came when I later observed — as I should have but did not the first time around — that the median RD values for the middle and upper portions of the 'scale' indicated a very spread, non-categorial distribution of the population. The means as well as the degree of categorial distribution of the populations are given in Table 6 below.

TABLE 6: **Comparison of mean referential distance (RD) values and degree of categorial distribution for common anaphoric devices** (from Givón, ed. 1983; 1983b; 1984c; Sun and Givón 1985)

construction	mean RD (# of clusters)	clustering around the mean
a. zero anaphora	1.0	100% at mean
b. unstressed PRO	1.0	95% at mean
c. stressed PRO	2.5	90% between 2–3
d. Y-movement	2.5	90% between 2–3
e. DEF noun	7.0	25% at 1.0 35% scattered 5.0–19 40% at 20+
f. DEF-Noun with modifiers\(s)	10.0	55% scattered 5.0–19.0 45% at > 20
g. L-dislocated DEF-N	15.0	60% at > 20 25% at 4–9 13% at 10–19

The mean RD values that seem to hint at a graduated scale in Table 6 turn out to characterize reasonably homogeneous populations only for the four short-RD devices: zero-anaphora (a), anaphoric pronouns (b), stressed pronouns (c) and Y-movement (d). The populations of the mid-scale categories full-DEF-NP (e),(f), and to a lesser extent L-dislocation (g), turn out to scatter all over the map. In other words, referential distance is not a very precise predictor of the distribution of the mid-range and long-range devices, in spite of the facts that the differences between their mean values are significant.

What is at issue here is the fact that textual anaphoric distance (RD) *per se* is not a cognitive measure of the cognitive function "referent accessibility", but rather a convenient heuristic that correlates with it — roughly, up to a point. In this case, the real cognitive issue was and still is **mental accessibility** and **mental activation**. As I have argued elsewhere,[25] the cognitive sub-system that underlies the grammar of referential coherence is probably a discrete, activation-based system. In such a system, the main contrast is between continuing and interrupted activation. This cognitive contrast is coded by the

330 FUNCTIONALISM AND GRAMMAR

grammatical contrast between the two most consistently-categorial grammatical
devices — zero/pronoun vs. full NP:

(29) continued activation $\Longrightarrow$ zero/pro
terminated activation $\Longrightarrow$ full NP[26]

Further, the real issue is not referential activation but rather the activation of
thematic units — clause-chain or paragraph. Since these thematic units tend to
exhibit a continuing topical referent, it is likely that the activation of such a
referent is simply part of the mechanism for activating the thematic unit. But
mental activation, particularly within highly automated sub-systems such as
grammar, is probably not a scalar process, but rather a discrete on/off phenomenon.

7.6. Hypotheses about the text vs. hypotheses about the mind

7.6.1. The perils of distributional reductionism

In her comments on Sun and Givón's (1985) conclusions about the
functional distribution of the Mandarin OV order, Nichols (unpubl.) raised an
important theoretical issue, one that becomes relevant at this juncture. From
Nichols' perspective, Sun and Givón (1985) exemplified the perils of so-called
essentialism in linguistics. Essentialism, harkening back to Plato, is a belief in
the underlying single essence of variable phenomenological populations. In
biology, Mayr (1963) has defined the contrast between essentialism and
population-variationism in the following strong terms:

> "... Fixed, unchangeable "ideas" underlying the observed variability are the
> only things that are permanent and real. Owing to its belief in essence, this
> philosophy is also referred to as *essentialism* and its representatives as
> *essentialist* (typologists).[27] ... The assumptions of **population thinking** are
> diametrically opposed to those of the typologist...All organisms and organic
> phenomena are composed of unique features and can be described collec-
> tively only in statistical terms. Individuals, or any kind of organic entities,
> form populations of which we can determine the arithmetic mean and
> statistical variation. Averages are merely **statistical abstractions**; only the
> individuals of which the populations are composed have any reality ..."
> (Mayr 1963: 4; boldfacing added)

In linguistics, Nichols (unpubl.) has suggested, misguided essentialist thinking
is at the bottom of our attempt to find a categorial correlation between form
(OV) and function (definite). Nichols contrasts this doctrinal error with Labov's
text variationism:

"... Standard structuralist dogma imposes **essentialist** thinking, while what is usually needed for non-formalist grammatical analysis is **population** thinking. When **Jacobsonian structuralists** say that a form codes a meaning, they generally mean that the meaning is a necessary and sufficient condition for use of the form ... But in population-oriented terms, the meaning would be seen as a factor (usually one of several or many) ... Neither necessity nor sufficiency is important in population thinking. What matters is whether the putative effect of a factor on a distribution is significant..." (Nichols, unpubl., p. 5; boldfacing added)

In Nichols' view, we must make a choice between these two extremes. But there are perfectly cogent reasons why both extremes are absolutely essential in order to study the correlation between grammar and communicative function. Necessary, but applicable in different domains — methodology and theory.[28]

We owe to Bill Labov (e.g. Labov 1975) our resurgent understanding of why one cannot simply assume categorial, invariant, one-to-one form-function correlations. One must test such assumptions empirically as hypotheses — test them distributionally, in some actual piece of text, with proper statistics. And the text must have been produced in the course of communicating, rather than by linguists indulging in the production of crucial examples. This is where our empirical responsibility is at stake. But text distributions by themselves are not the investigation's end, but only its methodological means. Our hypotheses, explanations and theoretical constructs are fundamentally not about the text. To be theoretically meaningful, these hypotheses must say something about the mind that produces or interprets the text. And this is where a dose of good old essentialism indeed comes into play.

The mind of both the text producer and text perceiver must make **coding decisions** about which functions pair with which code units. Such decisions, in both speech perception and speech production, are made at a surprisingly fast rate — roughly one word per 250 milliseconds or around 1-3 seconds per clause. At that speed, coding and decoding decisions are useless below a certain threshold of near-categoriality. There is an enormous body of psychological literature on this subject, much of it not specific to language.[29] My own tentative conclusion in studying correlations between grammar and heuristically-defined communicative functions is that somewhere around the level of 80% correlation between form and function, speech-perceivers begin to bet on a 100% categorial distribution and ignore the residue. In studies of diachronic change, this is the point where high use-frequency, the precursor to grammaticalization, is converted into categorial grammatical 'rules'.[30]

In processing information of all types, the mind may require some minimal threshold-level of **code fidelity**. And it is just as absurd to go with Nichols' extreme position and assume that the level of code fidelity could ever be as low as 8%, as it is to go with Chomsky's assumption that it must always be 100%. Somewhere between the two — and much closer to 100% than to 8% — a certain minimal level of categoriality is maintained, if the normal rate of speech processing is indeed what it seems to be. The much lower levels of form-function association we observe in our text-distribution studies are probably the artifact of our heuristic definitions of "function".

The original Mandarin study by Li and Thompson (1975) certainly illustrate the need, for even the best intuitive functionalists, to avail themselves of population-distributional methods. Equally well, competent Labovian studies illustrate just as vividly the opposite point — how the mere facts of text distribution can be theoretically vacuous, unless coupled with a liberal measure of old-fashioned essentialism. Consider for example Estival's (1985) summary of "syntactic priming" in the use of passive clauses in English narrative:

> "... Syntactic priming also plays a role at least in discourse production ...
> Weiner and Labov (1983) found that the passive alternant is more likely to
> be chosen by the speaker if there is a passive in the immediate discourse
> preceding the sentence ..." (Estival 1985: 7)

Estival (1985) reported highly significant statistical correlation between current and preceding uses of passive clauses, contending herself with the label 'syntactic priming' but otherwise neglecting to explain why the text-distributional facts were the way they were. But the facts may have indeed had a rather 'essentialist' underpinning.[31]

In our concern for explaining the workings of the communicating mind, some measure of essentialism is (forgive the pun) essential. The speech perceiver's mind is unlikely to detect — by *Chi*-square or other inductive means — weak form:function correlations such as the 8% correlation from definite to OV in Mandarin. Nor is the speaker's mind likely to utilize such weak correlations in making on-line coding decisions under real-time pressure. Presumably, the speech-processing mind should have much less trouble coding and de-coding the near-categorial association between contrastive topic and OV. A prudent, theoretically well-argued measure of essentialism is indeed indispensable in constructing explanatory hypotheses about the communicative function of grammar. That is, if we hope some day to bridge the methodological gap between the study of heuristically-defined artifacts (discourse contexts) and the study of the grammar-using, communicating mind.

7.6.2. The perils of cognitive reductionism

The line of reasoning I have pursued so far, insisting that proposed communicative functions be cognitively plausible, is open to two natural misinterpretations. Both fall under the rubric of **cognitive reductionism**. The first is a theoretical misinterpretation that will be dealt with in Chapter 8 below — that somehow anchoring communicative functions in the mind detracts from their inter-personal, interactive, social nature. This is an unfortunate non-sequitur, and the sooner it is laid to rest, the better. The second misinterpretation is methodological, and may be best illustrated with one more case study.

The notion of 'topic' ('theme') has been one of the most productive heuristics in studying the use of grammar in discourse processing. Decomposing this heuristic into more precise functional notions — both communicative and cognitive — has led to the realization that the grammar of referential coherence is systematically associated with two distinct cognitive domains — **memory** and **attention**. These two cognitive domains are intimately connected to what text-oriented linguists have traditionally identified as, respectively, the **anaphoric** and the **cataphoric** aspects of reference:[32]

(30) **Cognitive correlates of referential coherence**:
    a. **anaphoric** = access to the referent in some existing
                mental structures (= **memory**)
    b. **cataphoric** = activation of the referent for subsequent
                use (= **attention**)

The lack of clear separation between these two cognitive entity has led to recurrent confusion about the nature of 'topic' or 'theme'.[33] But confusion aside, there remains a vast potential for reductionism in the illicit inferential leap from **association** to **identity**:

(31)   **Cognitive reduction: From association to identity**:
    "Communicative function A is shown to be consistently associated with a particular cognitive operation X. Therefore Function A is nothing but operation X".

The perils of cognitive reductionism may be seen in a recent study by Tomlin (1991). In an elegant experimental study, Tomlin demonstrated a strong statistical association between the cuing of visual attention to an event participant and the assignment of grammatical-subject role in subsequent verbal descriptions:

(32) cued agent   ⟹   agent subject = active clause
      cued patient ⟹   patient subject = passive clause

Tomlin the went on to conclude:

> "... Since the general idea of "theme" and "topic" is intuitively so congru-
> ent with general ideas of attention, and since the specific manipulation of
> attention provided here produces such a strong effect in the production of
> speakers, there seems to be no particularly compelling reason to sustain a
> pragmatic category called theme or topic unless one is to re-define clause-
> level theme as "the referent which is focally attended at the moment of
> utterance formulation ..." (Tomlin 1991: 16)

A number of lower-level methodological reason's suggest that Tomlin's
conclusions are both premature and problematic:

(a) The attention-cuing experimental manipulation used by Tomlin was visual
— an arrow pointing at one participant in a pictorial event. But most text is not
produced as an on-line description of visual events, but rather as mentally-
assembled recollection or invention.

(b) The prototypical passive clause has no agent, but typically only a patient.
Tomlin's passive sentences all had agents, in this resembling more inverse
clauses.

(c) A cross-linguistic comparison of direct-active, passive and inverse clauses
(see Chapter 3 as well as Givón, ed. 1994) reveals the following functional
differences:

(i)   Inverse clauses, unlike passives, are typically agent-preserving.
(ii) In inverse clauses the agent typically is not much less topical ("focal")
      than the patient. Although the patient of the inverse is usually more
      topical than the patient of the direct-active clause.
(iii) Inverse clauses are often non-promotional, i.e. their patient need not be
      the grammatical subject.
(iv) Unlike inverse clauses, passives tend to severely suppress the topicality
      of the agent, without necessarily raising all that much the topicality of the
      patient.

Tomlin's experimentally-elicited passives thus reflect the natural communicative
properties of neither passives nor inverses.

(d) The most prototypical subjects in natural discourse are coded as either zero
or anaphoric pronoun. This is true not only of the subjects of active-direct

clauses, but also of the subjects/topics of passive and inverse clauses. The prototypical natural propensity of subjects is **referential continuity**, thus also **attentional continuity**. Tomlin's visual events were presented in isolation, and their topical ('activated') participants were thus referentially and cognitively **discontinuous**. Given that discontinuity, the speakers coded the subjects of both active and passive clauses as full NPs.

A more serious problem centers on the reduction of potentially-many complex communicative functions to a single cognitive variable. Grammar is often much richer, specific and detailed than cognition. How, for example, would one characterize in terms of attention the difference between the highly topical referents in the following constructions:

(33) a. **Neutral subject:**   **The fish** was eaten (by the frog)
      b. **L-dislocated topic:**   **The fish**, the frog ate it
      c. **R-dislocated topic:**   The frog ate it, **the fish**
      d. **Y-moved topic:**   **The fish** the frog ate
      e. **Cleft-focused topic:**   It was **the fish** that the frog ate

The patient referent is topical — thus "the focus of attention" — in all these constructions. But only in one of them, the passive (33a), is it the grammatical subject. Clearly, the grammar of topical reference codes many nuances of communicative — thus ultimately cognitive — function that cannot be reduced into a single cognitive variable.

Probably the most implausible thing about reducing "topic" to "activated referent" is the simple question of communicative goal: Why would a speaker want a hearer to attend to a referent? There could be many reasons for this, and it is hard to see what is to be gained by reducing all of them to a single cognitive operation, even when it partakes in all of them. Attention or 'activation' — visual or otherwise — is a relatively barren mental entity. It partakes **as one component** in many complex mental transactions, some pre-linguistic and cognitive, others communicative. Consider:

(34) a. Hey look at **that guy!** (pointing)
      b. Now what its **that**? (gazing)
      c. Listen to **that!** (tilting the head)
      d. Did you hear **that**?
      e. What I'm about to tell you is **this**: ...
      f. So all it boils down to is you bought a **Pontiac**?
      g. **That** was the whole story.

Some of the referents to be activated in (34) are anaphoric, others are cataphoric. Some are situational, others are textual, some are visual, others auditory. Some are grammatical subjects, others are objects. To leap from strong association to identity seems an unnecessary inference, perhaps once again a leap from a one-way conditional to a bi-conditional association.

If we are to make sense some day of the complex interaction between cognition and communicative function, reduction of the latter to the former is surely counter-productive. Much like the relation between structure and communicative function, "correlation between A and B" dissolves into tautology unless both A and B are defined independently of each other.

7.7.   Closure

In attempting to understand the communicative function of grammar, one can indulge in several kinds of methodological reductionism. Following the structuralist and naive iconists, one can reduce functions into observed structures. Following the surface-bound text linguist and conversational analyst, one can reduce functions into their heuristic stand-ins — discourse contexts. Finally, following the experimental psychologist's tight design, one can also reduce communicative functions into sparse cognitive operations. All three reductions are natural, understandable, tempting, but they are temptations we must resist. In one way or another, all three spring from the failure to distinguish between two types of inductive coincidence — the biased one-way conditional (association), and the bi-conditional (identity). Most reductions are not strictly wrong, only partially right. They spring from an attempt to see a part as the whole. And in some contexts this is surely a laudable parsimony. Two quotations from Stephen J. Gould come to mind:

> "... The solution to great arguments is usually close to the golden mean ..." (Gould, 1977, p. 18)

> "... I doubt that such a controversy could have arisen unless both positions were valid (though incomplete) ..."
> (Gould, 1977, p. 59)

Notes

*) I am indebted to Dwight Bolinger, Dori Payne, Sandy Thompson and Russ Tomlin for helpful discussions, and to Johanna Nichols for initially raising my hackles.

1) Even here, the limits of the linguist's intuition are already obvious in the case of negation (2b), where the pragmatics of the negative speech-act had been totally obscured by its logic (Givón 1979a, ch. 3).

2) I'll take it for granted that 'text' could be either written or spoken, and either conversational ('collaborative') or non-conversational.

3) See Dik (1978), Foley and van Valin (1984), *inter alia.*

4) In spite of their obvious pitfalls when practiced exclusively, both functional intuitionism and structural iconism retain legitimate — indeed important — roles in the process of hypothesis formation. Intuition is the wellspring of hypothesis formation (Hanson 1958). And the iconism of grammar probably hovers around 80%-90% (see further below).

5) The theoretical grounds involve the assumption that the association must be strong enough both ways in order to be part of both speech perception (form to meaning) and speech production (meaning to form). We will discuss this in Section 7.5.1.5.2. below.

6) The size of the text is determined by the frequency of the A,B and P,Q in the text and the amount of variation found in their respective associations. There is no way of determining this in advance. One may consider an arbitrarily-chosen length of text as a pilot study, to be augmented if necessary by additional text.

7) Like all hypotheses, our original hypothesis (6) no doubt has multiple logical consequences, and testing all of them is potentially an endless task:

"... The game of science is, in principle, without end. He who decides one day that scientific statements do not call for any further test, and that they can be regarded as finally verified, retires from the game ..." (Popper 1959: 53).

8) The process of theoretical reasoning and repeated testing eventually must extend into experimental psycholinguistic work, since "communicative function" must eventually decompose into mental operations that are performed in the mind/brain of the speech producer or comprehender (see Chapter 8).

9) In other words, language seems to tolerate ambiguity but avoid synonymy (see Marchand 1968).

10) Actually, as we claimed, not "definite" but rather "topical", since the category **NON-REF indefinite** in our sample behave very much like **REF-definite**. See directly below.

11) See Givón (1990b, Chapter 16).

12) This was indeed the distributional profile of both our spoken and written Mandarin samples.

13) Given a lifetime and enough ingenuity, one — or one's peers — could devise endless falsificatory tests, if Popper (1959) is to be taken seriously.

14) See Kuhn (1962).

15) For an exhaustive discussion of the contextual interaction between data and hypotheses, see Hanson (1958).

16) One may wish to argue, as I have done in Givón (ed. 1983), that contrastiveness is one sub-species of **low informational predictability**. In other words, it represents a context where the speaker assumes — or actively sets up — certain expectations on the part of the hearer, then proceeds to release information that is contrary to those expectations. More likely, contrastive constructions are also topicalizing (Givón 1990b, Chapter 16).

17) See also Chapter 2.

18) The assumption that the speaker's communicative intent is fully determined in advance of text production is an idealization, given the highly interactive nature of face-to-face communication (see Chapter 8).

19) There are presumably other contrastive-topicalizing grammatical mechanisms in Mandarin, such as independent pronouns, clefting, or emphatic stress. While similar, their functions are not identical to that of the OV order.

20) Several recent studies of object-fronting constructions suggest that they may serve an inverse-voice function (Givón ed. 1994; also Chapter 3).

21) See Chapter 3.

22) See Yang and Givón (1984).

23) See Chapter 3.

24) See Chapter 8, below. Fox's numerical analysis (1985: 46-47 and Table 5) further support this interpretation in showing the effect of feature clustering, i.e. of piling up gradually all four sub-variables of discourse dis-continuity. When all four are present, the predictability from form to function — which for theoretical reasons we never expect to be fully categorial — improves immensely. And the fewer of the four features are present, the less dramatic this predictability is.

25) See Givón (1990b, ch. 20; 1992) as well as Chapter 8 below.

26) The situation is a bit more complex because full NPs that are not marked as cataphorically important/topical do not lead to discontinued activation (see *ibid*).

27) For Mayr, the term "typologist" signifies the exact opposite of what it has come to signify in late 20th Century linguistics.

28) From a methodological perspective, one argues here against reductionism, i.e. the idea that a scientific methodology must perforce be "pure". For a similar plea against extreme reductionism in methodology, and for the empirical utility of methodological pluralism, see Feyerabend (1970). What Feyerabend points out, in his context, closely parallels my argument below: Both extreme inductivism (Nichols' text distributionalism) and extreme deductivism (Nichols' essentialism)

misrepresent the reality of empirical science. Feyerabend's later position (1975), however, is nihilistic: Since no method is by itself perfect, all methods are useless. This is a quintessentially reductionist conclusion — all or nothing.

29) See discussion of grammar as an automated processing system in Chapter 8 below. The attention vs. automaticity literature has specified the conditions under which information processing switches from attended to automated processing. In general, automated processing tends to rise in areas of **high frequency** and **high predictability**; that is, where the signals and the message show a high — near categorical — correlation over repeated exposures. Skilled performance acquired over one's lifetime — chess playing, dancing, music, typing, and many linguistic sub-components such as phonology and grammar — becomes progressively automated under such conditions.

30) See discussion in Givón (1977; 1979a, ch. 5; 1985b). The general observation in grammaticalization may be summed up as:

"Whatever speakers do more frequently during communication,
grammars tend to code more distinctly."

31) There is a strong tendency for the topicalized subjects-of-passive to be inanimate or non-human. The passive construction in English is often used as an "inverse", to topicalize a patient. When the topicalized patient persists as the topical referent in a clause-chain, the predicates that most naturally go with it are not-agentive ones, including chained passives. Chains of such inverse clauses have been described elsewhere (Dryer 1994).

32) See Chapter 8 below.

33) For a review of the early history of this confusion see Givón (1988). Chafe (1987) has contributed to the confusion more recently with his intuitive notion of "focus of attention", by failing to distinguish between referents that are accessible in memory and thus available for future re-activation, and those that are, currently activated.

8

Coming to Terms with Cognition:
Coherence in Text vs. Coherence in Mind

8.1.   Introduction*

We begin this chapter by confronting, this time from a theoretical perspective, the very same problem tackled earlier from a methodological perspective: the relation between text-based heuristic definitions and process-based cognitive definitions of communicative function. The domain within which the problem is examined is that of text coherence. Most linguists and experimental psychologists derive their understanding of text coherence, such as it is, almost exclusively from the study of well-edited written text,[1] and the behavior of text comprehenders. Both traditional tilts are of course understandable. Coherence is much easier to demonstrate *prima facie* in a well-written text, where repeated cycles of careful editing have produced maximally-consistent global structures. Coherence is also much easier to investigate experimentally by manipulating, controlling and recording the behavior of text comprehenders. One must recognize, however, that the price of methodological convenience in both disciplines may be rather steep. The phenomenon of text coherence as a natural cognitive process may be distorted beyond recognition; so that one winds up studying artifacts of either text editing or experimental design, and often of both.

What I hope to do in this chapter is to introduce a measure of realism into the discussion of discourse coherence, by reminding us all of the incredible complexity that a serious empirical study of coherence must entail, and how such complexity can only be handled by combining the methodological resources of several disciplines. My approach may be characterized by the following theses:

(a) **Single vs. multiple strands**: Text coherence is a complex, composite meta-phenomenon, involving multiple strands. While each of the strands may be discussed or manipulated independently, coherence is fundamentally an epi-phenomenon.

(b) **Product vs. the process**: Coherence is fundamentally *not* an objective property of the produced text. Rather, that text is a by-product of the mental processes of discourse production and discourse comprehension, which are the real loci of coherence.

(c) **Single vs. multiple perspectives**: Text coherence is fundamentally a collaborative process, involving two minds attempting to achieve, simultaneously, many goals. Some of those goals may be in conflict, and the collaboration between the two interlocutors toward resolving such conflicts and achieving their respective goals is a matter of degree.

(d) **Production vs. comprehension**: One must index one's study of the mental processes of text coherence separately to discourse production and discourse comprehension.

(e) **Written vs. oral discourse**: Fundamentally, the production of spontaneous oral communication is the most revealing medium where a realistic, cognitively revealing study of text coherence should be located.

(f) **Knowledge-driven vs. grammar-driven processes**: Human discourse production and comprehension involve two distinct processing channels: one older, slower and vocabulary-driven; the other younger, faster, and grammar-driven.

(g) **Local vs. global coherence**: In both processing channels, both local and global aspects of coherence are involved.

Of these seven, I will focus more narrowly on (a), (f) and (g). Thesis (b) remains the underlying *leitmotif* of the study. The other three — (c), (d) and (e) — will be either taken for granted or be supported primarily by cited references. I will begin by recapitulating some of what text-sensitive linguists know from studying the external artifact — the recorded or written text. How to extrapolate from the product text to the mental processes that produce and comprehend it remains a key methodological issue.

8.2.   Coherence and grounding

8.2.1.   Coherence strands in the external text

From a methodological, heuristic perspective, coherence may be defined as an observable property of the external, recorded text:

(1)   **Coherence as continuity**:
"Coherence is the **continuity** or **recurrence** of some element(s) across a span (or spans) of text".

Of the many elements that can recur across text, six more concrete elements are the easiest to track; and their coherence is thus the easiest to measure. They are:

(a) referents
(b) temporality
(c) aspectuality
(d) modality/mood
(e) location
(f) action/script

In processing the first five elements of coherence — (a), (b), (c), (d), (e) — **grammar** is massively involved, a subject we shall return to in considerable detail further below. The use of grammar as an instrument of discourse coherence has salutary consequences for both the text analyst and the text comprehender. For the text analyst, tracking recurrent elements through the text is facilitated by their predictable association with grammar. One needs to only study the **distribution of grammar in text**; and this is a clear methodological windfall. For the text comprehender, overt grammatical signals — syntactic constructions, morphology, intonation — *cue* the text processor, they *guide* him/her in the construction of a coherent mental representation of the text; and this is a vital cognitive boost.

8.2.2.   Coherence as a mental entity

A number of separate issues must be considered if one is to treat coherence not only as a methodologically-useful observable artifact of the external text, but also as a cognitive phenomenon in the mind that produces and comprehends the text. First, there are **cognitive operations** that must occur in both text production and text comprehension. These operations do not of themselves constitute text coherence. Rather, they *impose* or *guarantee* whatever coherence we find in the external text. Second, there are at least two **mental text-traces** that one must consider. And each of the two stands, at least potentially, in some isomorphic relation to the external text:

    (a) **working memory buffer** ('immediate recall')

    (b) **episodic memory** ('longer-term recall')

While I intend to confine most of my remarks to the latter, perhaps a few words could be said about the former.

8.2.2.1. The working memory buffer

It is fairly well established that the working memory buffer for text is severely limited, perhaps retaining no more than 2-5 clauses at a time, or roughly 8-20 seconds of verbatim text (Gernsbacher 1985; Squire 1987; Carpenter and Just 1988; Just and Carpenter 1992; *inter alia*). By 'verbatim' one means not only the vocabulary but also the surface **grammatical form** of utterances. During the short time-span of the buffer, whatever portion of the 'external' speech signal that is at all to survive in longer-term memory must be translated rapidly, into some other form of episodic mental representation. This dual system is no doubt essential for both the text producer and text comprehender, although their mental episodic representation need not be identical.

Surface information of grammatical cues probably does not survive beyond the working memory buffer, and thus most likely does not reach episodic memory. One may consider the grammatical signals associated with natural language clauses as the **mental processing instructions** [2] that guide the speech comprehender toward constructing a coherent, structured mental representation of the text. Put another way, grammatical signals are part of the **transfer mechanism** used for placing the clausal information at some coherent — connected, grounded — location in episodic memory. They are thus responsible for at least some of the connectivity — or coherence — of the mentally represented text.

8.2.2.2. Episodic memory

Unavoidable metaphorical usages such as 'mental trace', 'mental storage', 'mental model' or 'mental representation' need not conjure up an image of binding **isomorphism** between the external text and its episodic mental representation. Nor should these metaphors imply any particular **stability** of that representation over time. Both of these issues remain wide open, and are probably a matter of degree. In describing the sub-cortical hippocampus-based (medial temporal lobe) neurological mechanisms that supports at least the early phases of episodic memory, Squire and Zola-Morgan (1991) observe:

> "...This system is fast, has limited capacity, and performs a crucial function at the time of learning in establishing long-term declarative memory. Its role continues after learning during a *lengthy period of reorganization and consolidation* whereby memories stored in neocortex [the hippocampus is sub-cortical; TG] eventually become independent of the medial temporal memory system. This process, by which the burden of long-term (permanent) memory storage is gradually assumed by [the] *neocortex*, assures that the *medial temporal lobe system* is always available for the acquisition of new information..." (p. 1385; emphases are mine; TG; see also Squire 1987)

Not only is the information in episodic memory malleable during a protracted period of "reorganization and consolidation", but retrieval of this information for reflection or speech production, even from the more permanent neocortical storage, is heavily dependent on the **context** within which it is accessed or 'reproduced'.[3] The flexibility and context-dependence of longer-term episodic recall are indeed well documented (see e.g. Loftus 1980).

However little we know about the real details of text representation in episodic memory, either hippocampal or neocortical, I will take it for granted that text is represented at least in part as a **network of connected nodes**. This network structure displays at least two well-known features — hierarchy and sequentiality.[4]

(2) **Mental text structure**:
   a. **Hierarchy**:
      Episodic text representation has at least some depth of hierarchical organization, so that nodes ('chunks') are connected both 'upward' and 'downward' to other hierarchically adjacent nodes — clauses to their governing chains, chains to their governing paragraph, etc.[5]
   b. **Sequentiality**:
      Episodic text representation displays at least some sequential chaining at each hierarchic level, so that nodes are connected to both preceding and following sequentially-adjacent nodes — a clause to a preceding and following clause, a chain to a preceding and following chain, etc.

Both the degree of hierarchic depth and the length of sequential chains remain wide-open empirical issues. It is easy to demonstrate that both vary enormously from one external text to the next.[6] And there is no reason to assume that they do not vary even more extensively from one mental text representation to the next. Further, other — idiosyncratic — connections, neither hierarchic nor sequential, probably also exist between nodes in the network.

I will be concerned here primarily with the use of episodic representation during the on-line processing of incoming discourse. For this use, the longer-term neocortical episodic representation of the text is probably irrelevant. It is the early and extremely flexible episodic representation in the hippocampus-based system that concerns us most here.

8.2.3. Coherence as grounding

8.2.3.1. Preamble

If one accepts the assumption that mentally-represented text has some sequential-hierarchic network structure, one can see why coherent episodic representation is the chief guarantor of fast on-line access to episodic information during both text production and text comprehension. The guarantee of on-line access to individual nodes in the network of mental text lies in their **connectivity** or **grounding** to other nodes in the network. From the perspective of the text receiver ('hearer'), connectivity allows for coherent storage. From the perspective of the text producer ('speaker'), connectivity makes it possible to produce a text that the hearer can comprehend. Following Gernsbacher (1990), I will assume then that text comprehension is synonymous with the construction of a **structured mental representation** of the text. That is:

(3)   **Coherence as grounding**:
   a. In order to guarantee fast on-line access to nodes in the mental representation of text, nodes must be **grounded** at least to some degree. That is, a node must be connected to either some sequentially adjacent, hierarchically adjacent, or non-adjacent node(s) within the mental text-structure.
   b. The more connections a node has — the more grounded it is — the more **mentally-accessible** it is.

The grounding of information nodes in the mentally-represented text, especially during on-line text comprehension, involves two main directions —

anaphoric ('backward') and cataphoric ('anticipatory'). **Anaphoric grounding** has been studied much more extensively. It involves connecting incoming new information chunks to some **existing mental representation** — either of the text or of other mental entities. The second, **cataphoric grounding**, has been studied in much less detail. It involves the opening of pending connections in yet-to-be completed structure, in anticipation of a text that is in the process of being constructed (Gernsbacher 1990). Somewhat paradoxically, incoming text-nodes are grounded cataphorically to text-nodes that have not yet been processed, although some may have already been stored in the immediate recall buffer. In the space below, I will briefly flesh out the notions of anaphoric and cataphoric grounding.

8.2.3.2. Cataphoric ('anticipatory') grounding

Traditionally, cataphoric grounding has been discussed almost exclusively in terms of **indefinite reference**,[7] and then mostly in terms of the *absence* of anaphoric grounding. A more careful study reveals that cataphoric grounding is a much more extensive grammar-cued phenomenon, involving referential, temporal and thematic coherence.

In the grammar of **referential coherence**, referent NPs are identified as either those that will be **important, topical**, and thus **persistent** in the subsequent discourse, or those that will be unimportant, non-topical, and thus non-persistent. Topical referents are most commonly given special grammatical marking, while non-topical ones are left unmarked. As an example of this grammar-cued contrast, consider the use, in spoken American English, of the indefinite articles 'a(n)' and 'this' in the introduction of new indefinite NPs into the discourse. A typical example of this contrast can be seen in the following Dear Abby letter (Wright and Givón 1987):[8]

(4)   **The indefinite articles *a(n)* vs. *this*:**

"Dear Abby: There's **this guy** I've been going **with** for near three years. Well, the problem is that **he** hits me. **He** started last year. **He** has done it only four or five times, but each time **it** was worse than before. Every time **he** hits me it was because **he** thought I was flirting (I wasn't). Last time **he** accused me of coming on to *a friend* of **his**. First **he** called me a lot of dirty names, then **he** punched my face so bad **it** left me with a black eye and black-and-blue bruises over half of my face. It was very noticeable, so I told my folks that the car I was riding in stopped suddenly and my face hit the windshield.

Abby, **he**'s 19 and I'm 17, and already I feel like *an old married lady* who lets her husband push her around. I haven't spoken to **him** since this happened. **He** keeps bugging me to give **him** one more chance. I think I've given **him** enough chances. Should I keep avoiding **him** or what?

Black and Blue".

The referent introduced by 'this' recurs as the most central in the subsequent narrative (aside from the speaker herself). The referents introduced by 'a' do not recur in the subsequent text.

The cataphoric persistence of 'a'-marked vs. 'this'-marked indefinite referents in the oral English has been studied in narratives produced by 8–12-year old native speakers of American English. The results are summarized in (5) below.

(5)   **Mean topic persistence (TP) of the indefinite 'a'-marked and 'this'-marked subjects and objects in spoken English**; (expressed as number of times the same referent recurred in the subsequent 10 clauses; Wright and Givón 1987)

grammatical coding	mean TP value	N
'this'-subject	6.95	**28** (65%)
'this'-object	2.40	15
total 'this'		43 (100%)
'a'-subject	1.54	13
'a'-object	0.56	**94** (88%)
total 'a':		107 (100%)

There is a clear interaction between grammatical subjecthood and the indefinite article 'this': 65% of 'this'-marked NPs also appeared as subjects, while 88% of 'a(n)'-marked NPs occurred as non-subjects. Indeed the contrast of grammatical roles — subject vs. direct object vs. others — is one of the most important cataphoric grammatical signal for both indefinite and definite NPs. To illustrate this, consider the cross-language comparison of topic persistence of referents given in Table (6) below. The survey represents distributions in 5 unrelated languages. The **topic persistence** of subject and object NPs in active-transitive clauses is expressed as their recurrence in the following 10 clauses of text. The results are expressed as the contrast in frequency between low-persistence referents — those that persist only 0–1–2 times (0–2) in the following 10 clauses, and high-persistence referents — those that persist more than twice (>2).

(6) **Cataphoric persistence of subjects and objects of transitive clauses in Sahaptin, Panare, Bella-Coola, Korean and Spanish**[9]

	occurrences in the following 10 clauses					
	0-2		>2		total	
language	N	%	N	%	N	%
Sahaptin						
subj	9	19.6%	37	**80.4%**	46	100.0%
obj	21	**61.8%**	13	38.4%	34	100.0%
Panare						
subj	9	31.0%	20	**69.0%**	29	100.0%
obj	19	**65.5%**	10	34.5%	29	100.0%
Bella Coola						
subj	27	21.4%	99	**78.6%**	126	100.0%
obj	82	**65.1%**	44	34.9%	126	100.0%
Korean						
subj	53	35.3%	97	**64.7%**	150	100.0%
obj	106	**72.0%**	44	28.0%	150	100.0%
Spanish						
subj	19	19.0%	81	**81.0%**	100	100.0%
obj	70	**70.0%**	30	30.0%	100	100.0%

Other grammatical devices may also be used for the cataphoric grounding of topical indefinite referents. A common one is restrictive relative clauses in combination with the indefinite article:

(7) a. A man **with no shoes on** came into the office and...
    b. A woman **who spoke no English** then stepped forward and...
    c. Someone **who's very anxious to meet you** is coming over tonight...
    d. A guy **I haven't seen in years** has just called me and...

In addition to tagging the newly-introduced NP as an important topic in the subsequent discourse, the information in the REL-clause makes the referent **salient, grounded,** so that it can now be attached at a relevant location in the mental representation of the incoming text.

8.2.3.3. Anaphoric grounding

8.2.3.3.1. Preamble: Definite reference

Speakers code a referent as definite when they assume that it is **identifiable** or **accessible** to the hearer. By 'accessible' one means that it is represented in — and can be retrieved from — some pre-existing mental structure in the hearer's mind. When speakers re-introduce a referent in such a context, they ground it by various grammatical devices. Such grounding serves to establish a **mental connection** between the referent's occurrence in the current text-location and its previous **anaphoric trace** in some extant mental structure. Grammar-guided anaphoric devices most commonly ground re-introduced referents into three types of mental structures:

(8)　**Mental structures for anaphoric grounding:**
　　(a) Model of the current speech-situation
　　(b) Model of permanent generic-lexical knowledge
　　(c) Episodic model of the current text

We will take up these three types of anaphoric grounding in order.

8.2.3.3.2. Grounding to the speech situation

Grounding referents — or other coherence elements — to the current speech-situation is achieved by indicating their spatial relation to the two participants in the discourse — speaker and hearer, or by indicating their temporal relation to the times of speech. This involves well-known **proximity** and **orientation** devices such as:[10]

(9)　a.　**The interlocutors:**
　　　'I', 'you', 'we', 'y'all'
　　b.　**Other referents:**
　　　'this one', that one', 'that one over there'
　　c.　**Location:**
　　　'here', 'there', 'way over there'
　　d.　**Time:**
　　　'now', 'then', 'long ago, 'in the future'
　　　'today', 'yesterday', 'tomorrow'
　　　'this week', 'last week', 'next week'

8.2.3.3.3. Grounding to generic-lexical knowledge

Culturally shared, generic-lexical knowledge is represented mentally in the permanent semantic memory. Referents may be grounded to this mental structure in two distinct ways. First, some referents are **globally accessible** because they are uniquely identifiable to all members of the relevant speech community ('culture', 'sub-culture', 'village', 'family') at all times. Some examples of such referents are:

(10) **Globally-accessible generic definites:**

referent	relevant social unit
a. **The sun** came out.	all humans
b. **The president** has resigned.	a nation-state
c. They went to **the cemetery**.	a community
d. **The river** is frozen over.	a community
e. Call **the sheriff**!	a county
f. **The Gods** are angry.	a religion
g. **Daddy** is home!	a family

Generic access to definite referents is frequently intermixed with episodic text-based access, yielding a hybrid system of **double grounding**. A double-grounded referent is accessible partly through an anaphoric connection to its episodic trace in the episodic representation of the current text, and partly through connection(s) to generic-lexical knowledge. This hybrid type of grounding is often referred to as **framed-based** or **script-based** reference (Anderson, Garrod and Sanford 1983; Yekovich and Walker 1986; Walker and Yekovich 1987). Typical examples are:

(11) **Double-grounded frame-based reference:**
    a. My boy missed **school** today,
        he was late for **the bus**.
    b. He showed us this gorgeous **house**,
        but **the living room** was too small.
    c. She went into a **restaurant**
        and asked **the waiter** for **the menu**.

The definite referent 'the bus' in (11a) receives its anaphoric grounding from two separate sources — the antecedent referent 'school' in the preceding text, plus generic-lexical knowledge of the frame 'school' and its sub-component 'bus'. Similarly in (11b), the definite referent 'the living room' receives its anaphoric grounding in part from the antecedent referent 'this gorgeous house' in the preceding text, and in part from generic-lexical knowledge of the frame 'house' and its sub-component 'living room'. Likewise in (11c), both definite referents 'the waiter' and 'the menu' receive their grounding in part from the antecedent referent 'a restaurant' in the preceding text, and in part from generic-lexical knowledge of the frame 'restaurant' and its sub-components 'waiter' and 'menu'.

Frame-based referential access is often accomplished through conventional knowledge of whole-part, possessor-possessed relations:

(12)   **Whole-part, possessor-possessed frame-based access:**
       a. She grabbed **the fish** and chopped off **its head.**
       b. **John** just got a job working for **his father.**
       c. **The house** was a mess, **the roof** leaked.
       d. **She's** upset. **Her kids** keep flunking highschool.
       e. **The table** is missing **one of its legs.**
       f. **My wife** called and said...
       g. **Your house** is on fire.

In (12f, g), the anaphoric antecedent is not accessible from the current text itself, but rather from the speech situation, i.e. the identity of the speaker and hearer. But the use of frame-based knowledge to affect full grounding of the definite referent is of the same type.

8.2.3.3.4. Grounding into the current text

By far, the bulk of the grammar of anaphoric grounding involves access to anaphoric traces in the episodic mental model of the current text. Out of this vast array, one can separate several clusters of devices that seem to specialize in cuing access to rough locations — or configurations — in the mental text structure. One can illustrate the use of such devices by citing again the characteristic anaphoric gap — or **referential distance** (RD) — of various reference-coding grammatical devices. This purely heuristic measure records the gap, in number of clauses backward, between the referent's current text-location and its last previous occurrence.

(13) **Comparison of mean referential distance (RD) values and degree of categorial distribution for common anaphoric devices** (from Givón, ed. 1983; 1983b; 1984b; Sun and Givón 1985)

construction	mean RD (# of clauses)	degree of clustering around the mean
a. zero anaphora	1.0	100% at mean
b. unstressed PRO	1.0	95% at mean
c. stressed PRO	2.5	90% between 2–3
d. Y-movement	2.5	90% between 2–3
e. DEF noun	7.0	25% at 1.0 35% scattered 5.0–19 40% at 20+
f. DEF-Noun with modifier(s)	10.0	55% scattered 5.0–19.0 45% at >20
g. L-dislocated DEF-N	15.0	60% at >20 (25% at 4–9) (13% at 10–19)

As noted in Chapter 7, referential distance is primarily a heuristic measure of convenience. Distance by itself is not necessarily of great cognitive significance. Rather, distance tends to coincide with some mental entities — both structures and operations. The main division in (13) is probably between devices that signal **maximal continuity** (13a, b) and those that signal **discontinuity** (13c–g):

maximal continuity ⟹ zero anaphora,
                                         unstressed pronoun

discontinuity   ⟹ stressed pronoun,
                                         full lexical noun

As an example of how this major distinction is deployed in text, consider the following passage of fiction. Of the referents that play any significant role in the narrative,[11] continuous ones are bold-faced, and discontinuous ones are italicized:[12]

(14)   "...**He** circled it wearily as a wolf, **[Ø]** studying it from all
        angles, and when finally **he** stopped within a dozen feet of *the
        dead man*, **he** knew much of what had happened at this place.
        The dead man had ridden a freshly shod horse into the playa
        from the north, and when **[Ø]** shot **he** had tumbled from the
        saddle and *the horse* had galloped away. *Several riders* on
        unshod ponies had then approached the body and *one* had
        dismounted to **[Ø]** collect the weapons..."

Cognitively, the maximal-continuity anaphoric devices signal the default choice
of **continued activation** of the current topical referent. From the perspective I
will pursue here, this means continuing to attach incoming new information
under the same **thematic chain-node**. The topical referent is the **node label** of
the thematic chain. Discontinuous anaphoric devices, on the other hand, signal
the **terminated activation** of the current topical referent, and the activation of
another topic for which there exists an anaphoric mental trace. Among such
devices, the short-distance devices (13c, d) tend to signal the activation of
another referent *without* terminating the current chain. An example of such a
use of a stressed pronoun can be seen at the end of (14) and its continuation:

(15)   ... *Several riders* on unshod ponies had then approached the
        body and *one* had dismounted to **[Ø]** collect the weapons.
        The clothing had not been stripped off, nor was *the body* mutilated..."

The full indefinite NP 'several riders' in (15) terminates the activation of the
preceding chain *and* its topical referent ('the dead man'), and opens a new
chain, becoming its topical referent. The stressed pronoun 'one' then singles out
one member of this group briefly, but this is done without terminating the
thematic chain. The chain is then terminated, returning implicitly to the earlier
topic 'the dead man'. This is done indirectly by double-grounding the frame-
based reference, via 'the clothing' and 'the body'.

    As an example of the use of the other short-distance discontinuous referent
device, Y-movement ('contrastive topicalization' (13d)), consider:

(16)   "...After buying a copy of *The Racing Times* at a Manhattan
       newsstand, Ed Piesman, a dentist and an avid horseracing fan,
       said he preferred the new paper to the venerable *Daily Racing
       Form* because 'the columnists are much better' and some of the
       statistics 'are much much better'.
            But the news dealer who sold him the paper said people like
       Dr. Piesman are few. **'The Racing Time, I sell two a day,**
       maybe five when there is a big race', said Ashok Patel, whose
       stand at 72nd Street and Broadway is adjacent to an off-track
       betting parlor. **'The Daily Racing Form, I sell 40 or 50 a
       day'**..."[13]

Two topical referents persist throughout the paragraph, 'The Racing Time' and
'Daily Racing Form'. When they are switched for contrast, the object-fronting
Y-movement construction is used — without terminating the paragraph.[14]

Several long-distance anaphoric devices are characterized by the following
conflation of functions:

(a) Like other full-NP definites, they are topic-switching devices, de-
    activating the current topic/node.
(b) Their anaphoric topic is re-activated after a long gap of absence
    (i.e. of cognitive de-activation).
(c) The mental trace of the re-activated topic in the episodic memory
    is found in **another chain**, across at least one chain boundary, but
    often across a paragraph boundary.
(d) The long-distance anaphoric device signals the opening of a new
    thematic chain/node, in which the re-activated referent is the topic
    ('node-label').

As illustration of a long-distance anaphoric device, consider the use of L-
dislocation (13g) in informal spoken American English:[15]

(17) H: ...Well my dad was born in Sherman, that's close to where
     [...] is. He was born in Sherman in 1881, and he died in
     '75. Yeah. And ah, so, ah of course, **my great grandfather,
     they came in there**, I think, y'know, part of them from
     Tennessee and part of them from Illinois. And I don't really
     know much about that far back, Tom. **But my grand-dad,
     he was a hard-shelled Baptist preacher**, and he just,
     y'know, farmed and ranched.
     T: In Texas?
     H: Yeah, yeah.
     T: So he was already in Texas?
     H: They must've come there when he was small, y'know,
     'cause he spent...
     T: Your great grandfather moved and your grandfather was
     really raised in Texas.
     H: Yeah, yeah. In other words, about three generations of us...
     were in Texas...
     T: In Texas...
     H: And of course we eh, **my dad, all he ever did was farm
     and ranch**...

Some grammatical devices are better described as **theme switching** or
paragraph-initial devices. Rather than coding the re-activated topic, they
signal the beginning of a new thematic paragraph. Consider, for example, the
use of fronted adverbials in:[16]

(18) "...Their trail when they left Wells' body lay in the direction he
     himself was taking, and that meant the waterhole was off-limit
     for Shalako unless he wished to *fight* them for it, and no man
     in his right mind started a *fight* with Apaches.
     When the time for *fighting* came, the man Shalako *fought*
     with a cold fury that had an utter impersonal quality about it.
     He *fought* to win, *fought* with deadly efficiency, with no
     nonsense about him, yet he did not *fight* needlessly.
     Despite his weariness and that of the horse, he began
     backtracking. Peter Wells was not likely to be alone, so his
     presence indicated a camp nearby, and a camp meant water.
     Yet Shalako puzzled over his presence there at such a time..."

Both new paragraphs in (18) are introduced by pre-posed ADV-clauses. In both, thematic discontinuity overrides referential continuity, so that in spite of the continuing main participant ('Shalako', 'he'), a new thematic paragraph is initiated.[17]

8.2.4. The extreme bounds of coherence

It is possible, at least for those who interpret coherence as an objective property of the external text, to view coherence as akin to 'grammaticality' in the Chomskian sense — a text either has it or doesn't have it. Within the framework of network-like mental text structure I am proposing, it is more useful to view text coherence as a matter of degree. One could then set up the theoretical extreme upper and lower bounds of coherence, then see how various kinds of text stack up vis-à-vis such bounds.

A useful description of the extreme bounds of coherence can be extrapolated from Wittgenstein's (1918) discussion of tautology and contradiction in logic. The upper bounds of coherence is logical **tautology**, as in:

(19)   John came home, John came home...

In 'text' (19), all nodes in the second clause — subject, verb, locative — cohere maximally with corresponding nodes in the preceding clause. The second clause is thus maximally grounded, and the text maximally coherent — but also maximally redundant.

One type of lower bounds of coherence is the logical sense of **contradiction**, as in:

(20)   John came home, John didn't come home...

In 'text' (20), all nodes in the two clauses seem to cohere maximally — except for the crucial modal node of truth value, which thus makes the two clauses logically incompatible as members of the same text.[18] The more common cognitive, pragmatic sense of incoherence involves the absence of recurrent element(s) across the text, as in:

(21)   John went to Italy, the cow jumped over the fence...

Most coherent — interpretable — texts fall somewhere in the middle between the two extremes of total redundancy and utter incoherence. In moving across adjacent clauses, one encounters some recurring and some non-recurring elements.[19] But neither the amount of new (= disjointed) information nor the amount of old (= connecting) information in a single clause is totally unconstrained. The constraint on the amount of new information in the clause may be given as (Givón 1975b; Pawley and Syder 1983; Chafe 1986, 1987a):

(22) **The one-chunk-per-clause constraint**:
"Clauses in natural text tend to have **only one chunk** (usually
a word) of new information per clause".

If one accepts the clause as the incremental unit of processing new textual
information (Givón 1984b, ch. 7; Chafe 1986, 1987a, 1987b), then (22) can be
viewed as a constraint on the amount of new information that can be added to
mentally-represented text during a single processing increment.

The second constraint, at the other end of the scale, governs the amount of
old information in the clause, and may be given as (Givón 1984b, ch.7; 1990b,
ch. 20; Chafe 1987a):

(23) **The at-least-one-chunk-per-clause constraint**:
"Clauses in natural text tend to have **at least one chunk** (usually a word) of old information per clause".

The most common element of old (= connecting) information in the clause is
its main topic, most often the subject; the vast majority of clauses in natural
text have subjects; and the vast majority of subjects are definite — i.e. connecting information. There are good reasons to suspect that principle (23) represents
the **minimal grounding requirement** for coherent interpretation of the clause,
rather than an optimal level. The number of grounding connection in an average
clause is probably larger, and referential coherence is only one grounding
connection in the clause.[20]

If multiple grounding of a clause is indeed the norm, then it can be cast as
a principle of grounding, coherence and mental access:[21]

(24) **Multiple grounding, coherence and mental access**:
"The more grounding connections the clause has, the more
mentally accessible it is, and thus the more coherent it is
relative to the text in which it is embedded".

8.3. Knowledge-driven vs. grammar-cued coherence

8.3.1. Preamble

In a recent review, Walter Kintsch (ms) has suggested that two parallel
processing channels are active simultaneously during text comprehension. One,
the "strong method", is driven by domain knowledge contained in the specific
lexical information (nouns, verbs, adjectives, adverbs) in the clause. The other,

the "weak method", is driven by the **grammatical information** in the clause. Kintsch contrasts the two channels as follows:

> "...We have finally found a use for syntax in a psychological processing model. It provides the comprehender with a 'weak' but general method for comprehension, to be complemented by the 'strong' knowledge-based and domain-specific methods. As in problem solving, weak and strong methods have their respective advantages and uses, and the complete comprehender would not forego either..." (Kintsch, ms, p. 23)

Perhaps a more apt characterization of the contrast between grammar-driven and knowledge-driven text comprehension is that of "rough-grained" vs. "fine-grained" processing, respectively. One may illustrate the relation between the two processing modes with an analogy from transportation. Suppose you are heading toward a particular house on a particular street in a particular neighborhood of a distant city. You travel first on the freeway — fast, efficiently, with relatively little conscious attention — until you reach the city, your rough-grained destination. Now you must exit the freeway and negotiate your way through main streets and then side streets, attending carefully to traffic signals and street names, until — slowly, laboriously — you reach your fine-grained destination.

8.3.2.   Grammar as an automated discourse-processing mode

One must note that text comprehension — the construction of a coherent mental representation of the current text — need not rely on grammar cues at all. It is well established that there exist two modes of discourse processing in human language — the **pre-grammatical** and the **grammatical**. The pre-grammatical mode is both ontogenetically and phylogenetically prior (Givón 1979, ch. 5; 1989, ch. 7; 1990; Blumstein and Milberg 1983; Lieberman 1984; Schnitzer 1989; Bickerton 1990). The two processing modes may be compared as follows in terms of their structural, functional and cognitive properties:

(25) Pre-grammatical vs. grammatical discourse processing

properties	grammatical mode	pre-grammatical mode
STRUCTURAL:		
a. **grammatical morphology**	abundant	absent
b. **syntactic constructions**	complex/ embedded	simple/ conjoined
c. **use of word-order:**	grammatical (subj/obj)	pragmatic (topic/comment)
d. **Pauses:**	fluent	halting
FUNCTIONAL:		
e. **processing speed:**	fast	slow
f. **Mental effort:**	effortless	laborious
g. **Error rate:**	lower	higher
h. **context dependence:**	lower	higher
COGNITIVE:		
i. **Processing mode:**	automated	attended
j. **acquisition:**	late	early
k. **evolution:**	late	early

The slow, analytic pre-grammatical mode of discourse processing is heavily **vocabulary driven**. This tallies with the fact that vocabulary is acquired before grammar, in both first and second language acquisition. Thus, pre-grammatical children, adult **pidgin** speaker and **agrammatical** aphasics comprehend and produce coherent connected discourse, albeit at slower speeds and high error rates than those characteristic of grammatical language. As an example of coherent pre-grammatical child episodic text, consider the following, from a 2-year-old child:[22]

(26)   [anticipating a trip]
       In atnga.   Sit dawn. tan ki.
       in airplane sit down turn key
       '(We'll go) in the airplane, sit down, turn the key,

       Vruum vruum! Tan tu da rayt. Atnga!
       vr.   vr.   turn to the right airplane
       'And vroom vroom! (We'll) turn to the right. Airplane (flies)!'

As an example of coherent adult second-language pidgin, consider:[23]

(27)   "...oh me?...oh me over there...
       nineteen-twenty over there say come...
       store me stop begin open... me sixty year...
       little more sixty year... now me ninety...
       nah ehm... little more... this man ninety-two...
       yeah, this month over... me Hawaii come-*desu*...
       nineteen seven come... me number first here...
       me-*wa* tell... you sabe gurumeru?...
       you no sabe gurumeru?...
       yeah this place come...
       this place been two-four-five year...
       stop, ey... then me go home... Japan...
       by-n-by... little boy... come...
       by-n-by he been come here... ey...
       by-n-by come...
       by-n-by me before Hui-Hui stop...
       Hui-Hui this... eh... he... this a...
       Manuel... you sabe-*ka*..."

As an example of coherent narrative produced by an agrammatic aphasia
patient, consider (Menn 1990: 165):

(28)   "...I had stroke... blood pressure... low pressure... period... Ah...
pass out... Uh... Rosa and I, and... friends... of mine... uh... uh...
shore... uh drink, talk, pass out..."
"...Hahnemann Hospital... uh, uh I... uh uh wife, Rosa... uh...
take... uh... love... ladies... uh Ocean uh Hospital and transfer
Hahnemann Hospital ambulance... uh... half'n hour... uh... uh
it's... uh... motion, motion... uh... bad... patient... I uh... flat on
the back... um... it's... uh... shaved, shaved... nurse, shaved
me... uh... shaved me, nurse... [sigh]... wheel chair... uh...
Hahnemann Hospital... a week, a week... uh... then uh...
strength... uh... mood... uh... up... uh... legs and arms, left side
uh... weak... and... Moss Hospital... two week... no, two
months..."

In the absence of morpho-syntax (grammar), the most reliable clues for
establishing text coherence in pre-grammatical discourse processing are the
lexical words in the clause. These clues do not disappear in the presence of
grammar, in fluent, adult speakers. Rather, as Kintsch (ms) suggests, vocabulary-guided inferences remain a **parallel processing channel** alongside grammar-cued inferences.

8.4.   Local vs. global coherence

Much of the experimental psycholinguistic work on text coherence has in
fact centered on **vocabulary-driven** global processes, i.e. Kintsch's domain-
specific general knowledge inferences. This is especially conspicuous in the
work on **causal inference** (Trabasso and van den Broek 1985; Trabasso and
Sperry 1985; Fletcher and Bloom 1988;), as well as in earlier discourse-oriented
work (Rummelhart 1975; Johnson-Laird 1980; van Dijk and Kintsch 1983;
Morrow, Greenspan and Bowers 1987; Glenberg et al. 1987). The same focus
on knowledge-driven global coherence is apparent in the "story grammar" paradigm (Mandler 1978, 1982; Mandler and Johnson 1977; Johnson and Mandler
1980; Stein 1982; Stein and Glen 1979), or its near equivalent "story schema"
(Shank and Abelson 1977; Wilensky 1980, 1982; De Beaugrande 1982).

In a recent review, McKoon and Ratcliff (1992) refer to vocabulary-driven
global inferences as "elaborative inferences", "instrumental inferences" or
"inferences from situation models". They characterize this global approach to
text coherence as follows:

"...It is widely believed that readers automatically construct inferences to build a *relatively complete* mental model of the situation described by the text ..." (1992: 17–18)

In outlining their minimalist, localistic alternative, McKoon and Radcliff suggest that vocabulary-driven global inferences are somehow "not automatically encoded" during text comprehension, and do not depend on the immediate recall buffer. In this, global inferences presumably contrast with local inferences, which are "automatically encoded" during text comprehension and depend on the immediate recall buffer.

Whatever the ultimate status of this distinction, it is worth noting that the sense of "automatic encoding" used by McKoon and Ratcliff (1992) could not be the same one we used earlier in referring to grammar as an "automated discourse-processing mode". To begin with, the experimental text-frames used by McKoon and Radcliff have little to do with grammar-driven inferences. Rather, they contrast local vs. global vocabulary-driven inferences. Further, many processes subsumed under lexical access, whether under **spreading activation** (Collins and Quillian 1969, 1972; Rips, Shoben and Smith 1973; Smith *et al.* 1974; Collins and Loftus 1975; Glass and Holyoak 1975; Smith 1978; *inter alia*) or under **multiple activation** (Swinney 1979) are said to involve considerable automaticity. So that it could not be the case that all components of knowledge-based inference are "not automatically encoded".

In the remaining portions of this paper, I will outline and illustrate how both vocabulary-cued and grammar-cued text processing involve both local and global aspects of coherence. Further, I will suggest that flexible, opportunistic, negotiated aspects of coherence (cf. Goodwin 1986, 1988, 1992, in press; Coates 1987) may pertain to both its local and global structure. If my analysis turns out to be correct, then we must conclude that:

- Discourse has *both* local and global coherence structure.
- Grammar must have evolved as a mechanism for speeding up the processing of *both* local and global aspects of text coherence.
- Vocabulary-cued — Kintsch's "knowledge-driven" — text processing remains a parallel channel of text processing.

When grammar-cued processes can get us there faster, lexical knowledge may be merely redundant. But beyond a certain point, vocabulary-guided processing is indispensible for fine-grained text comprehension. Further, in a number of well-known instances the use of grammatical and lexical information is intertwined. And finally, quite often the very same grammatical device clues a mixture of local and global coherence.

8.5.   Mechanisms of coherence

8.5.1.   Preamble

We return now to deal with two central issues in the study of text coherence as a mental process — vocabulary-guided vs. grammar-cued coherence, and local vs. global coherence. The evidence that I will survey will be primarily of the kind that text-oriented ('functional') grammarians consider as their stock-in-trade: the distribution of grammatical and lexical information in well-defined environments in the recorded "external" text. The methodological slant of such work is relatively explicit (see Chapter 7): Specific text environments are interpreted as **communicative tasks**. And specific grammatical devices that coincide with such environments are interpreted as the **automated signals** that trigger the **cognitive mechanisms** that perform these tasks.

It is obvious that the connection between text environments, communicative tasks, grammatical signals and cognitive mechanisms is at the moment largely inferential. But the claims I make are explicit, and thus open to further empirical testing. What I intend to demonstrate here are three interlocking sets of facts:

• All major coherence strands involve both vocabulary-guided and grammar-cued processes.
• All major coherence strands display both local and global coherence processes.
• Both vocabulary-guided and grammar-cued coherence involve both local and global processes.

8.5.2.   Spatial coherence

8.5.2.1. Vocabulary-guided spatial coherence

It is relatively easy to show vocabulary-guided spatial coherence in text, and further, that such spatial coherence could be both local and global in scope. Consider:

(29)   a. **More local**:
        They left the **living room** and went **directly** into the **kitchen**.
     b. **More global**:
        In **Los Angeles**, they found a big mess and fired the manager. In **Chicago** the following week, things were looking much better.

As is typical of vocabulary-guided inferences, frame-based information plays an important role in identifying the spatial coherence as more local in one case, more global in another. Thus, the knowledge that a kitchen tends to be adjacent to the living room (29a) is implicit in the cultural frame "typical American home". Likewise, the knowledge that Los Angeles is geographically non-adjacent to Chicago (29b) comes with the cultural frame "U.S. geography".

The status of spatial prepositions in English is problematic, in the sense that they may be considered either grammatical or lexical-semantic. But regardless of their status, some prepositions cue local and some less-local spatial configurations. Thus, for example, 'in(side)', 'at', 'on (top of)', 'under', 'near (by)', 'in front of' and 'behind' tend to code more local spatial relations, where the figure is relatively close to its spatial ground. On the other hand, 'far (from)', 'away (from)', 'out(side) (of)', 'to(ward)' and 'from' tend to code more global spatial relations, where the figure is more remote from its spatial ground. Finally, some verbs incorporate spatial-orientation features in their lexical meaning. Thus:

> (30)   a. So he **came** to the house and...
>   (> I was there; he came **toward** me)
>   b. So he **went** to the house and...
>   (> I was not there; he went **away** from me)

8.5.2.2. Grammar-cued spatial coherence

Situation-based spatial reference is obviously confined to the immediate speech situation. Even so, it can be both more local and more global:

> (31)   a. Give me **this** book. Now **that** one you can keep.
>   b. You sit **right here**, and you **here** and you **here**. Now every-
>   body else please sit **way over there**.

Similarly, text-based spatial reference can be both local and global. Typical local spatial references are:

> (32)   a. He came to **the house** and stayed **there** for a week.
>   b. He kept out of **the office** but stayed **nearby**.
>   c. He went up **the hill**, and **that's where** he found the body.
>   d. They went further down, and **right there** they found...

More-global grammar-cued spatial reference may be seen in:

(33) a. This is all for **the Gulf desert**. Now **elsewhere** this Tuesday
          evening...
      b. So he camped **at the fort**. But the rest of them moved
          further away and...
      c. All was quiet in **Transylvania**. But **other** countries were not
          quite as lucky.

Quite often, spatial coherence is established by a mix of vocabulary-guided
and grammar-cued means. And this mix may involve more-local or more-global
spatial reference:

(34) a. **Local mixed-cues spatial coherence**:
          He left **his cubicle** and stepped **into** the **lounge right** across
          the hall and...
      b. **Less local mixed-cues spatial coherence**:
          He left **his cubicle** and **left** the **building**. On the **other side**
          of the **street** he hailed a cab and...

In (34a), the location nouns 'cubicle', 'lounge' and 'hall' furnish part of the
spatial coherence information, guided by the relevant frame-based knowledge
of "office". But the grammatical cues 'into', 'right' and 'across' further
reinforce the more local spatial interpretation. In (34b), the location nouns
'cubicle', 'building', 'side', 'street', together with 'cab' and the verbs 'left' and
'hail' furnish part of the spatial coherence information, again guided by frame-
based inferences. But the grammatical cue 'other' reinforces the more global
spatial interpretation.

Note, further, that at particular junctures in discourse — typically at the
opening of a discourse, a chapter or an episode — the whole **spatial framework** for an impending text is laid out in some detail. An example of such
spatial orientation ('scene setting') at a story-initial context can be seen in (35)
below, the second paragraph of a novel:[24]

(35) "...Seven days of [Ø] riding the ghost trails **up out of Sonora,
          down from the Sierra Madre, through Apache country,**
          keeping **off the sky lines** and watching the beckoning fingers of
          the talking smoke..." (p. 1)

In signalling spatial coherence in (35), a mixed array of lexical and grammatical means are employed.

Spatial re-orientation often takes place at paragraph-initial environments. One of the most common device there is a pre-posed adverbial with an intonational pause (comma):[25]

(36) a. ...Meanwhile **back on the ranch**, the crew is busy with fall roundup...
      b. ...**At all other locations**, the AP reports, order has been restored...
      c. ...Finally, **at the house where they found the body**, the missing gun all of a sudden turns up...

In each case, grammatical and lexical signals are combined. In each case, the fronted adverbial performs at least two communicative functions:
  • It signals the termination of the preceding thematic paragraph and the initiation of another.
  • It affects spatial re-orientation.
In each case, the spatial re-orientation contains specific global coherence clues, ones that refer backwards — anaphorically — to spatial information in the preceding paragraph or even further back. In (36a), this is implicit in both 'back' and 'the ranch'. In (36b), it is implicit in 'other'. In (36c), it is implicit in the restrictive REL-clause 'where they found the body', which refers back to an event assumed to be already accessible in episodic memory.

8.5.3. Temporal coherence

8.5.3.1. Vocabulary-guided temporal coherence

Vocabulary-guided temporal coherence is most often intermixed with grammatical signals, such as prepositions. The coherence may be strictly local, as in:

(37) a. On **Tuesday** she was late, on **Wednesday** she was late again, and on **Thursday** she didn't show up at all.
      b. You go to work in the **morning**, at **noon** you take a short lunch break, and in the **afternoon** you...
      c. They started calling him at **five** and they kept till **six** and he finally showed up at **seven**.

When vocabulary-guided temporal coherence is less local, the simultaneous use of grammatical devices such as pre-posed adverbials is almost obligatory, as a paragraph-initial or chain-initial device:

(38) a. ...So they made a deal and signed the papers.
The following **Tuesday**, at **eight** in the **morning**, the guy
calls and says...
b. ...So he went to sleep. **Two hours later**, she...
c. ...And so things went on this way the whole winter.
Next **spring**, a new chief was appointed...

Again, implicitly or explicitly, anaphoric connections are made by the temporal
adverb, tapping into information accessible in episodic memory. The anaphoric
clues are partly embedded in the lexical time-word — 'Tuesday', 'eight',
'morning', 'hour', 'spring'. Often, the clues involve modifiers such as 'following'
(38a), 'later' (38b) or 'next' (38c).

8.5.3.2. Grammar-cued temporal coherence

8.5.3.2.1. Tense-aspect and temporal coherence

Most non-pidgin languages code at least two major distinctions of temporal
coherence through their tense-aspect-modality system. These distinctions contrast three tense-aspectual markers:

(a) preterit ('perfective', 'past')
(b) progressive ('durative')
(c) perfect ('anterior')

The **preterit** aspect codes the more common temporal *norm* of discourse,
whereby events are recounted in the same **sequential-temporal order** in which
they occurred (Hopper 1979). These sequential events are, further, **temporally
adjacent**, so that the temporal coherence relation between them is strictly local.
The in-sequence norm can be then contrasted with two counter-norms. The
progressive aspect codes events that are **simultaneous** with other events. Such
events are by definition non-sequential, but due to their extreme temporal adjacency
their temporal coherence is by definition rather local. The contrast between the
preterit-sequential and progressive-simultaneous aspects is illustrated in:

(39) a. **Sequential (preterit-past):**
After she came home, he **cooked** dinner,
and they ate and went to bed.
b. **Simultaneous (progressive-past):**
When she came home, he **was cooking** dinner.
Then they ate and went to bed.

A more natural example from written narrative also illustrates the much higher text-frequency of the in-sequence preterit norm:[26]

(40) "...Within the mouth of the draw he *drew* reins again. With his first glance he *recognized* the body for what it was, but only when he *was* quite sure that he *was* alone *did* he approach it. He *circled* it as wearily as a wolf, **studying** it from all angles, and when he finally *stopped*, within a dozen feet of the dead man, he *knew* much of..."

The **perfect** aspect codes **counter-sequence** events, more specifically events that occur earlier but are placed later in the verbal depiction. Consider the contrast between (41c) and (42c) below:

(41) **Simple-sequential past**:
   a. She came back into the room,
   b. looked around,
   c. **spotted** the buffet
   d. and went to get a sandwich....

(42) **Perfect past**:
   a. She came back into the room
   b. and looked around.
   c. She **had spotted** the buffet **beforehand**.
   d. She went to get a sandwich...

The difference between the sequential preterit and the counter-sequential perfect in (41) and (42) may be given diagrammatically as:

(43) a. **Actual order of events**:
         ...A,B,C,D...
      b. **Order of narration in the preterit**:
         ...A,B,C,D...
      c. **Order of narration with the perfect**:
         ...A,C,B,D...

A more natural illustration of the contrast between the sequential preterit and the counter-sequence perfect in narrative can be seen in:[27]

(44) "...He *circled* it wearily as a wolf, studying it from all angles, and when finally he *stopped* within a dozen feet of the dead man, he *knew* much of what **had** happened at this place.
The dead man **had** ridden a freshly shod horse into the playa from the north, and when shot he **had** tumbled from the saddle and the horse **had** galloped away. Several riders on unshod ponies **had** then approached the body and one **had** dismounted to collect the weapons..."

Table (45) below summarizes the frequency distribution of the major tense-aspects in two English texts.

(45) **The distribution of tense-aspect-modality in low-brow fiction and academic text in English**[28]

	academic		fiction	
category	N	%	N	%
past (sequential)	2	2%	74	**56%**
irrealis	18	**20%**	8	6%
habitual (sequential)	62	**70%**	/	/
durative	/	/	43	**32%**
perfect	7	8%	8	6%
total:	89	100%	133	100%

In the fiction text, most sequential events were coded by the preterit-past, but the presence of dialogue provides for a relatively large portion of progressive-coded events. In the academic text, the sequential material — primarily stative and timeless — was coded primarily by the habitual.

8.5.3.2.2. Temporal adverbial connectors

Another grammatical sub-system used in the coding of temporal coherence are adverbial connectors. Those can be as small as single-word conjunctions, such as '(and) then', 'later', 'afterwards', 'soon', 'earlier (on)' and others. Most of these connectors have an implicit anaphoric temporal reference, some more local, some more global. The latter tend to be associated with more major thematic transition. Thus compare:

(46) a. He had a quick dinner **and then** got up and left.
      b. He ate dinner, **then** slept, **then** got up and left.
      c. He ate dinner. **Later (on)** he got up and left.
      d. He ate a good dinner. **Afterwards** he slept for 8 hours.
      e. They ate dinner. **Soon** the dishes were cleared and...
      f. He ate dinner. **Earlier on** he had slept for 8 hours.

Almost all the temporal connector in (46) are sequential. The lone exception is the counter-sequential 'earlier (on)' (46f), further amplified by the perfect aspect.

8.5.3.2.3. Temporal adverbial clauses

The last grammar-cued device used extensively in establishing temporal coherence in discourse are temporal ADV-clauses. The subordinator of such clauses provides the specific cataphoric temporal relation between the adverbial and main clause. This relation is in one sense local, since it pertains to the very next clause:

(47) **Temporal links of adverbial clauses**:
      a. **Precedence**:
         Before she came, he left.
      b. **Subsequence**:
         After she came, he left.
      c. **Simultaneity**:
         While she was working, he left.
      d. **Point coincidence**:
         As she was coming in, he saw her.
      e. **Terminal boundary**:
         Till she left, he worked steadily.
      f. **Initial boundary**:
         (Ever) since she came, he's been ignoring her.
      g. **Intermediacy**:
         Between her starting the project and
         her quitting in a huff, nobody slept.

But the temporal relation could be more remote, and thus in a sense also more global:

(48) **Way before** she came, he had already left.
      Long after she left, he came back.

Pre-posed ADV-clauses tend to be used as **coherence bridges** at the onset of a new thematic clause-chain or paragraph. Their more global, anaphoric coherence strands are not cued by the adverbial subordinator itself. Rather, they are signalled by a combination of grammatical and lexical cues inside the adverbial clause. This is especially true in presupposed ADV-clauses, i.e. those that have a past or perfect tense-aspect:

(49) a. After **he said that**, she decided...
      b. When **such a disruption occurs**, they immediately...
      c. Having **told us this incredible tale of woes**, he...
      d. During **her next visit**, the Queen said...
      e. In the **last attempt to assassinate him**, they tried...
      f. When **they finished telling her about it**, she said...
      g. After **what she told him** finally sank in, he got up...

8.5.4. Thematic coherence

Thematic coherence is most likely an epi-phenomenon. It may be an additive consequence of all the more concrete strands of coherence falling together; still, it is not likely to be the mere sum of its various parts. In this section I will illustrate one aspect of thematic coherence that is primarily vocabulary-guided, and a number of aspects that are heavily grammar-cued. Each one turns out to involve both local and global coherence.

8.5.4.1. Vocabulary-guided action coherence

By action coherence I mean here culturally-shared, conventional, generic knowledge of **sequential action schemata** ('scripts', 'routines'). Both thematically and syntactically, such sequences display maximally-tight coherence — typically with continuing reference, location, temporality, aspectuality, modality and perspective:

(50) a. She opened the fridge, took out the milk carton, poured herself a glass and drank.
      b. He put on his pajamas, got in bed, turned off the light and went to sleep.
      c. They shot the deer, skinned it, quartered the carcass and hung it to cure.

In each case in (50), reversing any local sequential order will disrupt the thematic coherence. Respectively:

(51) a. *She opened the fridge, poured herself a glass of milk, took out the milk carton and drank.
      b. *He put on his pajamas, got into bed, went to sleep and turned off the lights.
      c. *They skinned the deer, shot it, quartered the carcass and hung it to cure.

But the very tight local coherence relations in routinized action-frames tends to mask some highly global governing **script knowledge**. Thus in (51a), there is nothing inherently incoherent about pouring oneself a glass before taking the milk-carton out of the fridge. One can transfer liquids from one container to another inside a fridge. It is only in the more global context of the routine "going for a glass of milk" that the order is incoherent. Similarly in (51b), there's nothing inherently incoherent about going to sleep (but not falling asleep, or waking up later) and then turning the lights off. It is only in the more global context of the routine "going to bed at night" that the order becomes incoherent. And similarly in (51c), there is nothing physically impossible about skinning an animal and then shooting it. It is only in the more global context of the habituated routine "hunting game animals" that such an order becomes incoherent.

8.5.4.2. Grammar-cued thematic coherence

As noted earlier, human discourse is multi-propositional, with clauses making up chains, which in turn make up paragraphs (etc.).[29] One of the grammatical sub-systems that helps cue this hierarchic organization of discourse combines **conjunctions**, intonation and pauses — which in the written language are mimicked as **punctuation** —[30] and paragraph indentation. These devices are inherently cataphoric: The grammatical cue is placed between the two clauses, signalling the degree of thematic continuity of the next clause.[31]

Given the strong correlation between thematic and referential continuity, consider now the results of one study of low-brow English fiction text, where referential continuity across various grammatically-cued inter-clausal transitions was recorded.

(52)   **Referential continuity across adjacent clauses separated by**
zero, comma, period and paragraph indentation; with 'and'
and 'then' in written English (Hayashi 1989)

conjunction type	% subject switch (DS) across the conjunction
and	15%
, and	70%
. And	81%
and then	16%
, and then	36%
. and then	100%
,then	50%
.Then	56%
. PARAG/Then	100%
comma (alone)	10%
period (alone)	72%

An equally strong association exists between conjunctions that are thematically continuous ('and') and referential continuity, and between conjunctions
that are thematically disruptive or contrastive ('while', 'but', 'though', 'yet')
and referential discontinuity. Table (53) below summarizes the results of one
distributional study.

(53)   **Referential continuity across adjacent clauses separated by**
various conjunctions in written English (Hayashi 1989)

conjunction	% subject switch (DS) across the conjunction
and (all punctuations)	29%
, while	77%
but (all punctuations)	85%
, though	100%
. Yet	100%

The conjunctions that signal greater thematic continuity presumably cue more local coherence, while those that signal greater thematic disruption cue more global coherence — since they are typically found at chain or paragraph boundaries.

8.5.5. Referential Coherence

8.5.5.1. grammar vs. Lexicon, local vs. Global

The largest portion of the grammar of discourse coherence in most languages is connected, in one way or another, to the grammar of referential coherence. The following list of grammatical devices is by no means exhaustive:

(54)   **Main sub-systems in the grammar of referential coherence:**
       Without lexical information
   (a)   zeros, agreement, pronouns
   (b)   same-subject (SS) cataphoric morphology
       Combined with lexical information
   (c)   different subject (DS) cataphoric morphology
   (d)   determiners, articles, numerals
   (e)   grammatical case-roles (subject, direct object)
   (f)   role-changing constructions (passive, inverse, antipassive, dative-shift)
   (g)   existential-presentative constructions
   (h)   restrictive modifiers (relative clauses, adjectives)
   (i)   word-order devices (L/R-dislocation, Y-movement, cleft)

Among these devices, the major dichotomy is between those that signal **continued activation** of the current topical referent, and those that signal it **terminated activation**. Statistically, this dichotomy overlaps to a large extent (but not absolutely) with the dichotomy between continued thematic chain and terminated thematic chain, respectively. The dichotomy thus also coincides (again not absolutely) with the split between local referential coherence (continuity) vs. global referential coherence (discontinuity).

The dichotomy between grammatical devices that signal continued reference vs. those that signal disrupted reference also coincides, in the main, with the dichotomy between purely grammatical referential devices (54a, b), and those that combine grammar-cuing with lexical information (54c–i). The most obvious source of lexical information in the latter group is the lexical noun itself. Compare:

(55) **Grammar without lexical cuing (continuing reference):**
    a. **Zero:**
    ...The woman came in and [Ø] stopped...
    b. **Anaphoric pronoun:**
    ...The woman came in and stopped.
    Then **she** moved again...

(56) **Grammar combined with lexical cuing (terminated reference):**
    a. **Indefinite noun (modified by an adjective):**
    ...The woman came in and stopped.
    There was a tall man sitting there...
    b. **Demonstrative plus noun:**
    ...The woman came in and stopped.
    "There's something wrong with **this room**"
    she thought...
    c. **Definite noun:**
    ...They went in together. The woman stopped,
    But **the man** kept going...
    d. **Definite noun (modified by a REL-clause):**
    ...The woman came in and stopped. She saw
    the man who had questioned her earlier sitting there...
    e. **Word-order device (L-dislocation):**
    ...The woman came in and stopped. She was finally home.
    But **the man, he** never came back...
    f. **Grammatical role and voice change (passive):**
    ...The woman came in and braced herself for a long wait.
    The man was still being searched, so it seemed...

Combining lexical cues with grammatical ones is indispensible when reference is terminated (56). Even when the next topical referent to be activated has an accessible antecedent in some extant mental representation, a search for that antecedent must be instituted. Purely grammatical information cannot be conclusive, as it was in signaling continuing reference (55). Thus, the grammatical device "full NP" *per se* (56) could only signal discontinuing reference. Other grammatical devices signal definiteness, i.e. accessibility of the co-referent in some existing mental model (56b, c, d, e, f). Other grammatical devices yet may narrow the search down to episodic memory (56c, d, e, f). Others yet may point the search more finely beyond the current thematic chain (56d, e. f). But still, no final identification of the antecedent can occur without full specification of the actual lexical noun. This is Kintsch's "strong method" of referential identification, the final haul to an exact mental destination.

Above and beyond the head noun, other lexical clues for referential identification may be furnished by **restrictive modifiers**. Thus in (56d) above, the specific vocabulary items in the REL-clause "who questioned her earlier" guide the more fine-grained search for coreference, under the assumption that the proposition "A man questioned the woman" is still accessible in the hearer's episodic memory.

8.5.6.   Text frequency, markedness and cognitive default

In this section I briefly review the frequency distribution of zeros and anaphoric pronouns vs. full NPs in coherent discourse. Two facts are conspicuous about the two continuing reference grammatical devices. Functionally, they mark a continuing referent, one that was also topical in the preceding clause. Structurally, they display zero lexical expression of that referent.

The distribution of zero/pronouns vs. full NPs in natural text reveals that referential continuity is the more frequent norm, and discontinuity is the counter-norm. Consider first the distribution of zero/pronouns vs. full definite nouns in Ute, English, and two English-based pidgins.

(57)   **Text frequency of clauses with anaphoric subject pronouns (incl. zero) vs. full subject nouns in spoken Ute, spoken English and two spoken Pidgins**[32]

	zero/pronoun		def-nouns		total	
	N	%	N	%	N	%
Ute	288	**93.5**	20	6.5	308	100.0
English	540	**74.4**	185	25.6	725	100.0
Spanglish	109	**68.9**	54	31.1	163	100.0
Filipinglish	132	**73.3**	4	26.7	180	100.0

When the sample of full NPs includes indefinite nouns, the predominance of zero/pronouns is a little less pronounced. As illustration, consider the frequency distribution in Sacapultec Mayan (DuBois 1987)[33]

(58) The distribution of grammatical subjects, objects and
      'others' in the zero-pronoun and full-NP categories in
      Zacapultec (from DuBois 1987)

| grammatical category | NP type | | | | | |
| | zero/pronoun | | full-NP | | total | |
	N	%	N	%	N	%
transitive SUBJ	169	**93.9%**	11	6.1%	180	100.0%
intransitive SUBJ	136	**51.9%**	126	48.1%	262	100.0%
all subjects	305	**60.0%**	137	40.0%	442	100.0%
dir. objects	96	**54.3%**	81	45.7%	177	100.0%
others	24	13.4%	154	**86.6%**	178	100.0%

What table (58) reveals is the predominance of referential continuity — **93.9%**
continuous referents — of the subject in the transitive clause. Such subject are
semantically almost entirely human agents. Intransitive subjects, in contrast,
more commonly introduce new — discontinuous — participants into the discourse, and are also less likely to be human agents. The level of continuous
reference there drops to around **50%**, and matches the level found in direct
objects. The 'other' categories, indirect objects of various types, are almost
categorially non-continuous, with only **13%** zero/pronouns.

The predominance of the subject-coded participant in coherent text can
also be shown by the following distribution in spoken English narrative.

(59) **Number of participant-referents per clause in
      spontaneous oral English narrative**[34]

# of REFs per clause	N	%
1 (SUBJ only)	39	38.6%
2 (SUBJ & OBJ)	54	53.4%
3 (SUBJ, OBJ, OTH)	8	8.0%
>3	/	/
total:	101	100.0%

The distribution of total NPs in the various grammatical roles in the text in (59)
can be now computed as:[35]

(60) **Frequency distribution of various grammatical NP roles in spontaneous oral English narrative**

NP role	#	%
SUBJ	101	59.0
OBJ	62	36.0
OTHERS	8	5.0
total:	171	100.0

The grammatical subject, the clause's **primary topic**, codes the event participant that is the most continuous — both anaphorically and cataphorically. NPs occupying this pivotal grammatical role constitute 60% of all referents in text. Direct objects, the clause's **secondary topics**, constitute the bulk of the rest (36%). Non-topical "others" make up a negligeable residue (5%).

The conclusions that one may draw from the various distributions presented above are as follows:

• The grammatical cues that signal referential continuity are the most frequent referent-coding devices in text.
• Zero lexical marking of referents is a concomitant of the referent's cognitive status as **currently active**.
• Zero lexical marking is thus the **default choice** in the grammar of referential coherence, the **unmarked** case.
• There is a strong association between the high-continuity grammatical device and grammatical subjecthood.
• Even with the less-continuous direct objects (and subjects of intransitive clauses) thrown in, the ratio of all topical referents per clause approximates **1 topic per clause**.

These conclusions beg for a comprehensive hypothesis about the cognitive role of topical referents in the representation and retrieval of text in episodic memory.

8.6. The grammar of referential coherence as mental processing cues

8.6.1. Preliminaries

In this section I sketch out more explicitly the cognitive interpretation of the grammar of referential coherence, an interpretation that has been implicit in the preceding discussion. I will take it for granted that the clause is the minimal unit for accruing new language-coded information into episodic memory. And further, that a clause in connected discourse always has one topical referent (most commonly its grammatical subject). The function of the clausal topical referent may be now given as the hypothesis:

(61) **Function of the clause's topical referent**:
      (a) Adjacent clause-nodes that belong to the same equi-topic chain in mentally represented text are attached under their governing **chain-node**.
      (b) The clausal topic serves as the **node label** or **filing address** for the clause, insuring that it gets attached under its rightful chain-node.
      (c) As long as the incoming information is filed under the same chain-node, the same topic remains **activated**.
      (d) In order to discontinue one clause-chain and initiate another, the currently-active topic must be **de-activated**, and a new one **activated**.
      (e) Only **one chain-node at a time** can be activated, insuring unambiguous addressing of incoming new information.

The significance of using nominal referents — rather then other coherence strands such as locations, times, actions or abstract themes — as the chain-node labels lies in the conflation of four factors that are not wholly independent of each other:

- Nominal referents are **perceptually-cognitively salient**.
- Nominal reference is **acquired early in ontogeny**.
- Nominal reference **evolved early in phylogeny**.
- Nominal referents code **culturally central** entities, in particular those that are prototypically concrete, individuated, spatially compact; and in particular:
  The prototype subject-agent: human, active, conscious, willful.
  The prototype object-patient: concrete, compact, manipulable, usable.

8.6.2.   Cognitive model

8.6.2.1.   General operations

I will assume that the grammar of referential coherence, in so far as it involves the episodic mental model of the current text, cues two main mental operations:

- **Attentional activation operations (cataphoric):**
  Opening (activation) or closing (de-activation) text-nodes
  for attaching incoming new information.
- **Search & retrieval operations (anaphoric):**
  Searching in the episodic text representation for the anaphoric
  grounding of referents.

By activating a topical referent, one activates the text-node labeled by the referent. Three possible operations are subsumed under 'attentional activation'.

(62) **Main attentional instructions:**
  a. **continue activation** of the currently active topic/node
  b. **terminate activation** of the currently active topic/node
  c. **activate** a currently inactive topic/node, by either:
   (i) activating a **new referent** (indefinite)
   (ii) re-activate an **existing referent** (definite)

Memory search and retrieval operations apply only in the case of (62c-ii) — when a currently inactive definite referent is re-activated. The re-activation of a definite referent requires searching for its anaphoric antecedence in some relevant mental structure (speech-situation model, lexical knowledge model, episodic text model). A precondition for re-activating a definite referent is that its anaphoric antecedence be accessible. In other words, a definite referent can only be re-activated if its current text-location is **grounded** to its antecedent text-location in the episodic mental model of the current text.

The main grammar-cued mental operations relevant to referent activation are summarized in (63) below as a series of ordered, binary choices. For each binary choice, one option is assumed to be the **unmarked** ('default') case. This is the more frequent choice in natural text, the one that is cognitively less costly. The other option is the **marked** case, the less frequent choice in natural text, the one that is cognitively more costly.

(63)   **Major grammar-cued mental operations for referential coherence**

[U = unmarked = default]
[M = marked]

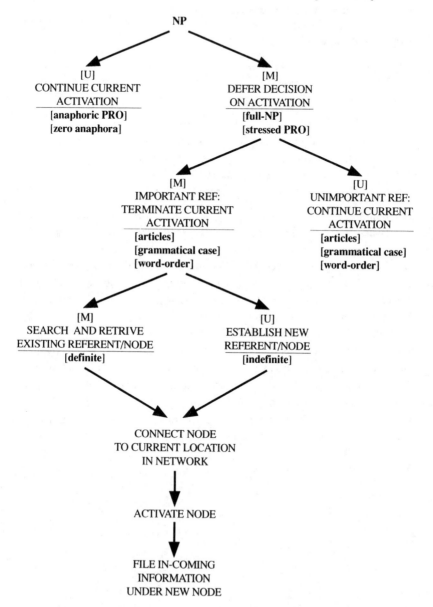

NP

[U]
CONTINUE CURRENT
ACTIVATION
[anaphoric PRO]
[zero anaphora]

[M]
DEFER DECISION
ON ACTIVATION
[full-NP]
[stressed PRO]

[M]
IMPORTANT REF:
TERMINATE CURRENT
ACTIVATION
[articles]
[grammatical case]
[word-order]

[U]
UNIMPORTANT REF:
CONTINUE CURRENT
ACTIVATION
[articles]
[grammatical case]
[word-order]

[M]
SEARCH AND RETRIVE
EXISTING REFERENT/NODE
[definite]

[U]
ESTABLISH NEW
REFERENT/NODE
[indefinite]

CONNECT NODE
TO CURRENT LOCATION
IN NETWORK

ACTIVATE NODE

FILE IN-COMING
INFORMATION
UNDER NEW NODE

The grammar-cued operations outlined in (63) are to be interpreted as the following set of processing instructions:

(64) **Major grammar-cued mental operations for referential coherence**

    (a) if **ZERO/PRO** ⟹ continue current activation (keep filing incoming information under same node)

    (b) if **FULL NP** ⟹ (i) defer activation decision
                          (ii) determine referent's importance

    (c) if **UNIMPORTANT** ⟹ (i) do not activate
                          (ii) continue current activation (keep filing incoming new information in the current active node).

    (d) if **IMPORTANT** ⟹ then
                      de-activate the current active node.
                      then

    (e) if **INDEF** ⟹ (i) do not search for antecedence;
                      (ii) initiate a new text-node;
                      (iii) activate the new referent/node;
                      (iv) attach the new referent/node to the current text-location;
                      (v) attach incoming new information under the new node;

    (f) if **DEF** ⟹ determine the source of definiteness among the three disjunctive options:
                      (i) Speech situation mental model
                      (ii) Generic-lexical mental model
                      (iii) Episodic text mental model;
                      then

    (g) (i) search for antecedent in appropriate mental model;
          (ii) ground the antecedent to its co-referent in the current text location;
          (iii) initiate a new text-node, labeled by the grounded topical referent;
          (iv) activate the new referent/node;
          (v) attach the new referent/node to its current text-location;
          (v) attach incoming new information under new node;

8.6.3. Some general principles

The cognitive model outlined above, of grammar-cued attentional activation of text-storage nodes, abides by a number of general principles. The first one involves the relationship between a topical referent and the text-node of which it is the **activating label**:

(65) **Node activation via referent-activation**:
      "A text-node in episodic memory is activated, and thus is open for storage of in-coming new information, when its topical referent, or node-label, is activated".

The second principle identifies the activation of text-nodes as a **limited capacity** mental process, a property one would expect of any attentional subsystem:[37]

(66) **One-node-at-a-time constraint**:
      "Only one text-node is open — activated — at any given time".

Principle (66) probably applies at any given hierarchic level within the mental text structure. So that only one chain-node at a time is open for attaching clause-nodes; only one paragraph-node at a time is open for attaching chain-nodes, etc. The next principle relates the grounding of referents that serve as node-labels — both indefinite (new) and definite (old) referents — with their activation:

(67) **Grounding as condition for activation**:
      "A node — and thus the referent-label that activates it for text-storage — must be grounded before it can be activated for text-storage.
      a. A new (indefinite) referent is grounded only to its **current text location** in the episodic structure still under construction.
      b. An old (definite) referent is attached to its **current** location in the episodic text structure; but it must also be grounded to some other location in some **pre-existing** mental structure".

The grounding of a referent-node to its current text location is by definition a local operation. The second type of grounding, applying only to definite NPs, involves more global connections between non-adjacent location in the current text-structure, or between two different structures.

8.7. Discussion

8.7.1. Local vs. global coherence

I think both the experimental work on text processing and the grammar-in-discourse work by linguists strongly suggest that coherence involves both local and global processes. This seems to be as true of vocabulary-guided ('knowledge-based') processes as it is of all major grammar-cued processes. Putting the two types of coherence against each other as mutually exclusive alternatives is not a viable approach.

8.7.2. Vocabulary-guided vs. grammar-cued coherence

The hybrid model of language processing and text coherence suggested by Kintsch (ms.) is probably the right approach to pursue. Information about the coherence structure of text is thus processed through two parallel channels:

(a) Knowledge-based inferences, supported by the lexical vocabulary of the clause.

(b) Grammar-cued inferences, supported by the syntactic structure, grammatical morphology and intonational cues of the clause.

If the clause is indeed the basic processing unit for language-coded information, then both processing channels aim at the very same cognitive task:

(68)   **Main on-line task in text processing**:
       "Determine where and how to attach the new information in the clause in the episodic mental representation of the current text".

The vocabulary-guided channel relies on the automatic activation of lexical meanings. That activation is always there, since it is necessary for understanding the **propositional information** of the clause, regardless of where and how that information is stored in episodic representation. Text production and comprehension can proceed by relying exclusively on this channel, as is the case in early child language, second language pidgin, and agrammatic aphasia. The vocabulary-guided channel is also slow, context-dependent and error-prone.[38] Nonetheless, it is a fine-grained processing channel. It guides the processor to exact mental destinations, and it is attuned to fine shades and gradations of meaning and context.

The grammar-cued channel is a later ontogenetic addition to the arsenal of language processing, and probably also a later phylogenetic addition. It is a rough-grained processing route, moving the bulk at high speed and lower error rates in a relatively context-free fashion.[39] But it very seldom gets the processor to exact, final mental destinations. To reach those, the processor must rely on the ever-present, automatically activated, vocabulary-coded "knowledge-based" channel.

The only discourse context where lexical information seems clearly superfluous for establishing text coherence is the default context of continued current activation. This is the context where lexical information is consistently "deleted" from the clause. But this is also the context where grammatical clues are dispensed with, and where one most consistently finds:

- zero-coded NPs
- reduced (non-finite) verbal morphology
- zero-coded thematic conjunctions.

This paucity of signals in both processing channels is possible because the default mental task of continued current activation requires no further operations. The task in unambiguous — attach incoming clausal information to the same, currently-activated, text-node. Constraint (66) — "one node at a time" — insures that this **most frequent** processing task is cognitively **least ambiguous**. That such a task is also linguistically the **least marked**, i.e. requires minimal coding, is only to be expected.[40]

The traditional notion that zeros and pronouns "create ambiguity" is, from a cognitive point of view, an upside-down rendition of the facts. It is only in the least ambiguous processing tasks that one can safely resort to zeros and pronouns, because their lexical identity is already activated.

8.7.3.   Why is anaphoric grounding necessary?

One of the most striking features of text coherence is the seemingly absolute **anaphoric grounding** requirement (67): Currently-topical referents that have antecedence in mentally represented prior text must be grounded to that antecedence. This requirement creates coherence connections that are often distant and in that sense global. And these distant connections cut across the hierarchic node-structure of the text. Requirement (67) may be recapitulated as:

(69)   **The anaphoric grounding constraint**:
      "When an important topic is re-introduced into the discourse, access to the information filed under its antecedent text-location must be assured".

But why such a rigid constraint? The answer is, I think, fairly obvious. If a referent is an important topic, its topicality and relevance must be justified upon activation in its current text location. As we have seen, this type of justification is systematically furnished for indefinite referents upon their first introduction into the discourse: They are cataphorically grounded by such information. But the information that justifies the importance and relevance of a definite referent with prior text antecedence has already been furnished at least once — at its prior text location. Obligatory anaphoric grounding makes that information available again — at the referent's current text location. This dispenses with the need to re-assemble the information again and again from scratch. Anaphoric connections between a referent's current and prior text locations are time-saving devices in the processing of coherent discourse. They make it possible to tap into grounding information that has already been assembled and stored in episodic text — when it again becomes relevant.

8.7.4. Grammar, episodic storage and working memory: The thematic flexibility of episodic representation

In their most recent review of the cognitive status of the working memory buffer, Just and Carpenter (1992) describe it as a **limited capacity** mechanism, in terms of both storage and processing. These two aspects of the buffer are thus in competition for a limited amount of "activation". While not explicitly stated in the review, the most likely limited capacity here is probably some species of attention.

The recall capacity for surface linguistic form, and thus for grammatical clues associated with the clause, is severely limited (Gernsbacher 1985; Carpenter and Just 1988; Just and carpenter 1992; *inter alia*). These limits are somewhere in the range of 2–5 clauses **moving buffer**, or 8–20 seconds,[41] beyond which grammatical form is *not* preserved. Within the 8–20 second time-span of working memory, the grammatical information associated with the clause must be translated into the clause's location and manner-of-attachment in episodic mental representation. The clause's grammatical clues may thus be considered a **translation mechanism**; they insure the coherent encoding of incoming information in episodic memory. The limited buffer capacity suggests that, with grammar, such translation occurs within the range of 8-20 seconds, and that grammatical cues are unnecessary beyond that point. But couldn't they still be useful?

There are at least two good reasons why grammatical clues are not stored in episodic memory. The first reason is evolutionary: The grammar-free storage of episodic text develops long before grammar in the child; it is supported by the same hippocampus neurology in pre-human, pre-grammatical primates; and it had no doubt evolved earlier in the phylogenesis of the human brain (see

Chapter 9). In other words, coherent episodic mental representation has always been grammar-free.

There is a more compelling reason why the original grammatical information coming with each clause should not be preserved in episodic memory: It may actually be communicatively harmful to preserve such information. Grammar is a translation mechanism that helps contextualize clausal information in its *current* communicative context: current speech situation, current goals, current perspective, current text, current thematic structure. But once stored, the information is always — by definition — retrieved and re-used in *another* communicative context. This is true in the case of later retrieval and re-telling on another occasion (cf. Loftus 1980; Squire 1987; Squire and Zola-Morgan 1991; Slobin 1987; *inter alia*). But it is equally true in the case of repeated access and retrieval during the on-line processing of the same current text. The speech-situation context shifts constantly, as does the thematic context, even during the "same current text". This is particularly clear when one notes the shifting, flexible, negotiable nature of coherence in oral face-to-face communication (cf. Goodwin 1982, 1986, 1988, 1992, in this volume; Coates 1987, *inter alia*). A simple-minded example will illustrate how unstable the grammatical form is across consecutive turns that have 'the same' propositional reference. The grammatical signals associated with three core proposition in (70) below — "Guy want see Bill", "Bill want John..." and "John ask guy..." — are bold-faced:

(70) JOHN: **There-s a** guy **here who** want-s to see **you.**
      BILL: **Why do-es he** want **to** see **me?**
      JOHN: **You** want **me to** ask **him?**
      BILL: **Yeah, why do-nt you** ask **him.**

Storing propositional information in episodic memory together with the grammatical clues that were originally attached to it would render the information rather confusing, since those grammatical clues are incompatible with the proposition's current communicative context. The sharp decay of grammatical signals beyond the short-term buffer is thus not a loss, but rather a vital communicative necessity.

8.7.5. Closure

Transforming the study of text into the study of mind is a delicate and complex undertaking. Methodologically, it requires letting go of early, heuristic, text-based definitions and methods and replacing them with their cognitive counterparts. Theoretically, it entails deserting hypotheses about the behavior of utterance-populations in text (words, grammatical devices) in favor of hypotheses about the population of processing activities in the mind/brain. This progression — from text-centered to mind-centered method and theory — is both natural and necessary. As elsewhere in science, one studies an invisible process by observing its visible artifacts. As elsewhere in science, the theory that one constructs is not about the visible artifacts, but rather about the invisible process responsible for them.

It has been a common gambit in discourse studies to posit a stark dichotomy between the study of the observable communicative transaction — the interaction and its textual by-product — and the study of the cognition that underlies the communicative transaction. Such a dichotomy is false and distortive, in that it disregards the fact that the ultimate object of our study is not the speech situation per se, but rather the speech situation as it is mentally represented. To the extent that this is not merely a truism, it suggests that our task in discourse studies is even more complex than hitherto envisioned, since it now embraces not only the mental representation of text but also the mental representation of the interaction — including the interlocutor's projected knowledge and intentions. If we are serious about the term "mental models", we may have to worry about mental models of mental models.

Notes

* I am indebted to Bruce Britton, Wally Chafe, Marcelo Dascal, Morti Gernsbacher, Chuck Goodwin, Walter Kintsch, Jean Mandler, Tony Sanford and Dan Slobin for helpful comments on earlier versions of this chapter.

1) Among linguists, the perspective of well-edited, written, narrative text is implicit in much of the early work on coherence (cf. Longacre 1971, 1976; Halliday and Hassan 1976; Grimes 1975; *inter alia*).

2) This approach to grammar as an automated discourse-processing mode follows Givón (1979, ch. 5; 1989, ch. 7; 1990, ch. 20). It is well known that non-grammatical, vocabulary-guided clues are responsible for a considerable portion of text coherence, especially in pre-grammatical communication (early child discourse, second language pidgin, agrammatic aphasic speech).

3) Dan Slobin (in personal communication) has noted that speakers and hearers bring a different context — goals, frames, relevance considerations — into verbal interaction. The mental text-trace that survives in episodic memory is heavily dependent on these varying contexts.

4) See e.g. van Dijk and Kintsch (1983); Gernsbacher (1990); *inter alia*. One may argue that there is at least a partial one-way conditional relation between the two, so that:

"if hierarchic, then sequential"

(but not necessarily vice versa)

The 'chunking' process that produce hierarchic representation — apparently in any modality and at any level — of sequential information beyond a certain length, is well documented (cf. Chase and Simon 1973; Chase and Ericsson 1981, 1982; Ericsson, Chase and Faloon 1980; Ericsson 1985). So that to all intent and purpose, for sequences beyond a certain minimal length of 3-4 items, one may interpret the relation between hierarchy and sequence as a *bi-conditional*.

5) See Carpenter and Just (1988) for a review of the role of chunking, i.e. the creation of hierarchic structure for long term storage (cf. Chase and Ericsson 1981, 1982; Ericsson, Chase and Faloon 1980; Ericsson 1985).

6) Some texts are 'flat' or 'shallow', other have deeper hierarchical structures. Some node-sequences (at whatever hierarchic level) are long, others are short.

7) Similar devices also exist in most languages to distinguish definite NPs that are slated to be more important ('persistent', 'topical') in the subsequent discourse from those that are slated to be unimportant ('non-persistent', 'non-topical').

8) The indefinite (unstressed) 'this' is not used in formal or written English. The letter cited here was written by a teenager using an informal oral style.

9) The data were taken from: Sahaptin (Sahaptian) oral narrative, Rude (1994); Surinam Carib (Carib) oral narrative, Gildea (1994); Bella-Coola (Salish) oral narrative, Forrest (1994); Korean written narrative, Lee (1994); Spanish written newspaper prose, Hidalgo (1994).

10) The grammar of *deixis* is much more extensive, and may involve the tense-aspect modality system and other verbal inflections, as well as other grammatical sub-systems.

11) Several full-NP referents are thematically incidental or unimportant, and were not bold-faced. Thematic importance ('topicality') tends to correlate statistically with "playing the subject role in a clause".

12) From L'Amour (1962, p. 7).

13) *The New York Times,* Daily Business Section, June 3, 1991, p. C1.

14) For a discussion of various contrastive topicalizing devices, see Givón (1990b, ch. 16).

15) From the conversation of a retired New Mexico rancher, recorded ca. 1978 (see Givón 1983b).

16) From L'Amour (1962: 8). For more details about the use of pre-posed ADV-clauses as thematic-discontinuity devices see Thompson (1985), Ramsay (1987), or Givón (1990b, ch. 19).

17) A somewhat similar situation was studied experimentally by Tomlin (1987).

18) The cognitive notion "same text" is akin to the logician's "same meta-level" (Russell's (1919) "same type") or the text linguist's "same universe of discourse".

19) When two adjacent clauses are disjointed in a coherent text, coherence — i.e. recurrent elements — must exist between the adjacent chain nodes or paragraph nodes that govern them. The same goes for higher level of hierarchic depth (if any).

20) See further below. Even when the clause contains only two main elements — an old-information subject and a new-information verb — chances are the verb carries tense-aspect-modality markers that signal other (temporal, thematic) grounding connections.

21) There may be time costs for processing each grounding connection, and some upper limit per clause. A clause can presumably be *over-grounded*, with confusion arising as to which direction of connectivity is more weighted, more relevant, or stronger. Marcelo Dascal (in personal communication) notes that one implication of constraints (23) and (24), taken together, may be that the ideal clause-size is two chunks, one new information, the other old (grounding) information. The issue is fundamentally not one of logic, and must be resolved empirically.

22) Recorded by L. C. Givón, 5–20–81 (cf. Givón (1990a).

23) Hawaii Japanese-English Pidgin; from transcripts supplied by D. Bickerton; see also Bickerton and Givón (1976).

24) L'Amour (1962: 1).

25) The use of pre-posed adverbials to signal the opening of a new paragraph has been discussed earlier above.

26) From L'Amour (1962: 7).

27) L'Amour (1962: 7).

28) The fiction text was L'Amour (1962: 83–85). The academic non-fiction text was Haiman (1985: 21–23).

29) For the relation between clauses, chains and paragraphs, see Grimes (1975), Longacre (1971, 1976), Chafe (1986, 1987a, 1987b), Givón (1990b, ch. 19).

30) For the use of punctuation, intonation and grammar in signalling thematic continuity, see Chafe (1987a); Givón (1990b, ch. 19). For cognitive aspects of pausing, see Eisler-Goldman (1968).

31) We have already noted how the grammar of reference, tense-aspect-modality and adverbials collaborates in signalling inter-clausal, inter-chain and inter-paragraph coherence. In other languages, the grammar of clause-chaining and paragraphing involves other devices, such as verb serialization, cataphoric switch-reference morphology, and more vs. less finite verb morphology — thus also tense-aspect-modality. See again Givón (1990b, ch. 19).

32) After Givón (1983b; 1984c).

33) Excluded from DuBois' original Table 2 are NPs occupying the role of *possessor*. These are not grammatical arguments of the clause, but rather modifiers within the noun phrase. Similar figures have also been reported for Modern Hebrew (Smith, in press).

34) Life-story of a retired New Mexico rancher; first two typed pages of transcript; see Givón (1983b). The count excluded single NPs coming under their own separate intonation contour (see discussion in Chafe 1987a). All the 8 3-participant clauses had one time-adverb, which strictly speaking is not a clausal *participant*, but was counted as one here.

35) A similar computation can be done with the Sacapultec distribution in Table (58).

36) The model presented below follows, in the main, the one presented in Givón (1990b, ch. 20) and Givón (1992).

37) See Posner and Snyder (1974); Schneider and Shiffrin (1977). Since grammatical cues seem to be to quite an extent a sub-conscious, automated system (rapidly decaying; immediate-recall dependent; not preserved episodic memory), the attentional sub-system involved here is probably a more modal-specific species of covert attention (Inhoff *et al.* 1989; Posner and Petersen 1990; Nissen and Bullemer 1986).

38) An estimate of the role of grammar in the processing rate of language-coded information is that it speeds up processing by a factor of 5 to 10 (with error rates factored in).

39) Grammar-cued processing is not, strictly speaking, wholly context free. Rather, the relevant notion of "context to be scanned" is reduced in grammar-cued processing to scanning for fewer, more conventionalized, more discrete structural clues of syntax, morphology and intonation.

40) For the relation between informational predictability (or frequency) and code quantity see Zipf (1935), Givón (ed. 1983, 1985a) or Haiman (1985).

41) Approximating from Swinney's (1979) figure of 250 msecs per lexical word, and an average of 4 words per clause in fluent spoken language.

9

On the Co-evolution of
Language, Mind and Brain

9.1.   Introduction*

For anyone accustomed to the great multivariant richness of either biology
or culture, the extreme reductionist accounts of language evolution that emanate
periodically from the academic market-place are a recurrent puzzle. Like all
complex biologically-based phenomena, human language is shaped by competing functional imperatives that most often yield middle-ground adaptive
compromises. One notes such competition and compromise in the diachronic
process of grammaticalization, where expressive elaboration and code-transpar-
ency ('iconicity') are pitted against processing speed (economy; Haiman 1983).
One notes it in language acquisition, where inborn constraints interact with
inductive, input-guided discovery (Baldwin 1994). One notes it in discourse
processing, where more automated, grammar-cued pathways interact with more
analytic, knowledge-guided strategies (Kintsch 1992). One also notes it in the
dynamic balance between homogeneity and diversity of biological and cultural
populations, where adaptive pressures toward cohesion and uniformity balance
against equally adaptive trends toward diversity and speciation (Bonner 1988).
A reductionist approach to causation singles out one variable in a complex
equasion — tool making, social grooming, collaborative hunting, child rearing
and cultural transmission, learning, cognitive capacity, randomly-mutated
neurology, laryngeal anatomy — and proclaims it *the* determinative cause of an
enormously complex and protracted adaptation. In our collective attempt to
understand the evolution of human language, this compulsive search for single-
cause explanations remains a seductive intellectual program.

This chapter aims to remind us all of the startlingly old idea that, like all
complex biological change, the evolution of human language must have been an

interactive, multi-factored process. This perspective is uncontroversial in either evolutionary biology or historical linguistics. In the former, the interaction between random mutation, adaptive behavior and natural selection has been accepted even by main-stream neo-Darwinians. Thus Ernst Mayr (1982) observes:[1]

> "...Many if not most acquisitions of new structures in the course of evolution can be ascribed to selection forces exerted by newly acquired behaviors. Behavior, thus, plays an important role as the pacemaker of evolutionary change..." [p. 612]

The interactive nature of bio-evolution is often motivated by the inter-dependence among multiple components of complex biological design. In this connection, Futuyma (1986) observes:

> "...there are numerous selective factors besides those imposed by the external ecological world. Chief among these are the internal relationships among biochemical and developmental pathways, and among different organs, that impose selection by requiring that new features be compatible with the rest of the organism's internal organization..." [p. 19]

Analogous complex causalities have been observed in diachronic syntactic change,[2] as well as in the interaction between synchronic rules of grammar.[3]

In this chapter I will survey data from a wide range of disciplinary sources and methodological traditions, in order to bring it all to bear on specific issues in language evolution. My central thesis — that the supportive neurology specific to the processing of human language is an evolutionary outgrowth of the **visual information-processing system** — is not strictly speaking novel. In particular, my conclusion that the human lexical code began its evolution as an iconic visual-gestural system — has been anticipated by many before (Hewes 1973a, 1973b, 1974; Stokoe 1974; see also Armstrong *et al.* 1994). What may be novel is the range of hitherto disparate facts that fall together into a unified coherent account, once the central hypothesis is adopted.[4]

I will also suggest that two distinct cycles of symbolization took place in the evolution of human language. The first involved the evolution of a well-coded lexicon, the second the evolution of grammar. In both cases one can detect an initial stage of more natural, iconic ('non-arbitrary') coding, followed by a shift toward a more arbitrary symbolic code. In both instances, I will argue, the early iconicity as well as the late symbolism had an unimpeachable adaptive motivation. Further, the very same sequence of changes — from more iconic to more symbolic coding — is invariably observed in the evolution of coded communication in pre-human species — from bees to mammals to

primates. And finally, there are excellent cognitive grounds, having to do with
the development of automated information processing, for precisely this kind of
a developmental sequence, a process that John Haiman (1992a, 1992b) has
called ritualization or emancipation.

9.2.   The functional components of human communication

The well-coded[5] human communicative system combines a number of
mutually-interacting functional modules that can be divided first into two major
components:
   (a) The cognitive representation system
      (i)   The conceptual lexicon
      (ii) Propositional information
      (iii) Multi-propositional discourse
   (b) The coding systems:
      (i)   The peripheral sensory-motor coding system
      (ii) The grammatical coding system
We will discuss them in order.

9.2.1.   The cognitive representation system

The cognitive representation system of human language is organized into
three concentric components:
   • The conceptual lexicon
   • Propositional information
   • Multi-propositional discourse

9.2.1.1.   The conceptual lexicon

The human lexicon is a repository relatively time-stable culturally-shared
well-coded knowledge about our external-physical, social-cultural and internal-
mental universe. By 'relatively time-stable' one means knowledge that is not in
rapid flux. By 'culturally shared' one means that when launching into communication, speakers take it for granted that words have roughly the same meaning
for all members of the same speech community.[6] By 'well-coded' one means
that each chunk of lexical knowledge is more-or-less uniquely — or at least
strongly — associated with its own perceptual code-label.

The conceptual lexicon is most likely organized as a network of intercon-
necting nodes. Given a certain level of homophony ('ambiguity'), the unique-

ness of the code-meaning connections is not absolute, but is rather a strong tendency (see chapter 2). An ambiguous word automatically activates several meanings, at least under some experimental conditions (Swinney 1979). An activated word-node presumably activates closely-related nodes in a **spreading activation** pattern (Neeley 1990). But the degree ('distance') to which lexical-semantic activation spreads remains a matter of considerable debate.

Within the lexical-semantic network, nodes stand for individual concepts, each with its own distinct meaning and code-label. By "concepts" one means types of conventionalized experience, rather than individual token subsumed under those types. The conceptual lexicon is just that — a repository of conventional, generalized experience types. 'Generic' and 'conventional' go hand in hand: The process of conventionalization subsumes abstraction and generalization.[7]

A lexical concept may represent a relatively time-stable entity — physical object, landmark, location, plant, animal, person, cultural institution or abstract concept — thus typically a *noun*. Or it may represent an action, event, processes or relations, thus typically a *verb*. It may represent a quality, property or temporary state, thus typically an *adjective*. Or it may convey some adverbial meaning, thus typically an *adverb*.

Cognitive psychologists have long recognized the conceptual lexicon under the label of **permanent semantic memory** (Atkinson and Shiffrin 1968). Both brain location and processing mode of this cognitive capacity are distinct from those of the **episodic memory** (Atkinson and Shiffrin 1968; Squire 1987; Petri and Mishkin 1994), in which input about uniquely-experienced events or uniquely-encountered entities is processed.[8] But a somewhat reciprocal relation holds between the two types of mental representation, so that:

(a) Developmentally, memory traces of unique but similar individual experiences presumably give rise, after sufficient repetition, to time-stable concepts, habits or skills. And

(b) In processing unique experiences, one recognizes the entities, states, events or relations involved in them as tokens of established lexical types.

9.2.1.2. Propositional information and clauses

Clauses ('simple sentences') combine concepts (words) to convey propositional information about relations, qualities, states or events in which entities partake. Such relations, qualities, states or events may pertain to the external world, to the internal (mental) world, to the culturally-mediated world, or to various combinations thereof. Propositional-semantic information about specific states and events is processed, at least initially, by the hippocampus-based **episodic memory** (Squire 1987; Squire and Zola-Morgan 1991; Petri and Mishkin 1994).

9.2.1.3. Multi-propositional discourse

As noted in Chapter 8, individual clauses are combined together into coherent discourse. Human discourse is predominantly multi-propositional, and its coherence is thus a property that transcends the bounds of isolated clauses. Multi-propositional information is also processed in the hippocampus-based episodic memory system. As illustration of the combinatorial relation of conceptual meaning, propositional information and discourse coherence, consider the simple-minded examples in (1), (2) and (3) below:

(1) **Concepts = words:**
   a. drive
   b. insane
   c. constant
   d. abuse
   e. maid
   f. kill
   g. butler
   h. knife
   i. hide
   j. fridge

(2) **Clauses = propositions:**
   a. The maid was driven insane.
   b. The butler constantly abused the maid.
   c. The maid killed the butler with a knife.
   d. The maid hid the knife in the fridge last night.

(3) **Multi-propositional discourse:**
   Having been driven insane
   by constant abuse,
   the maid killed the butler with the knife
   that she had hidden in the fridge the night before.

Taken by themselves, outside any propositional context, the words in (1a–j) convey only conceptual meaning. That is, you may only ask about them questions such as:

(4)   a. What does "drive" mean?
      b. Does "drive" mean the same as "abuse"?
      c. If someone is a "maid", can she also be a "butler", or a "woman"?
      d. Is "kill" related in meaning to "murder", and if so how?

Combined into clauses, as in (2a–d), the very same words now partake in the coding of propositional information. In addition to questions of meaning as in (4), the individual clauses in (2) may now prompt many questions of information, such as:

(5)   a. Was the maid driven insane?
      b. Who abused the maid?
      c. Who killed the butler?
      d. Who did the maid kill?
      e. What did the maid kill the butler with?
      f. Did the maid kill the butler?
      g. Where did the maid hide the knife?
      h. When did the maid hide the knife in the fridge?

Finally, the multi-propositional text in (3), in which the very same propositions of (2) are now combined, has discourse coherence. In addition to questions of meaning such as (4), and of information such as (5), one may now ask questions that pertain to coherence; such as:

(6)   a. Why did she kill him?
      b. How come she had a knife?
      c. Why had the maid hidden the knife in the fridge?
      d. Could she perhaps have talked to him first before taking such a drastic step?
      e. Was her action reasonable? Was it defensible in a court of law?

The questions in (6) may appear deceptively like those in (5). However, each question in (5) can be answered on the basis of knowing a single proposition in (2). In contrast, none of the questions in (6) can be answered on the basis of such atomic propositional knowledge. Rather, the knowledge of several propositions in the connected discourse (3), or even of the entire coherent text, is required in order to answer these questions.

A partial dissociation between conceptual meaning and propositional information is easy to demonstrate by constructing grammatically well-formed sentences that make no sense; that is, sentences whose words are perfectly meaningful each taken by itself, but still do not combine into a cogent proposition, as in Chomsky's ubiquitous example:

(7)   Colorless green ideas sleep furiously

The meaning-clashes that make proposition (7) bizarre — 'colorless green', 'green ideas', 'ideas sleep', 'sleep furiously' — are all due to the considerable semantic rigidity (specificity) of individual words. The relation between lexical meaning and propositional information is thus an inclusion relation or a one-way conditional. That is:

> "One can understand the meaning of words independent of the proposition in which they are embedded; but one cannot understand a proposition without understanding the meaning of the words that make it up".

The partial dissociation between propositional information and discourse coherence can be just as easily demonstrated, by stringing together perfectly informative but incoherently combined propositions. Re-scrambling the coherent paragraph in (3) thus yields:

(8)   a. Having killed the butler with the knife
       b. by constant abuse,
       c. the maid had been driven insane
       d. and had hidden it in the fridge the night before.

No propositional-semantic anomaly is discernible in the individual clauses (8a–d). The bizarreness of (8) as connected discourse is only due to lack of cross-clausal coherence. The relation between propositional information and discourse coherence is thus also an inclusion relation or a one-way conditional. That is:

> "One can understand the meaning of clauses independent of the discourse they are embedded in; but one cannot understand the discourse without understanding the propositions that make it up".

9.2.2. The coding systems

9.2.2.1. Peripheral sensory-motor coding system

The peripheral sensory-motor coding system of human communication involves two components:

(a) **The decoder**: This component translate perceived incoming code ('input') into information. The perceptual modality of the incoming code may be auditory, visual (ASL, reading), or tactile (Braille reading). For two of these perceptual, auditory and visual, language-specific decoding modules have been identified in the relevant sensory areas in the cortex.

(b) **The encoder**: This component translates outgoing information ('output') into motor instructions. The motor modality of the output may vary: it may be oral-vocal, manual (typing, writing), or gestural (ASL). The motor programs associated with these coding modalities are probably language specific and governed by various sub-areas of the primary motor cortex.

9.2.2.2. The grammar coding system

9.2.2.2.1. Preamble

The grammatical code is probably the latest evolutionary addition to the arsenal of human communication (Givón 1979; Lieberman 1984; Bickerton 1990). While the evolutionary argument remains conjectural, it is supported by a coherent body of suggestive evidence. Ontogenetically, both hearing and signing children acquire the lexicon, and pre-grammatical ('pidgin') communication using the lexicon, much earlier than grammar. Natural second language acquisition follows the very same course. In the natural communication of pre-human species, the existence of lexical-semantic concepts of both entities (nouns) and events (verbs) must be taken for granted, if one is to make sense of behavior, communicative as well as secular. Some lexical concepts are already well-coded in natural animal communication (e.g. Cheney and Seyfarth 1990; Marler *et al.* 1991; *inter alia*).

Further, birds, dogs, horses, primates and other pre-human species are easily taught auditory or visual lexical code-labels for nouns, verbs and adjectives (see e.g. Premak 1971; Gardner and Gardner 1971; Fouts 1973; Terrace 1985; Greenfield and Savage-Rambaugh 1991; Pepperberg 1991; *inter alia*). And the seeming ease with which such lexical learning takes place strongly suggests that the underlying cognitive structure and its supporting neurology are already in place. In pre-human primates, the supporting neurology for both semantic and episodic memory is essentially the same one as in humans (Petri and Mishkin 1994). In contrast, observing the natural use of anything remotely resembling human grammar — morphology and syntax — in communicating animals, or teaching it to them, has been almost a uniform failure.[9]

9.2.2.2.2. Grammar as a code

The grammar of human language is a much more abstract and complex device than the sensory-motor codes of the lexicon. At its most concrete level, the primary grammatical signal involves four major devices:

(9) **Coding devices of the primary grammatical signal**:
   a. Morphology
   b. Intonation:
      (i) clause-level melodic contours
      (ii) word-level stress
   c. Rhythmics:
      (i) pace
      (ii) pauses
   d. Sequential order

Some coding devices — morphology (9a), intonation and stress (9b) — are more concrete. They involve the very same physical coding-devices (sounds, letters, or gestures) that code lexical meaning. But these concrete devices are integrated into a complex whole with the more abstract elements of the code — rhythmics (9c) and sequential order (9d). These more abstract elements of the grammatical code are probably second-order constructions, inferred from the more concrete signals.

Grammar is the coding instrument for both informational components that feed into episodic memory — propositional semantics and discourse coherence. What is extracted from the primary grammatical signal (9) is the complex grammatical, semantic and pragmatic organization of both individual clauses and multi-clausal discourse. That is, at the very least:

(10) **Information extracted from the primary grammatical signal**:
   a. Hierarchic constituency organization of the various components
   b. The grammatical category-labels of the components
   c. Scope and relevance relations among components
   d. Government or control relations among components

9.2.2.2.3. Pre-grammatical vs. grammaticalized communication

As noted in Chapter 8 above, humans can — under a variety of developmental or neurological conditions — communicate readily without grammar, using a well-coded lexicon with some rudimentary combinatorial rules. The difference — structural, functional and cognitive — between pre-grammatical and grammaticalized communication were summarized earlier above (chapter 8, table (25)), and are reproduced in (11) below:

(11)   **Pre-grammatical vs. grammatical discourse processing**
       (after Givón 1979a, ch. 5; 1993)

properties	grammatical mode	pre-grammatical mode
STRUCTURAL:		
a. **Grammatical morphology**	abundant	absent
b. **Syntactic constructions**	complex/ embedded	simple/ conjoined
c. **Use of word-order:**	grammatical (subj/obj)	pragmatic (topic/comment)
d. **Pauses:**	fluent	halting
FUNCTIONAL:		
e. **processing speed:**	fast	slow
f. **Mental effort:**	effortless	laborious
g. **Error rate:**	lower	higher
h. **Context dependence:**	lower	higher
COGNITIVE:		
i. **Processing mode:**	automated	attended
j. **acquisition:**	late	early
k. **evolution:**	late	early

Slow and analytic, pre-grammatical communication is heavily vocabulary-dependent and knowledge-driven. This tallies with the fact that vocabulary is acquired before grammar in both first and second language acquisition. Pre-grammatical children, adult pidgin speaker and agrammatical aphasics all comprehend and produce coherent, connected discourse, albeit at slower speeds and high error rates than is characteristic of grammaticalized communication. The identification of grammar as an automated, streamlined, speeded-up language processing system has long been recognized (Givón 1979a, ch. 5; 1989, ch. 7; 1991; Blumstein and Milberg 1983; Lieberman 1984; Schnitzer 1989). As an example of coherent pre-grammatical child narrative text, consider again the following, from a 2-year-old boy:[10]

> (12) [anticipating a trip]
>   In atnga.   Sit dawn. tan ki.
>   in airplane sit down turn key
>   '(We'll go) in the airplane, sit down, turn the key,
>
>   Vruum vruum! Tan tu da rayt. Atnga!
>   vr.   vr.   turn to the right airplane
>   And vroom vroom! (We'll) turn to the right. Airplane (flies)!'

As an example of coherent adult second-language pidgin, consider again:[11]

> (13) "...oh me?...oh me over there...
>   nineteen-twenty over there say come...
>   store me stop begin open... me sixty year...
>   little more sixty year... now me ninety...
>   nah ehm... little more... this man ninety-two...
>   yeah, this month over... me Hawaii come-*desu*...
>   nineteen seven come... me number first here...
>   me-*wa* tell... you sabe gurumeru?...
>   you no sabe gurumeru?...
>   yeah this place come...
>   this place been two-four-five year...
>   stop, ey... then me go home... Japan...
>   by-n-by... little boy... come...
>   by-n-by he been come here... ey...
>   by-n-by come...
>   by-n-by me before Hui-Hui stop...
>   Hui-Hui this... eh... he... this a...
>   Manuel... you sabe-*ka*..."

As an example of coherent narrative produced by an agrammatic aphasia patient, consider again (Menn 1990: 165):

(14) "...I had stroke... blood pressure... low pressure... period... Ah... pass out... Uh... Rosa and I, and... friends... of mine... uh... uh... shore... uh drink, talk, pass out..."
"...Hahnemann Hospital... uh, uh I... uh uh wife, Rosa... uh... take... uh... love... ladies... uh Ocean uh Hospital and transfer Hahnemann Hospital ambulance... uh... half'n hour... uh... uh it's... uh... motion, motion... uh... bad... patient... I uh... flat on the back... um... it's... uh... shaved, shaved... nurse, shaved me... uh... shaved me, nurse... [sigh]... wheel chair... uh... Hahnemann Hospital... a week, a week... uh... then uh... strength... uh... mood... uh... up... uh... legs and arms, left side uh... weak... and... Moss Hospital... two week... no, two months..."

In the absence of morpho-syntax, the bulk of the well-coded clues for establishing text coherence in pre-grammatical discourse are furnished by the lexical vocabulary. Although a small component of "proto-grammar" is already evident in pre-grammatical communication (see further below). And non-coded clues derived from the situational and generic-cultural contexts remain ever-present. Neither lexical information nor the situational and cultural contexts disappear in grammaticalized communication. They remains parallel processing channels alongside grammar (Kintsch 1992; Givón 1993). In the transition from pidgin to grammaticalized communication, the relative functional load of vocabulary and contextual clues for discourse coherence is diminished, with the slack picked up by grammar.

9.2.3. Summary of mapping between codes and functions

The peripheral sensory-motor codes are responsible primarily for signalling lexical-semantic meaning, but are also exploited in the grammatical code — in morphology and intonation. Of these two, the use of intonation is in all likelihood a carryover from its use in pre-grammatical communication.[12] The use of the sound-code for morphology is derived diachronically from its primary use to code lexical meaning: All grammatical morphemes ultimately arise from erstwhile lexical words (Givón 1971, 1979a ch. 5; Traugott and Heine eds. 1991; Heine *et al.* 1991; *inter alia*). But a similar lexical origin of grammatical morphology ('inflection') need not be the case in gesturally-visually coded language. Thus in American Sign Language (ASL), the bulk of grammatical inflections have most likely evolved directly from non-lexical gestural sources, bypassing the lexicon altogether (Petitto 1992).[13]

As noted above, grammar is the joint coding instrument for both propositional-semantic information (clauses) and discourse-pragmatic coherence (discourse). But the part of grammar responsible for propositional semantics is relatively small:

• semantic roles of participant
• semantic transitivity (state vs. event vs. action)

The bulk of the grammatical code is deployed in discourse pragmatics, signalling the coherence of information within its wider — cross-clausal, situational, cultural — context. The semiotic relation between the three main cognitive-functional components of human communication and the two main coding systems may be given schematically as:

(15) **Mapping relation between cognitive-communicative functions and well-coded signals in grammaticalized language:**

function		code
lexical meaning	⟺	sensory-motor
propositional semantics	⟺	
		grammar
discourse pragmatics	⟺	

The semiotic relation in pre-grammatical communication may be given as:

(16) **Mapping relation between cognitive-communicative functions and well-coded signals in pre-grammaticalized language:**

function		code
lexical meaning	⟺	sensory-motor
propositional semantics	⟺	(inferences from well-coded vocabulary and uncoded context)
discourse pragmatics	⟺	

9.3.   Pre-grammar as proto-grammar

Earlier discussion of pre-grammatical communication has tended to suggest that pidgin language did not only lack grammatical morphology, but also had rather haphazard combinatorial rules, and thus no syntax (Bickerton 1975, 1977; Bickerton and Odo 1976). Closer examination of pidgin communication reveals that it abides by several rather explicit syntactic rules that may be called **proto-grammar**. The common denominator of those rules is that they are extremely iconic — cognitively transparent, non-arbitrary — as compared with the considerably more arbitrary — symbolic — nature of grammatical morphology and syntactic constructions. The main rules of pre-grammar (or proto-syntax) are summarized below (following Givón 1979a ch. 5; 1984c; 1985a; 1989 ch. 3; 1990a; Haiman 1985a, 1985b):

(17)   **Intonation rules**:
    a. **Stress and predictability**:
       "Less-predictable information chunks are stressed"
    b. **Melody and relevance**:
       "Information chunks that belong together conceptually are packed together under a unified melodic contour".
    c. **Pause and rhythm**:
       "The size of the temporal break between information chunks corresponds to the size of the cognitive or thematic distance between them".

(18)   **Spacing rules**:
    a. **Proximity and relevance**:
       "Information chunks that belong together conceptually are kept in close spatio-temporal proximity".
    b. **Proximity and scope**:
       "Functional operators are kept closest to the operand to which they are relevant".

(19)   **Sequence rules**:
    a. **Order and importance**:
       "A more important information chunk is fronted".
    b. **Occurrence order and reported order**:
       "The temporal order in which events occurred will be mirrored in the linguistic report of the events".

(20) **Quantity rules**:
   a. **Zero expression and predictability**:
      "Predictable — or already activated — information will be left unexpressed".
   b. **Zero expression and relevance**:
      "Unimportant or irrelevant information will be left unexpressed".

The most interesting fact about the rules of proto-grammar is that, without exception, they are found intact in grammaticalized language.[14] Nothing is lost, but rather a considerable amount of machinery has been added. In grammaticalized language, the rules of proto-syntax sometimes occur by themselves. More often, however, they are integrated together with the more arbitrary (symbolic) devices of grammar — morphology, hierarchic-syntactic constructions, grammatical word-order.

9.4. Visual information processing in the primate cortex

9.4.1. Directionality and hierarchy

In the primate brain, visual information from the optic nerve and mid-brain reaches the primate cortex at primary visual center — area 17 of the *striated cortex* in the *occipital lobe*. From there on, processing moves roughly forward, toward more anterior cortical locations. But many feedback loops, backward pathways and sideways pathways exist, so that the entire system over 20 main processing centers is complex and interactive, rather than merely linear (Maunsell and Van Essen 1983; Kaas 1989).

9.4.2. Retinotopic spatial maps

The 2D iconic spatial representation of the retina is preserved in all the visual processing centers in the cortex, in what is known as **retinotopic maps**. But it is also transformed during the progression to more anterior locations. So that while a general 2D orientation is preserved, more anterior visual maps are more abstract, more selective and more dependent on the context within which the visual information is analyzed and integrated. These more abstract representations are progressively more amenable to top-down feedback from other cognitive sub-systems, as well as to information from other sensory modalities (Kaas 1989).

9.4.3. The two streams of visual information processing

Somewhere in the occipital lobe, the processing of visual information splits into two main "streams". The lower or **ventral stream** leads toward the front of the *temporal lobe* via an *inferior temporal* route. The upper or **dorsal stream** leads toward the *posterior parietal* lobe (Ungerleider and Mishkin 1982; Ungerleider 1985; Kaas 1989). A schematic representation of the two pathways is given in Figure 1 below.

FIGURE 1: **The two pathways of visual information in the primate brain** (Kaas 1989)

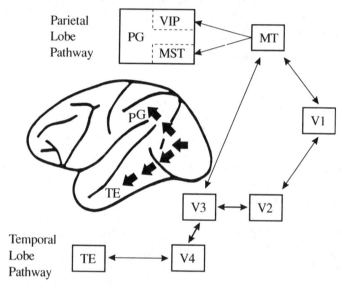

A simplified scheme of processing in visual cortex of macaque monkeys stressing two parallel path-ways, with the ventral stream for object vision and the dorsal stream to PG (parietal area "G") for visual attention and spatial relations. Modified from Ungerleider (1985). See text and Ungerleider (1985) for details and abbreviations.

The ventral (lower) visual processing stream is the **object recognition** pathway, identifying visually-perceived objects as belonging to particular types. Along this pathway, somewhere after visual areas V1 (area 17) and certainly by area V4 in the temporal lobe, distinct feature-analysis of visual objects begins to take place. This processing track is thus responsible for **semantic analysis** of visually-perceived entities. The dorsal (upper) visual processing stream analyzed the **spatial relations** between specific objects and **spatial motion** of specific objects. This processing track is thus responsible for analyzing specific visual **states** and **events**.

9.4.4. Correspondences between visual and linguistic information

The two streams of visual information processing correspond, rather transparently, to two major components of human linguistic information-processing. They are the visual precursors of the two components described in section 9.2. above as:

- object recognition = lexical concepts
- spatial relation/motion = propositional information
  about states or events

The correspondences are relatively straightforward. First, recognizing an object visually as member of a generic type is the visual equivalent — indeed the prototype — of **lexical-semantic identification.** In both processes, individual tokens of experience are classified as belonging to distinct types. In both, identification by type is pre-condition for meaningful storage of specific episodic information about specific tokens. That is, knowing the meaning of the vocabulary is a precondition for understanding a proposition.

Second, recognizing a spatial relation between objects, or between an object figure and its spatial ground, is the prototype of **episodic information** about states. Recognizing spatial motion of one object relative to another, or of an object figure relative to its spatial ground, is the visual prototype of episodic information about events. Declarative visual information involves not only recognizing objects as unique tokens (and members of distinct types), but recognizing their participation in unique states or events.

As we shall see below, other facts concerning brain's functional organization reinforce this identification. At this point, I will mention only two. First, the dorsal (upper) visual processing stream projects through the *medial temporal* region (MT), the *superior temporal* (ST), eventually to the *posterior parietal* (PP) area (PG). In terms of cortical evolution, area PG is a projection of the sub-cortical (limbic) hippocampus under the left medial-temporal lobe (Tucker 1991), the identified site of **episodic (declarative) memory** (Squire 1987; Squire and Zola-Morgan 1991; Petri and Mishkin 1994)). The projective organization of the sensory cortical areas is a general pattern, whereby older evolutionary 'rings' are much more richly inter-connected across sensory modalities, while their younger cortical projections — now taken to be the primary sensory areas — are much less inter-connected. Thus Tucker (1991) observes:

> "...The primary sensory cortices of vision, audition and somatothesis have few if any extrinsic connections, and each is connected with other areas of the brain only through connections with its adjacent [developmentally older] ring of supplementary sensory cortex. Thus the general coordination of the brain must be achieved by the densely inter-connected within-ring functional systems of the **more primitive**, rather than more highly differentiated, cortical networks..." (1991: 98)

Further, even in non-human primates, the object recognition (ventral) stream analyzes more than visually-perceived objects and their attributes. Thus Perrett *et al.* (1989) in their study of single-cell activation in monkeys have been able to differentiate between single cortical cells that respond to objects (nouns), and those that are activated by *actions* (verbs). Such differentiation occurs within the object recognition stream itself, in the *superior temporal sulcus* of the left-temporal lobe. And while the verbs involved — e.g. moving an object by hand towards mouth — are concrete and spatio-visual, they involve more abstract computations of purpose and causation. In this connection, Perrett *et al.* (1989) note:

> "...The coding of interrelationships that is inherent in goal-centered descriptions provides a framework through which the visual system can achieve a rich understanding of the world which embodies causation and intention..." (1989: 110)

The transformation of the ventral object-recognition stream in the inferior temporal lobe into a more generalized, conceptually richer and eventually cross-modal lexical recognition pathway had apparently began in pre-human primates.[15]

9.5.   Language-specific neurology in the left hemisphere

9.5.1.   Modularity and interaction

In this section I will sketch what can be prudently assumed about the localization, in the human brain's left cortical hemisphere, of specialized, automated language-processing functional modules. While choosing the term 'modules', I am inclined to reject both extreme reductionist approaches to modularity. In their recent review, Posner and Carr (1991) suggest three conditions for a strong assumption of modularity. A system is modular if it has:

- **Informational encapsulation**: Does not rely on help from other operations in its own input-output transformations.
- **Attentional self-sufficiency**: Possesses its own attentional resources.
- **Cognitive impenetrability**: Follows its own operational rules independently of higher-level strategic or volitional considerations.

Posner and Carr (1991) further suggest that these conditions are logically (and often factually) independent of each other. So that rather than an all-or-none forced choice, a system can be either 'modular' or 'interactive' to a degree.

In adopting a flexible approach to modularity, one recognizes that language processing in the left hemisphere is indeed organized distributively in many distinct functional-anatomical modules. Such a modular organization is indeed the hallmark of the left-hemisphere, which specializes in automated processing functions, linguistic as well as non-linguistic (Geschwind and Levitzky 1968; Geschwind 1970; Oujman 1991). Indeed, hierarchic modular organization is the hallmark of all specialized automated processing systems. In this respect the left hemisphere contrasts sharply with the less modular, less automated right hemisphere, which is less specialized, more global, and more context-dependent.[16] However, while the left hemisphere's language processing modules are specialized and distinct, they are also highly interactive in performing their assigned task. In this, they follow the pattern of the visual processing modules (Kaas 1989).

Do the human language-processing cortical modules form an encapsulated language-specific processing meta-module? A reductionist response to this question is probably misguided in two distinct senses. To begin with, at least two of the modules — the conceptual lexicon and episodic memory — retain important cross-modal connections. That is, they process both linguistic and non-linguistic information, so that input from one modality can be converted, at least under some circumstances, into another modality (see section 9.6.2.2. below). What is more, each one of the language-specific left-cortical modules — those responsible for peripheral sensory-motor coding and for grammar — occupies a brain location directly adjacent to its plausible phylogenetic and developmental pre-linguistic precursor.

9.5.2.   The semantic lexicon

9.5.2.1. Localization

Early studies of left-hemispheric lesions located meaning in *Wernike's area* in the left-temporal lobe, where lesions had been shown to produce hyper-grammatical verbal nonsense. The linguistic performance data obtained from lesion studies leave the interpretation of Wernike's aphasia open to two interpretations: Either it is involves a disruption of word-level lexical meaning, or of the semantic combinatorial mechanism. Chomsky's would-be sentence is a fair caricature of Wernike's aphasic speech:

(7)   Colorless green ideas sleep furiously

But we have no grounds for deciding whether the offensive pairings — "colorless green", "green ideas", "ideas sleep", "sleep furiously" — are due to failure in the processing of lexical meanings, or to failure of the combinatorial mechanism.

More recent studies of both positron emission tomography (PET) and evoked potential on the skull during word-processing reveal a more detailed picture. First, Petersen *et al.* (1988, 1989, 1990) and Posner *et al.* (1988, 1989) have identified a pre-frontal semantic area in the frontal lobe which is apparent-ly involved in the processing of single-word meaning — without activation in the Wernike region. More recently, studies by the same group (Fiez and Petersen 1993; Raichle *et al.* 1993) identified lexical-semantic modules in both Wernike's area and the pre-frontal cortex. The two suggested lexical-semantic modules and their approximate brain locations are indicated in Figure 2 below.

FIGURE 2:   **Brain location of the two reported lexical-semantic modules in the left hemisphere** (following Petersen *et al.* 1990; Posner *et al.* 1989; Raichle *et al.* 1993)

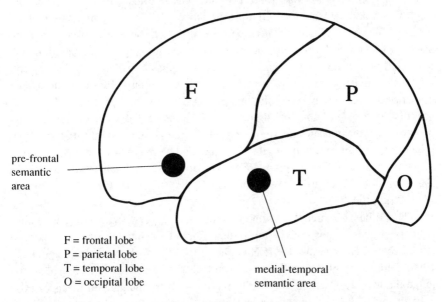

pre-frontal
semantic
area

F = frontal lobe
P = parietal lobe
T = temporal lobe
O = occipital lobe

medial-temporal
semantic area

The left medial-temporal word-meaning module, near the traditionally-recognized Wernike's area, sits astride the visual object-recognition (ventral) stream (Raichle *et al.* 1993). This is the very area where Perrett *et al.* (1989) had noted the differentiation, in monkeys, between single cells that are sensitive to objects (nouns) and those that are sensitive to actions (verbs). Further, the *inferior temporal* area (IT), toward which the ventral object-recognition stream projects also has projections to the subcortical *hippocampus* and *amygdala*, which is the site of episodic memory (Kaas 1989). Such connectivity is required for the interaction between lexical meaning and episodic ('declarative') information.

If one undertakes to interpret the linguistic lexicon and its attendant neurology as an evolutionary extension of the pre-linguistic system that processes visual information, however, then the connectivity between the pre-frontal semantic area and the medial-temporal semantic area remains to be explained.

9.5.2.2. Unified vs. bi-modal lexicon

Do language-using humans have two separate conceptual-semantic representation systems, one for processing visual information, the other for language-coded information? Or do they have a single cross-modal semantic lexicon? The bulk of empirical evidence bearing on the question comes from studies of lesion-induced aphasia, primarily from the pattern of association and dissociation of the performance of various aphasic patients. Some recent evidence comes in from positron emission tomography (PET) studies. The evidence, unfortunately, is conflicting, giving rise to two diametrically opposed schools of thought. One research tradition, represented by two converging groups of both aphasia and (more recently) PET studies, holds that the two modalities of information input — visual and verbal — have two distinct semantic lexicons (Warrington 1975; Warrington and Shallice 1979, 1984; Warrington and McCarthy 1983; Shallice 1988; Bub *et al.* 1988; Chertkow *et al.* 1990).

The other research tradition, looking at the very same cortical lesion patients, argues just as convincingly for a single cross-modal semantic lexicon (Riddoch and Humphreys 1987; Humphreys and Riddoch 1988; Riddoch *et al.* 1988; Funnell 1989; Funnell and Alport 1989). While I am not competent to judge the technical details of the still-ongoing debate, the general thesis of this paper rises or falls with the second group's perspective — a unified cross-modal semantic lexicon. This view of the lexicon is compatible with the bulk of evidence reviewed in this paper, as well as with more general considerations of the evolution of biological design (see further below). In essence, proponents of the cross-modal lexicon argue that all the dissociations between semantic processing of pictorially-presented and verbally-presented information are really dissociations between the more external modality-specific sensory processors — pictorial vs. written-linguistic, auditory vs. auditory-linguistic. All these modality-specific external processors feed into a single semantic lexicon. This view is represented schematically in Figure 3 below.

FIGURE 3:   The relation between modal-specific perceptual information channels and the cross-modal semantic lexi-
con (after Riddoch *et al.* 1988)

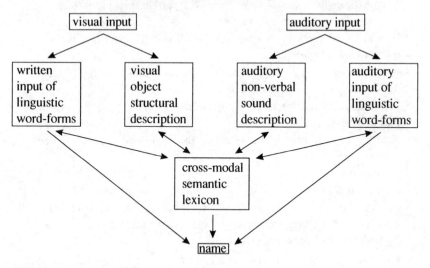

9.5.3.   Episodic memory

9.5.3.1. Localization

The brain localization of early episodic-declarative memory is relatively
well established. The study of both primate and human brain lesions identify
the sub-cortical *hippocampus* and directly-adjacent cortical structures such as
the *amygdala*, all under the left *medial temporal* lobe, as critical components of
both humans and primate episodic-declarative memory (Squire 1987; Squire
and Zola-Morgan 1991; Mishkin 1978, 1982; Mishkin *et al.* 1982, 1984; Petri
and Mishkin 1994). But as Petri and Mishkin (1994) suggest in their more
recent review, other brain locations are also involved.[17] This system is responsible for declarative, propositional, non-procedural, non-semantic memory of
specific states or events and the specific individual that participated in them.
"Episodes" may vary at length from a single state/event (or verbal clause) to a
coherent chain of states/events (or multi-propositional verbal discourse). And
the input modality in humans may be either visual-pictorial, auditory language
or written language. In monkeys, the only input modality is vision.

As Squire and Zola-Morgan (1991) note, early episodic memory displays the following functional properties:

- It is extremely malleable and involves further processing and re-organization of stored information.
- It is a limited-capacity processor in which storage-space and processing activity compete.
- It is emptied periodically and thus remains available for the processing of in-coming new information.
- It is thus a crucial intermediary between the more modality-specific immediate recall buffers ('loops'; see Baddeley 1986)[18] and longer-term episodic storage, most likely in the frontal or pre-frontal neo-cortex.
- Impairment in episodic recall due to hippocampus lesions is dissociated from both procedural and lexical-semantic knowledge.
- Hippocampus lesions do not impair the recall of old, long-established episodic knowledge, presumably because of the latter's different (frontal-cortical) localization.

The localization of the hippocampus-based early episodic-memory module in the left brain is extremely suggestive in terms of its necessary functional inter-connections. First, the hippocampus displays both functional-synchronic and evolutionary connections to the *posterior parietal* area (PP, PG) — the terminus of the dorsal visual-information stream of visual episodic information channel. Further, the hippocampus also has connections to the ventral visual object-recognition stream in the *inferior temporal* area (IT) (Kaas 1989). This connection is functionally crucial: If memory traces of specific states and events are to be stored in episodic memory in an interpretable form, it is not enough that the individual entities associated in the event are recognized *qua* individuals. They must also be classified as belonging to particular lexical-semantic types. Episodic comprehension — via visual or linguistic input — would be senseless without such a provision. The many cross-connections between the two visual processing streams thus guarantee interpretable episodic storage.

9.5.3.2. Modality of input

No controversy exists concerning the input modality of the hippocampus-based memory system. The very same system involved in episodic visual memory in monkeys is involved in visual and linguistic episodic memory in humans. Further, much like in the case of the cross-modal interpretation of the semantic lexicon, the short-term buffer ('loop') working-memory systems that feed into the modality-neutral episodic memory are described, at least by some investigators, as modality-specific (Baddeley 1986). This relationship is represented schematically in Figure 4, below.

FIGURE 4:   **Relationship between modality-specific immediate recall and cross-modal early episodic memory** (integrated from Baddeley 1986; Squire and Zola-Morgan 1991)

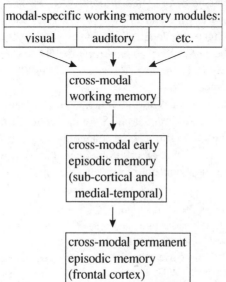

9.5.4.   **The peripheral coders and de-coders**

9.5.4.1. **Peripheral word-recognition modules**

     A growing consensus is beginning to emerge concerning the localization of the peripheral perceptual de-coders for auditory and written words. The localization of an **auditory (phonological) word-recognition** module in the left-temporal lobe near Wernike's area and the primary auditory cortex is well established (Geschwind 1970). This localization has been re-confirmed recently with added precision by two independent PET-scan studies (Howard *et al.* 1992; Raichle *et al.* 1993). Howard *et al.* (1992) specify the location of this module as follows:

"...The peak change is...at the junction between the superior and middle temporal gyri immediately beneath the primary auditory cortex in Heschl's gyrus, close but slightly more anterior to the classical location of Wernike's area..." (1992: 1777)

Two locations of a **visual written-word recognition** module have been proposed recently. First, a group of PET studies located the module in the *left-medial extra-striated* cortex, anterior to the primary vision center in the occipital lobe (Petersen *et al.* 1988, 1989, 1990; Posner *et al.* 1988, 1989; Posner and Carr 1991; Carr and Posner 1992). More recently, Howard *et al.* (1992) have challenged this localization, identifying instead a location in the *middle gyrus* of the *left-posterior temporal* lobe. This apparent contradiction seems to have been resolved by Raichle *et al.* (1993), who detected the involvement of both centers.

Both Howard *et al.* (1992) and Raichle *et al.* (1993) have observed a highly specific modular differentiation in the erstwhile diffuse Wernike's area, with distinctly localized auditory word-recognition module and written word-recognition module. Raichle *et al.* (1993) comment on this increased specificity and on the emerging new concept of Wernike's area:

"...several areas in the left posterior temporal cortex are involved in the processing of words. A more dorsal area(s) (Petersen *et al.* 1988, 1989; Wise *et al.* 1991) appear to be concerned with the processing of auditory words, whereas a more ventral area observed in the present experiment appears to be concerned with the processing requirements of visually-presented words..." (1993: 23 of ms.)

And further:

"...The appearance of activity in the left posterior temporal cortex is consistent with its well-established role in language processes that began with Wernike's seminal observations (Wernike 1874). However, the current findings challenge the concept that a single area located in this region has, as its major function, the analysis of words regardless of modality of presentation. Rather, this region of the human brain almost certainly contains a more complex array of processing areas..." (1993: 24 of ms.)

For the purpose of this discussion, it is important to note that both proposed visual word-recognition modules sit astride the ventral visual object-recognition stream, one in a more posterior location, the other in a more anterior one. Raichle *et al.* (1993) note this convergence:

"...From the present experiment there also appears a more ventral area which is active when subjects generate verbs from visually-presented nouns, but not during tasks involving the auditory presentation of words. The more ventral location of this latter area and its apparent involvement in visually and not auditorily-presented words would suggest that it may be part of the postulated ventral visual processing stream in the middle and inferior temporal cortices (Ungerleider and Mishkin 1982)..." (1993: of ms.)

A schematized pictorial representation of the various locations and their rough locations relative to each other is given in Figure 5, below.

FIGURE 5:   **Approximate localization of the perceptual speech-decoding areas relative to the primary auditory and visual cortex and Wernike's area** (following Posner *et al.* 1989; Carr and Posner 1992; Howard *et al.* 1992; Raichle *et al.* 1993)

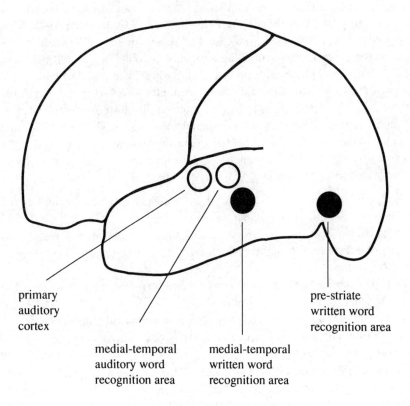

primary
auditory
cortex

medial-temporal
auditory word
recognition area

medial-temporal
written word
recognition area

pre-striate
written word
recognition area

420   FUNCTIONALISM AND GRAMMAR

9.5.4.2. The peripheral motor codes

The localization of both the oral-articulatory motor control and arm-hand-finger control for writing and gestured sign is fairly well established, in various locations on the lower portion of the motor cortex in the left-frontal lobe above Broca's area, although other left-cortical areas are also involved. With respect to the control of gestural linguistic signing, Kimura (1992: ch. 8) notes that it is impossible to dissociate the left-hemisphere lesions responsible for sign aphasia from those responsible for manual apraxia. While linguistic gestural signs may involve a distinct module, such a module is adjacent to the one that controlled non-linguistic signs and movements.

9.5.5. The grammar module and Broca's area

The grammar coding-and-decoding module at the lower end of the left-frontal motor cortex — Broca's area — has been discussed extensively. Agrammatic aphasia resulting from lesions in this region has been described by many (Zurif *et al.* 1972; Goodglass 1976; Bradley 1979; Kean ed. 1985; Menn and Obler eds, 1990; *inter alia*). In her recent review, Greenfield (1991) surveys the evidence concerning the localization around or above Broca's area of a variety of automated complex skills whose common denominator is roughly this: They all depend on habituated, automated, complex **rhythmic-hierarchic routines**. Some are complex motor skills, other are complex action-planning routines, hierarchic-object combination routines, hierarchic visual-tracking skills, or complex hierarchic tool-using routines. Greenfield's (1991) comparative survey of the human, non-human primates and human children can be summarized as follows:

• The homologue of Broca's area for automated complex routines is already present in non-human primates.
• In human neonates, the lower tip of Broca's area does not mature before the age of (roughly) two years, the age when grammar begins to develop.
• Human children lag in non-linguistic sequential-hierarchic skills until the age of grammar acquisition.
• In addition to the well-known strong neurological connection to Wernike's area (the *arcuate fasciculus*), Broca's area also connects to the *pre-frontal semantic area*.

Greenfield (1991) concludes that the use of Broca's area as a grammar processor is merely the last evolutionary (and ontogenetic) extension of much older pre-linguistic uses of the primary motor cortex for sequential-hierarchic skills.

Such phylogenetically-prior skills include coordinated motion, coordinated hand use, and coordinated oral-facial skills for oral articulation.

Two important implications emerge from Greenfield's (1991) comparative study. First, the physical contiguity of Broca's area to the primary motor cortex suggests a certain evolutionary continuity in the gradual emergence of specialized neurology that supports more abstract skills such as dance, music and language. One may thus view the evolution of a grammar-specific Broca's area as the most recent step in the gradual extension of automated sequential-hierarchic processing to more abstract cognitive skills.[19] Second, Broca's area is well connected to both semantic modules in the left cortex — Wernike's area in the temporal lobe, and the pre-frontal semantic area observed by Petersen, Posner, Raichle and their colleagues.

The connectivity between the grammar module and the lexical-semantic modules is critical for several independent reasons. To begin with, grammar is extremely sensitive to lexical semantics, especially to the more generic classificatory features of conceptual organization: concreteness, animacy, agency, humanity, countability and other classificatory features of nouns; telicity, intentionality, aspectuality, temporality, modality and other classificatory features of verbs; sensory, spatial, valuative, emotive and other classificatory features of adjectives.

Further, grammatical and derivational morphemes arise diachronically from lexical words. At the outset of such grammaticalization, the very same phonetic form is often used in a double capacity, to code either a lexical concept or a grammatical function. There remains a real possibility thus that morphology retains its representation within the semantic lexicon while establishing connections to the grammar module.

Finally, if the semantic module near Wernike's area turns out to involve the combinatorial aspect of clausal meaning (rather than the representation of lexical meaning), then vigorous interaction between such a combinatorial module and Broca's area, probably along the *arcuate fasciculus*, is a functional necessity, since part of grammar is involved in coding well-combined propositions.

9.5.6. Neuro-evolutionary considerations

9.5.6.1. Sub-differentiation and adjacency

In the evolution of biological design, including neurology, the most common pattern of change is that of extension by functional similarity. Existing functional modules re-adapted themselves to perform new but similar functions. This adaptation pattern, when stretched over a multi-step span, may eventually yield complete functional re-analysis of an entire module. Thus for example, the human lower jaw used to be part of an older vertebrate's gill plate. And the panda's prehensile 'thumb' is a modification of the *radial sesamoid* bone (Gould 1990).[20] The adaptation of an old structure to a new function may also be done by modifying only part(s) of the old module toward a new functional specialization (*homoplasy*). In the evolution of the vertebrate, mammal and primate brain, the process of gradual extension via functional sub-differentiation of an existing module is well attested. Equally well attested is the retention of spatial adjacency between newly diverged sub-modules of an erstwhile single module. The striking adjacency of all language-related brain modules to plausible pre-linguistic precursor is a compelling fact of the human left-cortical organization. Such persistent adjacency finds its natural explanation in the central hypothesis of this paper — that the human language-processing system evolved first as a gradual extension of the visual information processing system. The brain localization of the various language-related modules relative to their suggested pre-linguistic precursors, is recapitulated in Figure 6. below.

FIGURE 6: **Approximate localization of the language-related brain modules in the left hemisphere relative to their pre-linguistic precursors** (following Posner *et al.* 1989; Carr and Posner 1992; Howard *et al.* 1992; Raichle *et al.* 1993; Greenfield 1991; Kaas 1989)

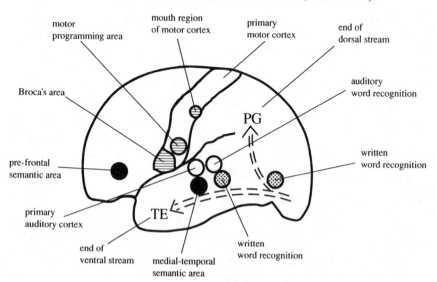

What is remarkable about this layout is that each language-specific module in the left-hemisphere is either a direct adaptation of an earlier pre-linguistic use, as in the case of semantic and episodic memory or is located in close proximity to its putative pre-linguistic precursor. A summary of the suggested evolutionary relationships runs as follows.

(a) **The semantic lexicon**:

The ventral visual object-recognition stream leads from the pre-striate area through the medial-temporal lobe, projecting forward through the inferior temporal lobe. Of the two proposed semantic areas, the Wernike's area sits directly astride this route in the medial-temporal region. The connectivity of the second proposed semantic module, in the pre-frontal cortex, remains to be explained.

(b) **Episodic memory**:

The dorsal visual processing stream for spatial relations (states) and motion (events) is a projection of the hippocampus. This accounts for the phylo-genetically older visual input of episodic memory. The medial-temporal cortical areas directly above the hippocampus, some of which are involved in its operations, are adjacent to the primary auditory cortex and the auditory word-recognition module. This accounts for the human-specific auditory input into episodic memory.

(c) **Visual word-recognition**:

Both the pre-striate (posterior) and medial-temporal modules involved in written word recognition sit directly along the ventral visual object-recognition stream.

(d) **Auditory word recognition**:

The auditory word-recognition module in the medial temporal lobe is adjacent to Wernike's area, to the primary auditory cortex, and — most important — to the more ventral visual word-recognition module.

(e) **The articulatory motor coders**:

Both the oral-facial motor control module and the writing/gesture hand-control modules sit at the lower end of the primary motor cortex, just above Broca's area.

(f) **The grammatical coder/decoder**:

Broca's area sits directly adjacent to other areas that control automated complex hierarchic activities of varying degrees of abstraction.

9.5.6.2. Input adjustment

The central component of my evolutionary hypothesis is that the first lexical code of human language was not the currently-prevalent arbitrary, symbolic auditory-oral code, but rather a more iconic visual-gestural code. The change to an auditory-oral code must have occurred later on, under different adaptive pressures. Neurologically, such a change must have involved a relatively superficial adjustment in the input modality of the two core cognitive components of language.

(a) **Input into episodic memory**:

Pre-human (and early human) episodic memory probably already processed auditory input from the primary auditory cortex, integrating it into a unified declarative representation of states and events. The differentiation of a lower (ventral) portion of the auditory cortex to become a language-specific word-recognition module may have involved parallel changes, in the medial-temporal primary auditory cortex and in its sub-cortical connections to the hippocampus.

(b) **Semantic memory**:

The extension of the visual object-recognition capacity of the ventral visual processing stream toward more abstract, richer, cross-modal semantic categori-zation is probably pre-human and pre-linguistic (cf. Perrett 1989). The sub-differentiation of this visual input channel to accommodate both visual objects and object-coding gestures is a relatively small adjustment — provided the gestures were initially extremely iconic. This may again be viewed as a case of gradual sub-specialization. The location of a written-word recognition module along the same ventral stream suggests that even within the visual modality, extending the evolutionary transformation toward recognition of more abstract symbols is not only feasible but has in fact occurred.

9.5.6.3. Re-training by adjacency

The location of the two word-recognition modules — auditory and visual — adjacent to each other in the medial-temporal region suggests another developmental model — the re-training of a new module by an adjacent older module. There is a well-known precedent for this in the neurological evolution of the barn owl. In the mid-brain of the barn owl, four areas of spatial informa-tion processing are adjacent to each other (Takahashi and Konishi 1986; Takahashi 1989):

(a) A non-iconic auditory input area (no spatial maps)
(b) An iconic auditory input area (spatial maps)
(c) An iconic auditory-visual area (spatial maps)
(d) An iconic visual area (spatial maps)

The rough visual structure of the optic tectum of the barn owl is given in Figure 7, below.

FIGURE 7:   **Approximate configuration of visual and auditory areas in the optic tectum of the barn owl[21]**

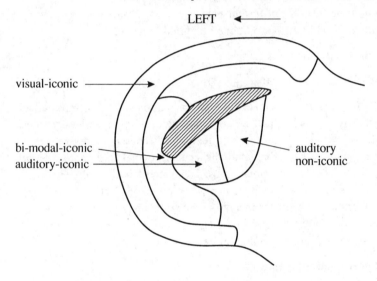

Knudsen (1985, 1989) and Knudsen and Knudsen (1990) have shown that the barn owl's auditory spatial-orientation ability can only develop through early training by the visual system. Owl chicks raised without visual input during the first 90 days of their life are incapable of creating 2D iconic spatial maps from auditory input alone. In other words, it is the presence of visually-derived 2D spatial maps in the visual layer of the *optic tectum* that trains the adjacent auditory center — via an intervening bi-modal region adjacent to *both*. Given this precedent, I suggest that the adaptation of a lower region of the primary auditory cortex in the medial temporal region to a linguistic sub-specialization of auditory word-recognition was due to its proximity to a pre-existing visual-gestural word-recognition module. That is, re-training by adjacency.

9.6.   The co-evolution scenario

This section outlines the main steps in what must have been the evolution of the human communication system. The multiple ingredients of this protracted adaptation must be discussed separately. Nonetheless, one must bear in mind that, as in complex bio-behavioral evolution elsewhere, the socio-cultural, cognitive, communicative, behavioral and the neurological aspects of language probably evolved in parallel rather than serially. These profoundly interdependent, interactive changes thus co-evolved. The outline presented here is but the bare skeleton, to be fleshed out further below by consideration of the cultural-adaptive context within which well-coded hominid language arose.

9.6.1.   Cognitive pre-adaptations

9.6.1.1. The conceptual lexicon

There is no reason to assume that earlier hominids did not have a rich conceptual lexicon of perceptual, spatio-temporal, concrete and even more abstract entity-types (nouns); of spatio-temporal, concrete and even more abstract state/event-types (verbs); and of sensory, spatial and more abstract attributes (adjectives). The communicative behavior of both birds and mammals, both in nature and under human instruction, cannot be coherently interpreted otherwise. Abstract concepts of intentionality, temporality, conditionality, causality, knowledge, desirability, obligation, purpose and the like permeate pre-human cognition and communication.

9.6.1.2. Propositional information

The vast classificatory schema of the conceptual lexicon is not in itself the contents of communication, but only the world-view that is its precondition. Pre-human communication is profoundly propositional and intentional. By directing the interlocutor's attention toward an entity, the communicating individual seldom if ever points to generic-lexical identity. Rather, s/he points to a state, event or action in which the entity is a participant. Pre-human pointing is thus "saying something about" the pointed entity. And while the speech-act value of pre-human "saying something about" is predominantly non-declarative, it is already profoundly propositional. The propositional nature of the pre-human cognition is even more striking when one considers its neurological basis — the dorsal visual-information stream and the hippocampus-based episodic memory. This system of processing and retaining mental traces of specific states and events is profoundly declarative.

9.6.2. The rise of a well-coded lexicon

9.6.2.1. Preamble: Well-coded signals

Having a well-coded lexicon means having consistent, unique associations between lexical concepts and sensory-motor code units. By 'unique' one means that a code unit must connect and thus activate a unique conceptual target, in preference to other available targets.[22] By 'consistent' one means that the unique semiotic (thus neurological) relation is stable and does not vary from one act of communication to the next. At the very least, different tokens of the same conceptual type and repeating occurrences of the same token must reveal roughly the same semiotic (and neurological) relation. In principle, consistency of semiotic pairs may be a matter of degree. Much evidence from child language acquisition, second language learning, diachronic change and synchronic variation demonstrates the existence of ambiguous, less-than-fully specified lexicalization in the same individual. But for a coding system to become an automated left-hemisphere module,
it must attain a certain threshold of consistency or predictability.

9.6.2.2. From pre-lexical to lexicalized coding: Attention-getting and referent-pointing

One of the earliest and most common communicative device used in both pre-human and early-childhood communication, gestural or vocal, is the generalized strategy of simultaneous attention-getting and referent-pointing. This strategy is employed for a dual purpose:

- attracting the attention of the interlocutor, then
- pointing their attention to an intended target, be
  it an entity, state or event.

In domesticated dogs, this strategy involves three distinct if often simultaneous behaviors, two of them gestural, one often vocal:

(21) **Pre-lexical generalized strategy of attention-getting and referent-pointing in domestic dogs:**[23]
   a. Motion toward the interlocutor followed by motion toward the intended referent.
   b. Gaze (and snout-pointing) toward the interlocutor followed by gaze (and snout-pointing) toward the intended referent.
   c. Yelping or barking either at the interlocutor or toward the intended referent.

Horses use similar combinations of gestural and vocal pointing, as do pre-human primates and human neonates.

Pre-human pointing behavior is conspicuous in its limitation to the immediate communicative environment. In this perceptually accessible space, a generalized signal of pointing in the direction of a visible referent may suffice to uniquely identify it as the intended focus of attention. Spatially or temporally remote referents are utterly un-pointable in this evolutionary stage. Another drawback of the pre-lexical pointing strategy is of course that the propositional message, what the communicator intended to "say about" the pointed referent, remains uncoded. Attention may be successful drawn to the intended entity, but the intended action must be inferred from the context, be it the shared speech situation or shared generic knowledge. Due to this context dependence, only highly predictable, stereotypical messages can be successfully communicated.

The great advantage of switching to a better coded pointing strategy is evident in early child communication, when pointing progresses roughly through the following stages:

(22) **Developmental sequence of shifting from pre-lexical to lexicalized referent pointing in human neonates**[24]

earlier

a. Grabbing an object
b. Reaching for an object
c. Reaching in the direction of an inaccessible object
d. Manually pointing toward an inaccessible object
e. Gesture (d) plus a generalized vocal cue
f. Gesture (d) plus a specific lexicalized vocal cue
g. Specific lexicalized vocal cue alone

later

The developmental sequence in (22) reveals one of the most general mechanisms in the development of well-coded communication — the shift from non-communicative ('secular') to communicative behavior.

9.6.2.3. From 'secular' to communicative behavior

The most prevalent mechanism for creating a well-coded system of communication involves re-interpretation by the interlocutor of everyday ('secular') behavior as a communicative act. This process leads eventually to the **ritualization** of erstwhile secular behavior (Andrews 1972; Cullen 1972; *inter alia*). The ritualization of secular behavior is most commonly a gradual multi-step process, but may nonetheless be broken into (at least) several conceptually-distinct components (Haiman 1992a, 1992b):

- A complex thick band of co-occurring features of secular behavior co-occurs reliably with a unique referent.
- Attention is gradually narrowed from the entire thick band to a few or one of its salient features.
- The single salient feature is then re-interpreted (construed) as a communicative clue.
- All other features of the behavior are disregarded.

Ritualization is, by definition, a progression toward increased abstraction and arbitrariness of the communicative code. The very act of construing a hitherto secular behavior as communicative is the first step toward symbolization of that behavior.

The progressive development of ritualized communication may be illustrated with a simple example. Dogs signal aggression by raising their head and propping their ears *up and forward*. Horses broadcast aggression by lowering their head and flattening their ears *down and back*. Both species display quantity scales in coding the degree of aggression similar to those found in primates (Simonds 1974: 146). In horses, this scale is roughly as follows:

(23)   **Scalar coding of aggression in mares**[25]

weakest signal

a. flattened ears
b. (a) + lowered head
c. (b) + back turned to target
d. (c) + rear-legs kick
e. (d) + repetition

strongest signal

Horse societies display precise power hierarchies, and when a new mare joins an established social group, her precise place in the social scale must be established. This is accomplished by exchange of carefully-selected aggression signals between the new mare and established members. If the new mare is a dominant one, chances are the full-blown ('thick band') secular aggressive behavior (24e) will be employed. Gradually, the behavior is reduced up the scale through (24d), (24c) and (24b) all the way to the seemingly arbitrary signal (24a). Once the social hierarchy is re-established, only signal level (24a), or at most (24b), are observed.

The seeming arbitrariness of ear position as signal of aggression — dogs vs. horses — is understood only in terms of the precursor thick-band secular behavior: Dogs attack by biting, and signal aggression by raising their head and chest to create a maximally threatening frontal image — enhanced by the propped-up ears and raised hair. Mares attack by turning their back and hind-kicking, whereby the head is automatically lowered and extended forward, resulting in an automatic flattening of the ears. In both cases, the primary functional attributes of aggressive behavior (biting, kicking) are discarded when secular behavior is transformed into a communicative signal. The features that are retained were incidental to the original secular function. In their new capacity as communicative signals, the fact that these features are symbolic and arbitrary is not really damaging. Ritualization involves the creating of automated associations liberated from conscious contextual analysis. Once such connections are in place, once a well-coded communicative system has been acquired, iconicity and naturalness cease to be an advantage. As behavior becomes more systematically communicative, the arbitrariness and abstraction of the code invariably increases.

9.6.2.4. Early co-existence of auditory-vocal and visual-gestural codes

Pre-human mammals and human children in their first year of life employ both visual-gestural and auditory-vocal communicative signals (Blurton-Jones 1972; Carter 1974; Bates et al. 1975, 1979; Lamendella 1977). Distinct auditory-vocal lexicalization has already been observed in monkeys (Snowdon et al. 1982; Cheney and Seyfarth 1990). There is no reason to assume that early hominids did not display the same mix.

Lieberman (1984) has argued that the phonetic-phonological inventory of potential speech-sounds was severely constrained by the laryngeal-oral anatomy of homo sapiens' immediate ancestors, and that for this reason the onset of human language must have been delayed until the larynx had been re-configured in homo sapiens. There are good reasons for suspecting that the constraint on laryngeal-oral articulation may have not been functionally significant. First, the early well-coded human lexicon must have involved primarily concrete nouns and physical action verbs.[26] The increase in the size of early-human vocabulary must have been gradual, and — as in child language acquisition —

proceeded from the concrete to the more abstract. A relatively small inventory of either auditory-vocal or visual-gestural signals could have accommodated such a small early lexicon. In the following section I explain why the small, concrete early hominid lexicon must have been visually-gesturally coded.

9.6.2.5. The rise of visual-gestural coding

Since both audio-oral and visual-gestural coding modes were available to early hominids, an advocate of the visual-gestural early lexicon must establish the compelling initial advantage of the visual-gestural over the auditory-oral communication. The argument is relatively straight-forward.

(a) Neuro-cognitive pre-adaptation

Visual information processing had evolved as the main perceptual modality of vertebrates, mammals and primates. The visual channel was already in place in early hominids. Likewise, left-hemisphere control of dexterous, complex, automated manual action routines was also in place. Further, two visual-processing streams — semantic and declarative — were also in place, both highly automated and already connected in just the right way to the two core cognitive representation systems underlying human communication, episodic memory (hippocampus) and semantic memory (medial-temporal, pre-frontal). Both memory modules already transcend their early specificity to vision in non-human primates. The monkey's hippocampus integrates cross-modal information, as does the monkey's pre-frontal associative cortex. Processing an input of highly iconic gestures that codes a small lexicon of concrete objects and physical-spatial states and events would require relatively small modification of the existing mechanisms.

(b) Ease of associative learning

Gestural communication is, at least at its early onset, highly iconic. The neuro-cognitive adjustment between recognizing a frequently-encountered visual object and recognizing an iconic gesture depicting that object is relatively small. Visual object recognition itself is already highly automated, abstract and schematic. An iconic representation that preserves the most salient schematic features of objects is highly natural and thus requires minimal instruction. The referents of signs are maximally transparent. A non-arbitrary coding mechanism thus has a crucial advantage for learning and transmission, especially in early stages of development, acquisition and evolution.

9.6.3.   The shift to audio-oral coding

9.6.3.1. Adaptive advantages

While the visual-gestural channel has obvious advantages as a pioneer of early lexical coding, many of its initial advantages turn out to be long-term adaptive drawbacks.

(a) **Ritualization, automation, and loss of iconicity**

As we have noted earlier, frequent use of well-coded signals leads inevitably to ritualization; that is, to automation, signal reduction, abstraction and schematization. This is as true in the development of native human sign languages as it is in animal communication. Once in place, a long-standing gestural coding system inevitably loses its initial iconicity. And as such, it also loses its initial adaptive advantage.

(b) **The growth of abstract vocabulary**

With an expanding vocabulary that is increasingly abstract, visual-gestural coding loses another advantage of iconicity. The sign may suggest a visual configuration, but the abstract referent has none.

(c) **Freeing the hand and body for other activities**

Shifting from visual-gestural to auditory-oral communication would free the hands, so that communication may now proceed simultaneously with manual activities, and can in fact support them.

(d) **Transcending the immediate visual field**

Auditory-oral communication may proceed in the dark, in thick bush, over physical barriers that prevent visual contact. The auditory signal also retains its fidelity over a much greater distance than gestural signals.[27]

(e) **Parallel deployment of visual attention**

Auditory-oral communication frees visual attention for strategic deployment elsewhere. When necessary, communication can now proceed via the auditory channel alone, while both parties may deploy their visual attention elsewhere — emergencies, priorities, joint activities.

9.6.3.2. Neurological adjustment

Given the considerable adaptive advantages of switching the peripheral coding modality of language from the iconic visual-gestural to the symbolic auditory-oral, the requisite neurological adjustment is surprisingly small.

- An well-coded visual-gestural word-recognition module is already in place astride the ventral semantic-analysis stream in the left-temporal lobe.
- The primary auditory cortex is just above and near this visual module.
- The lexical-semantic code is already abstract and non-iconic; its transmission thus does not require an iconic channel.
- The two representation areas — semantic memory and episodic memory — already integrate cross-modal information.
- A sporadic use of vocal lexical signals is already present.

Given the conflation of all these behavioral and neurological factors, a gradual shift from visual to auditory lexical coding is a relatively mundane evolutionary gambit. It is also neurologically plausible, given the proximity of the visual (ventral) semantic module to the primary auditory cortex. The auditory word-recognition modules is located between those two, and may well have been developed by proximity re-training, the way the barn-owls auditory spatial maps are trained by adjacent visual maps.

9.6.3.3. Expansion and abstraction of the vocabulary

As noted above, one adaptive advantage of switching from an iconic to a symbolic coding modality is that the latter can now accommodate a larger and more abstract vocabulary. The need for such vocabulary is in turn motivated by the increasing complexity of cognitive and socio-cultural organization. It would be thus unnecessary to make either one of these two factors — non-iconic coding and abstract vocabulary — causally prior to the other. The two developments most likely converged and then reinforce each other, but probably had distinct ontologies. The pressure for abstracting, schematizing and ritualizing a code — any code — is inherent in the very process of creating a reliable code: repetition, reduction, conventionalization. Automated signal-detection modules do not scan for iconic similarities between signals and their referents. They scan for automatic activation triggers.

9.6.4. The shift in speech-act value

A crucial ingredient in the evolution of human language is the rise of declarative speech-acts. Pre-human and early childhood communication is predominantly manipulative — commands and requests. (Carter 1974; Bates *et al.* 1975, 1979). The socio-cultural context that allows a successful communicative system to operate without recourse to declarative propositions is that of the **society of intimates,** and can be summarized as follows:[28]

- Communication is only about referents within the immediate speech situation.
- Face-to-face communication is the overwhelming norm.
- Communication takes place among intimates who know each other well, indeed exhaustively.
- The society is small, kin-based and homogenous, with little social, cultural or occupational differentiation.
- Life is relatively slow-paced, and so is communication.
- Environmental, cultural and technological change is relatively slow, so that the knowledge pool is relatively stable, shared equally by all adult members.
- Most potential referents, participants and interlocutors are thus well known to everybody, as are the likely states, events and actions those referents are likely to partake in.

In this intimate socio-cultural context, there is not much background declarative information that is known to one speaker but not the other. When one group member needs to solicit action by another, not much declarative justification is required. When the main parameters of the society of intimates begin to shift toward a **society of strangers,** an increased need for explicitly-coded declarative information arises.

Pre-human communicating animals, such as parrots and primates, are cognitively quite capable of declarative speech-acts. But their naturally occurring speech-acts are overwhelmingly manipulative. They only produce declarative speech-acts under human instruction. In the ontogenesis of human communication, the shift toward increasingly declarative information coincides with growing physical, social, cultural and technological complexity and variety in the child's environment.

The adaptive advantage of declarative speech-acts is enormous, in facilitating crucial tasks in a more complex human society. Joint planning of future activities, cooperation and coordination of group tasks, learning from past experience of others, and instruction and transmission of cultural values and technical skills, all are enormously dependent on declarative information. These factors stand at the very core of a massive if gradual shift in the evolution of higher mammals — from reliance primarily on **genetic transmission** of adaptive traits, toward increased reliance on **cultural transmission** of acquired skills. The rise of a well-coded lexicon and eventually of grammar in the communication of early hominids must have occurred within an evolutionary context where declarative information furnished a great adaptive advantage (Goodenough 1990).

9.6.5.   The evolution of grammar

9.6.5.1. Preamble

Grammar is no doubt the last major developmental step in the evolution of human language. This is true ontogenetically, and must have been true phylogenetically (Givón 1979a; Lieberman 1984; Bickerton 1990). Like other evolutionary changes discussed above, the evolution of grammar must have involved a complex interaction between socio-cultural, communicative, and neuro-cognitive factors. Further, it must have depended crucially on the preceding evolution of a well-coded lexicon.

In this section I sketch out the major stages that must have occurred in the evolution of grammar. The evidence for the sequence is largely analogical — the same sequence is followed in language acquisition by both children and adults. Such a recapitulationist perspective is respectable in bio-evolutionary thinking, although it must be taken with a certain amount of caution (see Gould 1977). There is no reason why it should not be just as applicable to the evolution of language (Lamendella 1976; Givón 1979a: ch. 7; Lieberman 1984; Bickerton 1990).

In our earlier discussion of the role of grammar in human communication we noted that grammar is an instrument of speeded-up automated processing of language. And further, that grammar is primarily involved in the processing of multi-propositional discourse, cuing the various cross-clausal coherence in discourse. Neuro-cognitively, grammar is a **translation function** that insures rapid, well-structured encoding of multi-propositional information in episodic memory. The rise of grammar is thus intimately associated with two other trends in the evolution of human communication — the rise of multi-propositional discourse, and the need to speed up language processing. The rise of grammar is ontogenetically — and was no doubt phylogenetically — part of a complex sequence of changes. We will discuss their likely evolutionary order.

9.6.5.2. The pre-grammar mono-propositional stage

The so-called **one-word stage** of child communication described by Bloom (1973) is in essence a lexicalized version of natural non-human primate communication. The salient features of this communication system are:

- The reference of communication is limited to the immediate speech situation — here and now, you and I, this and visible that.
- The message is largely mono-propositional.
- Speech-acts are predominantly manipulative, but can already be declarative.
- Only one salient item is lexically coded per speech-act 'clause'.
- The coded element is most commonly (80%) a concrete noun, most commonly an agent, patient or location.

In this highly situation-anchored communicative mode, the single well-coded word stands for the entire proposition, which is thus multiply ambiguous. The ambiguity pertains not only to the speech-act, but also — given the almost universal absence of a verb — to the intended state/event/action itself. Various facets of the shared situational and generic contexts are relied on to disambiguate the one-word propositional message.

9.6.5.3. Proto-grammar and multi-propositional discourse

In child language acquisition, the next developmental step was identified initially as the 'two word stage'. It involves two parallel developments:

- **Two-word clauses**: Two well-coded words are used per clause, most commonly either two nouns, a noun and an adjective or a noun and a verb.
- **Multi-propositional discourse**: The message expands to two or more propositions that have cross-propositional coherence.

Child language at this stage is essentially of the **pre-grammatical pidgin** communication type discussed in section 9.2.2.3. above. Bowerman (1973) described this type of communication as follows:

> "...early child speech is 'telegraphic' — that is consists of strings of content words like nouns, verbs, and adjectives, and lacks inflections, articles, conjunctions, copulas, prepositions and postpositions, and, in general, all functors or 'little words' with grammatical but not referential significance... (Bowerman 1973: 3–4; see also Slobin 1970)

Clauses produced during the two-word stage may look like (Bowerman 1973: 237–239):

(24)

utterance	non-linguistic context
Kendall sit 'Kendall is sitting down'	K. describing ongoing activity
Mommy read 'Mommy is reading'	K. describing ongoing activity
Melissa car 'Melissa is going to get into the car'	Melissa is about to get into the car
Kendall chair 'Kendall's chair'	K. pointing at a chair
Mommy, telephone 'Mommy, a/the phone'	K. pointing phone out to M.

As noted earlier above, while morphology and complex, embedded syntactic constructions are absent from pre-grammatical communication, a distinct set of grammatical coding principles — the rules of **proto-grammar** — are nonetheless observed. These iconic, cognitively- transparent principles, are reproduced below:

(17) **Intonation rules**:
  a. **Stress and predictability**:
     "Less-predictable information chunks are stressed"
  b. **Melody and relevance**:
     "Information chunks that belong together conceptually are packed together under a unified melodic contour".
  c. **Pause and rhythm**:
     "The size of the temporal break between information chunks corresponds to the size of the cognitive or thematic distance between them".

(18) **Spacing rules**:
  a. **Proximity and relevance**:
     "Information chunks that belong together conceptually are kept in close spatio-temporal proximity".
  b. **Proximity and scope**:
     "Functional operators are kept closest to the operand to which they are relevant".

(19) **Sequence rules:**
  a. **Order and importance:**
    "A more important information chunk is fronted".
  b. **Occurrence order and reported order:**
    "The temporal order in which events occurred will be mirrored in the linguistic report of the events".

(20) **Quantity rules:**
  a. **Zero expression and predictability:**
    "Predictable — or already activated — information will be left unexpressed".
  b. **Zero expression and relevance:**
    "Unimportant or irrelevant information will be left unexpressed".

Principles (17)-(20) are profoundly iconic, much like the processing constraints that insure the retention of proximity, relative size and spatial relations in the retinotopic visual maps in the brain. But many of the rules of proto-grammar already indicate a shift from concrete spatial relations coded by vision to more abstract temporal relations ((17b, c), (18a, b), (19a, b)). Other rules of proto-grammar involve even more abstract features of functional relevance (18a, b) or importance ((17a), (19a), (20b)).

The intimate connection between the spatiality of retinotopic maps and temporality is noted by Kaas (1989), in his attempt the understand the adaptive value of iconic visual representation in the brain:

> "...One implication [of iconic maps] is that selection for *correlated activity* [i.e. co-temporal activation] would tend to create and preserve retinotopic and visuotopic organization... Neurons in the same retinal location are likely to *fire together*, both initially and because they are likely to interrelate by local, perhaps initially random, interconnections, and later in development because they have a higher probability of being *activated together* by the same stimuli..." (1989: 129; italics added)

The proto-grammar rules of pidgin communication thus reflect similar principles of isomorphic organization that one finds in the early processing of visual information. As in the evolution of the peripheral lexical code,[29] the later development of full-fledged grammar displays the same general drift, from the more natural iconicity of earlier stages to an increased arbitrariness and abstraction once the system is conventionalized.

9.6.5.4. Grammaticalization

9.6.5.4.1. Episodic trace of the current text

We have noted earlier above that grammar must have evolved in the context of expanded socio-cultural and informational complexity. Most specifically, grammar evolved as an instrument of processing of multi-propositional declarative discourse. Within this context, the adaptive advantage of grammar is the general advantage found in automation elsewhere: rapid, streamlined, error-free processing. Grammaticalized communication is thus one of the tools that made the complex, diversified society of strangers possible.

The rise of the well-coded lexicon and multi-propositional discourse, i.e. pre-grammatical pidgin communication, is not only an expression of the increased informational complexity of human society. It is also a profound transformation in the relevant notion of "communicative context". Until the advent of well-coded episodically-stored discourse, two aspects of context dominated human (and pre-human) communication: The generic conceptual knowledge shared by all members of the community, and the immediate speech situation shared by the specific interlocutors. Both of these remain extremely important in the processing of human language. But another systematic element was added to the notion 'communicative context' — the anaphoric trace of the **current text** in episodic memory.

During language comprehension, episodic-memory traces of the current discourse are used repeatedly, in anaphoric and cataphoric reference. These uses are heavily cued by grammar (see chapter 8). The new instrument of streamlined discourse processing, grammar, is not only an instrument of more efficient and accurate episodic representation. It also takes advantage of episodic text representation to further speed-up communication.[30]

9.6.5.4.2. The retention of proto-grammar: Combining iconic and symbolic elements in the grammaticalized code

Not a single coding principle used in early proto-grammar has been lost from more evolved, seemingly abstract grammar. They have all been retained as the iconic principles found in grammaticalized communication (Haiman 1985a, 1985b; Givón 1985a, 1989, 1990b, 1991d; *inter alia*). But they are now supplemented by and integrated with more arbitrary abstract rules, grammatical morphology and complex-hierarchic syntactic constructions.[31]

In the evolution of grammaticalized communication, the older iconic and cognitively transparent principles of proto-grammar are not simply dispensed with. Rather, they are retained and incorporated into the more complex new system, where they are integrated with the emerging symbolic conventions.

9.7. Discussion

9.7.1. Convergence

The best support for a new hypothesis comes from its ability to accommodate — and illuminate — a wide range of facts that until then seemed disparate and unconnected (Hanson 1965). From this perspective, the hypothesis proposed here — the evolution of the language-processing system of humans from the pre-existing of visual information processing — seems to allow precisely such a felicitous convergence.

a. **The pre-adaptation argument**

The main components for language processing — semantic and episodic memories, the two channels of visual information processing, and an automated visual object-recognition module — are already intact and functioning in pre-human mammals. In pre-human primates and presumably also early hominids, this visual information-processing system had already gone a considerable distance toward more abstract, cross-modal representation of information, probably with an added module in the left pre-frontal associative cortex.[32] It is unlikely, although of course still possible, that a complex bio-functional domain that has such an extensive — obvious, compatible, multi-modular — pre-adaptation will be re-invented from scratch elsewhere in the system. If that were the case, then the current location of the language-specific modules in the left hemisphere is totally arbitrary. All other things being equal, I think that the reason the language-processing modules are where they are in the left hemisphere is because that is where their immediate pre-linguistic precursors were, and still are.

b. **The sign language argument**

The incredible ease with which the visual-gestural channel can be recruited to take over the peripheral coding of human language in the case of hearing impairment, and the smooth integration of this peripheral component into the rest of the system, would be inconceivable unless an old routinized channel had already been in place. Children acquiring ASL as their first language lag neither in lexicon nor in grammar nor in speed of communication behind children acquiring audio-oral language. There is no precedent for such a profound neurological adaptation, not for the incredible ease with which it occurs during the child's first two years.

It doesn't take long for visual-gestural language to become increasingly arbitrary. Presumably the very same adaptive pressures toward arbitrariness and ritualization elsewhere also obtain in the development of gestural language: automaticity and speeded-up processing, signal reduction and abstraction. This is precisely what one finds in the evolution of both the lexical and grammatical signal in gestural language (Klima and Bellugi 1979; Petitto 1991). The developmental course of gestural human language thus recapitulates the evolutionary course of audio-oral language.

c.   **The written language argument**

As in the case of sign-language, the way in which hearing humans can shift perceptual modality in their acquisition of literacy would have been unlikely unless it capitalized — piggy-backed — on a pre-existing processing channel. This is not to suggest that the adaptation is trivial. Unlike the acquisition of gestural language, which relies heavily at the early states on natural iconicity, the acquisition of a totally arbitrary visual written code is a complex cognitive undertaking. In the natural evolution of writing in all five known centers where such a process is known to have occurred independently (China, India, Mesopotamia, Egypt, Maya), the historical progression proceeded invariably from early iconicity to later symbolism. All five writing systems began as pictorial representations. Their gradual move toward a more arbitrary code — either ideographic (Maya, China) or phonological (Mesopotamia, Egypt, India) — came later. As elsewhere, the initial rise of a new code benefits from maximal iconicity and cognitive naturalness. Only later does a code — perhaps inevitably — gravitates toward symbolism.

d.   **The developmental argument**

In a broad way, the ontogenesis of child lexicalization recapitulates the evolutionary route proposed here. Early vocabulary is always more concrete and sensory-motor. Increased abstraction follows later on. The same is true in the development of grammar in both first and second language acquisition. The more iconic, cognitively-transparent rules of proto-grammar eventually give way to — and integrate into — a more arbitrary system of grammaticalized communication.

e.   **The diachrony argument**

In the historical development of word-senses, the most common process is the metaphoric extension of more concrete spatial-visual senses toward more abstract senses (Lakoff and Johnson 1980). The same general trend is observed in the rise of grammatical morphology, where more concrete, spatial lexical meanings invariably give rise to temporal and eventually more abstract grammatical functions (Heine *et al.* 1991; Traugott and Heine (eds) 1991; *inter alia*). Similarly in the rise of grammatical rules, more cognitively-transparent iconic rules invariably precede more arbitrary symbolic rules (Givón 1979a chapters 5, 6).

f.   **The iconicity-to-ritualization argument**

In each developmental sequence — evolution, acquisition, diachrony — the early stages always involve the coding of more concrete concepts with more iconic coding means. The growth of more arbitrary symbolic codes then follows. This sequence is just as ubiquitous in animal communication as it is in human language. The general developmental trend in the genesis of animal communicative codes invariably involves the extraction of a more arbitrary communicative signal from erstwhile secular behavior that is by definition more iconic. A wonderful example of this is given by de Waal (1982), describing the course of one metaphoric lexical development in chimpanzees:

(25)   a.   **Secular gesture:**
        Grabbing an object by the hand
    b.   **Early communicative gesture:**
        Extending a grasping hand toward the object
        (= 'I want this', 'Give this to me')
    c.   **Late communicative gesture:**
        Extending the arm with the down-drooping hand toward a person
        (= 'I am beat an need sympathy', 'Give me moral support')

We have already noted instances of this move from iconicity to symbolism in the communication of horses. But the process is equally pervasive in lower taxa. As one illustration, consider the evolution of the communicative code of honey bees. In the most evolved communication of *apis mellifera*, the angle between the waggle-dance axis and the honey-comb's vertical axis stands in a more abstract — if still iconic — relation to the angle between the direction of food-source and the sun. This coding system apparently evolved from a much more iconic representation, one still found in *apis florea*. There, the waggle-dance is performed horizontally, and its axis points directly toward the food-source (von Frisch 1967; Gould and Towne 1987). Further, the *apis florea* horizontal pointing dance may itself be an early ritualization, of the merely-secular pointing toward the food-source in anticipation of take-off (Gould 1991). Similarly, distance indication by duration of the dance, number of waggles per cycle, and motion and sound intensity in *apis mellifera* (von Frisch 1967) may be a ritualization of earlier secular behavior — intense excited motion due to high sugar contents in recently-ingested food (Gould 1991).

The ritualization of communicative codes, the move from more iconic to more symbolic signals, represents a general biological phenomenon in the evolution of both behavior and communication. This tendency is apparent in the evolution of visual representation, beginning with the largely iconic retina and through the increasingly more abstract representation beyond area 17 of the mammal cortex (Kaas 1989). Ritualization is thus an adaptive consequence of speeded-up processing of high-frequency information in all bio-behavioral systems:

• Reduction and economy of signal
• Conventionalization and abstraction of signal

9.7.2. Why the change to auditory coding?

If one accepts the hypothesis that human language relied initially on visual-gestural lexical code, then one must explain the later shift to an auditory-oral channel. We have already noted that iconic codes carry initial adaptive advantages, but also eventual long-term drawbacks. The shift to a more arbitrary code, once communication is in the process of becoming automated and conventionalized, carries distinct advantages to the processing system itself: Economic of reduced signals, discreteness and saliency of signals, differentiation of communicative signals from secular behavior, automaticity and speed. In terms of the specific adaptation to auditory-oral signals, the adaptive advantages must have been:

• Accommodating large abstract vocabulary
• Freeing the hands for parallel activities
• Freeing visual attention for parallel activities
• Communicating over barriers, distances and in the dark

9.7.3. Modularity, gapped evolution and pre-adaptation

One of the least enlightening aspects of the discussion of the evolution of language has been the coupling of a bizarre version of neurological modularity with an equally bizarre approach to discontinuous evolution. These two features seem intellectually — if not logically — intertwined. Nobody can seriously ignore the fact that in the evolution of human communication, a complex set of language-specific brain modules have arisen, and a striking re-organization of both the neurology and the behavior has indeed taken place. But what had emerged is hardly a brand-new left-cortical encapsulated language module. Rather, a great number of pre-existing pre-linguistic modules had already been in place, with highly specific inter-connections. These pre-existing modules were then modified and re-adapted, most often predictably and perhaps gradually, extending their early information-processing capacity toward a language-coded input.

In the evolution of complex biological systems, relatively small quantitative changes in many lower-level modules often produce a spectacular qualitative jump in the overall bio-behavioral system. And what seems to the paleontologist a gapped evolution (cf. Eldredge and Gould 1972; Gould and Eldredge 1977) may be, to the population geneticist, the product of multiple contiguous steps (see Lande 1980, 1986; Charlesworth *et al.* 1982).

9.7.4.   Closure: Co-evolution and multiple causality

Human language did not evolve from the communicative system of pre-human apes. Rather, it arose through co-evolution of the neuro-cognitive mechanisms, socio-cultural organization and communicative skills of pre-human *hominids*. The search for a single-cause explanation to a process as complex as language evolution has been an unedifying reductive enterprise, as implausible empirically as it is dubious philosophically. Thus, Bickerton (1990) and Burling (1992) identify the cause as a genetic saltation creating the brain's cognitive-linguistic organ. Chase and Dibble (1987) consider the crucial step to have been an increased capacity for symbolism. Greenfield (1991) sees tool-using routines and complex hierarchic behavior, all governed by Broca's area, as the jump-starter. Lieberman (1984) weighs in with the evolution of the larynx and oral tract, thus the capacity for oral-auditory coding. And Dunbar (1992) considers language's role as an affective instrument of social grooming as the determinative step.

For a society in the grip of accelerating cultural and technological change, a growing dependence on interpersonal cooperation, and an increased reliance on cultural transmission of knowledge and skills, the adaptive advantage of a wellcoded, streamlined system of communication is more than obvious. The rise of such a complex system is a paradigm case of **co-evolution** — an interaction between multiple adaptive motivations, converging relevant contexts, and inter-dependent cognitive, neurological and genetic mechanisms. To reduce this complexity to simple linear causation is to misrepresent both its mundane biological foundations and its mind-boggling uniqueness.

THE FAR SIDE   By GARY LARSON

Some anthropologists believe that the discoveries of fire, shelter and language were almost simultaneous

Notes

*) I am indebted to Rich Marrocco, Mike Posner and Sherman Wilcox for comments on an earlier draft of this chapther.

1) While conceding the trail-blazing role of adaptive behavior, Neo-Darwinian biologists remain adamantly anti-Lamarckian, primarily because of their inability to pinpoint a mechanism compatible with random mutation. Such a mechanism has been proposed by non-biologists (see Hinton and Nowlan 1987; Givón 1989 ch. 10).

2) Givón (1977, 1991).

3) Givón (1979: ch. 4).

4) In the philosophy of science, the chief merit of abductive reasoning used in hypothesis formation is precisely this, that it makes many hitherto unrelated facts fall together into a coherent theoretical whole (Hanson 1958).

5) Simultaneously with well-coded ('linguistic') communication, humans and other communicating species also make constant access to many less well-coded sources of information. These parallel channels extract relevant information by inference from both the physical and social context, as well as from various facets of individual behavior. There are good reasons for believing that less well-coded 'secular' behavior is the evolutionary precursor of well-coded communication. This precursor remains available simultaneously with well-coded communication.

6) Both 'same meaning' and 'same community' are somewhat elastic notions.

7) Conventionalization eventually yields conceptual nodes that are sufficiently categorial but not absolutely so, given residual shading and gradation in meaning and category membership (see discussion of prototype clustering in chapter 6).

8) Neuro-psychologists such as Mishkin and Petri (1984), Mishkin et al. (1982), Squire (1987), Squire and Zola-Morgan (1991), Petri and Mishkin (1994) have re-named the distinction between semantic and episodic memory 'procedural' vs. 'declarative' knowledge, respectively. Given that lexical-semantic knowledge is as unaffected by hippocampus lesions as are various habituated skills, one may conclude that all non-episodic memory capacities have a common neurological basis (Petri and Mishkin 1994). But such a conclusion may be premature, in that non-episodic knowledge, whose formation depends on repeated exposure, may be sub-divided into smaller specific sub-modules (conceptual meaning, customs and conventions, habits, skills). Further, conceptual meaning may hold a privileged position within this cluster, since customs, conventions, habits and skills all presuppose conceptual knowledge, but not necessarily vice versa.

9) The lone purported exception is discussed in Greenfield and Savage-Rambaugh (1991). While it is an honorable attempt, chances are that the proto-grammar of pygmy chimpanzees bear some resemblance to *pre-grammar* of pidgin communication in humans, but not to grammaticalized communication (see further below).

10) Recorded by L. C. Givón, 5-20-81.

11) Hawaii Japanese-English pidgin; from transcripts of recordings by D. Bickerton; see also Bickerton and Odo (1976), Bickerton and Givón (1976).

12) This is true for several other more iconic elements of grammar (see further below).

13)   Klima and Bellugi (1979: chapters 9–12) include lexical compounding in grammar. This makes it appear that some grammatical processes involve erstwhile lexicon.

14)   See again (Givón 1985a; 1989 ch. 3; 1990a; Haiman 1985a, 1985b).

15)   Given the evidence of avian lexicalized communication surveyed by Pepperberg (1991), a lexicon of verb concepts may well exist in the pre-mammalian mid-brain. Given the column-like projection of mid-brain rings into corresponding higher cortical rings (Tucker 1991), an evolutionary scenario of lexical and declarative memory from sub-cortical (limbic) to cortical rings is not implausible.

16)   In this rough description I rely on an extensive review by Gloria Olness (1991); but see also Joanette *et al.* (1990).

17)   Among the other components cited are the *fornix, medial thalamus* and *orbital pre-frontal cortex*. The system thus involves a number of interactive sub-modules.

18)   Baddeley (1986) proposes both multiple modality-specific 'loops' and a central modality-neutral component of working memory. Just and Carpenter (1992) adopt the latter but reject the former, it is not clear to me on what grounds.

19)   Whether manual tool-use routines are the crucial evolutionary link, as Greenfield (1991) suggests, is another issue. In addition to tool manipulation, pre-human primates presumably had other pre-linguistic complex-hierarchic routines, such as foraging, hunting, grooming, fighting, coordinated travel or planned complex action. These are all just as complex and rhythmic-hierarchic as tool-use or tool-making, but also more abstract. A high degree of structural abstraction is also characteristic of many non-linguistic activities of humans, such as music, dancing, architecture, art or goal-oriented planning.

20)   Extension by functional similarity is also characteristic of historical change in grammar (see chapters 2, 3).

21)   Terry Takahashi (in personal communication).

22)   The preference may be absolute, or a matter of degree. The latter seems to be the case in *spreading activation*. However, one may argue that spreading lexical-semantic activation proceeds through secondary connections. The uniqueness requirement may thus be defined by primary activation through the peripheral code.

23)   From my own field observations.

24)   From my own field observations; see also Carter (1974), Bates *et al.* (1975, 1979), and Bloom (1973).

25)   From my own field observations; see also Givón (1990a).

26)   Most Swadesh-type lists of core vocabularies of any language family seldom exceed 300 items. In most pre-industrial linguistic communities, the existing vocabulary of roughly 5,000 words can easily be traced back — through compounding, derivation and semantic extension — to a core vocabulary of 200–300 words. In some languages this core may be even smaller. Thus, for example, some Papuan languages have less than 100 lexical verb-stems, from which all conventional state/event frames are built combinatorially (Pawley 1987). A similar situation can be seen in many Amerindian languages (cf. Athabascan).

448   FUNCTIONALISM AND GRAMMAR

27)   The typical gestural inventory in ASL involves hand-and-arm movements and facial gesture, typically in front of the face and chest (Klima and Bellugi 1979).

28)   Following Givón (1979a ch. 5).

29)   And in fact also in the evolutionary addition of more — and more anterior — visual processing modules in the primate cortex (Kaas 1989).

30)   This is another example of interactive, non-linear causation associated with complex evolutionary changes.

31)   C. S. Peirce (1940) was the first to note this mixed aspect of grammatical structure.

32)   The exact connectivity of the pre-frontal semantic module to the temporal ventral stream of semantic analysis (and Wernike's area) remains to be resolved. My hunch is that the connection is mediated through the mid-brain limbic system. The argument is for the moment purely analogical: In the dorsal visual-processing stream, the cortical channel that ends in the parietal lobe feeds into the sub-cortical hippocampus-based early episodic memory. That system eventually projects — for longer-term episodic memory — to a cortical frontal-lobe area (Squire and Zola-Morgan 1991). The connectivity between parietal/temporal cortical systems and related frontal-lobe modules may thus be mediated systematically through the mid-brain, which seems to be a general trend (Tucker 1991).

Bibliography

Abraham, W. (1992) "The aspectual source of the epistemic-root distinction in modal verbs", *Symposium on Mood and Modality*, UNM, Albuquerque, May 1992 (ms)

Akrill, J. L. (tr. and ed. 1963) *Aristotle's Categories and De Interpretatione*, Oxford: Clarendon Press

Alt, F. W., T. K. Blackwell and D. D. Yankopoulos (1987) "Development of the primary antibody repertoire", *Science*, 238

Andersen, H. (1966) *Tenues and Mediae in the Slavic Languages: A Historical Investigation*, Ph D dissertation, Harvard University (ms)

Andersen, H. (1973) "Abductive and deductive change", *Language*, 49

Andersen, H. (1974) "Markedness in vowel systems", in L. Heilmann (ed.) *Proceedings of the XIth International Congress of Linguists*, vol. II, Bologna: Il Mulino

Andersen, H. (1979) "Phonology as semiotics", in S. Chatman *et al.* (eds) *A Semiotic Landscape*, The Hague: Mouton

Andersen, R. (1979) "Expanding Schumann's pidginization hypothesis", *Language Learning*, 29

Anderson, S. (1976) "On the notion of subject in ergative languages", in C. Li (ed. 1976)

Anderson, S. R. (1977) "On mechanisms by which languages become ergative", in C. Li (ed., 1977)

Anderson, A., S. C. Garrod and A. J. Sanford (1983) "The accessibility of pronominal antecedents as a function of episodic shift in narrative text", *Quarterly J. of Experimental Psychology*, 35A

Andrews, R. J. (1972) "The information potential available in mammal displays", in R. A. Hinde (ed. 1972)

Anttila, R. (1977) *Analogy*, State of the Art Report #11, The Hague: Mouton

Aristotle, *De Partibus Animalium*, in R. McKeon (ed. 1941)

Aristotle, *De Interpretatione*, in J. L. Ackrill (tr. and ed. 1963)

Aristotle, *De Interpretatione*, in J. Barnes (ed. 1984)

Armstrong, D. F., W. C. Stokoe and S. E. Wilcox (1994) "Signs of the origin of syntax", *Current Anthropology*, 35.4

Atkinson, R. C. and R. M. Shiffrin (1968) "Human memory: A proposed system and its control processes", in K. W. Spence and T. Spence (eds) *The Psychology of Learning and Motivation*, vol. 2, NY: Academic Press

Austin, J. (1962) *How to Do Things with Words*, Cambridge: Cambridge University Press

Awobuluyi, A. (1973) "The modifying serial construction: A critique", *Studies in African Linguistics*, 3.1

Bach, E. (1965) "Structural linguistics and the philosophy of science", *Diogenes*, 51

Baddeley, A. D. (1986) *Working Memory*, NY: Oxford University Press

Baldwin, D. (1994) "Update on inductive mechanisms for language acquisition", University of Oregon, Eugene (ms)

Bamgbose, A. (1973) ""The modifying serial construction: A reply", *Studies in African Linguistics*, 4.2

Bamgbose, A. (1974) "On serial verbs and verbal status", *J. of West African Languages*, 9

Barnes, J. (ed. 1984) *The Complete Works of Aristotle*, Princeton, NJ: Princeton University Press

Bates, E. (1976) *Language in Context: The Acquisition of Pragmatics*, NY: Academic Press

Bates, E., L. Benigni, I. Bretherton, L. Camioni and V. Volterra (1979) *The Emergency of Symbols: Cognition and Communication in Infancy*, NY: Academic Press

Bates, E., L. Camioni and V. Volterra (1975) "The acquisition of performatives prior to speech", *Merrill-Palmer Quarterly*, 21

Bavin, E. (1992) "Mood and modality in Acholi and related Western Nilotic languages", *Symposium on Mood and Modality*, UNM, Albuquerque, May 1992 (ms)

Bever, T. (1968) "A survey of some recent work in psycholinguistics", in W. J. Plath (ed.) Specification and Utilization of a Transformational Grammar, SR-3, Yorktown Heights, NY: IBM Thomas J. Watson Research Center

Bever, T. and D. Townsend (1979) "Perceptual mechanisms and formal properties of main and subordinate clauses", in W. Cooper and E. Walker (eds), *Sentence Processing*, Hillsdale, NJ: Erlbaum

Bickerton, D. (1975) "Creolization, linguistic universals, natural semantax and the brain", paper presented at the *International Conference on Pidgins and Creoles*, University of Hawaii, Honolulu (ms)

Bickerton, D. (1977) "Pidginization and creolization: Language acquisition and language universals", in A. Valdman (ed.) *Pidgin and Creole Linguistics*, Bloomington: Indiana University Press

Bickerton, D. (1981) *Roots of Language*, Ann Arbor: Karoma

Bickerton, D. (1990) *Language and Species*, Chicago: University of Chicago Press

Bickerton, D. and T. Givón (1976) "Pidginization and syntactic change: From SOV and VSO to SVO", *CLS #12*, Chicago: University of Chicago, Chicago Linguistics Society

Bickerton, D. and C. Odo (1976) *Change and Variation in Hawaii English*, vol. 1: The Pidgin, NSF Report, Honolulu: University of Hawaii (ms)

Bloom, L. (1973) *One Word at a Time: The Use of Single-word Utterances Before Syntax*, The Hague: Mouton

Bloomfield, L. (1922) "Review of Sapir's *Language*", *The Classical Weekly*, 18

Bloomfield, L. (1933) *Language*, NY: Holt, Rinehart and Winston

Blumstein, S. and W. Milberg (1983) "Automated and controlled deficits in speech/language deficits in aphasia", *Symposium on Automatic Speech*, Minneapolis: Academy of Aphasia

Blurton-Jones, N. G. (1972) "Non-verbal communication in children", in R. A. Hinde (ed. 1972)

Bokamba, E. G. (1971) "Specificity and definiteness in Dzamba", *Studies in African Linguistics*, 2.3

Bokamba, E. G. (1976) *Question Formation in Some Bantu Languages*, PhD dissertation, University of Indiana, Bloomington (ms)

Bolinger, D. (1977) *The Form of Language*, London: Longmans

Bolinger, D. (1978) "Yes-no questions are not alternative questions", in H. Hiz (ed.) *Questions*, Dordrecht: Reidel

Bonner, J. T. (1988) *The Evolution of Complexity by Means of Natural Selection*, Princeton, NJ: Princeton University Press

Bowerman, M. (1973) *Early Syntactic Development*, Cambridge: Cambridge University Press

Bradley, C. H. and B. E. Hollenbach (eds, 1988) *Studies in the Syntax of Mixtecan Languages*, vol 1, Dallas: SIL/UTA [vol. 2, 1990; vol. 3, 1991; vol. 4, 1992]

Bradley, D. C. (1979) "Syntactic deficits in Broca's aphasia", in D. Caplan (ed.) *Biological Studies of Mental Processes*, Cambridge: MIT Press

Brainard, S. (1984a) "Ergativity and grammatical relations in Karao", in her *Karao Grammar*, PhD dissertation, University of Oregon, Eugene (ms)

Brainard, S. (1994b) "Voice and ergativity in Karao", in T. Givón (ed. 1994)

Bresnan, J. (1993) "Locative inversion and the architecture of UG", Stanford University (ms)

Bresnan, J. and J. M. Kanerva (1988) "Locative inversion in ChiChewa: A case study of factorization in grammar", Stanford University (ms)

Brown, R. and C. Hanlon (1970) "Derivational complexity and the order of acquisition in child speech", in J. R. Hayes (ed.) *Cognition and the Development of Language*, NY: J. Wiley & Son

Bruce, L. (1985) "Serialization: The interface of syntax and lexicon", Ukarumpa, PNG: SIL (ms)

Bub, D., S. Black, E. Hampton and A. Kertesz (1988) "Semantic encoding of pictures and words: Some neuropsychological observations", *Cognitive Neuropsychology*, 5.1

Burling, R. (1992) "Primate calls, human language and nonverbal communication" (ms)

Butt, J. and C. Benjamin (1988) *A New Reference Grammar of Modern Spanish*, London: Edward Arnold

Bybee, J. (1985) *Morphology*, TSL #9, Amsterdam: J. Benjamins

Bybee, J. (1992) "The semantic development of past tense modals in English", *Symposium on Mood and Modality*, UNM, Albuquerque, May 1992 (ms)

Bybee, J., W. Pagliuca and R. Perkins (1992) "Mood and modality", chapter 7 of *The Grammaticalization of Tense, Aspect and Modality in Languages of the World* (ms)

Byrne, F. (1987) *Grammatical Relations in a Radical Creole*, Creole Language Library #3, Amsterdam: J. Benjamins

Byrne, F. (1992) "Tense, scope and spreading in Saramaccan", *J. of Pidgin and Creole Languages*, 7.2

Carlson, R. (1990) *A Grammar of Supyire: Kampwo Dialect*, PhD dissertation, University of Oregon, Eugene (ms)

Carlson, R. (1991) "Grammaticalization of post-positions and word-order in Senufu languages", in B. Heine and E. Traugott (eds) 1991, (vol. 2)

Carnap, R. (1947) *Meaning and Necessity*, Chicago: University of Chicago Press

Carnap, R. (1950) *Logical Foundations of Probability*, Chicago: University of Chicago Press

Carnap, R. (1963) *The Philosophy of Rudolph Carnap*, ed. by P. A. Schilpp, La Salle, Ill.: Open Court

Carpenter, P. A. and M. A. Just (1988) "The role of working memory in language comprehension", in D. Klahr and K. Kotovsky (eds) *Complex Information Processing: The Impact of Herbert Simon*, Hillsdale, NJ: Erlbaum

Carr, T. H. and M. I. Posner (1992) "The impact of learning to read on the functional anatomy of language processing", *TR 92-1*, Institute of Cognitive and Decision Sciences, University of Oregon

Carter, A. (1974) *Communication in the Sensory-Motor Period*, PhD dissertation, UC Berkeley (ms)

Chafe, W. (1970) *Meaning and the Structure of Language*, Chicago: University of Chicago Press

Chafe, W. (1986) "Writing in the perspective of speaking", in C. R. Cooper and S. Greenbaum (eds) *Written Communication Annual*, Beverly Hills/London: Sage Publications

Chafe, W. (1987a) "Cognitive constraints on information flow", in R. Tomlin (ed. 1987)

Chafe, W. (1987b) "Linking intonation units in spoken English", in J. Haiman and S. A. Thompson (eds) *Clause Combining in Grammar and Discourse*, TSL #18, Amsterdam: J. Benjamins

Chafe, W. (1987c) "How we know things about language", in D. Tannen and J. Altais (eds) *Languages and Linguistics: The Interdependence of Theory, Data and Application*, Washington, DC: Georgetown University Press

Chafe, W. (1992) "Realis and irrealis in Caddo", *Symposium on Mood and Modality*, UNM, Albuquerque, May 1992 (ms)

Chafe, W. and J. Danielewicz (1987) "Properties of spoken and written language", in R. Horowitz and J. Samuels (eds) *Comprehending Oral and Written Language*, NY: Academic Press

Chafe, W. and J. Nichols (eds, 1984) *Evidentiality: The Linguistic Coding of Epistemology*, Norwood, NJ: Ablex

Chafe, W. and D. Tannen (1987) "The relation between written and spoken language", *Annual Review of Anthropology*, 16

Chapin, P. (1967) *On the Syntax of Word Derivation in English,* Ph D dissertation, Cambridge, Mass.: MIT (ms)

Charlesworth, B., R. Lande and M. Slatkin (1982) "A neo-Darwinian commentary on macroevolution", *Evolution*, 36.6

Chase, P. G. and H. L. Dibble (1987) "Middle paleolithic symbolism: A review of current evidence and interpretations", *J. of Anthropological Archaeology*, 6

Chase, W. G. and K. A. Ericsson (1981) "Skilled memory", in J. Anderson (ed.) *Cognitive Skills and their Acquisition*, Hillsdale, NJ: Erlbaum

Chase, W. G. and K. A. Ericsson (1982) "Skill and working memory", in G. Bower (ed.) *Psychology of Learning and Motivation*, vol. 16, NY: Academic Press

Chase, W. G. and H. A. Simon (1973) "Perception in chess", *Cognitive Psychology*, 4

Cheney, D. L. and R. M. Seyfarth (1990) *How Monkeys See the World*, Chicago: University of Chicago Press

Chertkow, H., D. Bub, A. Evans, E. Meyer and S. Marrett (1990) "Processing words and pictures in the brain studied with positron emission tomography", *Canadian Journal of Neuroscience* (submitted ms)

Chomsky, N (1957) *Syntactic Structures*, The Hague: Mouton

Chomsky, N. (1959) "Review of B. F. Skinner's *Verbal Behavior*", *Language*, 35

Chomsky, N. (1965) *Aspects of the Theory of Syntax*, Cambridge: MIT Press

Chomsky, N. (1968) *Language and Mind*, NY: Harcourt, Brace and World

Chomsky, N. (1971) *Problems of Knowledge and Freedom*, NY: Vintage Books

Chung, S. (1976) "On the subject of two passives in Indonesian", in C. Li (ed. 1976)

Chung, S. (1977) "On the gradual nature of syntactic change", in C. Li (ed. 1977)

Clark, E. (1971) "What's in a word?" in T. Moore (ed.) *Cognitive Development and the Acquisition of Language*, NY: Academic Press

Clark, H. (1969) "Linguistic processes in deductive reasoning", *Psychological Review*, 76.4

Clark, H. (1971a) "The primitive nature of children's relational concepts", in J. Hayes (ed.) *Cognition and the Development of Language*, NY: Wiley and son

Clark, H. (1971b) "The chronometric study of meaning components", *Colloques Internationaux du CNRS*, #206, *Problèmes actuelles en Psycholinguistique*, Paris: CNRS

Clark, H. (1974) "Semantics and comprehension", in T. Sebeok (ed.) *Current Trends in Linguistics*, vol. 12, *Linguistics and Adjacent Arts and Sciences*, The Hague: Mouton

Coates, J. (1983) *The Semantics of Modal Auxiliaries*, London: Croom Helm

Coates, J. (1987) "Epistemic modality and spoken discourse", *Transactions of the Philosophical Society*

Cole, P. (1976/1984) "The treatment of the causee in universal grammar", *I.J.A.L.*

Cole, P. and J. Morgan (eds, 1975) *Speech Acts, Syntax and Semantics 3*, NY: Academic Press

Collins, A. M. and E. F. Loftus (1975) "A spreading activation theory of semantic processing", *Psychological Review*, 82

Collins, A. M. and M. R. Quillian (1969) "Retrieval time from semantic memory", *J.V.L.V.B.*, 8

Collins, A. M. and M. R. Quillian (1972) "How to make a language user", in M. Tulving and W. Donaldson (eds) *Organization of Memory*, NY: Academic Press

Comrie, B. (1973) "The ergative: Variations on a theme", *Lingua*, 32

Comrie, B. (1976) "The syntax of causative constructions: Cross language similarities and divergences", in M. Shibatani (ed. 1976)

Comrie, B. (1977) "Ergativity", University of So. California (ms)

Cooper, W. and J. R. Ross (1975) "World order", *Papers from the Parasession on Functionalism*, University of Chicago: Chicago Linguistics Society

Cooreman, A. (1982) "Topicality, ergativity and transitivity in narrative discourse: Evidence from Chamorro" *Studies in Language*, 6.3

Cooreman, A. (1985) *Transitivity and Discourse Continuity in Chamorro Narrative*, PhD dissertation, University of Oregon, Eugene (ms)

Cooreman, A. (1987) *Transitivity and Discourse Continuity in Chamorro Narratives*, Berlin: Mouton de Gruyter [revised]

Cooreman, A. (1988) "Ergativity in Dyirbal discourse", *Lingua*, 26

Cooreman, A., B. Fox and T. Givón (1984) "The discourse definition of ergativity", *Studies in Language*, 8.1

Coots, J. H. (ed. 1982) *Special issue on 'Stories'*, *J. of Pragmatics*, 6.5/6

Craig, C. (1977) *The Structure of Jacaltec*, Austin: University of Texas Press

Craig, C. (ed. 1986) *Noun Classes and Categorization*, TSL #7, Amsterdam: J. Benjamins

Crouch, J. E. (1978) *Functional Human Anatomy*, 3rd edition, Philadelphia: Lea and Fabiger,

Cullen, J. M. (1972) "Some principles of animal communication", in R. A. Hinde (ed. 1972)

Dahlstrom, A. (1986) *Plains Cree Morphosyntax*, PhD dissertation, UC Berkeley (ms)

De Beaugrande, R. (1982) "The story of grammars and the grammar of stories", in J. H. Coots (ed. 1982)

de Waal, F. (1982) *Chimpanzee Politics: Power and Sex among the Apes*, London: Unwin/counterpoint

Dik, S. (1978) *Functional Grammar*, Amsterdam: North Holland

Dixon, R. M. W. (1972) *The Dyirbal Language of North Queensland*, Cambridge: Cambridge University Press

Dixon, R. M. W. (ed. 1976) *Grammatical Categories in Australian Languages*, Canberra: Australian Institute of Aboriginal Studies

Dixon, R. M. W. (1977) "The syntactic development of Australian languages", in C. Li (ed. 1977)

Dixon, R. M. W. (1987) *A Grammar of Boumaa Fijian*, Chicago: University of Chicago Press

Dore, J. (1976) "Speech acts and language universals", *J. of Child Language*, 2

Dryer, M. (1991) "Subject and inverse in Kutenai", in J. Redden (ed.) *Papers from the American Indian Languages Conference, UC Santa Cruz, Occasional Papers in Linguistics*, 16, Carbondale, Ill.: University of So. Illinois

Dryer, M. (1992) "A comparison of the obviation systems of Kutenai and Algonquian", in W. Cowan (ed.) *Papers from the 23rd Annual Algonquian Conference*

Dryer, M. (1994) "The inverse in Kutenai", in T. Givón (ed. 1994)

DuBois, J. (1985) "Competing motivations", in J. Haiman (ed. 1985)

DuBois, J. (1987) "The discourse basis of ergativity", *Language*, 63.4

Dunbar, R. I. M. (1992) "Co-evolution of neuro-cortex size, group size and language in humans" *Brain and Behavior Sciences*

Egerod, S. (1975) "Typology of Chinese sentence constructions", *Eighth Conference on Sino-Tibetan Languages and Linguistics*, UC Berkeley, October 1975 (ms)

Eisler-Goldman, F. (1968) *Psycholinguistics: Experiments in Spontaneous Speech*, NY: Academic Press

Eldredge, N. and S. J. Gould (1972) "Punctuated equilibria: an alternative to phyletic gradualism", in T. J. M. Schopf (ed.) *Models in Paleobiology*, San Francisco: Freeman, Cooper & Co.

Ericsson, K. A. (1985) "Memory skill" *Canadian J. of Psychology*, 39.2

Ericsson, K. A., W. G. Chase and S. Faloon (1980) "Acquisition of memory skills", *Science*, 208

Ervin-Tripp, S. (1970) "Discourse agreement: How children answer questions", in J. Hayes (ed.) *Cognition and the Development of Language*, NY: Wiley and Son

Estival, D. (1985) "Syntactic priming of the passive in English", in T. Givón (ed. 1985)

Feyerabend, P. (1970) "How to be a good empiricist: A plea for tolerance in matters epistemological", in B. Brody (ed.) *Readings in the Philosophy of Science*, Englewood Cliffs, NJ: Prentice-Hall

Feyerabend, P. (1975) *Against Method: An Outline of an Anarchic Theory of Knowledge*, NY: The Humanities Press

Fiez, J. A. and S. E. Petersen (1993) "PET as part of an interdisciplinary approach to understanding processes involved in reading", *Psychological Science*, 4.5

Fillmore, C. (1963) "The position of embedding transformations in grammar", *Word*, 19

Fillmore, C. (1968) "The case for the case", in E. Bach and R. T. Harms (eds) *Universals of Linguistic Theory*, NY: Holt, Rinehart and Winston

Fleischman, S. (1989) "Temporal distance: a basic linguistic metaphor", *Studies in Language*, 13.1

Fleischman, S. and L. Waugh (eds. 1990) *Categories of the Verb in Romance Discourse: Discourse-Pragmatic Approaches*, London: Croom Helm

Fletcher, C. R. and C. Bloom (1988) "Causal reasoning in the comprehension of simple narrative texts", *J. of Memory and Language*, 27

Fodor, J. and M. Garrett (1967) "Some syntactic determinants of sentential complexity", *Perception and Psychophysics*, 2

Foley, W. (1986) *The Papuan Languages of New Guinea*, Cambridge: Cambridge University Press

Foley, W. and R. van Valin (1984) *Functional Syntax and Universal Grammar*, Cambridge: Cambridge University Press

Forrest, L. (1994) "De-transitive clauses in Bella Coola: Passive vs. inverse", in T. Givón (ed. 1994)

Fouts, R. S. (1973) "Acquisition and testing of gestural signs in four young chimpanzees, *Science*, 180

Fox, A. (1983) "Topic continuity in Early Biblical Hebrew", in T. Givón (ed. 1983)

Fox, B. (1985) "Word order inversion and discourse continuity in Tagalog", in T. Givón (ed. 1985)

Fox, B. and P. Hopper (eds 1994) *Voice: Form and Function*, TSL #27, Amsterdam: J. Benjamins

Funnell, E. (1987) "Object concepts and object names: Some deductions from acquired disorders of word processing", in G. W. Humphreys and M. J. Riddoch (eds 1987)

Funnell, E. and D. A. Alport (1989) "Nonlinguistic cognition and word meanings", in D. A. Alport, D. G. Mackay, W. Pririz and E. Schearer (eds) *Language Perception and Production: Shared Mechanisms in Listening, Reading and Writing*, London: Academic Press

Futuyma, D. J. (1986) *Evolutionary Biology*, Sunderland, Mass.: Sinauer [2nd edition]

García, E. (1979) "Discourse without syntax", in T. Givón (ed. 1979b)

Gardner, B. T. and R. A. Gardner (1971) "Two-way communication with an infant chimpanzee", in A. Schrier and F. Stollnitz (eds) *Behavior of Non-human Primates*, NY: Academic Press

Gernsbacher, M. A. (1985) "Surface information loss in comprehension", *Cognitive Psychology*, 17

Gernsbacher, M. A. (1990) *Language Comprehension as Structure Building*, Hillsdale, NJ: Erlbaum

Geschwind, N. (1970) "The organization of language and the brain", *Science*, 170

Geschwind, N. and W. Levitzky (1968) "Human brain left-right asymmetries in the temporal speech region", *Science*, 161

Gildea, S. (1992) *Comparative Cariban Morphosyntax: On the Genesis of Ergativity in Independent Clauses*, PhD dissertation, University of Oregon, Eugene (ms)

Gildea, S. (1994) ""Inverse alignment" and "inverse voice" in Surinam Carib", in T. Givón (ed. 1994)

Givón, T. (1971a) "Historical syntax and synchronic morphology: An archaeologist's field trip", *CLS #7*, University of Chicago, Chicago Linguistics Society

Givón, T. (1971b) "Dependent modals, performatives, factivity, Bantu subjunctives and what not", *Studies in African Linguistics*, 2.1

Givón, T. (1972) *Studies in ChiBemba and Bantu Grammar*, Studies in African Linguistics, supplement #3

Givón, T. (1973a) "The time-axis phenomenon", *Language*, 49.4

Givón, T. (1973b) "Opacity and reference in language: An inquiry into the role of modalities", in J. Kimball (ed.) *Syntax and Semantics 2*, NY: Academic Press

Givón, T. (1975a) "Serial verbs and syntactic change: Niger-Congo", in C. Li (ed. 1975)

Givón, T. (1975b) "Focus and the scope of assertion: Some Bantu evidence", *Studies in African Linguistics*, 6.2 _

Givón, T. (1976a) "Topic, pronoun and grammatical agreement", in C. Li (ed. 1976)

Givón, T. (1976b) "Some constraints on Bantu causativization", in M. Shibatani (ed. 1976)

Givón, T. (1977) "The drift from VSO to SVO in Biblical Hebrew: The pragmatics of tense-aspect", in C. Li (ed. 1977)

Givón, T. (1978) "Language typology in Africa: A critical review", *J. of African Languages and Linguistics*, 1

Givón, T. (1979a) *On Understanding Grammar*, NY: Academic Press

Givón, T. (ed. 1979b) *Discourse and Syntax, Syntax and Semantics #12*, NY: Academic Press

Givón, T. (1980a) *Ute Reference Grammar*, Ignacio, CO: Ute Press

Givón, T. (1980b) "The binding hierarchy and the typology of complements", *Studies in Language*, 4.1

Givón, T. (1981) "Typology and functional domains", *Studies in Language*, 5.2

Givón, T. (1982a) "Tense-aspect-modality: The Creole prototype and beyond", in P. Hopper (ed.) *Tense — Aspect: Between Semantics and Pragmatics*, TSL #1, Amsterdam: J. Benjamins

Givón, T. (1982b) "Evidentiality and epistemic space", *Studies in Language*, 6.1

Givón, T. (1983a) "Language, function and typology", in S. Hattori and K. Inoue (eds) *Proceedings of the XIIIth International Congress of Linguists, Tokyo, 1982*, The Hague: CIPL

Givón, T. (1983b) "Topic continuity in spoken English", in T. Givón (ed, 1983)

Givón, T. (1983c) "Topic continuity and word-order pragmatics in Ute", in T. Givón (ed. 1983)

Givón, T. (ed. 1983) *Topic Continuity in Discourse: A Quantitative Cross-Language Study*, TSL 3, Amsterdam: J. Benjamins

Givón, T. (1984a) "Direct object and dative shifting: The semantics and pragmatics of case", in F. Plank (ed.) *Objects*, NY/London: Academic Press

Givón, T. (1984b) *Syntax: A Functional-Typological Introduction*, vol. I, Amsterdam: J. Benjamins

Givón, T. (1984c) "Universals of discourse structure and second language acquisition", in W. Rutherford (ed.) *Language Universals and Second Language Acquisition*, TSL #5, Amsterdam: J. Benjamins

Givón, T. (1985a) "Iconicity, isomorphism and non-arbitrary coding in syntax", in J. Haiman (ed. 1985)

Givón, T. (1985b) "Structure, function and language acquisition", in D. Slobin (ed.) *The Crosslinguistic Study of Language Acquisition*, vol. II, Hillsdale, NJ: Erlbaum

Givón, T. (ed. 1985) *Quantified Studies in Discourse*, a special issue of *Text*, 5.1/2

Givón, T. (1986) "Categories and prototypes: Between Plato and Wittgenstein", in C. Craig (ed. 1986)

Givón, T. (1988) "The pragmatics of word-order: Predictability, importance and attention), in M. Hammond, E. Moravcsik and J. Wirth (eds) *Studies in Syntactic Typology*, TSL #17, Amsterdam: J. Banjamins

Givón, T. (1989) *Mind, Code and Context: Essays in Pragmatics*, Hillsdale, NJ: Erlbaum

Givón, T. (1990a) "Natural language learning and organized language teaching", in H. Burmeister and P. Rounds (eds) *Proceedings of the Second Language Research Forum (SLRF)*, University of Oregon, Eugene

Givón, T. (1990b) *Syntax: A Functional-Typological Introduction*, vol. II, Amsterdam: J. Benjamins

Givón, T. (1990c) "Ute reflexives, complementation and clause integration", in J. A. Edmonson, C. Fagin and P. Mühlhäusler (eds.) *Development and Diversity: Linguistic Variation Across Time and Space* (C. J. Bailey Festschrift), Dallas: UT Arlington

Givón, T. (1991a) "The evolution of dependent clause syntax in Biblical Hebrew", in E. Traugott and B. Heine (eds, 1991, vol. II)

Givón, T. (1991b) "Serial verbs and the mental reality of 'event': Grammatical vs. cognitive packaging", in B. Heine and E. Traugott (eds 1991, vol. I)

Givón, T. (1991c) "Markedness in grammar: Distributional, communicative and cognitive correlates of syntactic structure", *Studies in Language*, 15.2

Givón, T. (1991d) "Isomorphism in the grammatical code: Cognitive and biological considerations", *Studies in Language*, 15.1

Givón, T. (1991e) "Some substantive issues concerning verb serialization: Grammatical vs. cognitive packaging", in C. Lefebvre (ed. 1991)

Givón, T. (1991f) "The pragmatics of word-order in Early Biblical Hebrew: Referential vs. thematic coherence", (ms)

Givón, T. (1992) "The grammar of referential coherence as mental processing instructions", *Linguistics*, 30.1

Givón, T. (1993) "Coherence in text, coherence in mind", *Pragmatics and Cognition*, 1.2

Givón, T. (ed. 1994) *Voice and Inversion*, TSL #28, Amsterdam: J. Benjamins

Givón, T. and A. Kimenyi (1974) "Truth, belief and doubt in KinyaRwanda", *Studies in African Linguistics, Supplement #5*

Glass, A. L. and K. J. Holyoak (1975) "Alternative conceptions of semantic memory", *Cognition*, 3

Glenberg, A. M., M. Meyer and K. Linden (1987) "Mental models contribute to foregrounding during text comprehension", *J. of Memory and Language*, 26

Goodenough, W. (1990) "Evolution of human capacity for beliefs", *American Anthropologist*

Goodglass, H. (1976) "Agrammatism", in H. Whitaker and H. A. Whitaker (eds) *Studies in Neurolinguistics*, 1, NY: Academic Press

Goodwin, C. (1979) "Interactive construction of a sentence in natural conversation", in G. Psasthjas (ed.) *Everyday Language: Studies in Ethnomethodology*, NY: Irvington

Goodwin, C. (1981) *Conversational Organization: Interaction Between Speakers and Hearers*, NY: Academic Press

Goodwin, C. (1986) "Audience diversity, participation and interpretation", *Text*, 3

Goodwin, C. (1988) "Embedded context", paper read at the *AAA* annual meeting, Phoenix, Nov. 1988 (ms)

Goodwin, C. (1992) "Transparent vision", paper presented to the *American Association of Applied Linguistics*, Seattle, Febr. 1992 (ms)

Goodwin, C. (in press) "Sentence construction within interaction", in U. Quastoff (ed.) *Aspects of Oral Communication*

Goodwin, C. and M. H. Goodwin (1987) "Concurrent operations on talk: Notes on the interactive organization of assessment", *IPRA Papers in Pragmatics*, 1.1

Goodwin, M. H. (1980) "Process of mutual monitoring implicated in the production of description sequences", in D. Zimmerman and C. West (eds) *Language and Social Interaction, Sociological Inquiry*, 50

Goodwin, M. H. (1987) "Byplay: Participant structure and framing of collaborative collusion", paper read at the *Conference on Action Analysis and Conversation Analysis*, Paris, 1987 (ms)

Gough, D. (1965) "The verification of sentences", *J. V.L.V.B.*, 5

Gould, J. L. (1991) "An evolutionary perspective on honey bee communication", *Symposium on the Evolution of Communication: Cross-Species Comparison*, University of Oregon, Eugene: Institute of Cognitive and Decision Sciences (ms)

Gould, J. L. and W. Towne (1987) "Evolution of the dance language", *The American Naturalist*, 130.3

Gould, S. J. (1977) *Ontogeny and Phylogeny*, Cambridge: Harvard University Press/-The Belknap Press)

Gould, S. J. (1980) *The Panda's Thumb*, NY: Pelican Books

Gould, S. J. and N. Eldredge (1977) "Punctuated equilibria: the tempo and mode of evolution reconsidered", *Paleobiology*, 3

Greenberg, J. (ed. 1966a) *Language Universals*, The Hague: Mouton

Greenberg, J. (1966b) "On some universals of language with particular reference to the order of meaningful elements", in J. Greenberg (ed. 1966a)

Greenberg, J. (1974) "The relation of frequency to semantic feature in a case language (Russian)", *Working Papers in Language Universals*, 16, Stanford: Stanford University

Greenberg, J. (1976) *Language Universals, With Special Reference to Feature Hierarchies*, The Hague: Mouton

Greenberg, J. (1978) "Diachrony, synchrony and language universals", in J. Greenberg *et al.* (eds 1978), vol. 2

Greenberg, J. (1979) "Rethinking linguistic diachrony", *Language*, 55

Greenberg, J., C. Ferguson and E. Moravcsik (eds, 1978) *Universals of Human Language*, Stanford: Stanford University Press

Greenfield, P. M. (1991) "Language, tools and brain: The ontology and phylogeny of hierarchically organized sequential behavior", *Behavioral and Brain Sciences*, 14.4

Greenfield, P. M. and E. S. Savage-Rambaugh (1991) "Imitation, grammatical development and the invention of protogrammar by an ape", in N. Krasnegor, M. Studdert-Kennedy and R. Schiefelbuch (eds) *Biobehavioral foundations of Language Development*, Hillsdale, NJ: Erlbaum

Grice, H. P. (1968/1975) "Logic and conversation", in P. Cole and J. Morgan (eds, 1975)

Grimes, J. (1975) *The Thread of Discourse*, Mouton: The Hague

Gruber, J. (1965) *Studies in Lexical Relations*, PhD dissertation, MIT, Cambridge, Mass. (ms)

Guo, J.-S. (1992) "The interactional structure of meaning: Children's use and development of the Mandarin modal*neng* (can)", *Symposium on Mood and Modality*, UNM, Albuquerque, May 1992 (ms)

Haboud, M. (1993) "Grammatical change and language contact in Ecuadorian highlands", University of Oregon, Eugene (ms)

Haiman, J. (1983) "Iconic and economic motivation", *Language*, 59.4

Haiman, J. (1985a) *Natural Syntax*, Cambridge: Cambridge University Press

Haiman, J. (ed. 1985b) *Iconicity in Syntax*, TSL #6, Amsterdam: J. Benjamins

Haiman, J. (1991) "The bureaucratization of language", in H. C. Wolfart (ed.) *Linguistic Studies Presented to John L. Finlay*, Winnipeg: Algonquian and Iroquoian Linguistics, *Memoir 8*

Haiman, J. (1992a) "Motivation, repetition and emancipation: The bureauc ratization of language", Macalester College (ms)

Haiman, J. (1992b) "Syntactic change and iconicity", to appear in *Encyclopedia of Language and Linguistics* (ms)

Haiman, J. (1992c) "Ritualization and the development of language", Macalester College (ms)

Hale, K. (1973) "Person marking in Walbiri", in *A Festschrift for Morris Halle*, NY: Holt, Rinehart and Winston

Hale, K. (1976) "Person marking in Walbiri", in R. M. W. Dixon (ed.) *Grammatical Categories in Australian Languages*, Canberra: Australian Institute of Aboriginal Studies

Hale, K. (1983) "Walpiri and the grammar of non-configurational languages", *Natural Language and Linguistic Theory*, 1.1

Hale, K. (1991) "Misumalpan verb sequencing constructions", in C. Lefebvre (ed. 1991)

Halliday, M. A. K. (1961) "Categories of the theory of grammar", *Word*, 17

Halliday, M. A. K. (1973) *Explorations in the Functions of Language*, London: Edward Arnold

Halliday, M. A. K. and R. Hasan (1976) *Cohesion in English*, London: Longmans

Hanson, R. N. (1958) *Patterns of Discovery*, Cambridge: Cambridge University Press

Harder, P. (1992) "Function and structure in language description", paper read at the Linguistics Colloquium, University of Oregon, Eugene (ms)

Harris, A. (1982) *Diachronic Syntax: The Kartvelian Case*, Vanderbilt University (ms)

Harris, Z. (1956) "Co-occurrence and transformations in linguistic structure", *Language*, 33.3

Hawkinson, A. and L. Hyman (1974) "Natural topic hierarchies in Shona", *Studies in African Linguistics*, 5.1

Hayashi, L. (1989) "Conjunctions and referential continuity", University of Oregon, Eugene (ms)

Heine, B. (1992) "Agent-oriented vs. epistemic modality: Some observation on German modals", *Symposium on Mood and Modality*, UNM, Albuquerque, May 1992 (ms)

Heine, B. (1993) *Auxiliaries: Cognitive Forces and Grammaticalization*, Oxford: Oxford University Press

Heine, B., U. Claudi and F. Hünnemeyer (1991) *Grammaticalization: A Conceptual Framework*, Chicago: University of Chicago Pres

Heine, B. and E. Traugott (eds, 1991) *Approaches to Grammaticalization*, TSL #19 (2 vols), Amsterdam: J. Benjamins

Hempel, C. (1959/1970) "The logic of functional analysis", in B. Brody (ed. 1970) *Readings in the Philosophy of Science*, Englewood Cliffs, NJ: Prentice-Hall

Hempel, C. and P. Oppenheim (1948/1970) "Studies in the logic of explanation", in B. Brody (ed. 1970) *Readings in the Philosophy of Science*, Englewood Cliffs, NJ: Prentice-Hall

Hetzron, R. (1971) "Presentative function and presentative movement", *Studies in African Linguistics*, supplement #2

Hewes, G. W. (1973a) "Primate communication and the gestural origin of language", *Current Anthropology*,

Hewes, G. W. (1973b) "An explicit formulation of the relationship between tool-using, tool-making and the emergence of language", *Visible Language*, 7.2

Hewes, G. W. (1974) "Language in early hominids", in R. Wescott (ed. 1974)

Hidalgo, R. (1994) "The pragmatics of voice in Spanish: The*se* construction and the*ser*-passive", in Givón (ed. 1994)

Hinde, R. A. (ed. 1972) *Non-Verbal Communication*, Cambridge: Cambridge University Press

Hinton, J. and S. J. Nowlan (1987) "How learning can guide evolution", Carnegie-Mellon University, Computer Science Dept. (ms)

Holmes, J. (1984) "Hedging your bets and sitting on the fence: Some evidence for hedges as support structure", *Te Reo*, 27

Hoosain, P. (1973) "The processing of negation", *J.V.L.V.B.*, 12

Hoosain, R. and C. Osgood (1975) "Response time for Yang (positive) and Yin (negative) words", Urbana, Ill.: University of Illinois (ms)

Hopper, P. (1979) "Aspect and foregrounding in discourse", in T. Givón (ed. 1979b)

Hopper, P. and S. Thompson (1980) "Transitivity in grammar and discourse", *Language*, 56.2

Hopper, P. and S. Thompson (1984) "The discourse basis for lexical categories in universal grammar", *Language*, 60

Howard, D., K. Patterson, R. Wise, W. D. Brown, K. Friston, C. Weller and R. Frakowiac (1992) "The cortical localization of the lexicon: Positron emission tomography evidence", *Brain*, 115

Humphreys, G. W. and J. M. Riddoch (1987) "Introduction: Cognitive psychology and visual object processing", in G. W. Humphreys and J. M. Riddoch (eds, 1987)

Humphreys, G. W. and J. M. Riddoch (eds 1987) *Visual Object Processing: A Cognitive Neuropsychological Approach*, London: Erlbaum

Humphreys, G. W. and M. J. Riddoch (1988) "On the case of multiple semantic systems: A reply to Shallice", *Cognitive Neuropsychology*, 5.1

Hyman, L. (1971) "Consecutivization in Fe'fe'", *J. of African Languages*, 10.2

Hyman, R. and N. A. H. Frost (1975) "Gradients and schema in pattern recognition", *Attention and Performance, V*, NY: Academic Press

Inhoff, A. W., A. Pollatsek, M. I. Posner and K. Rayner (1989) "Covert attention and eye movement in reading", *Quarterly J. of Experimental Psychology*, 41A(1)

Jackendoff, R. (1971) "Modal structure in semantic representation", *Linguistic Inquiry*, 2.4

Jacobs, P. (1994) "The inverse in Squamish", in T. Givón (ed. 1994)

Jakobson, R. (1932/1971) "Zur Struktur des russiches Verbums", reprinted in Jakobson (1971) *Selected Writings*, II, The Hague: Mouton

Jakobson, R. (1939/1962) "Zur Struktur des Phonems", reprinted in Jakobson (1962) *Selected Writings*, I, The Hague: Mouton

Jakobson, R. (1974) "Mark and feature", *World Papers on Phonemics*, Tokyo: Phonetic Society of Japan

Jakobson, R. and K. Pomorska (1980) *Dialogues*, Paris: Flammarion

Jakobson, R. and L. Waugh (1979) *The Sound Shape of Language*, Bloomington: Indiana University Press

James, D. (1982) "Past tense and the hypothetical: A cross-linguistic study", *Studies in Language*, 6.3

Jespersen, O. (1934/1965) *The Philosophy of Grammar*, NY: Norton

Joanette, Y., O. Goulet and D. Hannequin (1990) *Right Hemisphere and Verbal Communication*, NY: Springer-Verlag

Johnson, N. S. and J. M. Mandler (1980) "A tale of two structures: Underlying and surface forms in stories", *Poetics*, 9

Johnson-Laird, P. N. (1980) "Mental models in cognitive science", *Cognitive Science*, 4

Just, M. A. and P. A. Carpenter (1987) *The Psychology of Reading and Language Comprehension*, Newton, Mass.: Allen and Bacon

Just, M. A. and P. A. Carpenter (1992) "A capacity theory of comprehension: Individual differences in working memory", *Psychological Review*, 99.1

Kaas, J. H. (1989) "Why does the brain have so many visual areas?" *J. of Cognitive Neuroscience*, 1.2

Kalmár, I. (1980) "The antipassive and grammatical relations in Eskimo", in F. Plank (ed.) *Ergativity: Toward a Theory of Grammatical Relations*, NY/London: Academic Press

Kaswanti Purwo, B. (1988) "Voice in Indonesian: A discourse study", in M. Shibatani (ed. 1988)

Katz, J. J. and P. Postal (1964) *An Integrated Theory of Linguistic Description*, Cambridge: MIT Press

Kean, M.-L. (ed. 1985) *Agrammatism*, NY: Academic Press

Keenan, E. L. (1975) "Some universals of passive in relational grammar", *CLS #11*, University of Chicago: Chicago Linguistics Society

Keenan, E. L. (1976) "Toward a universal definition of 'subject'", in C. Li (ed. 1976)

Keenan, E. L. and B. Comrie (1972) "Noun phrase accessibility and universal grammar", paper presented at the *47th Annual Meeting of the Linguistics Society of America*, Atlanta, GA (ms)

Keenan, E. Ochs (1974a) "Conversational competence in children", *J. of Child Language*, 1.2

Keenan, E. Ochs (1974b) "Again and again: The pragmatics of imitation in child language", Los Angeles: University of Southern California (ms)

Keenan, E. Ochs (1975a) "Making it last: The use of repetition in children's discourse", *BLC #1*

Keenan, E. Ochs (1975b) "Evolving discourse: The next step", Los Angeles: University of Southern California (ms)

Keenan, E.Ochs and T. Bennett (1977) "Planned and unplanned conversation", *SCOPIL #5*, Los Angeles: University of So. California

Keenan, E. Ochs and T. Bennett (eds, 1977) *Discourse Across Time and Space*, *SCOPIL #5*, Los Angeles: University of Southern California

Kemmer, S. (1993) *The Middle Voice*, TSL #23, Amsterdam: J. Benjamins

Kim, A. H. (1986) "Semi-clausal modals in Korean verb morphology", Linguistics Colloquium talk, University of Oregon, Eugene (ms).

Kimenyi, A. (1976) *A Relational Grammar of KinyaRwanda*, PhD dissertation, UCLA (ms)

Kimura, D. (1992) *Neuromotor Mechanisms in Human Communication*, Oxford: Oxford University Press

Kintsch, W. (ms) "How readers construct situation models for stories: The role of syntactic cues and causal inference", in A. F. Healy, S. Kosslyn and R. M. Shiffrin (eds) *Essays in Honor of William K. Estes*, Hillsdale, NJ: Erlbaum

Kiparsky, P. and C. Kiparsky (1968) "Fact", in M. Bierwisch and K. Heidolph (eds) *Progress in Linguistics*, The Hague: Mouton

Klein-Andreu, F. (1990) "Losing ground", in S. Fleischman and L. Waugh (eds, 1990)

Klima, E. and U. Bellugi (1979) *The Signs of Language*, Cambridge: Harvard University Press

Knudsen, E. I. (1985) "Experience alters the spatial tuning of auditory units in the optic tectum during a sensitive period in the barn owl", *J. of Neuroscience*, 1

Knudsen, E. I. (1989) "Visual experience shapes auditory orienting behavior in developing owls", paper read at the *Symposium on Orienting: Phylogenetic, Developmental and Cognitive Perspective*, University of Oregon, Eugene (ms)

Knudsen, E. I. and P. F. Knudsen (1990) "Sensitive and critical periods for visual calibration of sound localization by barn owls", *J. of Neuroscience*, 5

Kornfeld, J. (1974) *The Influence of Clause Structure on the Perceptual Analysis of Sentences*, PhD dissertation, MIT, Cambridge, Mass.

Kuhn, T. (1962) *The Structure of Scientific Revolution*, Chicago: University of Chicago Press

Labov, W. (1975) "Empirical foundations of linguistic theory", in R. Austerlitz (ed.) *The Scope of American Linguistics*, Lisse: Peter de Ridder Press

Lakoff, G. (1970) *Linguistics and Natural Logic*, Studies in Generative Semantics, #2, Ann Arbor: University of Michigan, Linguistics Dept.

Lakoff, G. (1973) "Hedges: A study in the meaning criteria and the logic of fuzzy concepts", *J. of Philosophical Logic*, 2

Lakoff, G. and M. Johnson (1980) *Metaphors We Live By*, Chicago: University of Chicago Press

Lamendella, J. (1976) "Relations between the ontogeny and phylogeny of language: A neo-recapitulationist view", in S.R. Harnad, H.D. Stelkis and J. Lancaster (eds) *The Origins and Evolution of Language and Speech*, NY: New York Academy of Science

Lamendella, J. (1977) *Neuro-Functional Foundations of Symbolic Communication*, San Jose State University (ms)

L'Amour, L. (1962) *Shalako*, NY: Bantam

Lande, R. (1980) "Microevolution in relation to macroevolution", *Paleobiology*, 6.2

Lande, R. (1986) "The dynamics of peak shifts and the pattern of morphological evolution", *Paleobiology*, 12.4

Langacker, R. (1978) "The form and meaning of the English auxiliary", *Language*, 54.4

Langacker, R. (1987) *Foundations of Cognitive Grammar*, vol. I, Stanford: Stanford University Press

Larson, R.K. (1991) "Some issues in verb serialization", in C. Lefebvre (ed. 1991)

Leder, B. (1982) "The genetics of antibody diversity", *The Scientific American*, XX

Lee, I.-H. (1994) "The pragmatics of voice in Korean", in T. Givón (ed. 1994)

Lefebvre, C. (1991) "Take serial verb constructions in Fon", in C. Lefebvre (ed 1991)

Lefebvre, C. (ed. 1991) *Serial Verbs: Grammatical, Comparative and Cognitive Approaches*, SSLS #8, Amsterdam: J. Benjamins

Li, C. (ed. 1975) *Word Order and Word Order Change*, Austin: University of Texas Press

Li, C.N. (ed. 1976) *Subject and Topic*, NY: Academic Press

Li, C. (ed. 1977) *Mechanisms of Syntactic Change*, Austin: University of Texas Press

Li, C.N. and S.A. Thompson (1973) "Serial verb constructions in Mandarin Chinese: Subordination or coordination", *CLS Comparative Syntax Parasession*, University of Chicago, Chicago Linguistics Society

Li, C.N. and S.A. Thompson (1974) "Co-verbs in Mandarin Chinese: Verbs or prepositions?", *J. of Chinese Linguistics*, 2.3

Li, C. and S. Thompson (1975) "The semantic function of word-order: A case study in Mandarin", in C. Li (ed. 1975)

Li, C.N. and S. Thompson (1976) "Subject and topic: A new typology of language", in C. Li (ed. 1976)

Lieberman, P. (1984) *The Biology and Evolution of Language*, Cambridge: Harvard University Press

Limber, J. (1973) "The genesis of complex sentences", in T. Moore (ed.) *Cognitive Development and the Acquisition of Language*, NY: Academic Press

Loftus, E. (1980) *Eyewitness Testimony*, Cambridge: Harvard University Press

Longacre, R. (ed. 1971) *Philippine Discourse and Paragraph Studies in Memory of Betty McLachlin, Pacific Linguistics*, 22, Canberra: Australian National University

Longacre, R. (1976) *An Anatomy of Speech Notions*, Lisse: Peter de Ridder

Lunn, P. V. (1992) "Choosing the best description of the Spanish subjunctive", *Symposium on Mood and Modality*, UNM, Albuquerque, May 1992 (ms)

Lunn, P. V. and T. D. Craven (1990) "A contextual reconsideration of the Spanish *ra* 'indicative'", in S. Fleischman and L. Waugh (eds, 1990)

Mandler, J. M. (1978) "A code in the node: The use of story schemata in retrieval", *Discourse Processes*, 1

Mandler, J. M. (1982) "Another story of grammars: comments on Beaugrande's 'The story of grammars and the grammar of stories'", in J. H. Coots (ed. 1982)

Mandler, J. M. and N. S. Johnson (1977) "Remembrance of things parsed: Story structure and recall", *Cognitive Psychology*, 9

Marantz, A. (1983) "Comments on Givón's paper", in S. Hattori and K. Inoue (eds) *Proceedings of the XIIIth International Congress of Linguists, Tokyo, 1982*, The Hague: CIPL

Marchand, H. (1968) *The Categories and Types of Present-Day English Word-Formation*, University, Ala.: University of Alabama Press

Marler, P., S. Karakashian and M. Gyger (1991) "Do animals have the option of withholding signals when communication is inappropriate? The audience effect", in C. A. Ristau (ed. 1991)

Maunsell, J. H. R. and D. C. Van Essen (1983) "The connections of the middle temporal visual area (MT) and their relationship to a cortical hierarchy in macaque monkeys", *J. of Neuroscience*, 12

Mayr, E. (1963) *Populations, Species and Evolution*, Cambridge: Harvard University Press

Mayr, E. (1982) *The Growth of Biological Thought*, Cambridge: Harvard University Press

McCawley, J. (1988) *The Syntactic Phenomena of English*, Chicago: University of Chicago Press

McKeon, R. (ed. 1941) *The Basic Works of Aristotle*, NY: Random House [22nd edition]

McKoon, G. and R. Ratcliff (1992) "Inference during reading", *Psychological Review*,

McMahon, L. (1963) "Grammatical analysis as part of understanding a sentence", *J.V.L.V.B.*, 6

McMurtry, L. (1963) *Leaving Cheyenne*, NY: Penguin Books

Mehler, J. (1963) "Some effect of grammatical transformations on the recall of English sentences", *J.V.L.V.B.*, 6

Mejías-Bikandi, R. (1991) "Case marking in Basque", *International J. of Basque Linguistics and Philology (ASJU)*, XXV.2

Menn, L. (1990) "Agrammatism in English: Two case studies", in L. Menn and E. Obler (eds, 1990)

Menn, L. and L.K. Obler (1990) *Agrammatic Aphasia: A Cross-Language Narrative Source-book*, Amsterdam: J. Benjamins

Mishkin, M. (1978) "Memory in monkeys severely impaired by combined but not by separate removal of amygdala and hippocampus", *Nature*, 273

Mishkin, M. (1982) "A memory system in the monkey", *Philosophical Soc. of London [Biol.]*, 298

Mishkin, M., B. Malamut and J. Bachevalier (1984) "Memories and habits: Two neural systems", in G. Lynch and J.L. McGaugh (eds), *Neurobiology of Learning and Memory*, NY: Guilford Press

Mishkin, M. and H.L. Petri (1984) "Memories and habits: Some implications for the analysis of learning and retention", in N. Butters and L.R. Squire (eds) *Neuropsychology of Memory*, NY: Guilford Press

Mishkin, M., B.J. Spiegler, R.C. Saunders and B.J. Malamut (1982) "An animal model of global amnesia", in S. Corkin, K.L. Davis, H. Growdon, E.J. Usdin and R.J. Wurtman (eds) *Toward a Treatment of Alzheimer's Disease*, NY: Raven Press

Mithun, M. (1984) "The evolution of noun incorporation", *Language*, 60.4

Mithun, M. (1992) "On the relativity of irreality", *Symposium on Mood and Modality*, UNM, Albuquerque, May 1992 (ms)

Morrow, D., S. Greenspan and G. Bowers (1987) "Accessibility and situation models in narrative comprehension", *J. of Memory and Language*, 26

Neeley, J.H. (1990) "Semantic priming effects in visual word recognition: A selective review of current findings and theories", in D. Besner and G. Humphreys (eds) *Basic Processes in Reading: Visual Word Recognition*, Hillsdale: Erlbaum

Nichols, J. (unpublished) "On SOV word order in Mandarin", UC at Berkeley (ms)

Nissen, M.J. and P. Bulleme (1986) "Attention requirements of learning: Evidence from performance measures", University of Minnesota, Minneapolis (ms)

Ochs, E. (1979) "Planned and unplanned discourse", in T. Givón (ed. 1979b)

Olness, G.S. (1991) "Pragmatic-contextual difficulties as a correlate of deficits associated with right-hemisphere lesions", University of Oregon, Eugene (ms)

Osam, K.E. (1993a) "From serial verbs to prepositions in Akan", University of Oregon, Eugene (ms)

Osam, K.E. (1993b) "Grammatical relations in Akan", University of Oregon, Eugene (ms)

Oujman, G.A. (1991) "Cortical organization of language", *J. of Neuroscience*, 11.8

Palmer, F. R. (1979) *Modality and the English Modals*, London: Longmans
Palmer, F. R. (1986) *Mood and Modality*, Cambridge: Cambridge Univesity Press
Pawley, A. (1987) "Encoding events in Kalam and English: Different logics for reporting experience", in R. Tomlin (ed. 1987)
Pawley, A. and F. Syder (1983) "Natural selection in syntax: Notes on the adaptive variation and change in vernacular and literary grammar", *J. of Pragmatics*, 7
Payne, David (1991) "The classification of Maipuran (Arawakan) languages based on shared lexical retentions", *Handbook of Amazonian Languages*, vol. 3, The Hague: Mouton de Gruyter
Payne, D. L. (1990) "The Tupi-Guaraní inverse", in B. Fox and P. Hopper (eds 1994)
Payne, D. L. (ed. 1992) *The Pragmatics of Word Order Flexibility*, TSL #22, Amsterdam: J. Benjamins
Payne, D. L., M. Hamaya and P. Jacobs (1994) "Direct, inverse and passive in Maasai" in T. Givón (ed. 1994)
Payne, T. (1982) "Role and reference related subject properties and ergativity in Yu'pik Eskimo and Tagalog", *Studies in Language*, 6.1
Payne, T. (1994) "The pragmatics of voice in a Philippine language: Actor-focus and goal-focus in Cebuano", in T. Givón (ed. 1994)
Peirce, C. S. (1934) *Collected Writings*, vol. V, Cambridge: Harvard University Press
Peirce, C. S. (1940) *The Philosophy of Peirce*, ed. by J. Buchler, NY: Harcourt, Brace
Pepperberg, I. M. (1991) "A communicative approach to animal cognition: A study of conceptual abilities of an African Grey Parrot", in C. A. Ristau (ed. 1991)
Perrett, D. I., M. H. Harries, R. Bevan, S. Thomas, P. J. Benson, A. J. Mistlin, A. J. Chitty, J. K. Hietanen and J. E. Ortega (1989) "Framework of analysis for the neural representation of animate objects and actions", *J. of Experimental Biology*, 146
Petersen, S. E., P. T. Fox, M. I. Posner, M. Mintun and M. E. Raichle (1989) "Positron emission tomographic studies of the processing of single words", *J. of Cognitive Neuroscience*, 1.2
Petersen, S. E., P. T. Fox, A. Z. Snyder and M. E. Raichle (1990) "Activation of extrastriate and frontal cortical areas by visual words and word-like stimuli", *Science*, 249
Petitto, L. A. (1991) "From gesture to symbol: The relation between form and meaning in the acquisition of personal pronouns", Papers and Reports from Child Language Development (ms)
Petri, H. L. and M. Mishkin (1994) "Behaviorism, cognitivism and the neuropsychology of memory", *American Scientist*, 82
Popper, K. (1934/1959) *The Logic of Scientific Discovery*, NY: Harper and Row

470   BIBLIOGRAPHY

Posner, M. (1969) "Abstraction and the process of recognition", in G. H. Bowers and
  J. T. Spence (eds) *The Psychology of Learning and Motivation*, vol. 3, NY:
  Academic Press
Posner, M. (1986) "Empirical studies of prototypes", in C. Craig (ed. 1986)
Posner, M. I. and T. H. Carr (1991) "Lexical access and the brain: Anatomical
  constraints on cognitive models of word recognition", *TR 91-5*, Institute of
  Cognitive and Decision Sciences, University of Oregon
Posner, M. and S. Keele (1968) "On the genesis of abstract ideas", *J. of Experimental
  Psychology*, 77
Posner, M. I. and S. E. Petersen (1990) "The attention system of the human brain",
  Annual Review of Neuroscience, 13
Posner, M. I., S. E. Petersen, P. T. Fox and M. E. Raichle (1988) "Localization of
  cognitive operations in the human brain", *Science*, 240
Posner, M. I. and M. E. Raichle (1994) *Images of Mind*, NY: Scientific American
  Library
Posner, M. I., J. Sandson, M. Dhawan and G. L. Shulman (1989) "Is word recognition
  automatic? A cognitive anatomical approach", *J. of Cognitive Neuroscience*, 1.1
Posner, M. I. and Snyder (1974) "Attention and cognitive control", in R. L. Solso
  (ed.) *Information Processing and Cognition: The Loyola Symposium*, Hillsdale,
  NJ: Erlbaum
Postal, P. (1964) *Constituent Structure*, The Hague: Mouton
Premak, D. (1971) "Language in chimpanzee", *Science*, 172
Pu, M.-M. (forthcoming) "Zero anaphora and grammatical relations in Mandarin",
  University of Oregon (ms)
Rafferty, E. (1982) *Discourse Structure of the Chinese Indonesian of Malang, Linguis-
  tics Studies in Indonesian and Languages of Indonesia*, #12, Jakarta: Atma Jaya
  University
Rafferty, E. (1984) "Topicality and ergativity in Indonesian and Malay texts",
  University of Wisconsin, Madison (ms)
Raichle, M. E., J. A. Fiez, T. O. Videen, M. K. MacLeod, J. Pardo, P. T. Fox and S. E.
  Petersen (1993) "Practice-related changes in human brain functional anatomy
  during non-motor learning" *Cerebral Cortex*
Rajewsky, j., E. Forster, and A. Cumano (1987) "Evolutionary and somatic selection
  of antibody repertoire in the mouse", *Science*, 238
Ramsay, V. (1987) "The functional distribution of pre-posed and post-posed 'if' and
  'when' clauses in written discourse", in R. Tomlin (ed. 1987)
Rhodes, R. (1991) "The Algonquian inverse and grammatical relations" unpublished
  communication, UC Berkeley (ms)
Rhodes, R. and R. Tomlin (1992) "Information distribution in Ojibwa", in D. L.
  Payne (ed. 1992)

Rice, K. D. (1989) *A Grammar of Slave*, Berlin/NY: Mouton de Gruyter

Riddoch, M. J. and G. W. and Humphreys (1987a) "Visual optic processing in a case of optic aphasia", *Cognitive Neuropsychology*, 4

Riddoch, M. J. and G. W. Humphreys (1987b) "Picture naming", in G. W. Humphreys and J. M. Riddoch (eds 1987)

Riddoch, M. J., G. W. Humphreys, M. Coltheart and E. Funnell (1988) "Semantic systems or system? Neuropsychological evidence reexamined", *Cognitive Neuropsychology*, 5.1

Rips, L. J., E. J. Shoben and E. E. Smith (1973) "Semantic distance and the verification of semantic relations", *J.V.L.V.B.*, 12

Ristau, C. A. (ed. 1991) *Cognitive Ethology*, Hillsdale, NJ: Erlbaum

Roberts, J. R. (1990) "Modality in Amele and other Papuan languages", *J. of Linguistics*, 26

Roberts, J. R. (1992) "The category 'irrealis' in Papuan Medial Verbs", *Symposium on Mood and Modality*, UNM, Albuquerque, May 1992 (ms)

Roland, K. (1994) "The pragmatics of Modern Greek voice: Active, passive, inverse" in T. Givón ed. (1994)

Rosch, E. (1973a) "On the internal structure of perceptual and semantic categories", in T. Moore (ed.) *Cognitive Development and the Acquisition of Language*, NY: Academic Press

Rosch, E. (1973b) "Natural categories", *Cognitive Psychology*, 4

Rosch, E. (1975) "Human categorization", in N. Warren (ed.) *Advances in Cross-Cultural Psychology*, London: Academic Press

Rosch, E. (1978) "Principles of categorization", in E. Rosch and B. B. Lloyd (eds) *Cognition and Categorization*, Hillsdale, NJ: Erlbaum

Rosch, E. and B. Lloyd (eds, 1978) *Cognition and Categorization*, Hillsdale, NJ: Erlbaum

Rosch, E. and C. B. Mervis (1975) "Family resemblance: Studies in the internal structures of categories", *Cognitive Psychology*, 7

Ross, J. R. (1972) "The category squish: Endstation Hauptpoint", *CLS #8*, Chicago: University of Chicago, Chicago Linguistics Society

Ross, J. R. (1973) "Nouniness", in D. Fujimura (ed.) *Three Dimensions of Linguistics*, Tokyo: TEC Corp.

Ross, J. R. and G. Lakoff (1967) "Is deep structure necessary?", paper presented at the *First La Jolla Conference on Linguistic Theory*, May 1967 (ms)

Rude, N. (1985) *Studies in Nez Perce Grammar and Discourse*, PhD dissertation, University of Oregon

Rude, N. (1987) "Topicality, transitivity and the direct object in Nez Perce" *I.J.A.L.*, 52.2

Rude, N. (1988) "Possible sources of the Sahaptin inverse prefix*pá*-", University of Oregon, Eugene (ms)

Rude, N. (1989) "Inverse marking and ergativity in some Oregon languages", University of Oregon, Eugene (ms)

Rude, N. (1991) "Origin of the Nez Perce ergative NP suffix", *I.J.A.L.*, 57.1

Rude, N. (1992a) "Voice in Nez Perce and Sahaptin: Some functional differences", University of Oregon, Eugene (ms)

Rude, N. (1992b) "Word order and topicality in Nez Perce", in D. Payne (ed. 1992)

Rude, N. (1994) "The inverse in Sahaptin", in T. Givón (ed. 1994)

Rummelhart, D. E. (1975) "Notes on a schema for stories", in D. G. Bobrow and A. M. Collins (eds) *Representation and Understanding: Studies in Cognitive Science*, Hillsdale, NJ: Erlbaum

Russell, B. (1919) *Introduction to Mathematical Logic*, London: Rutledge

Sachs, H., E. A. Schegloff and G. Jefferson (1974) "A simple systematic for the organization of turn-taking for conversation", *Language*, 50

Salone, S. (1983) "The pragmatics of reality and unreality conditional sentences in Swahili", *J. of Pragmatics*, 7.3

Sapir, E. (1921) *Language*, Harcourt, Brace and World (Harvest ppbk.)

Savin, H. and E. Perchonok (1965) "Grammatical structure and the immediate recall of English sentences", *J.V.L.V.B.*, 4

Schachter, P. (1974a) "A non-transformational account of serial verbs", *Studies in African Linguistics*, supplement #5

Schachter, P. (1974b) "Serial verbs as verbs: A reply to a reply", *Studies in African Linguistics*, supplement #5

Schachter, P. (1976) "The subject in Philippine languages: Topic, actor actor-topic or none of the above", in C. Li (ed. 1976)

Schneider, W. (1985) "Toward a model of attention and the development of automatic processing", in O. Marin and M. I. Posner (eds) *Attention and Performance XI*, Hillsdale, NJ: Erlbaum

Schneider, W. and R. M. Shiffrin (1977) "Controlled and automatic human information processing, I: Detection, search and attention", *Psychological Review*, 84

Schnitzer, M. (1989) *The Pragmatic Basis of Aphasia*, Hillsdale, NJ: Erlbaum

Schumann, J. (1976) "Second language acquisition: The pidginization hypothesis" *Language Learning*, 26

Schumann, J. (1978) *The Pidginization Process: A Model for Second Language Acquisition*, Rowley, Mass.: Newbury House

Scollon, R. (1976) *Conversations with a One Year Old Child*, Honolulu: University of Hawaii Press

Searle, J. (1969) *Speech Acts*, Cambridge: Cambridge University Press

Sebba, M. (1987) *The Syntax of Serial Verbs*, Creole Language Library #2, Amsterdam: J. Benjamins

Shallice, T. (1988) "Specialization within the semantic system", *Cognitive Neuropsychology*, 5.1

Shank, R.C. and R.P. Abelson (1977) *Scripts, Plans, Goals and Understanding*, Hillsdale, NJ: Erlbaum

Shapiro, M. (1983) *The Sense of Grammar*, Bloomington: Indiana University Press

Shibatani, M. (ed. 1976) *The Grammar of Causative Constructions, Syntax and Semantics #6*, NY: Academic Press

Shibatani, M. (1985) "Passive and related constructions: A prototype analysis", *Language*, 61.4

Shibatani, M. (1988) "Voice in Philippine languages", in M. Shibatani (ed. 1988)

Shibatani, M. (ed. 1988) *Passive and Voice*, TSL #18, Amsterdam: J. Benjamins

Silverstein, M. (1976) "Hierarchy of features and ergativity", in R.M.W. Dixon (ed. 1976)

Simonds, P. (1974) *The Social Primates*, NY: Harper & Row

Slobin, D. (1966) "Grammatical transformations and sentence comprehension in childhood and adulthood", *J.V.L.V.B.*, 5

Slobin, D. (1970) "Universals of grammatical development in children", in W. Levelt and G.B. Flores d'Arcais (eds) *Advances in Psycholinguistic Research*, Amsterdam: N. Holland

Slobin, D. (1977) "Language change in childhood and history", in J. MacNamara (ed.) *Language, Learning and Thought*, NY: Academic Press

Slobin, D. (ed. 1985) *The Crosslinguistic Study of Language Acquisition*, Hillsdale, NJ: Erlbaum

Slobin, D. (1987) "Thinking for speaking", in J. Aske, N. Beery and H. Filip (eds) *Proceedings of 13th Annual Meeting, Berkeley Linguistics Society*, Berkeley: University of California

Smith, E.E. (1978) "Theories of semantic memory", in W.K. Estes (ed.) *Handbook of Learning and Cognitive Processes* vol. 6, Hillsdale, NJ: Erlbaum

Smith, E.E., L.J. Rips and E.J. Shoben (1974) "Semantic memory and psychological semantics", in G.H. Bower (ed.) *The Psychology of Learning and Motivation*, vol. 8, NY: Academic Press

Smith, W. (1992) "Spoken narrative and preferred clause structure: Evidence from Modern Hebrew discourse", UCLA, Applied Linguistics Dept. (ms) to appear in *Studies in Language*

Snowdon, C.T., C.H. Brown and M.R. Petersen (eds. 1982) *Primate Communication*, Cambridge: Cambridge University Press

Squire, L.R. (1987) *Memory and Brain*, Oxford: Oxford University Press

Squire, L. R. and S. Zola-Morgan (1991) "The medial temporal lobe memory system", *Science*, 253:1380-1386

Stahlke, H. (1970) "Serial verbs", *Studies in African Linguistics*, 1.1

Steele, S. (1975) "Past and irrealis: Just what does it all mean?", *I.J.A.L.*, 41.3

Steele, S. (1978) "The category AUX as a language universal", in J. Greenberg, C. Ferguson and E. Moravcsik (eds) *Universals of Human Language*, vol. 3, Stanford: Stanford University Press

Stein, N. L. (1982) "The definition of story", in J. H. Coots (ed. 1982)

Stein, N. L. and C. Glen (1979) "An analysis of story comprehension in elementary school children", in R. O. Freedle (ed.) *New Directions in Discourse Processing*, Hillsdale, NJ: Erlbaum

Stockwell, R. P., P. Schachter and B. H. Partee (1973) *The Major Syntactic Structures of English*, NY: Holt, Rinehart and Winston

Stokoe, W. C. (1974) "Motor signs as the first form of language", in R. Wescott (ed. 1974)

Sun, C. F. and T. Givón (1985) "On the so-called SOV word-order in Mandarin Chinese: A quantitative text study and its implications", *Language*, 61.2

Sweetser, E. (1984) *Semantic Structure and Semantic Change: A Cognitive Linguistic Study of Modality, Speech Acts, and Logical Relations*, PhD dissertation, UC. Berkeley (ms)

Swinney, D. A. (1979) "Lexical access during sentence comprehension: (Re)consideration of context effects", *J.V.L.V.B.*, 18

Syder, F. and A. Pawley (1974) "The reduction principle in conversation", Auckland University (ms)

Terrace, H. S. (1985) "In the beginning there was the name", *American Psychologist*, 40

Thompson, C. (1989) *Voice and Obviation in Athabascan and Other Languages*, PhD dissertation, University of Oregon, Eugene (ms)

Thompson, C. (1994) "Passive and inverse constructions", in T. Givón (ed. 1994)

Thompson, S. (1973) "Resultative verb compounds in Mandarin Chinese: A case for lexical rules", *Language*, 49.2

Thompson, S. A. (1985) "Grammar and written discourse: Initial vs. final purpose clauses in English", in T. Givón (ed. 1985)

Timberlake, A. (1978) "Hierarchies in the genitive of negation", *Slavic and Eastern European Journal*, 19

Tomlin, R. (1985) "Foreground-background information and the syntax of subordination", in T. Givón (ed. 1985)

Tomlin, R. (ed. 1987) *Coherence and Grounding in Discourse*, TSL 11, Amsterdam: J. Benjamins

Tomlin, R. (1991) "Focal attention, voice and word order: An experimental cross-linguistic study", *Technical Report TR-91-10*, Institute of Cognitive and Decision Sciences, University of Oregon

Tonegawa, S. (1985) "The molecules of the immune system", *Scientific American*, XXIII

Trabasso, T. and L. L. Sperry (1985) "Causal relatedness and importance of events", *J. of Memory and Language*, 24

Trabasso, T. and P. van den Broek (1985) "Causal thinking and the representation of narrative events", *J. of Memory and Language*, 24

Traugott, E. (1982) "From propositional to textual and expressive meaning: Some semantic-pragmatic aspects of grammaticalization", in W. P. Lehmann and Y. Malkiel (eds) *Perspectives on Historical Linguistics*, Amsterdam: J. Benjamins

Traugott, E. (1986) "On regularity in semantic change", *J. of Literary Semantics*, 15

Traugott, E. (1987) "From less to more in situated language: The unidirectionality of semantic change", *Proceedings of the International Conference on English Historical Linguistics*, V, Cambridge: Cambridge University Press

Traugott, E. (1988) "Pragmatic strengthening and grammaticalization", *BLS #14*, Berkeley: Berkeley Linguistics Society

Traugott, E. (1989) "On the rise of epistemic meanings in English: An example of subjectification in semantic change", *Language*, 65.1

Traugott, E. and B. Heine (eds 1991) *Approaches to Grammaticalization*, TSL #19.1/2, Amsterdam: J. Benjamins

Trithart, L. (1977) *Relational Grammar and ChiChewa Subjectivization Rules,* MA Thesis, Los Angeles: UCLA (ms.)

Troubetzkoy, N. S. (1958/1969) *Principles of Phonology*, tr. by C. Baltaxe, Berkeley: U.C. Press

Troubetzkoy, N. S. (1975) *Letters and Notes*, ed. by R. Jakobson, The Hague: Mouton

Tsunoda, T. (1985) "Ergativity and coreference in Warrungu discourse", *Nagoya University Working Papers in Linguistics*, 1

Tsunoda, T. (1986) *Topicality in Ergative and Accusative Languages*, Nagoya Working Papers in Linguistics, vol. 2, Nagoya: Nagoya University Press

Tsunoda, T. (1987) "Ergativity, accusativity and topicality", *Nagoya University Working Papers in Linguistics*, 2

Tucker, D. M. (1991) "Developing emotions and cortical networks", in M. Gunnar and C. Nelson (eds), *Developmental Neuroscience, Minnesota Symposium on Child Psychology*, vol. 24, Hillsdale, NJ: Erlbaum

Tversky, B. (1969) "Pictorial and verbal encoding in a short-term memory task", *Perception and Psychophysics*, 6

Tversky, B. (1975) "Pictorial encoding of sentences in sentence-picture comparisons", *Quarterly J. of Experimental Psychology*, 27

Tweedale, M. (1986) "How to handle problems about forms and universals in Aristotle's work", Auckland University, Auckland, NZ (ms)

Ungerleider, L. A. (1985) "The cortical pathways for object recognition and spatial perception", in C. Chagas, R. Gattass and C. Gross (eds) *Pattern Recognition Mechanisms, The Pontifical Academy of Sciences*, 21-37

Ungerleider, L. A. and M. Mishkin (1982) "Two cortical visual systems", in D. G. Ingle, M. A. Goodale and R. J. Q. Mansfield (eds) *Analysis of Visual Behavior*, Cambridge: MIT Press

van Dijk, T. and W. Kintsch (1983) *Strategies of Discourse Comprehension*, NY: Academic Press

Verhaar, J. (1983a) "Two aspects of pragmatics: Topicality and iconicity", in S. Hattori and K. Inoue (eds) *Proceedings of the XIIIth International Congress of Linguists, Tokyo, 1982*, The Hague: CIPL

Verhaar, J. (1983b) "Ergativity, accusativity and hierarchy", *Sophia Linguistica*, 11

Verhaar, J. (1985) "On iconicity and hierarchy", *Studies in Language*, 9.1

von Frisch, K. (1967) *The Dance Language and Orientation of Bees*, Cambridge: Harvard University Press

Walker, C. H. and F. R. Yekovich (1987) "Activation and use of script-based antecedents in anaphoric reference", *J. of Memory and Language*, 26

Warrington, E. K. (1975) "The selective impairment of memory", *Quarterly J. of Psychology*, 73

Warrington, E. K. and R. McCarthy (1983) "Category specific access disphasia", *Brain*, 166

Warrington, E. K. and T. Shallice (1979) "Semantic access dislexia", *Brain*, 102

Warrington, E. K. and T. Shallice (1984) "Category specific semantic impairment", *Brain*, 107

Wernike, K. (1874) *Der aphasische Symptomencomplex*, Breslau; trans. in *Boston Studies in Philosophy of Science*, 4

Wescott, R. W. (ed. 1974) *Language Origins*, Silver Springs, Md.: Linstok Press

Wierzbicka, A. (1981) "Case marking and human nature", *Australian J. of Linguistics*, 1

Wierzbicka, A. (1988) *The Semantics of Grammar*, Amsterdam: J. Benjamins

Wierzbicka, A. (1992) "A semantic basis for grammatical typology", in W. Abraham, T. Givón and S. Thompson (eds) *Discourse Grammar and Typology. Papers in Honor of John Verhaar*, Amsterdam: J. Benjamins (in press)

Wilensky, R. (1980) *Understanding Goal-Based Stories*, PhD dissertation, Yale University (ms.)

Wilensky, R. (1982) "Story grammars revisited", in J. H. Coots (ed. 1982)

Williamson, K. (1965) *A Grammar of the Kolokuma Dialect of Ijo*, West African Language Monograph #2, Cambridge: Cambridge University Press

Williamson, K. (1991) "The tense system of Izon", *Afrikanistische Arbeitspapiere*, #27, Cologne: Institut für Afrikanistik

Wise, R., F. Collet, U. Hadar, K. Friston, E. Hoffner and R. Frackowiac (1991) "Distribution of cortical neural networks involved in word comprehension and word retrieval", *Brain*, 114

Wittgenstein, L. (1918) *Tractatus Logico Philosophicus*, NY: The Humanities Press [1961]

Woodbury, A. (1975) *Ergativity of Grammatical Processes: A Study of Greenlandic Eskimo*, MA thesis, University of Chicago (ms)

Wright, L. O. (1932) "The *ra* verb form in Spain", *University of California Publications in Modern Philology*, 15.1, Berkeley: University of California Press

Wright, S. and T. Givón (1987) "The pragmatics of indefinite reference", *Studies in Language*, 11.1

Yang, L. and T. Givón (1994) "The evolution of the GET-passive in English", in B. Fox and P. Hopper (eds 1994)

Yekovich, F. R. and C. H. Walker (1986) "The activation and use of scripted knowledge in reading about routine activities", in B. K. Britton (ed.) *Executive Control Processes in Reading*, Hillsdale, NJ: Erlbaum

Young, P. and T. Givón (1990) "The puzzle of Ngabere auxiliaries: Grammatical reconstruction in Chibchan and Misumalpan", in W. Croft, K. Denning and S. Kemmer (eds) *Studies in Typology and Diachrony*, TSL #20, Amsterdam: J. Benjamins

Zavala, R. (1992) The Grammaticalization of Motion Verbs as Directionals or Modals in Mayan languages", MA Thesis, Linguistics Department, University of Oregon, Eugene (ms)

Zavala, R. (1993) "Se les esta moviendo el tapete: Gramaticalización de verbos de movimiento en Akateko", II Encuentro de Linguistica en el *Noroeste*, Universidad de Sonora, Hermosillo (ms)

Zavala, R. (1994) "Voice and inversion in Akatek (Mayan)", University of Oregon, Eugene (ms)

Zipf, G. K. (1935/1965) *The Psychobiology of Language: An Introduction to Dynamic Philology*, Cambridge: MIT Press [1965 edition]

Zubin, D. (1972) *The German Case System: Exploitation of the Dative-Accusative Opposition Comment*, MA Thesis, Columbia University (ms)

Zubin, D. (1979) "Discourse function of morphology: The focus system in German", in T. Givón (ed. 1979b)

Zurif, E., A. Caramazza and R. Myerson (1972) "Grammatical judgements of agrammatic aphasics", *Neuropsychologia*, 10

Index

semantic case-roles 191, 226
semantic frame 187
semantic inverse 78, 91, 92, 93, 98, 99, 101
semantic lexicon 412, 423
semantic memory 16, 396, 424
semantic transitivity 76
sensory-motor codes 400
sequentiality 345
serial order 177
serial verbs 300
serial-verb languages 205, 267, 279, 290
Shallice, T. 414
Shapiro, M. 26, 27
sign language 440
Silverstein, M. 103
Slobin, D. 39
Smith, W. 194
society of intimates 41, 42, 433
society of strangers 42, 434
spatial coherence 364
spatial motion 409
spatial relations 409
speech-acts (markedness) 40
speech-act value 433
speech-situation (grounding) 350
split ergativity 103, 104
split subjunctive 133
spreading activation 363, 396
Squire, L. 345, 409, 415, 416
Steele, S. 163
striated cortex 407
structural similarity 72
structuralism 5, 176
subjective certainty 115
subjunctive (mood) 112, 123, 141
subjunctive complements 130
subjunctive of low certainty 146
subjunctive of manipulation 133

subjunctive of uncertainty 133
subjunctive of weak manipulation 144
subordinate clause (subjunctive) 123
Sun, C.-F. 315
surface structure criteria 182
switch reference 87
switch-subject clause(s) 292
Syder, F. 167
synonymy 58, 321
syntactic complexity 225
syntactic demotion 83
syntactic scattering 300

T
Takahashi, T. 424, 425
tautology 308, 357
taxonomy 72
teleological 3
teleology 5
temporal coherence 367
tense-aspect (irrealis) 116
terminated activation 354, 375
Tesnière, L. 307
text 343
thematic coherence 36, 327, 372
Thompson, S.A. 210, 230, 314, 322, 332
Tomlin, R. 333, 334
topic hierarchies 91, 92
topic persistence 79, 348, 349
topic prominent (languages) 230
topic shifting 87
topicality 51, 77, 78, 230
topicality hierarchy 46
transitive event 76
transitivity 76
truth 111
Tucker, D. 410
typology (inverse) 84, 99, 100
typological variation 166